Tenant's Handbook of Office Leasing

Tenant's
Handbook
of Office
Leasing

Tenant's Handbook of Office Leasing

How to Plan, Negotiate, and
Enforce the Most Favorable
Lease Transaction Possible

Stanley Mark Wolfson

McGraw-Hill, Inc.

New York St. Louis San Francisco Auckland Bogotá
Caracas Lisbon London Madrid Mexico Milan
Montreal New Delhi Paris San Juan São Paulo
Singapore Sydney Tokyo Toronto

Library of Congress Cataloging-in-Publication Data

Wolfson, Stanley Mark.
    Tenant's Handbook of office leasing / Stanley Mark Wolfson.
       p.   cm.
    Includes index.
    ISBN 0-07-071542-4 (hb)
    1. Office leases—United States. 2. Landlord and tenant—United
States. I. Title. II. Title: Handbook office leasing.
KF593.C6W65 1992
346.7304'346—dc20
[347.3064346]   92-7730
                                                    CIP

1 2 3 4 5 6 7 8 9 0 DOC/DOC 9 8 7 6 5 4 3 2

ISBN 0-07-071542-4

*The sponsoring editor for this book was James H. Bessent, Jr., the editing supervisor
was Ann Armstrong Craig, and the production supervisor was Suzanne W. Babeuf.
It was set in Baskerville by Carol Woolverton, Lexington, Mass.*

Printed and bound by R. R. Donnelley & Sons Company.

As writing a book takes so much time,
A patient spouse can be sublime.
To my loving Nan, who helped its start,
This book is dedicated—and so is my heart.

Contents

A Note from the Author

I must confess that I am a tenant-oriented commercial real estate broker. My sympathy for the tenant probably stems from all the years I myself had to deal with landlords and real estate agents. The experiences were never very enjoyable. And I always felt at a disadvantage. I did not know enough about leasing office space and had to rely on the advice of my attorney and my real estate agent, so when they said, "You're getting a fantastic deal," I believed them.

Yet I always had the nagging feeling that it was not really so. Sooner or later (sometimes much later in a lease term), I always found out that a rent increase or similar lease provision was never quite worded in my favor as a tenant.

When my career branched out into consulting, I began doing some relocation consulting for office tenants. In my zeal to help the tenant and to correct all the mistakes I had made (and remembering the many times agents had withheld vital information or landlords had been less than truthful), I alienated a number of landlords. But I felt someone had to stick up for the tenant.

This bias followed me when I became a partner in a major commercial real estate company—and even before that, when I acted as a consultant for some real estate firms. Actually, it was during that consulting work that the idea for this book first took hold in late 1984 and early 1985. I had just created a special 12-week, 172-

hour training module for commercially oriented professional real estate brokers (PREBs).

The course was for newly hired or inexperienced agents and was inspired by discussions with a number of commercial PREBs. All of the PREBs described the sorry state of—and outright lack of—good, professional training for commercial real estate agents. Everyone learned how to be an agent on the job. If you didn't have a good mentor or senior agent to work under, you either didn't learn how or took considerably longer to learn. Success was based on being able to mimic a senior agent. Training by osmosis was rampant! A junior agent would follow a senior agent around like a puppy dog, do everything he or she was told, and "gofer" anything the senior agent wanted—and maybe, just maybe, the senior agent would throw the junior a crumb, a piece of a commission, even turn over a client.

It was not that firms didn't recognize the importance of training. There just wasn't much available, at least not specifically for the commercial real estate agent. Senior agents would often put on special programs for the junior agents, but they themselves had had no training and found it difficult to organize and convey to others the great wealth of information they had acquired over the years. Sometimes outside specialists were brought in. But these professionals—attorneys, construction specialists, and nationally known speakers on management and negotiations—while interesting, weren't able to teach the junior agents a great deal about their own newly adopted profession.

I also learned that most states that have licensing requirements for real estate agents and brokers concentrate on residential selling. In fact, most state laws and regulations are steeped in residential matters. Commercial real estate, even though it is a multibillion-dollar business in the United States, is a stepchild with little real regulation and almost no entry-level training opportunities.

Hence the intensive 12-week training course. The course was designed to present both the basics of commercial real estate and to teach selling and other required skills, such as understanding leases and performing rent escalation calculations.

I prepared two training manuals for the course, which altogether consisted of approximately 1200 pages of material aimed exclusively at entry-level and junior commercial real estate agents.

One of the objectives of the training program was to provide agents with detailed information on commercial lease clauses. Therefore, a manual was specially designed to explain the intricate and complex language in lease clauses and their related provisions.

That commercial lease clause manual was the basis for this book. Needless to say, the agent training I provide is geared toward helping tenants make favorable leasing transactions in the real estate market.

Stanley Mark Wolfson

1
Evening the Odds

The commercial real estate tenant is usually someone who negotiates and signs a lease with a landlord every five, ten, or twenty years. Many times the negotiations are perfunctory. The tenant wants to stay put and does not want to be hassled or interrupted by having to run around looking for space or moving to a new location.

Whether a small office user requiring a few hundred square feet or a megasize firm needing several hundred thousand square feet, every tenant is at a considerable disadvantage when dealing with someone in commercial real estate, which is a world unto itself. It takes many years of experience to become a professional commercial real estate broker, to learn the jargon and ins and outs of the profession, to develop an understanding of the complexities of lease clause language, and to become skilled in structuring a tenant-landlord financial transaction. The professional is immersed in the market every day, staying current on available spaces, new buildings, new project financing, property purchases, and the street talk and gossip between real estate brokers regarding the construction plans of developers and the relocation plans of tenants.

When commercial real estate brokers want to buy a "widget," they don't build one themselves. They go out and buy one from a widget maker. All too often, however, the widget maker considers him- or herself an expert in commercial real estate and decides to lease space on his or her own.

1

Never Negotiate for Yourself

The typical office tenants who go out into the real estate market on their own are also going to be negotiating for themselves. As any good negotiator will tell you, nothing is harder than negotiating on one's own behalf, which is why baseball players have negotiators and office tenants have professional real estate brokers (PREBs). When you negotiate for yourself, certain things become too personal. What may otherwise be innocuous words and body language can become personal affront. Inflexibility due to an "ownership mentality" sets in regarding the particular wording of a sentence, an amount of money, or an otherwise minuscule financial point. The "I've gotta have that piece of candy" syndrome, where personal wants and needs regarding something desired—office space in a particular building—becomes all-consuming and overrides good sense and judgment.

To get around this negotiating problem, many office tenants hire lawyers to help with the lease and to do the negotiating. Although this is indeed a better alternative than doing it yourself, it still has some difficulties. The biggest problem is that lawyers, unlike PREBs, are not out in the market every day. All too often a lawyer will get caught up in the nuances of the legal language of a lease clause or a particular negotiating point or stance, fixated on doing something "the right way."

Whom Does a Broker Work For?

It is up to the PREB to come to the rescue of the office tenant. An experienced and ethical commercial real estate broker can provide a tenant with excellent representation. However, in the majority of situations the broker will be getting paid by the landlord of the building in which a tenant takes office space. Many (especially lawyers) would construe this a direct conflict of interest, and in many cases it is. A broker who is taking a landlord's money may not want to upset the landlord by negotiating too good a transaction for a tenant—the typical euphemism is a "fair deal for both the landlord and the tenant." (Why isn't it ever a *great deal* for the tenant and a *fair deal* for the landlord? And why is it always

a "deal"? The expression makes a PREB sound like the stereotypi-
cal used car dealer. Look for a broker who has a vocabulary of
more than four-letter words. The term that should be used is
transaction, as in "I will get the best transaction on your behalf,"
rather than "I will get you the best deal.")

Since the landlord will be paying the broker's fee (known as a
commission) in the majority of office-tenant transactions, to
whom does the broker owe a fiduciary responsibility? In residential brokerage it is always to the person paying the fee. In a commercial real estate transaction the tenant should insist on a written agreement with the broker that spells out unequivocally that
the broker is representing the tenant, that the broker will be fidu-
ciarily responsible to the tenant, *and* that the broker will make
these facts known to—and will provide a copy of the agreement
to—the landlord in each building for which the tenant is interested in office space.

These things will help, but still all will not be perfect. By using a
broker, the tenant should get reasonable representation, but it
will be more important for the tenant to have full access to up-to-
date market information. Such information will give the tenant
an idea of what office space is available and what market transactions have recently occurred with other tenants in the same or
nearby office buildings (such information will include specifications on rental rates, square footage, and landlord concessions).

Tenants undertaking a commercial real estate transaction will
actually have to call on a number of professionals in order to arrive at the best transaction. They will need not only a real estate
broker, but also a lawyer, an accountant, a space planner, an interior decorator, a construction consultant, and a relocation consultant. To ensure that these professionals are working on the
tenant's behalf, the tenant should carefully interview each of
them in advance and check their references.

PREBs Are Salespeople

It is important to remember that the commercial real estate broker is first and foremost a salesperson. A broker carries a sales license. Although they may have to take a test to obtain the license
and are required to continue seeking educational credits, they

are salespeople. It is worth noting that the precursor of the salesperson's license was the peddler's license. A former partner of mine was fond of telling brokers they were nothing more than peddlers—they just happened to be in a business where the peddler can make lots of money.

Remember, too, that a broker's years of experience may not guarantee the tenant adequate, much less excellent, representation. It is not unusual to find brokers with many years of experience who have made a great deal of money and appear to be successful. One broker I knew who fit this description was also an excellent talker (a "schmoozer" in the jargon of the PREB), and he knew how to build long-term relationships. Even so, he had difficulty understanding many lease clauses. Many were the times he would run around to two or three different brokers in the office to "reclarify" the differences between a right to renew a lease, an option to expand, and a right, versus an option, to purchase a building.

As salespeople, brokers are glib—they are supposed to be. If their presentation seems superprofessional and extremely convincing, it is because they have had lots of practice and often have had extensive training in both selling and presentation techniques. As soon as you hear, "I can't believe the landlord is making you that good an offer" (or "deal"), or "It's a fantastic deal; it's the best one in the building," or "No one has ever gotten that good a deal from that landlord," or "You got the best deal going; no one will be able to match that deal in that building"—watch out!

Everyone likes to have his or her ego stroked. Everyone wants to know how great a "deal" he or she got and how it compares with others. But the salesperson's soothing words and assurances are merely the tools of the trade; they are part of the selling process.

Therefore the wise tenant will put some effort into choosing a broker. The process is no different from that of choosing any type of professional. You first check with colleagues, friends, and others you know in the business world and identify three or more potential brokers. Interview each firm, using a prepared standardized set of questions, and carefully check five or more references per broker, again, using a standardized set of questions.

Have each firm prepare a proposal for your specific needs, clearly delineating what its PREB will do for you, how that person will do it, and what distinguishes this broker from others.

Get Your Own PREB

Instead, tenants usually begin looking for new office space on their own. They invariably find a building they like and fix their sights on it. Now the owner of that building is likely to have a broker representing his or her interests. This broker, being a good salesperson, will begin wooing the prospective tenant, trying to get the tenant to negotiate a transaction and to avoid getting another broker involved (so there will be no need to share the commission). The good landlord broker will make assurances like "I'll get the best possible deal for you in this building," or "Just tell me what you need (want), and I'll go to bat for you with the owner," or "Let's sit down and talk, and I'll get the owner to make the deal."

This broker has been hired by, is working for, and is getting paid by, the building landlord. Do you really believe this person will be negotiating on your behalf? (If you do, let me know, because I can get you the title and deed to the Brooklyn Bridge.)

Yet, time and again, tenants will fall for this line and let the building's broker negotiate their leases. There really is no nice way to say it: Using a building's broker to negotiate a lease for you is foolish and stupid. Get your own broker! Get your own lawyer! Get your own representation!

And when the broker (or owner or anyone) looks you in the eye and tells you that because a commission will need to be paid to "your separate broker" and therefore you cannot or will not be able to get as good a deal, look that person back in the eye and say, "Poppycock." Virtually every office lease transaction has an expected commission budgeted. When you do not have broker representation, the building owner's broker gets to keep the whole commission; otherwise, it is shared with your broker.

Over the life of a lease, a good broker leading a tenant's representation team (lawyer, space planner, and so on) can save the client two, three, four, and even more times the commission dollars he or she earns.

A Legal Aside

A commercial real estate broker has a number of specific legal obligations and duties to both parties to a real estate transaction. One of the more important obligation of a PREB, from a tenant's perspective, is a legal requirement: The PREB must provide a factual and accurate disclosure of information regarding the premises or property, especially when asked a direct question about it. That is, a broker may not deceive a tenant either through misstatement or intentional misrepresentation of facts or information or by failing to disclose pertinent facts or information. Ignorance of the facts and deception by omission are not acceptable excuses.

This means the tenant is protected to some extent from being deliberately (or otherwise) misled into accepting certain premises or property. But the tenant can gain added protection by learning to ask the right questions and to recognize what to look for in the PREB's answers. If the tenant's questions are too broad and general, they will invariably meet with a general response. A request for specific information by a tenant requires a specific answer by the PREB. A PREB must be willing to admit to a lack of knowledge and be prepared to track down an exact answer to a tenant question at the tenant's request.

To extract useful information from a PREB, the tenant needs to ask specific questions and to insist on equally specific answers. Don't ask, "How much does space rent for in this building?" or "How much are other tenants paying for space in the building?" And never include the word *about* in a question, as in "About how much is the rent?" Questions like these allow a PREB to respond vaguely with "Space rents from $x to $y per square foot" or "Other tenants are paying about $x per square foot."

The proper way to ask the question is "Exactly how much are the other tenants in the building paying for rent?" or "Exactly how much rent was paid by the last tenant to sign a lease in the building?" If a PREB responds with an "about" answer or a range of values, insist on clarification or a more specific answer.

Of course, the PREB you are working with may not really know the answer. But you should urge the PREB to track down the necessary information. Sometimes the information may not be available because the landlord refuses to disclose the precise financial details of a previous leasing transaction. Even this situation can yield valuable information, however. When the PREB explains the difficulty, the landlord's evasiveness is a warning either of possible problems in other lease negotiations or of the inexperience or lack of ability of the PREB.

Protecting Your Interests

If you are planning to hire a broker and perhaps a commercial real estate lawyer to represent your interests, why do you need to bother with this book?

First, no matter whom you hire to represent *your* interests, the person who cares the most about your interests—is you.

Second, no matter how good your broker representation is, your PREB's primary aim will be to make the transaction happen. After all, no transaction, no commission. This is not to say that the broker will lie to you or be unethical—only that the broker knows all too well that the business of real estate consists largely of negotiation. The broker might make an assumption or a decision based on experience that would not be in the same direction you would have gone if you knew all your options.

Third, commercial real estate is a profession. You do not have the time for becoming an office-leasing expert or a legal expert able to check every lease clause for accuracy and legal compliance. You are a businessperson, an entrepreneur, a decision maker. You need enough information to make an informed decision that will benefit your business or organization. To understand an office lease, you need an easy-to-read and easy-to-use reference—one that will provide you with the full range of available options, alternatives, and opportunities in a completely unbiased manner.

This book has been written specifically for the businessperson (although the professional commercial real estate broker should find it both useful and interesting). Its goal is to help the office tenant better understand what is typically available in the marketplace. With this in mind, it is designed to help office tenants make better use of the legal and real estate services they must depend on in order to receive maximum benefits.

Lease Clause, Lease Provision

This book avoids excessive use of commercial real estate and legal jargon. There is virtually no legalese, nor are any legal conventions followed in the discussion of lease clauses.

In this book the term *lease clause* refers to major subject areas and broad concepts described and found in a lease document: "rent," "surrender of premises," "operating expenses," and the like. The term *provision* (as in "lease provision") is used to delineate ideas, subjects, and concepts found in a lease clause. Distinguishing between these terms helps in clarifying the different parts of a lease document. It is common practice in commercial real estate, however, to use the terms *lease clause* and *lease provision* interchangeably.

More Costs Less

This book will help you get as much as there is to get when leasing office space. This promise requires further explanation, though. To paraphrase a great American, you can get some of the things in this book all of the time, and you can even get all of the things in this book some of the time, but you cannot (nor should you) get all of the things in this book all of the time. Megatenants can get almost anything they want. Medium- to large-sized tenants can get almost all they need most of the time, but small space users have to work very hard to get as much as they can.

The information in this book will help any space user of whatever size achieve a better leasing transaction and maximize the value of a transaction. However, the reality of the commercial real estate marketplace is that different-sized space users will achieve different leasing transactions—financial and otherwise.

As a general business concept, the greater the quantity of something that is bought, the better the price or financial terms that are expected. For example, if one pencil costs 25 cents, then it is expected that a larger quantity, such as a dozen pencils, will cost something less then 25 cents each; a gross of pencils (12 dozen) is expected to cost even less per unit. This business concept applies to the commercial real estate market, where there tends to be a similar cost-to-quantity inverse relationship. That is, each square foot (or per unit) should cost less, the greater the quantity of square feet to be leased.

Even so, knowledge, not size, is often the deciding factor in how well a tenant does in a transaction. This book will help maximize the tenant's knowledge about what is available when structuring a leasing transaction.

What Is Small, What Is Large?

What distinguishes a small space user from a large space user? Small and large are judged in relation to the overall size of the building or project. For example, a 12,000-sq-ft space user could be considered a medium- to good-sized space user in a 120,000-sq-ft, 10-story building in which the individual floors measure 12,000 sq ft. This tenant would use a full floor and therefore be valuable from the perspective of the building's owner.

Many owners like to have large space users in order to limit the number of tenants and thus the number of negotiations they have to deal with in any one building. There is also a considerable savings in time for the owner since a smaller number of users can usually lease the majority of the building in a shorter period of time.

Other building owners prefer smaller space users. Even though it may take longer to lease all the space in a building when there is tenant turnover, the overall amount of space that has to be released at any particular time is less. In addition, most small space users are not hard negotiators. They tend to feel that they are in a weak position because of their size and are therefore more likely to pay higher rents and look for fewer concessions. Of course, this perception may not always be correct. Small space users may be vital in filling a particular niche in a building, and they may be able to negotiate extremely favorable lease terms, better than those obtained by medium- to large-sized space users.

The 12,000-sq-ft user in a 500,000-sq-ft or 1-million-sq-ft building project with 50,000-to-100,000-sq-ft signed floors would be a relatively small space user—but still a valuable one.

Is a Little Knowledge Dangerous?

This book will provide many office tenants with information and knowledge they never realized existed. The book opens up the world of commercial real estate brokerage and office leasing as it has never before been exposed.

Sometimes in the exuberance of trying to do good, one may achieve just the opposite result. Learning and understanding what was previously unknown, some readers may be tempted to overstep the boundaries of reasonableness. I urge the reader to use the information contained herein judiciously and to exercise some measure of control and good, fair, and reasonable judgment.

Whatever the negotiation, the best result is not to have a clear winner and a loser but to have both parties feel they have been treated fairly. If there is mutual respect on both sides, the parties will leave the negotiation satisfied.

2

Understanding and Defining the Premises

On the surface, defining or specifying what space a tenant will occupy in a building would seem to be a relatively straightforward matter. In fact, however, for many tenants this is anything but straightforward. Unfortunately, the inability to accurately and clearly define the space to be occupied can have a significant impact on cost to the tenant.

Basic Items to Consider

Specifying the Location

Include both the building's name (if pertinent) and a complete street address of the property or building in which space is being leased. A good business practice for all space users is to incorporate a full legal description of the property (land and building) into the lease or to attach it as an addendum. A full legal description eliminates any possible ambiguities regarding what building or property is being discussed. Furthermore, the full legal description will be needed if the tenant intends to record the lease. Recording the lease may be especially important to full building users and to tenants with equity participation or future options to purchase.

11

Define Where and What Space Is Being Leased

This section of the lease should specify locational characteristics. As explained below, the tenant should treat with caution any mention of the specific amount of space being leased.

The typical means of identification are suite or room numbers (when the space already exists and is built out) or, for a full floor user, a floor number. Depending on the landlord and the tradition in the given region, both building and floor common areas (e.g., lobby areas, fire and exit stairwells, and utility shafts) may be excluded from the description of the premises being leased.

For space that is yet to be constructed to the user's specifications, it is typical to specify a floor number and, if less than a full floor, the approximate dimensions of the space to be leased, along with some additional locational information (e.g., "the northeast corner of the building fronting on Main Street"). Often a suite number, even though one doesn't yet really exist, may be specified.

Sometimes the specification can be extremely vague and therefore open to future interpretation (usually to the detriment of the tenant). This is a common source of disagreement. For example, "approximately 2720 square feet located on the tenth floor" can mean absolutely nothing.

Special reasons for tenant caution include the following:

1. Do not automatically accept descriptions stating the exact number of square feet being leased (or just as bad, an inexact or approximate amount of square feet). This description will determine the rent dollars you will be paying, so you must fully understand how space is measured and what is included and excluded in the defined space. You are entitled to a clear definition of the rentable square feet and the usable square feet in the building.

2. The space or premises being leased are often defined as the "demised premises." The term comes from the demising wall, which is the wall that separates one tenant's space from another's or the wall defining the outer limits of the building itself. The premises being leased, whether the space already exists or is yet to be constructed, must be clearly defined in the lease document. It

should be written out in outline form and clearly marked on a blueprint or drawing of the floor plan for the floor on which the space is located. This floor plan identification should be attached to the lease documents as an exhibit.

Agree on the Exact Amount of Space

How will the premises be measured? What measurement standards will be used? What is the amount of usable square feet? Exactly how much space is the tenant leasing? Does the tenant really know, or has the tenant just accepted the landlord's figures for the amount of space?

Surprisingly few tenants really understand how the space in a building is defined. Even worse, few tenants really know or even check to see if they have the amount of space the landlord says they do. This translates into extra dollars paid in rent by the tenant and extra dollars in the landlord's pocket.

So how does the tenant verify the amount of space being leased? Ignoring for the moment the difference between a building's and an individual floor's common space and the difference between rentable and usable square feet, the tenant needs to make sure that the following details are specified:

1. The measurement standard used to establish the amount of space in the building, on a particular floor, or in a suite

2. How and when the space will be measured and who will measure it

3. When any agreed-to adjustment will be made to the amount of space paid for by the tenant

Measurement Standard.   How landlords actually measure the space in a building or a suite may vary not only from one region to another but also within the same city. Furthermore, a landlord may use different methods to suit his or her needs in different buildings.

There really is no national standard for measuring space. The Building Owners and Managers Association (BOMA) has published a proposed national standard. However, the Washington, DC Association of Realtors has its own published standard, as does the Real Estate Board of New York and those of other cities around the country. Each of these standards attempts to specify exactly how a measurement should be made (e.g., from the inside or from the outside surface of a wall; there are also definitions of the finished surface and the dominant portion of a wall). They also explain what determines whether a "major vertical penetration" (e.g., fire stairwell or elevator shaft) is included in or excluded from the measurement and what determines actual rentable area.

The tenant should insist that the method of measurement (even if it is the landlord's own special measurement system) be clearly specified in the lease document. The tenant should also obtain a detailed written copy of the standard and how it is to be applied.

Even with the measurement standard in hand, the tenant will find that no two space planners or architects (the professionals who usually measure the space) will come up with exactly the same result. Measurements will vary by 2 to 8 percent, which is deemed acceptable by most real estate professionals.

The tenant needs to guard against leasing premises described as, say, "suite #1024 consisting of 8525 square feet," without any documentation to back up that figure. The reason is simple! Over time, a landlord or building management company (sometimes by accident and sometimes not) rounds off or adjusts the amount of space specified to be in a particular office suite. For example, 1024 sq ft may become 1100 sq ft or even 1200 sq ft. When tenants lease an already built-out office suite or floor, they usually just count the spots where their employees are going to fit and make sure that there is enough room for file cabinets and computers and perhaps a lunchroom, a storeroom, a conference room, and a copy room. If everything fits, they accept the specified square footage as accurate. However, depending on how honest or how unscrupulous a landlord is, the specification of space may be 10 to 20 percent greater than the amount that really exists. A 100,000-sq-ft building could therefore bring in rent for a 120,000-sq-ft building. On a consulting assignment for a developer, I once found a 150,000-sq-ft building bringing in rent for just under

200,000 sq ft of space—about a 30 percent phantom increase in the space!

When it comes to how much space a tenant is leasing, the rule is "Let the tenant beware."

How and When Will the Space Be Measured, and Who Will Measure It?   Space can be measured in a number of ways. The most accurate one is called a field measurement. A space planner or architect measures the exact space in the building itself or on a particular floor. For office space that is already built out, the architect uses the measurement standard agreed upon by the landlord and the tenant.

It is in the tenant's best interest to have a space planner or an architect perform the actual measurement. Bear in mind, though, that unless there is an agreement to do so in advance, the landlord may not be willing to accept the results. Furthermore, unless there is an agreed-to cost-sharing arrangement, the tenant will wind up paying the whole tab (however, given some of the discrepancies that have been found, the cost of the measurement can easily be offset by the savings in rent).

Often the landlord will agree to have his or her own architect do the measuring, but this person may merely take measurements from the blueprints of the building, rather than measure the space on-site. This procedure is less than useful since the whole purpose of a measurement is to establish the size of the space that has actually been built. As any contractor will tell you, what is built is only close to what is supposed to be there. Given the vagaries of carpenters and brick masons, what are a few inches (or feet) between friends? Not much—unless you are the tenant paying for the phantom space.

The best time to measure space is when an area is being constructed to the tenant's specification. The ideal time is when the stringers and wall studs are all in place but before the walls are enclosed. At this point the final placement of walls that define the space is known, and allowances can be made if the measurement standard is based on the relationship to the outside finished surface.

Obviously, for the tenant of a full floor or a single building, the best time to take measurements is as soon as the building's outer wall or skin is in place (and the elevator shaft, stairwells, and utility rooms have been constructed or their exact size and placement are known). However, from a tenant's perspective, there is never a bad time to have space measured. Even if the space was previously occupied and is already constructed, it is worthwhile to include an on-site physical measurement as part of the rent payment requirement.

When and How Will Adjustments Occur After Measurement?   The main question many landlords ask after an on-site space measurement is "So what?"

So what if the lease document says the final amount of space being leased is subject to an on-site measurement. Unless the lease document also specifies exactly what steps will be taken after the measurement occurs (and even sometimes when it occurs), many a landlord will just ignore the tenant's protestations regarding the wrong amount of space and the overpayment of rent.

A lease document only specifies the amount or the approximate amount of space being leased and the monthly or annual rent payment to be made. Rarely does it include the possibility of a unilateral adjustment of rent payment by the tenant—for any reason. A tenant who unilaterally adjusted the rent, no matter what the reason, would be in default of the lease. The landlord could begin eviction proceedings or take other cure-of-default action specified in the lease.

Many landlords ignore a tenant's complaints and attempts to adjust the lease document, especially the amount of rent being paid. After all, what are you, the tenant, going to do about it? Are you going to stamp your feet and threaten to move out? Are you actually going to move out? Taking into account the frustration involved in a move, it is not an inexpensive proposition. Also, there is the question of whether you will find another space to fit your needs. Even worse, how do you get another landlord to accept you when you still have an operative and valid lease elsewhere—and it looks as though you're trying to skip out on the rent, regardless of the "right" reasons?

Of course, you could take the landlord to court; that is, you could sue the landlord for nonperformance or something of the sort. In most jurisdictions, it is relatively cheap to file a lawsuit; however, legal advice and expertise are very expensive. The landlord keeps a lawyer on a retainer and is accustomed to legal costs as a necessary expense of doing business. Most businesspeople are shocked to find out how much it costs to take a lawsuit to court and pursue it to some reasonable end—win, lose, or settlement. Even more important than the money is the amount of time that top management will have to invest, especially if the landlord decides to drag things out a bit and begin fact finding and deposition taking.

Will right prevail? Will the tenant win out after it's all over? Not necessarily. You'll need to check with legal counsel in your jurisdiction. The court may well accept a 2 to 5 percent (or greater) differential between the actual measurement and the amount of space specified in the lease (depending on exactly how the space is defined in the lease document).

Does a 5 percent miss mean much? Well, for every 1000 sq ft leased, 5 percent is 50 sq ft. For each $1 per square foot (psf) of annual rent, the extra cost to the tenant is $50 per year. Therefore, for an annual rent of $20 psf the cost for each 1000 sq ft of phantom space is $1000 a year, for $30 psf the cost is $1500 a year. The larger the space user, the more money laid out for imaginary square footage. For example, a 10,000-sq-ft user with a 5 percent actual-to-paid space differential would be paying an extra $500 per year for each $1 psf in annual rent. This is an extra $10,000 per year if the annual per-square-foot rent is $20, or an extra and unnecessary $100,000 over the 10-year lease term.

Just What Can a Tenant Do?   For this you need to get legal advice relevant to your jurisdiction. Here are some basic guidelines:

- Include a provision in the lease stating that the final measurement or agreed-to size of the space for which rent is to be paid is subject to a final measurement.

- Specify whether an on-site measurement is required or a measurement from final building construction drawings is sufficient.

- Specify who will be responsible for the measurement (i.e., tenant or landlord or both) and when the measurement is to occur.

- Clearly define the measurement standard that will be used for the space (see the discussion on rentable and usable square footage in this chapter), and include a copy of the standard as an addendum to the lease document.

- Specify who (landlord or tenant or both) will pay for the space planner or architect to do the measurement and whether it will be an average of separate measurements by the landlord's and tenant's individual architects.

- To establish a valid lease, include (specifying that they are estimates) the approximate number of square feet being leased (based on the appropriate descriptions and attached marked-up floor plan drawings), the agreed-to rental rate per square foot, with an estimated annual (or monthly or whatever, depending on the jurisdiction) rent amount.

- Include language indicating that actual rent payments will not begin until a lease addendum outlines the amount of square feet established in the actual measurement. This addendum would take the rent per square foot specified in the lease document and compute the necessary annual or monthly rent, as well as adjust final rentable and usable square feet calculations or percentage calculations necessary for tenant's proportionate share of appropriate expenses.

Note: An "after signing of the lease" addendum or certification document between landlords and tenants is not without precedent. In fact, addenda are made regularly, for example, notices of increases in rent, notices regarding annual payments for proportionate share of the building's operating expenses, and the landlord's approval and signed sublease document for the tenant's subleasing of space. The most common is an estoppel certificate, where the tenant certifies the possession of space and payment of rent to the building's mortgage lender. (This issue will be discussed in more detail later.)

Will Any of This Work?   The answer is, it doesn't hurt for the tenant to try. The tenant has a right to pay only for real space and his or her proportionate share of the general and common spaces of the building, not for phantom or nonexistent space. The majority of landlords will be forthright and honest about space measurement and will be willing to do whatever is reasonable to allay a tenant's concerns regarding the amount of space being leased. If the landlord looks hurt or acts as though his or her "honor" as a businessperson is being impugned, however—watch out. This can be a sign that the tenant is being conned and may wind up the lessee of nonexisting space.

And what of the PREB? Shouldn't that individual be helping the tenant and verifying the amount of space being leased? Part of the answer to this question is the very reason why this book was written.

Yes, the majority of brokers are honest. But even with honest and ethical brokers, a tenant's concern over a "measly" 2 to 5 percent possible difference in space measurement is just not worth the hassle. The less experienced or newer brokers usually have no idea that phantom space even exists (many are incredulous the first time they come across it), and what is more important, they have no idea what to do about it. As long as the space meets all the tenant's needs, few brokers bother commenting on or even warning their clients about phantom space. Remember, too, that PREBs are usually paid a commission or fee based on the total value of the lease, which is directly related to the amount of space being leased.

What Is Common Space?

The term *common space* usually refers to space of a general nature; that is, common space is not leased to any of the tenants and is for the common good or common usage of all or some of the tenants. Certain kinds of common space affect the amount of space a tenant winds up paying for. They also affect what is known as the rentable and usable space areas of the building and of each tenant's space.

In general, the landlord owns and controls the common spaces, but tenants have access to, and the use of, these spaces. Both landlords and tenants have a vested interest in maintaining common areas. Such areas create the general atmosphere that greets visitors and guests to the building and to the tenant's premises.

Common space can be divided into two main types: common space for the overall building and that for individual floors. The common space for the building consists of the entrance lobby, corridors to the lobby and office suites, stairwells, rest rooms for the building, general mail collection room, building health club or spa, plumbing or heating, ventilation, and air conditioning (HVAC) rooms used for the whole building, the roof, general terraces open to all tenants, storage rooms for the exclusive use of maintaining the building and operating plant, courtyards, atriums, adjacent parks, elevators, and any other area that is open to all tenants and their guests or that is for the general good of the whole building.

Common areas on a floor are more likely to be found in multi-tenant floors (i.e., floors that have two or more tenant premises). These common areas are usually telephone closets or rooms, HVAC rooms, corridors to tenant premises, floor rest rooms, or terrace areas that are only accessible from that floor.

Common space can play an important role for all the tenants and guests. Just how important it is will determine how it is maintained and how rentable and usable areas are defined. Common areas are often in a state of flux, constantly changing to meet various tenant or landlord needs. The common space on an individual floor can change as corridors are added or eliminated to expand or contract tenant premises. If retail areas are added to a building's main lobby, the common area available to all tenants will be reduced, with leased premises present that were not contemplated in the tenant's lease. Park areas might be eliminated or another building built on vacant land, corridors and side and rear building entrances might be closed or used for other than building access purposes, and general basement storage space might be converted to rentable storage space.

A tenant does not have much control over common space. Most leases contain either a specific common space lease clause or define and specify the use of common space as part of a building's rules and regulations, as promulgated by the landlord.

Typical buzzwords and phrases that crop up in common space lease clauses are "provided from time to time by the landlord," "provided for general nonexclusive use," "granting of tenant and guests, employees and invitees nonexclusive license to use said space in common with other entitled tenants," "provided without any liability," "Landlord may establish or change rules and regulations regarding common space use," "Landlord may change, add, close off, or eliminate said space without incurring liability or entitling tenant to a substitute or rent abatement," and "Landlord may create additional leased premises." The landlord may do whatever he or she wishes with a building's common areas as long as the tenants are not deprived of the use and benefit of their own premises.

All this works well for the landlord, but what about the tenant? In effect, the tenant has no rights regarding common space—with one or two exceptions. An important exception is when a tenant has leased premises because of the ambience or unique business environment created by a particular common area or common space. If that is the case, it is up to the tenant to have the lease document modified in order to ensure that the particular common area or building convenience will remain in existence throughout the term of the tenant's lease.

A good example of a common area and tenant benefit that can come or go at the whim of the landlord is a health club or spa. A health club is actually considered a building amenity rather than a true common space; however, to the extent that it is available to all tenants, because the space was initially set aside for the facility and is used to attract tenants, it is included here as a common area. This type of common area will often disappear unless it is clearly and specifically defined in the lease document.

The importance of common areas is reflected in how they are treated in the measurement of a tenant's premises. Common areas and building amenities must be paid for in some fashion, supposedly by all of the building's tenants. In some jurisdictions, for example, a building's lobby area is divided up and a portion included in the total rentable square feet for each premises. However, confusion can result. The individual tenant must make sure the apportionment of common space is fair to all of the building's tenants.

What Are Rentable Square Feet?

Rentable square feet is simply a way of expressing the amount of space the tenant will be renting. The main difficulty for most tenants lies in determining the number of rentable square feet. As explained earlier, there are many ways to measure space. Not only is there no national standard, but standards vary among jurisdictions and landlords (even the same landlord may use different methods in different buildings).

Rentable square feet can include the following:

1. Concrete or brick walls (e.g., if the standard specifies that the measurement will be made from the outside finished surface of a building's outer wall)

2. Air (e.g., if the measurement standard includes penetrations through the floor or ceiling slabs for an electrical or plumbing conduit of some minimum or maximum size or where the standard measures from an imaginary point outside an inward-slanting wall)

3. Parts of interior walls (depending on whether the measurement is taken from the inside or the outside finished surface of a corridor wall)

4. Common space both for the floor (e.g., corridors, rest rooms) and for the building (e.g., main building entrance lobby)

5. In some cases, nonexistent space (usually because there is no measurement standard or because the tenant does not check to see what he or she has actually leased)

Theoretically, the amount of total rentable square feet available in a building should not vary over the life of the building. After all, the building was constructed as a certain size and really shouldn't change. But even this is not necessarily true. Landlords often convert building common space such as basement storage areas and portions of building lobbies.

The total rentable square feet in a building will affect most tenants. Leases in excess of one year will often include some type of escalation provision allowing the landlord either to increase the base rent or to call on the tenant to pay his or her share of the increased operating costs, real estate taxes, and other variable or increasing building expenses. These increases are typically passed on to tenants in the same ratio as their share of the total building space leased (see Chapter 7). The tenant's proportionate share is the number of total rentable square feet being leased as a percentage of the total rentable square feet in the building.

Therefore, if the building's total rentable square feet is a constant, the sum of all space users and available space to lease should equal the total. This, of course, is just simple common sense. No higher mathematics needed here—right?

Only One Total Rentable Square Feet

Well, sort of.

First, the tenant must insist on having the number that forms the base for all expense sharing or all proportionate share calculations included in the lease document. And this number must be verifiable.

Second, if there is more than one kind of tenant or space user in a building or more than one classification of space (e.g., office, retail, storage), the tenant will need to use more than one base number to establish the building's total rentable square feet. Each base would be used to figure the proportionate share of expenses for each space classification. The tenant should be sure to have all the different types of total rentable square feet specified in the lease document; in other words, the available rentable square feet must total 100 percent after the space classifications are added up.

For example, in an office building that has retail space or a large shopping area, the office user should be aware that the retail lease will be significantly different from an office lease; for example, the retail tenant may be separately metered for electricity and will often have separate or supplemental HVAC. Therefore, although there might be one base number expressing the total rentable square feet in the building for use by all tenants in sharing property tax increases, there should be a separate base number for the distribution of increased operating expenses associated with building maintenance and operations. This is especially the case for janitorial services. Retail tenants typically contract separately for cleaning services, whereas office tenants usually have janitorial services performed as part of the building's operations.

Things can become even more complicated when there are large atrium areas with (and even without) retail space. Who is responsible for paying for the maintenance and operation of these areas? Everyone in the building? Or should a large part, if not all, of the expenses be assigned to the retail spaces since they get the most benefit? And what about two of the same kind of space users who use the space so differently that one significantly increases the costs of building maintenance and other expenses?

To complicate matters further, the total rentable square feet for the whole building may not really be a constant. The tenant must specify what procedure is to be used when the base number of total rentable square feet needs to be adjusted because a particular type of space has changed or has been added to the building. For example, what happens if the landlord permits a retail kiosk to be added to the main entrance lobby? What was not previously rentable square feet has now changed. The total rentable square feet of the building should change (increase) accordingly. Because this is the denominator for calculating each space user's proportionate share, this change should lower the proportionate percentage assignable to all space users. In some cases, a change or addition of space can change more than just one of the different total rentable square feet base numbers for a particular space user. For example, the landlord may convert a significant portion of a lobby area or previously unused basement or first-floor space to retail or other type of space (e.g., a lower or basement floor area into rentable storage space). Or the landlord may add on a particular type of space to the building.

Tenants should also take a close look at the treatment of a building's parking areas, especially if the parking is integrated into the building structure (e.g., roof parking or below-grade parking areas). Who pays for the maintenance and operating expenses of these areas (e.g., sweeping, trash pickup, possibly snow removal, line painting, surface repair, wall damage, painting, general upkeep)? Everyone in the building? Or only those who use the areas? What if the parking areas are leased out to a parking lot operator who charges for the use of the parking? Is this area still to be counted as part of the building?

In general, the base numbers used to calculate total rentable square feet should not include parking or other similarly utilized spaces. They should be specified separately and have their own base number.

The definition of what constitutes a building's common space and the determination of the total rentable square feet in a building have implications for a tenant's expenses and costs of leasing space. Tenants must guard against broad generalities that can cost them money. Every change in the calculation of a number or percentage should be thoroughly understood before the tenant agrees to any change. It is all too easy for a landlord to convert some previously nonrentable space, such as the lobby area, to rentable space, say, for retail purposes. Because this kind of space is different from the space in the rest of the building (which is office space in our example), the landlord will want the office tenant to agree that the total rentable square feet base number has decreased. However, if the office user's base number for the total amount of rentable square feet decreases, every office user will have to pay an even higher percentage of the building's expenses (because the denominator has shrunk). The amount of rentable space available for office space has not changed, though; rather, the total rentable square feet in the building has increased, and that should reduce certain costs (e.g., proportionate shares of real estate taxes) for the rest of the building's space users—not increase them!

Total Rented Is Not Total Rentable

Tenants must also make sure that the definitions being used refer to total *rentable* square feet, not total *rented* square feet. This difference is all too often glossed over by the landlord. The tenant who is unaware of this difference can wind up overpaying for space.

The total rentable square feet in a building constitutes all the space that can or will conceivably be leased. The total rented square feet constitutes the space that has actually been leased by space users up to that point in time.

The difference is important in calculating the tenant's proportionate share of operating expenses and real estate taxes. If space is not yet leased (or occupied), then the total rented square feet is less than the total rentable square feet. If total rented square feet is the basis for distribution, then at that time each tenant would pay for more of the expenses related to building maintenance and operations.

Although this may sound like a logical approach, it represents backward thinking. A tenant should only pay his or her proportion of expenses for the total rentable space in a building and not be concerned with occupied versus vacant space. Suppose that a building has 100,000 sq ft of rentable space but only 50,000 sq ft are rented. A tenant has leased 10,000 sq ft. The amount of space the tenant has as a proportion of the total building is 10 percent if the base is rentable square feet but 20 percent if the base is rented square feet.

Vacant space is the landlord's problem, not the tenant's. The tenant might be concerned if the landlord were going bankrupt because of not being able to lease the vacant space. Or if the tenant were one of the first to sign a lease in a building and the building or certain floors were still under construction, problems could arise—the "vacant building syndrome." That is, the tenant would have to put up with construction dust and noise, do without full building services, and share elevators with construction crews. But vacant space typically does not create the same types of expenses or service problems as occupied space: No janitorial services are needed, maintenance is minimal, and there is no heating and air conditioning.

The tenant must be on the watch not only for these problems, but also for those associated with the proportionate sharing of costs and expenses. The tenant must be aware and beware. The space user must see to it that total rentable square feet are carefully spelled out and that areas used for other purposes are appropriately specified in the lease document.

The tenant should not expect the landlord to be all that quick to adjust the proportionate share calculation or to be specific about what expenses are included or excluded for distribution. It is up to the tenant to keep tabs on what is happening in the building and to make certain the landlord has made the appropriate and accurate adjustments.

Usable Square Feet

But the complications of square footage don't end there! The next concept the tenant needs to grasp is that of usable square feet. The term *usable square feet* refers to the area that the tenant actually uses as a business environment for staff, inventory, furniture and equipment, and guests or customers. Usable square feet include any parts of the area that will be needed to construct walls to partition the space into work areas and to separate the space from other space users. The actual usable square feet are also a function of the measurement standard being used to define the building's space. A typical measurement standard will include things like columns and supports necessary for the structural integrity of the building. Obviously, a large concrete column measuring 2 ft on a side and taking up 4 sq ft of space doesn't really provide any usable space for the tenant. Nevertheless, it is included in the definition of usable square feet.

Usable square feet is a dynamic measurement that can change constantly (even in single-user buildings) as new spaces are created, partition walls added, partition walls removed, hallways created, and hallways deleted.

In practical terms, *usable square feet* means the space that is sufficient to provide the desired working or customer environment and provide space for staff and associated officeware. Usable square feet becomes significant when related to the concept of efficiency, both from the viewpoint of the use of space and from that of cost. The more efficiency and maximum utility a space offers, the lower the overall costs for the user.

How efficiently different spaces can be used is often a function of what is known as bay sizes and window mullion placements. *Bay size* refers to that space within any four points that define the structural or unmovable elements of the building (e.g., the interior space within four building support columns). A *window mullion* is the area or space between windows or where windows are joined together so that there is a place to anchor a dividing or partition wall. (Otherwise, the end of the wall partition would abut a window. Although special rubber gaskets and seals can be used to complete the wall partition, they will spoil the architectural intention and the "look" of the glass spanning the building's outer wall when viewed from outside the building.)

Not all buildings have window mullions to worry about; some have brick, masonry, or some other construction material separating the windows. In the buildings that do have them, the spacing between mullions is important for the efficient use of the interior space, especially if the interior space is to be divided with fixed wall construction or partitions. The distance between the mullions defines the typical size of space, such as an office, that can be built along a window wall. If mullions are 4 ft apart, for example, the space along them can be divided into multiples of four, such as four, eight, or twelve. Window mullions will usually be 4, 6, or 8 ft apart. The closer the mullions, the greater the flexibility the user has in deciding how the space will be divided and utilized.

The bay size, even more than the mullion distance, determines how efficiently the space will be used. Small bay sizes (e.g., 10 ft by 10 ft or 15 ft by 15 ft) do not permit an interior space to be subdivided into large clear open spaces, as for an auditorium or a meeting room. If columns are too close to an outer window or building walls, there will be less depth available for creating office space. Greater depth allows for a larger office space area that can also include nearby support staff. In addition, the space can be constructed without intruding on badly placed interior columns. Perhaps more important, greater depth also permits the space to be divided more reasonably, so that more offices can be constructed with window views.

The space planner or architect is the best person to consult about the efficient use of a particular space. And don't neglect to compare efficiency if more than one space is under consideration. Where there is an opportunity to use space more efficiently, there is also an opportunity to reduce expenses and save resources.

Rentable Versus Usable Square Feet

The ultimate measure of efficiency is how much the space costs to lease. The actual costs paid are a combination of the rent and various expense passthroughs, such as a building's operating expenses and real estate taxes. However, all of these costs are a direct function of the amount of rentable square feet of space assignable to the tenant. The more efficient a space, the more usable square feet a tenant has in relation to the rentable square feet the tenant is being charged for. It is particularly important for the space user to determine this relationship when comparing alternative spaces or buildings before actually leasing a space.

Naturally, the real estate profession has its own jargon regarding the difference between rentable and usable square feet. This jargon varies from one region to the next. The tenant must be absolutely sure he or she understands the terms being used to describe different spaces. In addition, the tenant will need to know what measurement standards, if any, are being used for a particular building and whether buildings are using different standards of measurement.

The terms generally used to distinguish usable from rentable square feet are *core factors, grossing-up,* and *loss factor.* All of these terms refer to the additional square feet the space user must pay for above and beyond the amount of space actually needed to provide the business environment. These terms can result in significant differences between the amount of space that is attributable to rentable and usable square feet.

The term *conversion factor* is a softer-sounding term for *grossing-up* and *loss factor,* just as *transaction* carries fewer overtones than *deal.* A definition of the conversion factor will be integrated in a region's formal measurement standard (e.g., BOMA's method of measurement or the Washington, DC, Association of Realtors measurement standard). It is also calculable in advance and is based on the actual measurements of a building floor using the amount of rentable versus usable square feet available.

Grossing-up refers to a factor that is applied to the amount of usable square feet being rented to get the amount of total rentable square feet of the building the user will be responsible for. *Loss factor* is just the reverse; it refers to the percentage of the space that is the difference between the rentable and usable square feet (see the following example).

The term *core factor* is real estate jargon (often regionally) for the amount of space in a building that space users will be assigned and pay rent for but will not be able to utilize as part of their business environment usable square feet—elevator lobbies of multitenanted floors, telephone closets, and so forth.

Many buildings require two conversion factors: one for single-building tenants or single-tenanted floors and another for multitenanted buildings or multitenanted floors. For example, multitenanted floors require additional hallways to provide access to the different tenant premises, but these would not be needed on a single-tenanted floor. Therefore, a single-tenanted floor has a higher ratio of usable space to rentable space than a multitenanted floor.

A *conversion factor* is usually defined as the usable square feet divided by the rentable square feet, or vice versa:

$$\text{Conversion factor } A = \frac{\text{rentable square feet}}{\text{usable square feet}}$$

$$\text{or} \quad \text{Conversion factor } B = \frac{\text{usable square feet}}{\text{rentable square feet}}$$

If the amount of rentable square feet on a floor is, say, 25,000 sq ft and the amount of usable square feet on the floor for a "typical" multitenanted floor is 21,500 sq ft, then applying the formula gives the following conversion factors:

$$\text{Conversion factor } A = \frac{25,000}{21,500} = 1.163$$

$$\text{or} \quad \text{Conversion factor } B = \frac{21,500}{25,000} = 0.86$$

Both conversion factor A and conversion factor B are decimal equivalents of two viewpoints describing essentially the same thing, namely, the amount of additional space that a tenant must pay for when renting space that is not available for actual use for business operations or environment. In the one instance, the amount of usable square feet would be grossed up to get the amount of rentable square feet; in the other instance, the total amount of rentable square feet has an attributable loss factor resulting in the usable square feet. (In some regions, the conversion factor is simply the building or floor core factor, giving the same results as described above.)

The only difference between the two conversion factors (and the related decimal equivalents) is that of perception. As every

PREB quickly learns, in the real estate business, *perception is reality.* If a tenant uses a full floor of space (the same 21,500 sq ft and 25,000 sq ft above), there are two possible perceptions or views: (1) The tenant will "only" have a 14 percent loss factor of the total rentable square feet, so the remaining amount will be usable square feet, or (2) there will be a 16+ percent grossing-up factor, which increases the amount of usable square feet to give the total amount of rentable square feet. Different conversion factor percentages result from the different denominators used to calculate the difference between the amount of usable and rentable square feet. That is, the difference between 25,000 sq ft and 21,500 sq ft is 3500 sq ft. This 3500 sq ft as a percentage of the 25,000 rentable sq ft is 14 percent of the total; the same 3500 sq ft is 16.3 percent when taken as a percentage of the 21,500 usable sq ft.

Using the two conversion factors gives the same results, as follows:

Grossing-up

Usable square feet × conversion factor A

$$= \text{total rentable square feet}$$

$$21{,}500 \times 1.63 = 25{,}005^*$$

Alternatively,

$$\frac{\text{Total rentable square feet}}{\text{Conversion factor } A} = \text{usable square feet}$$

$$\frac{25{,}000}{1.163} = 21{,}496$$

Loss factor

Total rentable square feet × conversion factor B

$$= \text{usable square feet}$$

$$25{,}000 \times 0.86 = 21{,}500$$

---

*Difference from actual 25,000 sq ft is due to rounding of decimal equivalent.

Alternatively,

$$\frac{\text{Usable square feet}}{\text{Conversion factor } B} = \text{total rentable square feet}$$

$$\frac{21{,}500}{0.86} = 25{,}000$$

The alternative computations are shown as they are most often associated with the conversion term *core factor.* The examples show how the core factor percentage is applied to either the total rentable or usable square feet to get the related usable or total rentable square feet, respectively.

Because of architectural diversity, there are no standards for core factors, grossing-up factors, loss factors, or conversion factors. However, the lower the conversion factor A (or the higher the conversion factor B), the more cost efficient the usable space will be in relation to the amount of total rentable square feet being paid for by a tenant. The measurement standard being used for a building will also create significant usable versus rentable square feet differences, especially when main entrance lobbies, balconies, parking areas, and atriums are included in the calculations. In addition, there are significant differences in space efficiency in single-tenanted versus multitenanted floors.

As an interesting aside regarding space efficiency, consider the use of space by large single-floor or multifloor space users. These space users are often willing to pay premium prices for being able to confine occupancy to one large floor. It is believed that a business will operate more efficiently when people are located on just one floor, since more departments will be "near" each other (they're called horizontal or departmental adjacencies) and there will be greater interaction between the staff.

In actuality, many supersized-floor users find that 50,000 or 100,000 sq ft is such a vast space that staff efficiency decreases. Tenants often find that a vertical adjacency (for example, contiguous floors with a connecting internal staircase) is more practical and efficient.

Supersized single floors are also cost inefficient when judged by the conversion factor of percentage of rentable versus usable square feet. This is due to the doubling or tripling of the space needed for the general building space (in some areas known as a double-core or triple-core building) needed to service the super-sized floor. For example, such space requires extra fire stairwells and extra elevators to ensure adequate evacuation. Two or even three separate banks of elevators are often required to improve floor access for employees, clients, and visitors. In addition, extra telephone closets, additional bathrooms, and additional air-handling units and closets will be required for the extra-large space. Often it takes more of these items to service the supersized floor properly than it does to service two floors of equal capacity. Cost inefficiencies result in regard to usable square feet.

A space user needs to consider three efficiency questions:

1. How many usable square feet are needed, and how well can this space be utilized to meet business operational and environmental needs?

2. How comfortable is the space for staff and business-related resources (e.g., furniture, machinery)?

3. What is the cost per square foot to the user on a *usable* square-foot basis?

It is this last item that will drive the PREB to a bicarbonate-of-soda break. As for the tenant, the efficiency of space can be measured accurately only when the cost of each usable foot is known. This is especially true when someone is trying to compare two different spaces for a leasing decision. Although there are many factors that can make one space more expensive and worth more than another space, there are also many things that can pad the cost of space without adding any value—that is, for the tenant.

3

Landlord's Right to Relocate Tenants

The lease clause that gives the landlord a right to relocate tenants usually applies more to small and medium-sized space users than to large space users, but large space users may be included.

The clause, which can be relatively simple or extraordinarily complex, is designed to protect and give total flexibility to a landlord. It enables the landlord to utilize a building's leasable space in a way that will maximize income. It is included in a lease purely for the benefit of the landlord. The tenant must fully understand the version of this clause included in his or her lease and have it crafted to ensure reasonable benefits. Without the possibility of such adjustments, the tenant may be severely inconvenienced, suffer significant business disruptions, and incur unexpected (as well as unfair) and large expenses.

Basically, this clause enables the landlord to relocate (or move) a tenant within a building to new and different space so that an additional or a large space user can be accommodated.

This is well and good for the landlord, but what about the tenant? From the perspective of a building or landlord broker, this clause is an absolute must. It provides opportunities for maximizing revenue. However, all too often the tenant's broker is "understanding" of the landlord's need for this clause and is quick to accept the version of the clause that is offered, not recognizing that other options are available to the tenant.

Major Items to Consider, and How Often

When May the Landlord Relocate the Tenant?

The landlord may want to relocate a space user for a number of reasons.

Relocation may become necessary when a building is under construction or is newly completed. By being able to move smaller tenants to another floor or to another area of the same floor, the landlord will be able to accommodate a larger tenant who might insist on a particular view or area of a building or who may want a full floor.

After a building is fully leased, relocation is an important part of a landlord's space management strategy. For example, a landlord needs flexibility when a number of small- to medium-sized space users move from the building, especially if they were all formerly on different floors. By being able to move other tenants around in the building, the landlord is able to consolidate and create a large space or even a whole building floor to accommodate or attract a large space user.

In a fully leased building the landlord wants to be able to accommodate expansion options or first rights of refusal to additional space for current tenants. For example, a tenant may have the right to expand his or her space to contiguous space in a particular year or time period. To meet this preplanned expansion or growth, the landlord must either find space users able to accept short-term leases or have the flexibility to move a tenant and thereby free up the required space at the required time.

Normally, this clause is used to maximize the leasing of a new building, and its use is more limited after a tenant has moved in.

You can do the following to reduce the risks of relocation:

1. Limit the landlord's right to relocate you to the time period before you take possession of the space or up to the date the lease commences.

2. Require a minimum amount of time for the landlord to notify you of the intention to relocate before you take possession of the original leased space or before the date the lease com-

mences. If a minimum period of time is not required, you may not find out about the relocation until a week or less before the originally scheduled move-in date.

3. Permit or restrict the landlord's relocation options after you have taken possession or during the term of the lease. (Will the landlord be permitted to relocate you at any time and for any reason?) Such limits may pertain to how soon after possession or the beginning of the lease term the first relocation can take place, or they may consist of previously approved reasons for any possible tenant relocation already specified in the lease document (if possible, include some test of validity for the induced relocation).

4. Have limits placed on how many times you can be relocated during the term of the lease. The lease should not be open ended, with an unlimited number of relocations permitted.

Time Frame of Relocation

How long a time period should be permitted for a relocation, and how much notice of a relocation should be given?

There are no pat answers to these questions. Each relocation will be governed by the given circumstances. However, the tenant should be sure that the lease provisions make it possible to continue operating the business as usual.

Here are some lease provisions concerning relocation that you should consider:

1. Insist that you be notified within a minimum period of time of the landlord's intention to relocate you. The length of this period will depend on how long it will take you to prepare for a move, to prepare new business materials, and to avoid any business disruptions.

2. Provide specific time periods when a notice of relocation or actual relocation is unacceptable because of the threat of serious business disruption. For example, a manufacturer's broker who is required to be at certain trade shows or an importer of seasonal goods (e.g., Christmas goods) would find a relocation during certain times of the year both inconvenient and disruptive. Other

businesses, such as temporary employment agencies, law firms, accounting firms, and courier services, may also find relocation unacceptable at particular times of the year.

Another point to spell out clearly is the actual time during the week that would be acceptable for a move. For example, many businesses prefer a weekend move to avoid disrupting business and the staff's activities. Other businesses may rely on weekend business and would prefer a weekday move late at night. It is up to the tenant to see that such specifications are included in the lease.

3. Make certain that any extensions on the time of relocation because of buildout or construction or because of necessary improvements in the relocation space are at your convenience. How long a relocation takes is often a function of whether the space being moved into is in an acceptable condition or is in the same condition as the space being vacated. If neither is the case, extensive renovation or special business-related construction or improvements may be required (e.g., wiring for computer systems, supplemental air conditioning for conference rooms, specialized equipment).

4. Before the actual relocation takes place, the language should clearly indicate that any new space must be comparable to or meet the same quality of construction and business environment as your current space. This will ensure, for example, that telephone wiring, telephone equipment and systems, computer wiring, and the proper number of office, storage, and equipment spaces are in place before you move in. This will keep to a minimum the time your business needs to become fully operational.

5. The lease should clearly state the amount of time you need to prepare for the relocation in addition to the time required for any construction or improvements of the new space. From a tenant's perspective, the time it takes to relocate depends on what has to be done before relocation can occur. For example, clients and vendors have to be notified of the change of address; new business cards have to be prepared for employees; new stationery or other printed materials have to be acquired; and specialty equipment, such as a printing press or product-testing machinery, has to be moved in advance and set up. (If the tenant has

certain relocation obligations, the landlord will want time limitations placed on the tenant as well.)

6. Make sure that landlord-granted benefits, concessions, or inducements will be extended for a time period acceptable to you, to account for any extension of the relocation time period and for the inevitable relocation hassles and disruptions. If relocation should occur during a rent abatement period, the rent abatement time period would be extended to account for both the relocation time and business disruption. An extended time benefit provision should be included whether the relocation is to take place before the lease commences or at some point during the term of the lease.

Who Pays for What?

The tenant must be sure that the lease indicates that any costs associated with or that result from a landlord-induced relocation are to be reimbursed or paid for by the landlord. This landlord payment requirement should be in force regardless of whether the relocation is permitted before or after the lease commences. Unless the notice of relocation or actual relocation occurs before the tenant has to set in motion any of the subsidiary tasks associated with moving to new space, there will be a long list of costs and business-related expenses that must be paid for.

The typical space user will incur at least three kinds of costs during a relocation:

1. *General moving expenses.* Moving costs fall into two categories: those related to the physical move itself and those that arise because of the relocation.
   a. Physical moving costs
      - Moving physical property, such as furniture, equipment, machinery, bookshelves (for a library), storage shelves, and business inventory
      - Disassembling, moving, and reassembling furniture and equipment such as book or library shelves, computer equipment, copy machines, printing presses, special furniture (e.g., large conference tables, credenzas, bar

areas), video and teleconferencing capabilities, and tele-communication equipment

    b. Nonphysical moving costs

- Printed business materials, typically business cards and stationery
- Relocation announcements, including the printing and mailing costs for notifying clients or customers and vendors of the relocation
- Other printed materials that may have to be changed or modified because of the relocation, such as catalogs, promotional materials, or published materials (e.g., newsletters, magazines or books)

2. *Business operation expenses.*

- Moving the office telephone systems or rewiring for telephones
- Special installation of the HVAC system
- Special handling (e.g., by manufacturers or approved representatives only) of equipment that requires special care or is oversized, such as computer mainframes, large copy machines, or printing presses
- Adjusting dedicated or high-voltage electrical circuits
- Special wiring for computers or telecommunication networks

3. *Special construction or work done to improve the business environment.* This includes changes made to the basic walls, ceilings, electric wiring, and doors. At times, it may not even be possible to move special items such as kitchen areas, conference rooms, glass walls, enhanced wall treatments (e.g., wainscoting, wallpaper), wood paneling, floor-to-ceiling wood doors, special ceiling treatments, ceiling moldings, upgraded floor coverings, electronic security or controls, built-in safes or security areas, and built-in cabinets, bookshelves, or counters. If they are replaced, the expense may be considerable.

4. *Business-related income and rent expense.* Business income and revenues are not really expense items except to the extent that they are interrupted as a result of the relocation. If that is a possibility, or when it actually occurs, to the extent the lost income was a result of a landlord-induced relocation, the landlord should be required to reimburse the tenant. Typically a tenant will determine how much income was lost on the basis

of the experience of the business in the preceding year during the same time period as the relocation. Therefore, the onus will be on the tenant to prove that income has been lost. If it was only delayed, then the tenant may still be entitled to some type of out-of-pocket expenses, but again, proof of the delay is required.

A tenant who finds that business cannot be conducted or that business operations will be delayed for some time, or even that relocation was a serious inconvenience, should expect to have related space utilization expenses abated. These expenses include rent for the space, building operations and maintenance costs, and any other proportionate share of expense items otherwise chargeable to the tenant.

A business can face hundreds of costs during a relocation, whether it is moving from one building to another or from one space to another in the same building. In a landlord-induced relocation, the landlord must reimburse the business for these expenses. But the burden of proof regarding appropriate expenses or lost income will rest with the relocating business.

It is up to the tenant to make sure the appropriate provisions are included in the relocation clause of the lease. The tenant should attempt to secure the broadest lease provisions possible regarding the landlord's reimbursement or direct payment for relocation-related expenses or lost income. Barring that, a specific listing of what a landlord will reimburse the tenant for is a good fallback position. (Actually, a listing of what the landlord will *not* pay for often works better for a tenant; this takes the form of broad language indicating that everything else will be reimbursed.)

In addition, the lease clause should state when (the time frame) and how the landlord will provide the reimbursement. Will the reimbursement occur within 30 days of the time that the tenant submits an invoice? And will the landlord pay the reimbursement directly to the tenant or arrange to credit it against future rent payments?

Is There Equality of Space?

The space user will be particularly concerned about whether the new or proposed space is at least equal to or better in quality than the original space. The quality will be judged by a number of factors:

1. Are the spaces of comparable size? Is the new space larger or smaller than the original space? If it is not the same size, what side effects will this have on the rent?

2. Are the spaces comparable from the standpoint of efficiency of use? Will the new location offer more or less usable space, and will business resources be used with more or less efficiency?

3. Does the new space provide an equal or better overall business environment? This includes the intangible aspects of the space, such as the layout, the storage areas, and all the nooks and crannies that over time have helped create a productive business environment for both the staff and the clients. Pay special attention to the finish and any features or buildout that either exist in the new space or are missing in the new one but existed in the original space.

4. Is the new space in a comparable location? Is it at a higher or lower floor? Does it have the same number of windows, window views, location of space on the floor (e.g., prime corner location or back corridor location)? What is the locational relationships to other tenants in the building, especially if vendor-client relationships exist?

5. From the standpoint of rent, is the value of the new space equal to, less than, or more than that of the original space? Will a "better" location mean paying a higher rent? Will the rent be adjusted downward for a less desirable location?

   The tenant must always insist that, except under extraordinary circumstances and only with his or her approval, the new rent will not be greater than that paid for the original space. This should be the case regardless of whether the new space is larger than the original space, because the relocation is at the behest of, and for the convenience of, the landlord. If the space is smaller and there is any reduction in quality, however, even if it is only a perceived reduction by the tenant, there should be an appropriate downward adjustment in the rent.

Equality of space is not always easy for the small- to medium-sized space user to achieve. To measure or establish all the many items that contribute to the quality of the business environment, the tenant must pay careful attention in the relocation lease clause to all areas and items of concern.

Since it is often difficult to describe space equality and comparability, the tenant may be better served by indicating what would not be acceptable in a relocation. For example, the tenant might specify that new space may not be located any lower than two floors from the current space; the amount of windowed wall space may not be reduced by more than 10 percent of the total linear wall space; the space on the east and south sides of the building is not acceptable; or the tenant cannot be moved into a space that consists of more than 5 percent less usable square feet than the current space (as defined by the original measurement standard).

Right to Terminate

Lease documents seldom contain termination provisions that favor the tenant. But since the burden of a relocation provision falls on the tenant, it would seem to be a fair trade-off to expect. Essentially the tenant would have the right to terminate his or her lease on the basis of certain unacceptable criteria related to the landlord-invoked relocation. The criteria would usually be taken from the items discussed above. The tenant would be permitted to terminate the lease if, for example, the new space increased the tenant's rent by more than 10 percent of the current rent, if the landlord refused to reimburse relocation expenses submitted by the tenant, or if the landlord were unable to provide an equal or a better quality of business environment in the new space.

A termination provision related to the relocation provision gives the tenant an extra measure of flexibility regardless of his or her size and negotiation strength. After all, a paying tenant is money in the bank to a landlord in most space rental markets.

To be effective, a termination provision must allow adequate time for the location of new space in a new building, for any expected special construction requirements, and for conducting the move itself. In addition, depending on when the relocation is to occur—for example, after the initial lease has begun—or on how many times a tenant has been forced to relocate, this provision would also require the landlord to reimburse the tenant for moving expenses and extraordinary construction or space improvements the tenant would have to make for the new space to be of equal quality to the old space.

Get It in Writing

Of course, if a tenant is to achieve all or some of these lease provisions, the relocation must be instigated by the landlord for the general reasons of improving space management and building revenue. If, however, the tenant was originally informed that the leased space was subject to another space user's prior claim (another business may have planned to expand into this space and the tenant may have been given a specific relocation time requirement), the tenant is less likely to achieve a favorable relocation clause. But it is not altogether out of the question. The relocation clause will have to be extremely narrow, specifying the exact limitations (e.g., time limitations) required for relocation and outlining the rights and needs of the tenant (e.g., dollar allowance).

All too often, the relocation lease clause is brief and favors the landlord entirely. It does not mention landlord liability and simply states that the tenant will relocate in some period of time when required to do so by the landlord. In the business world, market power is traditionally a function of size. But even the smallest space user should not give a landlord the dictatorial power to bounce a tenant around from space to space without (from the tenant's point of view) proper and adequate compensation.

A key ingredient often missing from a relocation clause, especially for relocations that occur after the lease commitment, is a clear statement of what, expressly when, and how adjustments will be made to the lease document. Will there be a new document? Will any required changes occur before or after the relocation? Will the change be ordained by an addendum to the current lease or through a whole new lease?

The tenant must also recognize that the relocation clause can have a domino effect on virtually every other lease clause—yet, little, if anything, is ever said about how adjustments will be made.

When will relocation expenses be reimbursed? When will the stated size of the premises be adjusted? When will the rent be adjusted? And when will all the other related and affected lease areas, especially those involving dollars, be adjusted?

Each party can trust the other and believe in the other's goodwill. Of course, tenants who do that also believe in the tooth fairy. For the protection of the tenant everything should (must) be as carefully spelled out and detailed in the lease as possible.

Landlords constantly cry foul and act as though space users are stealing the food from the mouths of their children. In fact, the tenant rarely gets everything that is asked for. On the subject of relocation, the tenant must be fully informed and forewarned.

Is What You See What You Get?

When a space user first visits a building, a number of factors, taken together, form the overall impression of what is considered a building's ambience. Often this ambience is what leads a tenant to lease space in a building. Frequently that decision is based on such intangible factors that it may be contrary to any analysis of efficiency and cost of space. In other words, even though the amount and quality of the space cannot match what another building offers and the rent is higher, this ambience is a deciding factor.

Ambience is a combination of how a building looks and feels to the tenant. It is a combination of the building's landscaping, the common areas, the availability of special services, and what is generally known as appurtenances, those items that seem to be attached to or belong to the building.

The tenant begins responding to a building through the surrounding view or neighborhood as he or she approaches the building (in real estate jargon, these surroundings make up a building's "curbside appeal"), and the response may be heightened by sidewalks, gardens, atriums, walkways, street lighting, accent lighting, entranceways, parking areas, parking convenience, lobby areas, hallways, stairwells, access to stairwells, entrance security, internal building security, bathrooms, in-building services, such as retail shops, exercise rooms, concierge services, directory listings (in the lobby, on each floor, and in elevator cabs), entry doors to space (in an office building often called the suite entry door), the number of elevators, internal elevator cab finishes, perceived speed of elevators, external views from the space under consideration, storage areas, loading docks, freight elevators, and delivery entrances or areas, and anything else that the space user sees as or believes to be part of the reason for choosing that particular building.

It is up to the tenant to ensure that what is seen or wanted is what he or she gets—and gets to keep. Many of the things that attracted a tenant to a building may not remain as they were originally seen—often because of subsequent actions of the landlord, but many times because not everything is under the landlord's control.

All too often, the beautiful window views that attracted the tenant are later obscured because another building has been built next door. Or beautiful gardens disappear because of new construction or building additions. Parking lots become crowded as they become shared lots with new buildings. Building entrances are changed to accommodate retail spaces or new construction. Lobby areas are redesigned to provide additional leasable space. Stairwells are moved, or access is restricted. Certain elevators can only be used by one or two large space users on the upper floors. Retail areas disappear. Building services are reduced.

A tenant must not ever take any attractive feature for granted. The tenant must never assume that everything will remain as it is forever—or at least for as long as he or she is leasing space in the building.

Can Anything Be Done?

Sometimes. But do you really want something to be done? The landlord argues that the common spaces are his or hers to control and wants a lease that provides for no other rights except those specified in the lease document. On the other hand, a large space user, especially a full building user, wants an understanding of what common space(s), building services, and appurtenances will continue during the term of the lease.

The landlord wants to control the building to the greatest extent possible. On the other hand, the tenant may have decided to lease space in the building because of the original ambience created by a combination of common space, building services, and appurtenances. With one or more of them no longer available, the tenant may wish to move to another building.

If the tenant feels strongly about some item, especially a building service, it should be included in the lease clause. The difficulty is that, inevitably, the provision for some feature will be forgotten or unintentionally omitted, and it will be that very feature that winds up disappearing or changing. This will create unnecessary enmity between the tenant and the landlord. As additional protection, the tenant should check out what the landlord has done with building services and amenities at other projects.

4
Use of Premises

The lease clause concerning the use of premises is one of the simpler, more innocuous lease clauses. It should not present any difficulties or problems whatsoever for the majority of tenants. This clause, although relatively brief as lease clauses go, does have a number of distinct parts that require close attention, however.

The main purpose of the use clause is to limit or define the use to which premises may be put by a tenant. Normally the clause states that the tenant will use and occupy the premises for, or solely for, some specified use. The specified use can be general: The premises will be used for general business office purposes. It can be even broader: The premises will be used for general business office, research and development, light assembly, and related purposes. This provision will also stipulate that the premises may not be used for any purposes other than those stated, without the prior written consent of the landlord.

As part of the defined permitted use of the premises, this clause may specify that the tenant will not use or occupy the premises in violation of the law or the certificate of occupancy issued for the building. There will also be a specified time period at the end of which the tenant, upon written notice of the landlord, will cease and discontinue any use of the premises that is determined by governmental authority to be in violation of the law. In effect, the landlord is ensuring that the tenant will meet all the requirements of the jurisdiction for conducting business, such as procuring a valid business operating license.

A general phrase that the landlord will include will require the
tenant not to engage in, use the premises for, or allow the premises to be used for any improper, immoral, unlawful or objectionable purpose and will further comply with all present and future
laws, ordinances, regulations, governmental orders (federal,
state, county, local), and any other public or quasi-public authority having any jurisdiction over the building or the premises. In
addition, the landlord will require the tenant, at his or her own
expense, to obtain and deliver a copy to the landlord of any applicable occupancy permits or use licenses in the event of any
change or addition to any law, ordinance, regulation, or governmental order. As a further limitation, the landlord may insist on
excluding specific things that the premises may not be used for,
for example, "The premises will not be used for any hazardous
purpose or for the manufacture of any commodity or the preparing or dispensing of any foods or beverages except as necessary
for the tenant's personal use within the premises."

Any hazardous business performed in the building can be a
great concern for a landlord. Buildings are issued fire and insurance ratings on the basis of their proposed and actual use. The
fire and insurance ratings affect the cost of insurance for the
landlord (and for the tenants as well). If the stated use or purpose
of the building changes, even if unintentionally, because of some
action by a tenant, the landlord may have higher insurance
rates—and extra unanticipated costs are not what landlords are
in business for.

Therefore, the landlord will want this clause to include language indicating that the tenant will not use the premises, nor
permit the premises to be used, nor allow anything to be done or
maintained within the premises that would change any of the fire
or insurance ratings of the building or would invalidate or increase the cost of the landlord's fire, liability, extended coverage,
or any other insurance policy covering the building or its contents. This provision will state: "In the event that, because of the
actions, the use of the premises, or conduct of business by the
tenant, the landlord's insurance costs for the building or its contents increase, the tenant may be deemed to be in default and
agrees to pay the landlord, on demand, as additional rent the
amount of any such increase."

As part of the general use requirements of the building and to create a standard for general tenant conduct, the landlord often will add two additional short provisions to this lease clause. The first will state that the tenant will not permit or allow to be committed any waste in or upon the premises, shall keep the premises in first-class repair and appearance, and shall maintain the premises in a clean, healthful, and safe condition. The second provision will indicate that the tenant will conduct business and control its agents, employees, guests, invitees, and customers in such a manner as not to create any nuisance on the premises or in the building or to interfere with, annoy, or disturb other tenants in the building or the landlord's management of the building.

The use of premises lease clause is normally straightforward and is nothing more than a minimal form of protection for the landlord, allowing him or her to maintain and control the legality of the tenant's conduct in the building. Sometimes, as shown above, this clause also attempts to define and create a standard of equality and fairness for all tenants. In defining that standard, however, the landlord is creating the rules the tenant is agreeing to abide by.

When an overly detailed or onerous clause is found by the tenant, it should be changed to meet the tenant's needs so that it does not create any hardships for the tenant's business operations and operating environment. In some instances, the statement of use may be either too vague or too restrictive. When in doubt, the tenant should either provide additional descriptive details to clarify the vagueness or add more general language to tone down a restriction.

For example, when the use of the premises is strictly defined in such a way that the premises shall only be used for the publication of books and periodicals, the tenant would be well advised to modify this clause to something like "The premises shall be used for general office purposes, including the publication of books and periodicals." This would give the tenant greater flexibility for business operations. If the tenant's publishing business slows down but the tenant can maintain the business by selling a specially developed in-house order-processing system, the tenant will want the use clause to provide for this possibility by having a nonrestrictive use that allows for broad business concepts such as consulting.

The landlord may be particularly restrictive in the provision stating the tenant will not annoy other tenants and waste will not be permitted. The landlord may even specify that the occupants permitted on the premises will not exceed the number that the building's systems and equipment were designed to accommodate. The restriction might state that the number of occupants in the premises shall not be greater than one person per x hundred rentable square feet. If the tenant's business might ever experience explosive growth that would require having many more employees jammed into the allotted space, the tenant needs to ensure that this provision is more general.

5
Term and Possession

The clause covering the term of the lease is often one of the shortest clauses in a lease document. Its length will depend on how many areas it covers. More important, the term clause specifies when the lease—and thus the landlord's and tenant's obligations to each other—begins and ends.

Although a lease may be agreed to and signed by the landlord and tenant, the actual lease obligations may not begin until some future date, which may or may not be based on some future event. The tenant should be sure that the lease document specifies beginning and ending dates that are legally correct for the local jurisdiction.

When the lease actually starts is defined as the *lease commencement date,* which may or may not be related to the *delivery of premises (or possession) date,* which may or may not be related to the actual occupancy of the premises by the tenant (or the *tenant occupancy date*). And these particular dates may or may not have any relationship to when a tenant begins to pay rent. If at all possible, the lease commencement date should be a specific time and date; for example, "This lease shall commence at 12:01 a.m. on the first day of January 1999 (the lease commencement date)."

The next step is to define the term or length of the lease. Here, again, a specific date and time are required: "The lease shall expire at 12:00 midnight on the thirty-first day of December 2008 (the lease expiration date)." And just to cover all the bases, the actual term being specified should also be provided: "The term of this lease shall be for ten (10) years."

The tenant should avoid any ambiguity in the term of the lease and when the lease begins and ends. However, this is not always easy to do. The difficulties stem from the fact that there may be a delay in the landlord's turning over the space to the tenant.

For the tenant, the point is whether or not he or she has possession or beneficial use of the premises (discussed later in this chapter) and whether the actual use of the premises coincides with the date on which the lease commences. The tenant must make certain that he or she has use or possession of the space before any lease obligations begin and that contingency is clearly specified in the lease.

All kinds of good reasons can delay a tenant's possession or use of the premises. In an already completed and tenanted building, for example, the current tenants may not have moved out (and will not do so for an extra month or two because the new space they've leased is not yet ready for them), or the existing premises may require some repair, alterations, or reconstruction to meet the tenant's needs. If the premises are in a brand-new building, the landlord may have to build out the space to the tenant's specifications. Whatever the reasons, the tenant must pay particular attention to the length of the delay, whether it is likely to become unreasonable, how it will affect the term of the lease, and how it will affect the lease obligations of the tenant and the landlord.

Depending on the exact situation regarding the premises, the landlord will want some flexibility; he or she will want to be able to delay the new tenant's possession of the space without losing the tenant, especially if the delay is beyond the landlord's control. The main consideration for the tenant is how the term of the lease itself will be affected, if at all. There are usually three basic ways of handling delays:

1. The lease term can remain the same, but there will be new lease commencement and expiration dates.

2. The lease commencement date and the lease term can remain the same, but tenant obligations will be delayed until possession of the premises actually takes place.

3. The lease commencement date can remain the same, but the lease expiration date will be extended day-for-day of the delay so that the lease term will still be the same.

The tenant needs to decide whether a shortened lease term because of a delayed possession would be in his or her best interests. That decision must be viewed in conjunction with all the other lease clauses and especially the various tenant and landlord obligations.

For example, if the lease commencement date and lease term stay the same but the tenant's possession date is delayed, what happens to the concessions that the landlord granted the tenant? If rent abatement starts on the lease commencement date but the tenant does not get to possess or use the space for two or three months, unless specific wording to the contrary is included in the lease, the tenant will be forced to use up some (or all) of the rent abatement and get no use from the premises.

What the tenant must watch out for are any lease obligations that would apply to the period before the actual beneficial use or possession of the premises. For example, a tenant may find that even though rent is not payable until possession occurs (this is not automatically the case, by the way; it must be specifically stated in the lease document), he or she may be obligated to pay other expenses beginning on the date the lease commences, such as building operating expenses, real estate taxes, pro rata share of common area expenses, and perhaps even some portion of required insurance.

The tenant needs to decide how important an actual expiration date or a fixed lease term might be in relation to the lease term and any occupancy delay. Part of this decision will be affected by how the tenant benefits from any landlord-granted concessions. For example, there may be a fixed lease term for the period the tenant actually pays rent, with an additional period added for any lease-abatement period. In this instance, a 10-year lease term could actually be a 10½- or 11-year term when the rent-abatement period is included. Similarly, a fixed 10-year period for which there is rent abatement for six months or one year has no effect on the lease term, but only on how many months the tenant pays rent.

Why is all of this important? Depending on the market, a lot of money can be saved. If rental rates rise to or above the inflation rate, then a long-term lease with low or no rent increases is of significant value to a tenant. The longer the tenant can pay a rent lower than the market rent, the better off the tenant will be. Having a 10-year lease term reduced because of a fixed expiration date—coupled with a delay in the tenant's possession—is not often in the tenant's best interests.

Notification

When a tenant is not able to get into a space, it is usually for one of two reasons: Either the previous tenant did not leave on time, or the landlord is unable to prepare the premises to the new tenant's specifications on time. In either of these instances the landlord will undoubtedly provide suitable protection—for the landlord.

If the problem is a current or previous tenant (and depending on what a tenant agrees to regarding how the term will be specified), the lease clause might say something like this: "If the landlord is unable to deliver possession of the premises for reason of the holding over or retention of possession by any tenant or occupant, the lease commencement date shall be extended for such period of time as may be reasonably necessary to enable landlord to evict such tenant or occupant and to deliver possession of the premises to the tenant."

In this case the tenant wants to be sure that it is the landlord's responsibility to evict the previous tenant. The tenant should only be concerned with the space and should not accept possession or occupancy until it can actually be used.

If alterations and construction are taking longer than expected, depending on the extent of the construction and the work agreement between the landlord and tenant (the workletter), the landlord will want to give minimum notice to the tenant regarding the availability of the premises. The tenant, however, will want maximum notification time. In this connection, the lease also needs to define clearly when the premises will indeed be considered to be constructed properly and ready for occupancy.

The landlord will usually agree to give the tenant 10 days' notice of the anticipated date on which the premises will have all construction substantially completed. In addition, that notice will serve as delivery of possession to the tenant. A simple statement to this effect is not necessarily in the tenant's best interests.

Possession of the Premises

The new tenant's greatest concern is that the premises (or, with a new building, the building itself) will not be ready for occupancy. Availability is often difficult to predict for premises in a new building. Determining when the premises will be ready for occupancy can be tricky (key phrases are *substantial completion* of the required construction and *beneficial use* of the premises), and there are a number of pitfalls to watch out for.

Complications arise when tenants have their own contractor rather than the landlord building out their space or when tenants ask for an extensive or complex buildout that may require specialized tradespeople or materials that have to be specially ordered. In a landlord-provided lease clause, the phrase "substantial completion of the premises" (for new or existing space) will be defined as the level at which, in the landlord's view, all the necessary, reasonable, and standard construction items have been substantially completed in accordance with the tenant's construction plans (and attached workletter). The landlord's assessment will be guided by the landlord's architect's "punch list" (a list of any missing, incomplete, or unacceptable work or materials) for any incomplete standard items or improvements. All nonstandard, special-order items or above-standard constructions will be exempted from the architect's punch list. The premises will be substantially complete when the punch list items are deemed to be items of adjustment that do not, or will not materially, interfere with the tenant's use of the premises, even though such items are yet to be completed.

Therefore, in the typical substantial completion provision it is the landlord who decides when the majority of the construction work has been done. The tenant who does not exercise any control over the definition of "substantial completion of the premises" may find his or her space only partly completed. Such a situation can greatly affect staff productivity, as well as general business and customer relations. The tenant needs to negotiate three main items regarding the premises:

1. The architect's punch list compiled for the tenant must be in substantial agreement with the landlord's punch list; otherwise, the two architects must reconcile the differences.

2. Any and all special-order items or special construction work must be listed and agreed to by the architects of both the landlord and tenant before construction, or they may not be excluded from the punch list. This can be a key point for a tenant, especially when the landlord will be the one doing the construction. In effect, without some type of prespecified level of construction, the landlord can control all standard construction items.

3. When the landlord is responsible for the alterations to or construction of the premises, a provision should specify that the landlord is so responsible, and "substantial completion" should be defined as denoting that the alteration or construction work has passed all required local codes and ordinances and, when applicable, that the landlord has procured a certificate of occupancy for the premises.

The lease should also contain a provision stating that if the tenant consents to a lease commencement date that is subsequent to the landlord's completion of the punch list items, the landlord agrees to complete all the punch list items to the reasonable satisfaction of the tenant within 30 days of the tenant's occupancy (or possession date).

As in any lease provision, unless there is some force behind the language, the tenant will have little clout when things are not done as they are supposed to be. So what if the landlord does not complete all the work within 30 days! So what? Monetary incentives or penalties are necessary to put force behind the provision.

In this case the additional language might be phrased as follows: "If the punch list work is not completed to the tenant's satisfaction within the specified period of time, the tenant, in addition to any other remedies available, will be entitled to one day of rent abatement for each day after the specified time period in which the punch list items remain incomplete. Furthermore, the tenant will have the right, but not the obligation, to have all uncompleted punch list items finished to his or her reasonable satisfaction and at his or her expense. However, all such tenant documented costs and related expenses may be used as a credit to or an offset of the next due rent or additional rent payments to the landlord."

Acceptance and Beneficial Use

Not only does "substantial completion" have to be precisely defined, but the language of the lease must state what is meant by tenant "acceptance" of the space and tenant's "beneficial use" of the premises. This could either supplement or supersede the language concerning substantial completion.

This item is especially important to a tenant who needs to get into a space as soon as possible and is willing to accept space that would not otherwise be considered complete. The supplemental language would make the commencement date contingent on both tenant acceptance and beneficial use. Understandably, this additional language may not be acceptable to a landlord, whose principal goal is to control the process. The landlord will want substantial completion to be the rule for the delivery of possession to the tenant and thus the lease commencement date. However, some middle ground can often be achieved.

Language favoring the tenant will specify that the taking of possession of the premises will be contingent on acceptance of the space by the tenant and also on substantial completion of all alterations or construction by the landlord for purposes of establishing the lease commencement date.

Alternatively, the tenant can define acceptance of the space as the point at which beneficial use by the tenant begins. Beneficial use will be said to have begun when the tenant actually uses the premises, as evidenced by the moving of furniture, furnishings, inventory, equipment, or fixtures onto the premises.

Even under these particular provisions, work may still have to be done on the space after the landlord's work is finished. To the maximum extent possible, the tenant wants to avoid paying rent or using up a rent-abatement period while space remains vacant. Therefore, the tenant should try for a lease commencement date that begins at some negotiated amount of time (e.g., 30 days) after it is agreed that substantial completion of the premises (or of the building, as discussed shortly) has occurred.

The tenant will need to make sure that the language of the lease permits the tenant to have access to the premises during the period before the lease commencement date, especially for the tenant's contractors. Moreover, the lease must define this as preparation work and not as the tenant's taking possession or having beneficial use of the premises, even if certain equipment will be installed.

Certification

It is in both the tenant's and the landlord's interests to require that, on the lease commencement date, or upon the request of either the landlord or the tenant, the landlord and tenant shall both promptly execute, acknowledge, and deliver to each other a written declaration certifying the lease commencement date and the lease expiration date, as required by the lease document, and that there will be no landlord or tenant obligations as specified in the lease document until that time.

The mutual certification is, of course, more advantageous to the tenant than a notice that needs to come only from the landlord. It means that the landlord cannot unilaterally specify a lease commencement date based on his or her interpretation of "substantial completion" or "beneficial use" of the premises. A landlord-tenant certificate provides an absolute and agreed-to date on which the lease—and hence landlord-tenant obligations—will begin.

Vacant and Ready-to-Use Space

When premises are being relet or sublet and will not be subjected to delaying alterations or construction, the lease commencement date will be the same as the date on which the space is accepted, and an expiration date (and thus the lease term) will be specified.

In this case the tenant must carefully examine the property, hiring whatever expert is needed to determine the usefulness and suitability of the space (e.g., an architect or a mechanical engineer). Rarely are premises taken by a tenant sight unseen. Rather, the tenant usually has to make multiple visits to a property to be sure that everything is intact and meets the tenant's needs and requirements—from the surrounding area and neighborhood environment and amenities to the property location, general building appeal, size of the space, and necessary building and business operational needs.

When there is vacant and ready-to-use space, the landlord will be careful to protect him- or herself against a possible future claim that a property was delivered in an unsuitable or unacceptable condition. The language of the lease will accordingly specify that the tenant accepts the property (or premises) on an "as is" basis. No mention will be made of landlord obligations for alterations, construction, or other improvements. It will also state that the tenant certifies that the property has been examined by the tenant personally and by experts chosen by the tenant and that the mechanical, electrical, structural, and any other necessary systems of the building and the premises have been found to be in acceptable and useful condition.

For the tenant, the lease provided by the landlord should also indicate what needs to be checked in the "as is" condition before the lease document is signed.

Possession—The Building

When a tenant is dealing with a new building and is going to be one of its first occupants, the lease should contain a separate provision regarding the substantial completion or beneficial use of the building and, where applicable, the surrounding property (e.g., parking areas), as an additional factor in establishing the proper lease commencement date. From the tenant's perspective, even though premises may be ready for occupancy, the total property must be suitable for business operations. Even more important, the tenant has to consider whether the hassles of an incomplete building and construction on the surrounding property are detrimental to staff morale and client-customer relations.

Although pioneering in a new location or building can be exciting, the inconvenience can quickly become annoying. An incomplete parking area, a barricaded street, an unfinished lobby, only one or two elevators in operation, no landscaping, interruptions to the mechanical system—these and more can be the penalty for accepting premises in an incomplete structure too early.

A tenant may feel harassed if for the first six months of occupancy only one of four elevators is in working condition and that one has to be shared with work crews. What is even worse is having to subject one's clients or customers to all the detritus of an incomplete lobby area. Is this inconvenience really worth all those great landlord-granted concessions, such as the six months of rent abatement? The tenant must think ahead, not only about the office space itself, but also about the parking areas, landscaping, streets and sidewalks, the building's general structure (e.g., roof, walls, and foundation), and the building's mechanical, electrical, and service systems (e.g., HVAC, elevators, utilities, and plumbing).

It is up to the tenant to insist that the substantial completion provision in the lease refers to both the building and its surrounding property for purposes of establishing a lease commencement date. This provision, too, can be contingent on a property and building punch list (in accordance with the original base building plans). Both the landlord's and tenant's architects must agree that the disruption to the tenant's business operations will be minimal and inconsequential. Furthermore, the provision must state that all property and building work conforms to all necessary local jurisdiction building codes and ordinances and has passed all required inspections and that the landlord has obtained the necessary building occupancy permits. (Note: A tenant should particularly be careful when a local jurisdiction has issued a temporary occupancy permit because some additional work needs to be done. The tenant does not want to find out that he or she has to move out "temporarily" because a temporary permit was not converted into a permanent occupancy permit in the allotted time.)

The tenant must decide how long a waiting period is acceptable: Moving into the space may be necessary for business operations to continue; on the other hand, business may suffer because the building is incomplete. For example, the tenant may not want to delay moving into a new space just because a lobby is not finished, since such a delay could cost far more in financial terms than a little inconvenience.

Each tenant must decide for him- or herself what level of annoyance, inconvenience, and hassle from an incomplete property or building is acceptable. The controlling factors are usually the lease commencement and expiration dates. However, other alternatives can be negotiated. For example, there can be an acceptable lease commencement date and lease term with the possession of the premises by the tenant, but certain tenant obligations such as rent payments can be delayed until the building is substantially completed. Likewise, landlord-granted concessions such as a rent-abatement period can be delayed and then begun when the building is substantially completed.

And What If It Is Late?

What happens if a new building runs into construction problems that cause a serious delay so that the tenant will not be able to move in for another six months, a year, or more? Or what if the vacating tenant runs into this problem in his or her new space and stays on, preventing the new tenant, you, from moving in six months or more beyond the original plan? Or what if the landlord, for whatever reasons, is slow to finish building out the premises?

But how are "slow" and "delayed" to be defined? For some tenants, a delay of just two or three months can cause considerable difficulties and have a large ripple effect.

As shown, the landlord will favor language that merely changes the lease commencement date. Depending on the region and the landlord, the lease may keep the same expiration date and thus shorten the term or the lease, or it may keep the term of the lease the same by also moving the lease expiration date.

In any case, the landlord will also specify that if there is a delay and the tenant is prevented from taking possession of the premises, the tenant will have no claim against the landlord, and the landlord will have no liability whatsoever for this failure to deliver the premises. Furthermore, the landlord's provision will often state that even in the event of a delay, the lease shall remain valid and not be rendered void by the delay.

Late Because Premises Remain Occupied

The extent of the problem for the tenant depends on what potential exists for delay. If another tenant already occupies the space, the tenant should not accept any continuing rights by the landlord to extend the possession time. Instead, the tenant should make sure that the lease provides for a timely eviction by the landlord, with any extension time frame specified.

Otherwise, the tenant should have a right to cancel the lease immediately. The tenant must avoid being kept on a string, so to speak, by a landlord who continues to permit a current tenant to extend the lease or have an excessive holdover in the space. This could happen if the holdover rent is excessive and the landlord knows the new tenant will not be able to walk away easily. Or more likely, the current tenant may be relocating to another one of the landlord's buildings, which makes it in the best interests of the landlord to grant the current tenant a lease extension.

Late Because Premises Are Being Renovated

Another common situation is when the premises must be altered or constructed by the landlord. The potential for delay is particularly strong in these circumstances. Construction involves many variables: Plans and construction documents have to be drawn up, materials ordered, and workers hired. As an additional complication, the tenant's buildout may be complex, with alteration and construction delays virtually inevitable.

The landlord, who may be faced with delays beyond his or her control and who may have a significant investment tied up in the ongoing preparation of the premises, will understandably want to safeguard against losing the tenant. Even when construction is involved, the landlord should be able to give an absolute outside date for finishing everything, both in the building and on the premises. Often the landlord will do so, although the date given might be a year or more from the actual expected date.

No Excuses When Space Is Vacant

If the premises are vacant and ready, there should be no reason whatever for any serious delay in having the tenant move in. Therefore, nothing in the lease should permit the landlord to provide for a delay, without either imposing a severe penalty on the landlord or giving the tenant the right to cancel the lease.

If the landlord has a current tenant who wants to expand into the vacant space or if there is a great amount of vacant space in the building and a large space user is being sought or is considering the building, a small space user will lose out.

Tenants Have Rights, Too

The tenant has certain rights regardless of the reason for the delay or the premises situation. For the tenant, the difficulty is to persuade a landlord to go along with any provision that favors the tenant and can result in the tenant's not accepting the premises or even canceling the lease. The landlord will be loath to lose any control.

The tenant must evaluate his or her own needs and requirements regarding the proposed relocation. Often delays have financial consequences for the tenant. The opportunity for getting a favorable lease provision regarding delayed possession of space is a function of the power and leverage of the tenant (bigger is better!) and market conditions (how much vacant space exists in the market).

Tenant Right to Cancel

When possible, the tenant will want the right to cancel a lease if delays in possession are excessive. The right to cancel can be a two-edged sword, however. Sometimes this right will give the tenant ample time to find new space without any tenant-incurred monetary expense (other than the lost opportunity costs associated with having to begin over again to look for space in lieu of being able to conduct business).

On the other hand, however, even if the tenant has the right to cancel after, say, a year's delay in preparing and constructing new premises, the timing might be such that it would be impossible for the tenant (perhaps because of size) to find new space in the additional time remaining on a current lease. This would mean going into a holdover period and facing the usual doubling of the rent during this period. It often is more efficient to stick it out with the landlord and get the space built out. When such a situation occurs, the tenant needs to have a penalty provision against the landlord.

Getting the Landlord to Pay for Delay

The delay can be expensive for the tenant, considering, for example, the storage costs of furniture and equipment, supplies and materials ordered for the new premises but put on hold, the extra rent paid in the current space over the rent in the new premises because of the holdover situation, or the extra expenses involved in moving to a temporary space (relocation costs, increased rent) because the new space is not ready and the tenant is unable to stay on in the current space.

To the extent that a delay can be shown to be due to the actions—or inactions—of the landlord, the tenant should request a lease provision that makes the landlord responsible for the reimbursement of these costs. The reimbursement could be in cash or in the form of a credit on future rent payments.

Nothing works better in getting a relocation delay reduced to a minimum than a clause requiring the landlord to reimburse the tenant's expenses. As an additional incentive, the lease could include a monetary penalty (or its equivalent) tied to the length of delay. For example, for every day the premises are not ready beyond some specified reasonable period of delay, the tenant would receive or have forgiven a day of future rent payment (in addition to any rent abatement).

But a tenant will find it difficult to get any payments from a landlord without enormous economic leverage or the help of market forces. And even when such a concession is won, the tenant could still lose, depending on the extent of the penalty payment, because the landlord might find it more advantageous to delay possession of the premises long enough to force the tenant to give up and go elsewhere—thereby relieving the landlord of the penalty payment.

When a Situation Is Beyond Control

Whatever strictures or penalties are put into a lease, there is always the possibility that circumstances will move beyond either the tenant's or the landlord's control. This is where the so-called act of God or force majeure (a force beyond control or an unexpected event) clause comes in. This clause may appear anywhere in the lease and it will usually apply to all the landlord's obligations under the lease. However, it is often added to the section on the lease execution date when the landlord is altering or constructing the premises.

This provision excuses any delay and often specifically states that any alterations or construction or inability of the landlord to complete the work will be granted a time extension equal to the time period of the delay when the delay is the result of

1. Any strikes, lockouts or labor disputes
2. The inability to obtain labor, materials, fuel, electricity, or any other needed services or any reasonable substitutes
3. Acts of God, civil commotion, fire, accidents, or any other casualty
4. Laws, regulations, or any kind of governmental actions (local, state, regional, and federal)
5. Any other cause or condition that is beyond the landlord's reasonable control

This lease provision is relatively easy to justify. And it's difficult for tenants to argue with—after all, it is so reasonable.

What most tenants fail to recognize is that this same clause can be included for the benefit of the tenant. It can apply to the tenant's ability to take possession of the premises, the lease commencement date, and any tenant obligations under the lease, including the payment of rent. The tenant would be granted an extension equal to the period of the delay due to the same act of God or force majeure provision.

Such a provision is extremely important to all tenants, but especially so for tenants relocating from one jurisdiction to another (whether intrastate or interstate). It gives the tenant some protection should certain events delay the move or relocation. Typical events that could affect a tenant include labor or truckers' strikes, adverse weather (e.g., tornadoes, high winds, snowstorms), riots, a telephone workers' strike, utility disruption to the building, and the like.

6
Rent and Rent Increases

The amount of rent a tenant pays would seem to be straightforward. The tenant and landlord negotiate for a rent that is satisfactory to both parties, and the tenant then pays the rent, usually at regular intervals: each month, quarter, half-year, or year. The initial base rent is actually a fairly uncomplicated concept, and the necessary lease provisions to describe it are therefore short and straightforward.

What is complicated for the tenant is trying to figure out exactly what he or she agreed to pay and whether, and by how much and how often, the rent will increase—and what is included when it does go up. Even more complicated is trying to compare different leases when a number of premises are under consideration. Unfortunately for the tenant, there is no standard way that landlords compute rent and rent increases. The complex interrelationships between the many ways rent increases can be calculated and the various property expenses that can enter into the rent, such as building operating expenses and real estate taxes, can easily confuse even the seasoned PREB.

Basic Rent

The basic rent lease clause includes some standard provisions.

What Is the Amount of the Rent?

The amount should be specified in sufficient detail to avoid any possible misunderstanding of what is really to be paid by the tenant. Excessive details are preferable to a single statement of a lump-sum amount. The ideal is to show the per-square-foot (psf) cost of the space, the total annual rent, and the base amount that must be paid on a required regular interval (e.g., monthly).

When Is the Rent Due, and How Often?

If rent is due on a monthly basis, for example, this provision will state: "The rent specified is to be paid in equal monthly installments, in advance, on the first day of each calendar month." Rent payments can be made on virtually any schedule—monthly, quarterly, semiannually, annually, or any other agreed-to schedule.

How Will the Rent Be Prorated?

A lease can start on any day of the month. A system of proration will be in effect so that a smaller first or last scheduled payment can be made (e.g., a smaller first or last month's rent for a monthly payment schedule).

The proration schedule can have various forms. The two most common forms are as follows:

1. The rent for each day before the first day of a calendar month (or after the last day, for the months past the end of a lease) is to be calculated at $\frac{1}{30}$ of the scheduled monthly rent.

2. The rent for each day before (or after) is calculated on the basis of $\frac{1}{365}$ of the annual rent. Obviously, the more accurate and the finer the calculation, the better it is for the tenant. For example, a $12,000 annual rent ($1000 per month) would, using a $\frac{1}{30}$ calculation, be equal to a cost of $33.33 per day, while the more accurate annual calculation using $\frac{1}{365}$ results in a rent of $32.88 per day.

Where Is the Rent Paid?

The exact place that the rent is to be paid is often specified in a "notices" lease clause. But it does not hurt to include the details in the rent clause. This provision would state the following:

1. *To whom is payment to be made?* Is payment to be made directly to the landlord or to the landlord's representative? This point is important to the tenant. The tenant does not want to get caught up in disagreements between a landlord and a management company, with the landlord suddenly claiming that the rent has not been paid because the management company was fired and has not sent on your rent payments. To avoid this problem, ask the landlord to include a notification period for any changes regarding the destination of payments, for example, "The landlord will notify the tenant at least 30 days prior to the due date of any rent payment of any change."

2. *Where is payment to be made?* Will payment be picked up at the tenant's premises? Is it to be delivered to the management office in the building? Or is it to be delivered or sent to another, specifically stated address in the same city or somewhere else? This item, too, is important to the tenant. The tenant will want adequate notification in the event the landlord or the management company moves. A rent payment could be considered late if sent to the former address. Although the tenant may be legally and technically correct, it is wise not to get caught up in a dispute with the landlord.

3. *When is payment considered to have been made?* Is payment considered to have been made when it is mailed or when it is received at the office? The tenant needs to know when a payment will be considered late.

When Is a Rent Payment Considered Late?

The tenant must be careful not to accept a landlord's interpretation of a "just and reasonable" time period in the case of payment. Like every other lease provision, this one is fully negotiable.

How late is late? Sometimes "the date the amounts are due" in a lease may mean the date after which payments are considered late. A practice that is fairly common and acceptable to landlords is to state that a payment is not late until 10 days after "the date the amounts are due" (the grace period). The tenant should ask that these 10 days be business days, although using calendar days is traditional. At any rate, the tenant should be sure the provision permits an automatic extension to the first following business day when the grace period ends on a holiday or weekend.

There is no standard way of handling late penalties, late charges, or interest on late rent, although certain penalties or excessive interest may violate jurisdictional laws and be disallowed if challenged in a court of law. For this reason, the landlord's lease provision may go to great lengths to guard against future difficulties. It might specify, "The tenant hereby acknowledges that late payment by tenant to landlord of rent and any other sums due hereunder will cause landlord to incur costs not contemplated by this lease," or "The parties hereby agree that such late charges represent a fair and reasonable estimate of the costs landlord will incur by reason of late payment by tenant."

For a tenant, a flat late charge, if reasonable, may often be best. With a flat charge, it will not matter to the tenant when the late payment is actually made. That is, there is no incentive to pay late charges quickly. For this reason, the landlord will want the late charge to be pegged to some percentage of the total amount due, such as 3 percent. The landlord prefers a percentage over a flat fee, especially if rents increase on a regular basis because of a built-in annual rent escalator.

It is only when late charges continue to accrue that the tenant has an incentive to pay the rent on time or before a payment is considered late. For this reason, the landlord will also want to include a provision for interest to be paid on all amounts due from the due date until paid. This motivates the tenant to pay so as not to continue to incur additional expenses. The interest rate can be specified in a variety of ways, including a flat percentage rate or a number of percentage points over a bank's prime rate.

The tenant should remember that there is no standard way of treating these items. The tenant must negotiate them and be as comfortable as the landlord with them.

Additional Rent

The lease provision entitled "Additional Rent" was created by landlords to cover any amounts the tenant might owe under the lease, including, for example, rent increases, operating expenses, and even repairs. To the landlord, the logic is inescapable: Any money owed as "additional rent" is subject to the same severe remedies as rent that is past due. This means it can be subject to the standard legal action available to anyone for any debt.

To separate the different kinds of money that can be owed under a lease, the tenant should work toward having precise definitions of *rent* and *additional rent*. Then the tenant should attempt to limit the definitions to actual basic rent and any rent increases and escalations. The tenant's compromise position is to allow the definition of *additional rent* to include rent-related items such as operating expenses and real estate taxes. It is up to the landlord to convince the tenant that other items should be included in the definition.

Some Important Legalese

The rent lease clause will normally contain some legal language regarding the rent payment. Two common phrases in this category are *lawful money* and *no deductions*.

Lawful Money. Many landlords add a simple provision stating that all monies owed by the tenant must be paid in lawful money (or legal tender) of the United States. Depending on the other provisions within this clause and the landlord's prior experience with other tenants, this provision may allow a landlord to take forms of payment other than actual cash as payment for the rent. The bank check, for example, is an instrument businesses across the country use to pay each other. However, a bank check is not legal tender of the United States. It is not until the check clears the banking system and the landlord's account is credited for the proper amount that the landlord can make a withdrawal in legal tender (or until the landlord takes the check to the tenant's bank and exchanges it for actual cash).

Theoretically, then, the tenant is not meeting a lease provision even though the landlord accepts the tenant's check. If the check does not properly clear the banking system (e.g., for lack of sufficient funds), the rent is not considered paid. Subject to other lease provisions, the tenant would be considered late with the rent and in probable default of the lease. After enough checks are bounced, the landlord may no longer accept the tenant's checks as payment.

No Deductions. Other standard verbiage states: "All rent and additional rent shall be paid without demand, deduction, abatement, or set-offs."

This is what keeps a tenant from holding back any rent or additional rent or placing it in an escrow account because he or she is dissatisfied with the landlord. The tenant may pursue any other remedy except for holding back rent. So the tenant should be careful about what is included in, and why the landlord does not want to exclude something from, the "additional rent" lease provision and definition.

Rent Types

The commercial real estate jargon associated with leases and rent includes the terms *gross lease, full-service lease, net lease, absolute net,* and *flat rent.* The trouble is that there is nothing standard about this jargon. That is, there is no standard definition in the country of a full-service lease. Even more surprising, sometimes a term can mean something different to two PREBs working in the same jurisdiction. If the PREB is not certain of the meaning, how is the tenant supposed to know?

The tenant must request as clear a definition as possible from each person using the term *full-service rent.* The tenant must not assume that once *full-service rent* has been defined by one landlord, another landlord will use the term to mean the same thing. Although it is difficult enough to compare the true costs of different lease transactions when the definitions vary, it will be impossible to make such comparisons without them.

Note that the jargon used often applies to the lease or the rent.

For example, the full-service lease is so called because it contains a full-service rent.

Before different leases can be compared, the way rent dollar amounts are expressed must be clearly understood and must be arrived at in some standardized way. The standard used by the commercial real estate industry is to express rent in terms of square feet. Then it is relatively easy to express rents as a total to be paid monthly or annually. However, even the square foot has its pitfalls and is not quoted identically throughout the country.

The first point to note is whether the rent per square foot is quoted on an annual, a monthly, or some other basis. For example, a rent of $10 psf on an annual basis will be $0.83 psf on a monthly basis. For 10,000 sq ft, the annual rent works out the same: $10 × 10,000 = $100,000 per year; $0.83 × 10,000 × 12 months = $100,000 (rounded) per year. (For simplicity, and to avoid quantitative, qualitative, and jurisdictional differences, a standard annual $10 psf rent is used in the calculations in the rest of the book. With the $10 basic unit, the reader can use the sample calculations provided as a multiplier for calculating rents of $20, $30, $40, $50, or $100 psf.)

The tenant must also be careful, when rent is being quoted by the square foot, to find out what kind of square foot is being considered and whether the square feet of different leases are comparable. An annual rent of $10 psf quoted on a usable per-square-foot basis is not the same as an annual rent of $10 psf quoted on a rentable per-square-foot basis. (See Chapter 2 for a discussion of the difference.) Commercial PREBs usually quote rents on the basis of a rentable square foot, but they don't always do so. (The rentable per-square-foot basis will be used for all calculations throughout the remainder of this book.) The tenant must be sure to establish the proper basis being used by a PREB and should remember that not all landlords necessarily follow these same standards.

Flat Fixed Rent

The most basic type of rent is flat rent, also known as fixed rent, flat fixed rent, and gross rent (e.g., gross lease). The flat fixed rent refers to a fixed amount paid on some regular schedule (e.g., a monthly basis); that is, the rent amount will not change for the full term of the lease, and this amount will include all costs and expenses the tenant must pay for leasing the premises. The flat fixed rent can be expressed either as a price per square foot of space or a total monthly, annual, or other rent amount. The flat fixed rent is typically used for short-term commercial space, for example, in a one-year lease on a small office or warehouse. At least for the short term, a landlord will be more comfortable knowing the majority of the costs and expenses associated with a leasehold. Therefore, the confidence that no money will be lost may induce a landlord to provide a flat fixed rent to a tenant.

Graduated Rent

The flat fixed rent, once the most widely used type of real estate rent, is impractical in today's more complex real estate market. For one thing, landlords are unwilling to take all the risk in regard to costs and are requiring tenants to bear related responsibilities for costs and expenses. Tenants would have premises rent sticker shock if a flat fixed rent were applied to long-term leases, providing landlords with the relative comfort of knowing that the amount paid would cover all current and any future and unanticipated costs and expenses associated with a building's occupancy.

The graduated rent, also known as a stepped-up rent, is often used for leases of moderate length. This rent is just an upgraded version of the flat fixed rent. At fixed increments, typically made on an annual basis (but possibly on a semiannual or a quarterly basis), an increasing flat fixed rent is paid covering the basic rent and all costs and expenses associated with the premises. An example of this would be a five-year lease payable in monthly increments, with the annual rent set at $10 psf in the first year, $11 psf the second year, $12 psf the third year, $13 psf the fourth year, and $14 psf the fifth year. Table 6-1 compares the per-square-foot total monthly and total annual rent for premises measuring 10,000 sq ft.

The graduated version of the flat fixed rent tells the landlord in advance exactly what his or her income stream will be. Meanwhile, the tenant knows exactly what his or her occupancy costs

Table 6-1. Monthly and Annual Rent Compared for 10,000-Sq-Ft Premises

Year	10,000 sq ft		
	Psf rent ($)	Monthly rent ($)	Annual rent ($)
1	10.00	8,333.33	100,000
2	11.00	9,166.67	110,000
3	12.00	10,000.00	120,000
4	13.00	10,833.33	130,000
5	14.00	11,666.67	140,000

will be over the full term of the lease. This type of rent puts all the risks associated with occupancy costs and expenses onto the landlord's shoulders. For long-term leases (those in excess of two or three years), most landlords, under the pressure of varying economic and market conditions, have developed a rent system that makes the tenant responsible for some—or all—of the costs and expenses associated with occupying both the premises and the building. These expenses, known as operating expenses or expense passthroughs, may include virtually all the costs and expenses associated with the building (and premises), such as utilities, cleaning, janitorial services, real estate taxes, and repairs. (See Chapter 7 for a discussion of expense passthroughs and operating expenses.)

The two terms most frequently used to contrast interrelating rent and expenses are *full-service rent* (or *full-service lease*) and *net rent* (or *net lease*).

Full-Service Rent or Lease

A full-service rent or lease implies that the rent includes all the initial operating passthrough expenses related to the premises and the building that are, and will remain, the responsibility of the landlord. But what about the expenses that exceed the initial expenses and are therefore considered the tenant's responsibility? What basis is used to calculate these costs? The method used here is often known as the expense stop or the base year approach. (It is discussed in Chapter 7.)

Net Lease

A net lease is usually one that stipulates a basic rent for the premises and that passes on to the tenant all related premises and building operating expenses, for direct or indirect payment. The rent in a net lease may also be referred to as "net rent." If that is the case, the net rent will only be the basic rent for the premises and will be devoid of any premises and building expenses.

When the term *net lease* is used as jargon, many PREBs describe separately a net rent, a net-net rent (also known as a double net rent), and a net-net-net rent (also known as a triple net rent or an absolute net rent)—all of which are subsets of a full-service lease.

Net Rent

In this context, net rent is the rent for the basic premises and for all related premises and building operating expenses except for one major operating expense, which is either passed through to, or paid directly by, the tenant. A fairly typical expense in this category is the utility cost (e.g., electricity or gas). In this case the rent would then be said to be "net of electric."

Double Net Rent

The net-net, or double net, rent is the same as the net rent except that there are two (or more) major operating expenses either passed through to, or paid directly by, the tenant. The most typical expenses in this category would be a utility (e.g., electric or gas) and janitorial services.

Absolute Net Rent

The net-net-net, or triple net or absolute net, rent most nearly embodies the concept of the net lease. That is, basic rent is charged for the premises, but all expenses related to the premises and the cost of running the building are passed through to, or are directly paid by, the tenant. In effect, *triple net rent* is jargon for the rent referred to in the net lease, whereas *net rent* may suggest something less than the rent referred to in a net lease.

Graduated Rent Revisited and Rent Bumps

When rent includes expense passthroughs, many a landlord will expand upon the graduated, or stepped-up, rent and make it even more complex. The graduated rent will work as it did before, increasing in predetermined increments, but with two additions or exceptions. First, operating expenses will be passed on to the tenant in the manner described under full-service rent and net rent. Second, the graduated base rent may be subject to various increases or escalations (discussed later in this chapter). The rent does not have to be, and usually is not, a fixed flat amount at each new level.

An offshoot of the graduated rent is the rent bump. The rent bump differs from the graduated rent only in that the bumps can occur in an irregular manner and can vary in amount. For example, an annual rent may be increased (bumped) by $2 the second year and by $7 in the eighth year of a lease (see the sections on rent increases in this chapter).

The graduated rent and rent bumps can play a vital role in various economic situations and competitive markets. These rent arrangements are creative solutions for at least two tenant situations. In the first, the tenant is at the end of an old long-term lease and has enjoyed significant below-market rents for a considerable time (without knowing it). Comes the time to renegotiate the lease or look for new space, and premises rent sticker shock syndrome occurs. Many organizations will be unable to meet modern rent realities without undergoing significant economic adjustments or experiencing some instability. In the second situation, the tenant wants or needs significant concessions or inducements to accept particular premises. This situation often occurs because of the tenant's expectations, which are influenced by what he or she has read or heard about market transactions, or because of economically driven competitive pressures on the premises. The landlord wants to, and often needs to, accommodate the tenant but also needs to ensure somehow that the building will remain economically viable.

Enter the graduated rent and rent bumps, which allow tenants and landlords to meet their respective needs by being able to start basic rents at artificially low rates and increase them over time in such a way that the end result, when averaged over the whole term of the lease, will be in accord with economic and market reality. Exactly how this works is shown in Chapter 9.

Comparing Leases

Temporarily ignoring any operating expenses and other expense passthroughs, the rent a landlord receives is designed to pay for the principal and interest on the property's mortgage, other costs related to the property that cannot otherwise be passed through to the tenant, and the landlord's profit.

In rational economic times, the amount paid on a regular basis for the mortgage principal and interest is a fixed amount that is the same in the first year as in the tenth year of the mortgage (subject to various landlord financial options, such as refinancing). Some landlords may have a commercial adjustable rate mortgage (ARM) that has a changing annual (or monthly or quarterly) interest fee. (The implications and complications of having to pay changing interest are addressed in Chapter 7.)

The landlord would like to protect from the ravages of inflation profits and money received for expenses. That is, the landlord would like the value of one dollar of profit in the tenth year of a lease to be the same as that of one dollar of profit in the first year of the lease.

Net Effective Rent

Because the concept of the value of money over time is so important to the landlord, the tenant should be aware of all the complications it can introduce into a lease. Complex rent computations make it difficult to compare different transactions. Where one lease may offer a low base rent, another may have a graduated rent or a different rent escalation and operating expense pass-throughs. Unless there is some basis for comparing the different kinds of leases, the tenant may even choose the most expensive lease, when considered over a full lease term, because of some supposedly attractive landlord concessions (e.g., rent abatement or seemingly lower expense passthroughs that wind up increasing faster than expected).

The tenant needs some way of comparing two or more monetary effects. In commercial real estate, the method, which is called a net present value (NPV) analysis, is used to calculate the net effective rate. Adding up all the rent that would be paid over the term of a lease, adjusting for all the landlord concessions and inducements and for tenant costs and expenses, and then simply dividing by the number of years in the lease and the amount of square feet is not very accurate. NPV analysis provides a more accurate net effective rent by factoring in all the alternatives of different leases. Despite the differences in lease terms and conditions, this type of analysis makes it possible to compare the overall value of leases. The results are usually shown on a per-square-foot basis, so it does not matter if premises are of a different size or if the term of the lease is not the same.

A tenant-based NPV analysis will provide a different view of the financial implications of a lease than a landlord's NPV analysis. The tenant will be concerned with cash outflows, what it will cost every month to rent the premises and what the total costs will be over the life of the lease. The landlord will be more concerned with revenues, cash flow, and profits. The landlord will want to make sure that his or her profits will not be eroded by inflation, that the investment under consideration is better than another investment, and that the tenant's lease at hand will generate a fair return when compared with another tenant's lease.

Net Present Value Explained

NPV analysis examines a stream of income over time and tries to determine what the total value of all the money, as it becomes available, would be if an alternative financial strategy were employed. The basic purpose is to estimate the return that can be earned on this income or the costs that can be incurred, depending on whether the money is owned and to be invested or will be borrowed and then paid back. The result of the analysis is a current dollar value.

Suppose that a dollar invested today earns 10 percent a year for 10 years. Knowing what the value will be in 10 years' time, how much would someone be willing to lend today to someone who will want to pay back exactly $1 in 10 years' time? To give someone $1 today, only to be paid back the same $1 in 10 years' time would not make economic sense, since that $1 today could be invested to earn money. Also, given the concept of inflation, $1 today is not going to have the same buying power in 10 years' time. In other words, the lender here is interested in knowing these values in terms of current dollars.

Table 6-2 shows as an example a five-year lease for 10,000 sq ft of space utilizing an annual base rent of $10 psf as a standardized rent multiplier and a rent increase of 5 percent per year (the standardized rent multiplier permits the reader to consider a $30 rent by simply multiplying the results by 3).

On a per-square-foot basis, this $552,700 would yield a simple net effective rent of $11.05 ($552,700 ÷ 5 years ÷ 10,000 sq ft), which is also equal to the average of all the rents each year ($10.00 + $10.50 + $11.03 + $11.58 + $12.16 = $55.27 ÷ 5 years). If this money could be invested, or if this amount of money could be borrowed, there would be interest earned or interest to pay. The NPV accounts for the cost of this economic opportunity. For

Table 6-2. Total Aggregate Rent for 10,000-Sq-Ft, Five-Year Lease with 5 Percent Per Year Rent Increase

Year	Base rent ($) with 5% per year increase (psf)	Annual rent ($) (× 10,000 sq ft)
1	10.00	100,000
2	10.50	105,000
3	11.03	110,300
4	11.58	115,800
5	12.16	121,600
	Total aggregate rent	552,700

calculating the NPV, the individual must specify a percentage number, such as an interest rate on money or the inflation rate, which represents expectations of economic conditions. Suppose that 8 percent is used to calculate the NPV:

$$\frac{\text{NPV of \$552,700 using an 8\%}}{\text{interest (or inflation) rate}} = \$438,048$$

$$\frac{\text{Net effective rent (annual)}}{\text{(constant payment)}} = \$10.97 \text{ psf}$$

An NPV of $438,048 is the amount that needs to be put into an alternative investment that is earning 8 percent interest. To keep calculations simple, the sample rent payment shown in Table 6-3 is made in a lump sum at the end of each year immediately after the interest has been earned. Another way to look at this concept is to consider what amount of money a landlord might be willing to accept at the beginning of the lease term as an alternative to the total aggregate rent that he or she would otherwise receive over the full five-year term of the lease. For the landlord, that decision might depend on the alternative investments that could be made with the money, ensuring that the mortgage and interest would still be paid or could be prepaid. Prepayment would free up for immediate use today's value of the profit that would otherwise be earned over the full term of the lease.

Table 6-3 shows the NPV amount of money invested in an interest-bearing account that pays out a lump sum, as was calculated above, for rent at the end of each year, without any further payments by the tenant. As the figures show, the NPV is the amount that needs to be invested at an economic opportunity return of 8 percent to pay off the total five-year lease obligation.

The (annual) net effective rent, shown in the equation above as $10.97 psf, is called the constant payment. This amount cannot be calculated until the NPV is known. This amount *is not* the NPV divided by the number of square feet and the number of years of the lease (which in this example would give $8.76 psf, showing how extremely skewed the more simple computation would be). The tenant must watch out for any analysis that presents an NPV utilizing a "simplified" net effective rate calculation and present-

Table 6-3. Concept of Net Present Value (in Dollars)

Year	Account balance beginning of year	Annual* interest (8%)	Account* balance with interest	Lump sum rent payment at year end (see text)	Account balance end of year
1	438,048†	35,043	473,091	100,000	373,091
2	373,091	29,848	402,939	105,000	297,939
3	297,939	23,835	321,774	110,300	211,474
4	211,474	16,918	228,392	115,800	112,592
5	112,592	9,008	121,600	121,600	0*

*Rounding effects on accuracy are ignored.
†NPV.

ing the results in terms of a per-square-foot amount. It is incorrect and totally misleading.

The constant payment is the more accurate way of calculating the net effective rent. This is the per-square-foot cost to the tenant over the full term of the lease after accounting for economic opportunity costs.

In this example, $10.97 is a more accurate reflection of the current per-square-foot value of the full lease value than the simple average of $11.05 calculated earlier.

Just what is this constant payment? It is the amount of money, expressed in terms of square feet, that would be needed to pay off, as a regular annual payment, the NPV amount ($438,048) if it could be borrowed at an 8 percent interest and used to pay off a lease in one lump sum. It is like any other type of installment payment—say, for a car or a home mortgage. In this case, the payment is $10.97 psf, which translates to an annual payment of $109,700 (on 10,000 sq ft) for five years. The total payments therefore amount to $548,560. One may well wonder why this is less than the original annual amount of $552,700 (see Table 6-2). The reason is that a constant payment is being made. Because of this, a larger payment is made in the earlier years than would otherwise be paid with the rent calculation, and smaller amounts are paid in the later years than would be required with a variable rent amount. Obviously, in this example, the tenant who could borrow the NPV amount at 8 percent interest and pay off the lease in one lump sum would be better off because the total of the payments to repay the loan would be less than the five-year cost of the lease. If, however, the tenant had to borrow the money at 10 percent interest, he or she would wind up paying more than the total value of the lease. (Note: If borrowed money is paid back monthly rather than annually, the total amount required, or paid back, is less than the total required for the annual payment.)

The constant payment, or net effective rent, provides an amortized, standardized basis of comparison for evaluating the complex interrelationships of different lease terms and conditions. NPV analysis will be used throughout this book to illustrate net effective rent for various rent increases and landlord concessions and inducements.

Fixed Rent Increases and Escalators

Given the fixed nature of certain items that the landlord pays with rent money (i.e., mortgage principal and interest), the landlord, recognizing the concept of net present value or the decreasing value of money over time, will want to protect and, to the extent possible, increase the relative value of his or her profits. (Landlord concessions and inducements and operating expense passthroughs will, for simplicity's sake, continue to be excluded from this section. Only mortgage principal and interest, un-reimbursed costs and expenses, and profit will be considered for increases in the rent.)

A tenant's basic rent can be increased in many ways to provide protection for the landlord. However, not every method will be considered reasonable by the tenant.

In addition, it is possible that, given a particular economic climate, a landlord will rent premises without any starting profit. Rather, the landlord will expect the profit to come over time through a rent increase or escalator. Often a PREB will explain to a tenant that the market or economic conditions have forced a landlord to rent space at below-market rates and at no profit. In some instances, this may be true. However, the landlord is not in business to lose money. Somewhere, somehow, a profit will be made—it may just take some time. A landlord may forgo profits for the first few years of a lease. However, given the fixed nature of the expenses that the bulk of the rent must go toward, and depending on the type of rent escalation, the landlord is able to achieve an end result that can be quite profitable. This direct cash profit does not reflect property appreciation and increased investment value, neither of which is normally passed on to tenants (except when the tenants have significant market and economic power and are able to participate in the equity of the property).

For computational purposes, the annual $10 psf standardized base rent multiplier will continue to be used in conjunction with a five-year lease. However, all calculations will be shown only on the square-foot rent, without regard to the size of the premises. In addition, different rent situations, with and without profit, will be considered for different possible effects.

Fixed Percentage Increase

A fixed percentage rent increase is patently unfair to a tenant, even when there is no initial landlord profit. To be fair, the amount of the increase must, and can, be adjusted to meet the needs of both the landlord and the tenant. Tables 6-4 and 6-5 illustrate the different ways of increasing rent and the outcomes. The tables use a flat 5 percent rent escalator and an annual rent of $10 psf. In one example it is assumed that the landlord makes no profit in year one and a 15 percent profit thereafter; in the other example a 15 percent profit starts immediately. We must also decide whether the increase is to apply to the original base rent or to the most recently increased rent. If the latter method is used, the percentage increase compounds itself so that the next increase also applies to the previous increase, as well as to the base rent. Because the rent initially goes to cover fixed expenses, any increase in rent thereafter goes toward the landlord's profits.

In Table 6-4 the landlord does quite well, because the 5 percent increase is compounded and the total benefit flows to the landlord. In Table 6-5 the nature of a fixed percentage increase

Table 6-4. Fixed 5-Percent Increase Applied against Each
Previous Year's Increased Rent (in Dollars)

Year	5% compounded rent increase (psf)	Landlord profit of 0% of first year's rent (psf)	Landlord profit of 15% of first year's rent (psf)
1	10.00	0	1.50
2	10.50	0.50	2.00
3	11.03	1.03	2.53
4	11.58	1.58	3.08
5	12.16	2.16	3.66
	Total profit	5.27	12.77

against a base rent works the same as a flat fixed annual increase
of, in this instance, $0.50 psf. Obviously Table 6-5 shows a better
result than Table 6-4 for the tenant. Although the difference in
the fifth year seems small, just $0.16 for 10,000 sq ft, this is $1600
in additional costs, with a total rent expense of $121,600 ($12.16
× 10,000 sq ft), which amounts to 1 percent of the total rent for
that year. This 1 percent extra, multiplied by more and more
square feet, can add up to a considerable amount.

In both examples the landlord seems to be gaining a healthy

Table 6-5. Fixed 5-Percent Increase Applied against the Base
Rent of Year One (in Dollars)

Year	5% compounded rent increase (psf)	Landlord profit of 0% of first year's rent (psf)	Landlord profit of 15% of first year's rent (psf)
1	10.00	0	1.50
2	10.50	0.50	2.00
3	11.00	1.00	2.50
4	11.50	1.50	3.00
5	12.00	2.00	3.50
	Total profit	5.00	12.50

profit. Note that with the starting profit of 15 percent, the increase goes entirely into profits. The question is, what is a fair return for the landlord to make on the premises? Assuming that the starting profit of 15 percent is a fair amount, the next question is, how much does this profit need to increase to compensate for the decreasing value of money?

Reasonable Landlord Profit

If a reasonable return to the landlord is, say, a 10 percent increase in profit each year in order to maintain the 15 percent profit margin, then the profit portion of the rent will increase as shown in Table 6-6. This profit margin is added to that portion of the original annual $10 psf base multiplier rent that was fixed. With a 15 percent profit margin, the remaining 85 percent of the base rent is fixed at $8.50 psf (Table 6-7).

The second example provides a consistent landlord profit of 15 percent of the base rent amount without any erosion of the profit itself (assuming the 10 percent increase each year matches the rate of inflation). It is interesting that the total profit due to the landlord for five years of $9.17 psf (Table 6-6) is $4.17 psf more than the landlord would get starting with a zero percent first-year profit in Table 6-5 ($5 psf total profit), but $3.33 psf less than the landlord actually gets if he or she starts with a 15 percent profit of the base rent ($12.50 psf total profit).

Table 6-6. Profit Rate with 10-Percent Return

Year	Landlord profit ($) with 10% return each year (psf)
1	1.50
2	1.65
3	1.82
4	2.00
5	2.20
Total five-year profit	9.17

Table 6-7. Profit Margin Added to Fixed Portion of Base Rent (in Dollars)

Year	Fixed amount of base rent (psf)	Added profit (psf)	Total annual psf rent	% increase over previous year's rent
1	8.50	1.50	10.00	
2	8.50	1.65	10.15	1.5
3	8.50	1.82	10.32	1.7
4	8.50	2.00	10.50	1.7
5	8.50	2.20	10.70	1.9

These examples begin to show the complexities that arise and have to be considered when looking at different lease terms and conditions. The tenant must be wary of glib explanations from the landlord (and the PREB) regarding the amounts and applications of various rent increases and escalators.

It would be simple if the landlord explained what items made up the base rent and disclosed the expected profit. As in any business, however, this type of disclosure is unlikely. The tenant will need to question and become familiar with every nuance of the lease, must rely on the experience of his or her PREB (never the PREB representing the landlord), and must be sure that the PREB provides a complete financial spreadsheet showing the appropriate calculations of the escalating rent for every year of the lease.

Put on a Maximum Amount of Increase

As Table 6-7 also shows, the actual rent increase needed to maintain a profit for the landlord is approximately 1.7 percent of the total base rent. Strange as it may sound, this fixed net escalation of close to 2 percent is not an unrealistic rent increase. Since it is relatively rare for a landlord to "give away" a space, the tenant should not even think about the no-profit scenario. As a guideline, the longer the length of the lease, the smaller the percentage rent escalator should be.

Flat Fixed Escalator

A flat fixed escalator works in much the same way as the fixed percentage increase applied against the initial base rent, as shown in Table 6-5. This escalator is just a fixed dollar value that is applied to the escalated rent of the previous year. Therefore, it becomes in effect a decreasing percentage increase over the term of the lease (Table 6-8). The fixed escalation works reasonably well for short-term leases.

The great difficulty with the fixed income is that it has no relationship to varying economic conditions and can still provide either windfall profits or highly eroded profits for a landlord. The flat fixed dollar escalator is the basis for the graduated, or stepped-up, rent.

Graduated, or Stepped-Up, Rent

The distinguishing feature of graduated rent is the possibility for varying the magnitude of the increase creating the graduated rent on an annual (or more frequent) basis (Table 6-9). The graduated rent adds an element of flexibility that is not available with the other types of escalators discussed above.

Table 6-8. Fixed Rent Escalator

Year	Fixed $1-psf increase in rent ($)	% Income previous year's rent
1	10.00	
2	11.00	10.0
3	12.00	9.1
4	13.00	8.3
5	14.00	7.7

Table 6-9. Graduated Rent (in Dollars)

Year	Increased rent (psf)	Graduated amount of increase at beginning of year
1	10.00	
2	10.50	0.50
3	11.00	0.50
4	12.00	1.00
5	13.50	1.50

Rent Bumps

A special version of the graduated rent increase is the rent bump, which permits a variable increase in rent at irregular intervals (Table 6-10). The rent bump increase offers both the landlord and tenant more flexibility since it enables them to start with a lower than market rent and adjust to the market rent later in the term of the lease. However, graduated rent and rent bump increases can easily be abused by landlords. The justification for a particular increase may be vague and no longer valid by the time the increase actually occurs. Because there are fixed increases, however, a landlord who miscalculates could wind up with less than the anticipated profit.

Table 6-10. Rent Bump (in Dollars)

Year	Increased rent (psf)*	Increase (bump) at beginning of year (psf)
1	10.00	
2	11.00	1.00
3	11.00	
4	12.50	1.50
5	13.00	0.50

*Standardized $10.00 psf annualized rent used.

Graduated Rent and
Rent Bumps with a
Percentage Increase

Graduated rent and rent bump increases can also be integrated with a percentage increase to help the landlord achieve extraordinary rent results. Table 6-11 combines Table 6-10 with Table 6-4; it shows what can happen to the landlord's profit in Table 6-4.

Table 6-11. Fixed-Percentage Rent Increase with Rent Bumps (in Dollars)

Year	Annual rent (psf)	5% increase of adjusted rent	Rent bump	Actual annual rent (psf)	Landlord profit at 0% of first year's rent (psf)	Landlord profit at 15% of first year's rent (psf)
1	10.00			10.00		1.50
2	10.00	0.50	1.00	11.50	1.50	3.00
3	11.50	0.58		12.08	2.08	3.58
4	12.08	0.60	1.50	14.18	4.18	5.68
5	14.18	0.71	0.50	15.39	5.39	6.89

Table 6-11 is meant to be an exaggeration. However, it is something a tenant might agree to. The final rent seems excessive, compared with the fixed-percentage increase or the graduated rent examples. Note that the percentage increase was calculated before the rent bump increase. It could just as easily have been calculated after, with the percentage increase being taken on the rent bump, and the result being an even higher rent. The landlord profit columns are self-explanatory.

Tenant and Landlord
Certainty

The fixed-increase rent types are more viable for tenants occupying smaller spaces and for shorter-term leases. Few larger space users or tenants with long-term leases would accept a fixed-percentage rent increase. However, the graduated rent or rent bumps are more acceptable to these tenants because they serve important purposes (see Chapters 7 and 9). The main redeeming feature of these types of rent increases is that they provide certainty. The landlord knows what his or her rent income and thus cash flow will be. Likewise, the tenant knows what his or her rent costs will be each year and the maximum costs for the entire lease period.

Use of Indexes for Rent Increases

The sophisticated tenant will want any percentage increase to have a maximum cap or be tied to some measure that reflects economic conditions. These would prevent the landlord's rent from declining and yet ensure that rent increases would reflect economic realities. These types of increases will be based on an index of some type.

An endless variety of indexes can be used to provide rent escalators. Indexes can include bank indexes, stock indexes, and various economic indexes, such as the Consumer Price Index (CPI), the Wholesale Price Index, a change in a regional or national bank prime rate, the Federal Reserve's cost of funds rate, the Standard and Poor's 500 or another stock index, the changing interest rates for U.S. Treasury notes and bonds, and anything else that can be thought up, such as the increase in a union contract for porter's wages (this is actually used, but it is a regionally specific index).

Perhaps the most important aspect to keep in mind in choosing an index is its need to reflect the tenant's expectations of economic reality accurately. After an index is chosen, the tenant should make certain the lease clause clearly defines every aspect of the index to be used: its exact name, where it can be found, how to use it, and what time periods are being referred to. It is also important to specify an alternative index in case the chosen index is discontinued.

To find out whether a proper description has been provided, the description of the index and other information should be turned over to a staff person, who should be asked to locate and provide a copy of what is specified. If the person cannot, either the description is unclear or the index is not readily available—or perhaps you need a new staff person.

Often a lack of clarity in the description of the index will work to a tenant's favor. In the event of a dispute with a landlord, a tenant will often prevail if the index has not been clearly presented and if the intent and process are ambiguous. However, it works to the tenant's advantage to avoid landlord-tenant disputes that require a court's reconciliation.

Consumer Price Index

Perhaps the most commonly used economic index for rent escalation purposes is the CPI. This index is published on a regular basis by the U.S. Department of Labor's Bureau of Labor Statistics. There are a number of variations, such as the CPI-U and CPI-W, which represent all urban consumers and wage earners, respectively. Furthermore, the index is presented both on a national level and for urban and metropolitan areas. However, not all indexes are necessarily published on the same regular basis.

When an index is published can be quite important. For example, if the lease commencement date is in May and that is also the basis for the rent increase, what is used if there is no index published for May? Also, when exactly are the indexes published? For example, an April index may not actually show up until June.

The specific details of the various indexes and their exact workings are left to the reader to investigate. Our examples will use the CPI without regard to the accuracy of the numbers used.

How the CPI Works

The current national all-urban consumer index has a base year of 1982 to 1984 equal to 100. As the CPI measures the value of a market basket of various goods and services, the base year for the index can be important. The idea behind the base year is that in 1982–1984, regardless of the actual price of a product, for example, a pair of shoes, it is reset to 1.00 in the base year. From this point, each change in the index measures the percentage change in the price of the article, or in this case, the total market basket of goods. The base year index of 1.00 times 100 percent equals a base year number, or index of 100. If in 1987 a given market basket of goods is said to be 115, it indicates that prices have increased 15 percent when measured in 1987 over the prices in effect in the base year. The CPI is not additive from year to year but cumulative for the two points of time being considered.

To measure the change in the CPI is relatively straightforward:

$$1984 \text{ index} = 100 \qquad 1990 \text{ index} = 140$$

- Difference between indexes = 40 (140 − 100)
- Amount of change equals difference divided by base year index = 0.40 (40 ÷ 100)
- Percentage change from 1984 to 1990 = 40 percent (0.40 × 100)

Therefore, something that costs $1.00 in 1984 costs $1.40 in 1990. Similarly,

$$1981 \text{ index} = 190 \qquad 1993 \text{ index} = 210$$

- Difference between indexes = 20 (210 − 190)
- Amount of change equals difference divided by base year index = 0.1053 (20 ÷ 190)
- Percentage change from 1991 to 1993 = 10.53 percent (0.1053 × 100)

Therefore, something that cost $1.50 in 1991 cost 10.53 percent more in 1993, or $1.66.

The cumulative rather than nonadditive effect of the CPI can be seen in Table 6-12. As shown in the table, the total of the annual increases for the first five years would be 26.3 percent (6.2 + 5.2 + 8.0 + 6.9 = 26.3 percent). However, the cumulative effect of the CPI is actually a 28.9 percent increase when calculated from year 1 to year 5. For the full 10-year period shown, the additive

Table 6-12. Sample CPI (Percent)

Year	CPI*	Annual increase over previous year (%)	Cumulative increase from year one (%)
1 1992	145		
2 1993	154	6.2	6.2
3 1994	162	5.2	11.7
4 1995	175	8.0	20.7
5 1996	187	6.9	28.9
6 1997	197	5.3	35.9
7 1998	209	6.1	44.1
8 1999	222	6.2	53.1
9 2000	238	7.2	64.1
10 2001	254	6.7	75.2

*The specified CPI indexes are not actual. They have been created for purposes of the examples in this book.

effect is 57.8 percent, while the cumulative impact from year one to year ten is 75.2 percent, a significant difference.

Using the CPI

The CPI index may be used as a rent escalator in lieu of a fixed percentage increase. The supposition is that the economic index provides a more realistic estimate of the economic forces affecting the value of money. This protects the landlord's profits and other expenses from being eroded and provides a realistic rent increase for the tenant that mirrors economic factors.

Perhaps the biggest difficulty in using any index as a rent escalator is in how it is applied. This seems to confuse tenants, landlords, attorneys, and PREBs alike. In fact, the explanation of how the escalator is to be applied is often written in a lease provision incorrectly or is so confusing that it causes different results when used by different individuals.

Because there are at least three ways to apply an index as a rent escalator, with numerous variations, no preferred sample is provided here. Rather, it is up to the tenant and his or her PREB to sit down with the appropriate lease provision and work through every year of the lease term using the rent escalation language to determine the annual and total lease effects. Even though the lease reflects the unknowns of a future index, it is relatively easy to use estimated data, as presented in Table 6-12.

The tenant may well be surprised by the results. The language of the lease provision will be so convoluted that either calculating the same answer consistently will be impossible or the result will be an unintended astronomical rent increases.

A typical lease provision might state the following: "The basic monthly rent shall be adjusted each year by a maximum of 30 percent of the change in the index known as the 'United States Bureau of Labor Statistics, Consumer Price Index, for Urban Wage Earners and Clerical Workers' (CPI-W), all items (1982–1984 = 100), hereafter referred to as the 'Index,' provided, however, that the amount payable by the tenant under this lease shall not be less than the stated base rent. Such adjustment of the base rent shall be accomplished by adding to the base rent the result of the calculation, which shall be the product of the base rent and 30 percent of a fraction, the numerator of which shall be the difference between the index published for the month immediately preceding the adjustment date of the year for which such adjustment is to be made and the index published for the corresponding month preceding the first month of the lease term (to be known as the 'Base Index'); and the denominator, which shall be the base index."

CPI Applications

There are three major ways to apply the CPI increase:

1. Use the percentage increase in the index between the appropriate month in the current lease year being calculated and the same month in the base index year (e.g., lease commencement month) and apply it to the base year rent. (In Table 6-12 the comparable calculation would be to take the percentage increase between year five and year one for an increase of 28.9 percent, which would be applied to increase the base year

rent.) This application is called the fixed, or static, base year escalator.

2. Use the percentage increase in the index between the appropriate month in the current lease year being calculated and the same month in the previous year of the lease and apply it to the previous year's increased rent (known as the previous year's adjusted base rent). (In Table 6-12 the comparable calculation would be to take the percentage increase between year three and year two, for an increase of 5.2 percent, which would be used to increase the adjusted base rent from year two to arrive at the adjusted base rent for year three.) This application is called the adjusted, moving, or rolling base year escalator.

3. The third version, a combination of types one and two, should never be accepted by a tenant. It is the most onerous of the increases, as will be shown in Table 6-15 in "Effects of Rent Escalator." This version takes the percentage increase as calculated in the static base calculation (i.e., for the current calculated year back to the base year) but applies it to the previous year's adjusted base rent as specified in the rolling base calculation. It applies a compounded or cumulative index increase against an already compounded increased rent. This version is not standard practice. It came about because of a mistake in just a few words in a lease provision. The lease provision was attempting to define the method of applying the static base method, but instead of saying that the percentage increase in the index would be applied to the base year's rent, it mistakenly said the increase was to be applied to the previous year's adjusted base rent. Not much of a mistake, just a couple of words. (See what happens in the examples in "Effects of Rent Escalator.")

When Does Index Calculation Take Place?

The tenant should be aware of when the landlord will actually calculate the index and when the rent increase will be effective. For example, when using the CPI, the appropriate month's data will not be available for 60 to 90 days. Thus, a March rent increase date could not be calculated until June or July. However, the effective date of the rent increase will still be in March. Therefore, a lease will often require the tenant to pay in one lump sum the two, three, or more months of rent increase retroactive to the effective date of the increase. This is often an unwanted surprise and undue burden for the tenant.

As an alternative to the lump-sum retroactive payment, the landlord may estimate the amount of the increase and have the tenant start paying the estimated increased rent on the effective date until the actual calculation can be made, at that point making the necessary adjustments. Depending on whether the landlord's estimate is high or low, there may be an unwarranted delay in the actual calculation. Since the landlord is being paid an increase, there may be no incentive to make the adjustments.

An alternative tenants prefer is to have the lump sum of the increase for the few months retroactive to the effective date, amortized and paid over the following 12 months of the lease. In this example, when the increase for March is known in July, the increased rent starts in August, with an additional one-twelfth of the total amount of the five months of rent increase that is due.

A compromise alternative that is not advocated is to choose the effective month for calculating the increase as one, three, or four months prior to the lease commencement month (or whatever month is effective for calculating the rent increase—for example, the month the premises are occupied). For example, if March is the rent increase month, the amount of the rent increase would be based on the month of December. Other than an initial first-year calculation bias regarding an inexact index, which may result in a slightly over- or understated index, any initial bias will be smoothed out in the following years through automatic averaging that occurs over a 12-month period.

What Happens When the Index Goes Down?

Another question to consider is how the rent would be affected if an economic-based index, such as the CPI, were to go down—although such a trend is almost impossible. (The index must be chosen with care: A volatile index could well work against a tenant.) The landlord will want to include a lease provision stipulating that in the event of a decrease in the index, the then-current adjusted base rent would not change. In other words, the landlord wants the index to work only one way: in his or her favor. But remember what the index is used for. It is not there just to increase the rent automatically; it is there to reduce the consequences of economic erosion due to time. A decreasing index is providing economic benefit, but when it is not used to decrease the rent, only the landlord is benefiting.

The tenant should be sure that all movements or changes of the index affect the rent in the same way. If the rent can be increased, it can and should also be decreased as appropriate.

The usual landlord compromise for this proper tenant position is to allow the index to work in either direction but with a lower floor so that the rent will in no case be allowed to fall below the original base rent.

How Much of the Index Should Be Used?

Assuming that the tenant and landlord have chosen an appropriate index and that the index and lease provision has been checked to ensure that it is accurate and has been properly calculated, how much of the index should be used to calculate the rent increase? The reader is directed back to the section on fixed percentage increases and Tables 6-4 and 6-5 to see the effects of a large percentage increase on landlord profits.

Because the purpose of the rent increase is to protect the landlord from the effects of economic erosion, it obviously should not apply to that part of the rent related to the landlord's fixed costs and expenses. Assuming a consistent 10 to 20 percent increase in the landlord's profit and other costs and expenses not chargeable to tenants, the percentage of increase when applied to the total rent should be limited, on the high side, to a maximum of 2 to 3 percent. An increase of 1.5 to 2 percent would be about right for the majority of tenant situations.

The tenant or the tenant's PREB must therefore do a little homework and find out the amount of the average annual percentage increase for the past five or ten years in the economic (or other) index that has been chosen as a rent escalator. For example, the average increase over a five- to eight-year period for the CPI tends to be about 6 to 7 percent. (Of course, there have been years in which the index was 8, 9, or 10 percent or more.)

Once the average increase is known, the tenant needs to be sure that the language in the lease providing for the use of the index as a rent escalator limits the percentage of increase that can be applied in the calculation. For example, if the average increase were 6 to 7 percent and the acceptable rent escalator were about 2 percent, then no more than 30 percent of the index would be used. If the percentage increase in the index were 6 percent, 30 percent of 6 percent would give a rent escalation of 1.8 percent— right where it's wanted.

Obviously, tenants and landlords will have different interpretations of what is the true average percentage increase. Landlords will want to stress how low this index has been known to go. Taking, for example, a 4 percent index increase, 30 percent of that increase would permit a mere 1.2 percent rent increase, which, from the landlord's perspective, would "unfairly penalize the landlord." The tenant must be sure, when a low increase in the index is pointed out, to likewise point out a high percentage increase in the index, such as a phenomenal 12 percent increase in the CPI during a high inflationary period. Taking 30 percent of the 12 percent increase would permit a 3.6 percent overall rent escalation.

The point is that the rent increase is to be based on an average. There will always be highs and lows, and these exceptions must be acceptable to both the tenant and the landlord; that is what makes an average work.

In the following examples, 30 percent of the CPI created in Table 6-12 is used.

The Effects of the Rent Escalator

Three interesting observations can be made about Tables 6-13 and 6-14. First, it does not matter whether a static or rolling base escalator is used when 100 percent of the increase in an index is used. The results are the same. Why? Because, as in Table 6-14, the full increase each year is being applied not only against the

Table 6-13. Fixed, or Static, Rent Base Escalator

	Full CPI cumulative increase*			30% of cumulative increase		
Year	Base rent† (psf) ($)	Full cumulative CPI increase (%)	Adjusted base rent (psf) ($)	Base rent† (psf) ($)	30% of cumulative CPI increase (%)	Adjusted base rent (psf) ($)
1	10.00	—	10.00	10.00	—	10.00
2	10.00	6.2	10.62	10.00	1.86	10.19
3	10.00	11.7	11.17	10.00	3.51	10.35
4	10.00	20.7	12.07	10.00	6.21	10.62
5	10.00	28.9	12.89	10.00	8.67	10.87

*Data are from Table 6-12.

†The previous standardized annual $10 psf base rent multiplier is used. The reader needs only to multiply results by the appropriate factor for various rent amounts.

NOTE: Type 1 rent escalator; see text. Percentage increase taken from appropriate increase year back to base year and applied against base rent.

Table 6-14. Adjusted, or Rolling, Rent Base Escalator

	Full CPI annual increase*			30% of annual increase		
Year	New base rent† (psf) ($)	Full single-year CPI increase (%)	Adjusted base rent (psf) ($)	New base rent† (psf) ($)	30% of single-year CPI increase (%)	Adjusted base rent (psf) ($)
1	10.00	—	10.00	10.00	—	10.00
2	10.00	6.2	10.62	10.00	1.86	10.19
3	10.62	5.2	11.17	10.19	1.56	10.35
4	11.17	8.0	12.06	10.35	2.40	10.60
5	12.06	6.9	12.89	10.60	2.10	10.82

*Data are from Table 6-12.

†The previous standardized annual $10 psf base rent multiplier is used. The reader needs only to multiply results by the appropriate factor for various rent amounts.

NOTE: Type 2 rent escalator; see text. Percentage increase taken from appropriate increase year back to previous year and applied against previous year's adjusted base rent.

Table 6-15. Combined—Fixed or Static Base Year Increase Applied to Previous Year's Adjusted Base Rent

	Full CPI cumulative increase*			30% of cumulative increase		
Year	New base rent† (psf) ($)	Full cumulative CPI increase (%)	Adjusted base rent (psf) ($)	New base rent† (psf) ($)	30% of cumulative CPI increase (%)	Adjusted base rent (psf) ($)
1	10.00	—	10.00	10.00	—	10.00
2	10.00	6.2	10.62	10.00	1.86	10.19
3	10.62	11.7	11.86	10.19	3.51	10.55
4	11.86	20.7	14.32	10.55	6.21	11.21
5	14.32	28.9	18.46	11.21	8.67	12.18
6	18.46	35.9	25.09	12.18	10.77	13.49
7	25.09	44.1	36.15	13.49	13.23	15.27
8	36.15	53.1	55.35	15.27	15.93	17.70
9	55.35	64.1	90.83	17.70	19.23	21.10
10	90.83	75.2	159.13	21.10	22.56	25.86

*Data are from Table 6-12.
†The previous standardized annual $10 psf base rent multiplier is used. The reader needs only to multiply results by the appropriate factor for various rent amounts.

base rent, but also against the additional portion that is the rent increase. Therefore, the adjusted base rent is being compounded. This works out the same as the cumulative increase (which is the compounded effect of the increase in the index).

Second, there is a marked difference between using a full index increase and using only a portion of the index increase. At the end of five years in either Table 6-13 or Table 6-14 the rent increase is $2.00 psf or greater. For a 10,000-sq-ft space this is $20,000; for 100,000 sq ft it is $200,000. Given the fixed nature of certain landlord costs of the original base rent, that increase would be additional landlord profit.

Third, when using some percentage of the index increase (in this case 30 percent), the adjusted rolling base will produce a lower rent for the tenant. This will always be true and should be the preferred tenant option.

To impress upon the tenant how important it is to check the calculations in the lease provision, Table 6-15 combines the two methods. The absurdity of using a full index increase as a rent escalator is shown as well. Table 6-15 shows the calculations for a full 10 years. As can be seen, the more modest 30 percent of the index increase will more than double the rent by the end of the lease term. (Note: The economic index increases used are in the relatively realistic range of 6 to 8 percent.) When using the full index increase, with the extra compounding effect, the rent at the end of the 10 years is too astronomical even to contemplate.

Economic Consequences

Because market and economic conditions are dynamic, there can never be one solution, such as a perfect rent escalation method, that works for everyone everywhere.

The real estate market is never static. Its property values can slide from sky-high appreciation to depressed levels. In a turnaround market the investor often needs to be patient and willing to take a long-term view of an investment.

Under certain market conditions a base or absolute net rent may barely cover a property's debt service and allow a landlord to break even. This is when a base rent escalator becomes critical to a landlord; over time, it will provide the profit otherwise missing from having made the distasteful economic decisions necessary to lease vacant space at reduced rents.

In the end, although a landlord may have to forgo profits for a number of years, except in periods of overvaluation, commercial real estate tends to continue appreciating over time. In poor economic times, the patient landlord with some staying power will realize the reward built into appreciating real estate and the increased profits to be made from base rent escalators.

Tenants enter a market to look for new premises only every three, five, ten, or sometimes twenty years. They are at a distinct disadvantage in not being up to date or involved with the changing real estate market conditions that have surrounded them. Tenants, justifiably, often depend on an attorney or a PREB to help them achieve the best and most realistic transaction in a current market.

To achieve such a transaction, of course, one must be sure that things like rent escalation provisions work as they are supposed to. At a minimum, a PREB (or an attorney) should provide the tenant with a complete financial spreadsheet showing—on an annual basis and using tenant-approved assumptions regarding economic consequences and rent escalation increases—the estimated financial implications of the appropriate lease provisions over the full term of the lease.

If you do not have a PREB (or other individual) who is willing to do this, you have the wrong person—get another one!

What Happens to Rent Escalations During a Rent-Abatement Period?

Exactly how does a rent escalator work during a rent-abatement period? The answer could have significant monetary implications to a tenant.

If a tenant starts out at the standardized annual $10 psf base rent multiplier and has one year of rent abatement, what rent is paid immediately after the rent-abatement period? The answer would be $10 psf *if* a tenant-preferred provision stipulated that the rent escalator was to start at the same time that the tenant actually started paying the base rent (this must be stated separately in case of complications in the operating expense base; see Chapter 7). This tenant-preferred provision would automatically adjust the initial setting of the base month and year for purposes of an economic index rent escalator.

Without this tenant-preferred provision, it is more likely that, with a rent escalator of 5 percent for the year, the tenant will find out that immediately at the end of the rent-abatement period (assuming it is for one year) the annual rent due will be $10.50 psf. The only enjoyment the tenant gets from the hard-fought negotiations over a starting rent of $10 psf is never to have paid it.

7
Operating Expenses

The rent a tenant pays for space has three broad purposes: (1) to pay for the debt service incurred for the property (e.g., mortgage principal and interest), (2) to cover any and all costs and expenses incurred in maintaining and operating the property on behalf of the tenants, and (3) to reimburse the landlord directly for his or her time, resources, and entrepreneurship, as well as provide a return on the investment (i.e., profit and other miscellaneous expenses). The type of rent being paid (as described in Chapter 6) depends on whether all the costs and expenses are lumped together into one regular payment to the landlord, are collected partly by the landlord, or are paid directly by a tenant to various service providers.

Just as rent escalators are used to reduce the economic erosion of the landlord's profit, some means may be used to have the tenant pay for any increases in the maintenance and operating costs and expenses related to the tenant's occupancy of a property, building, and premises. In this chapter the broad term *operating expenses* will be used to refer to these expenses; it includes real estate and other appropriate taxes, maintenance and janitorial service, insurance, utilities and associated services, and other related costs and expenses. Whether these operating expenses are collected as basic rent or as "additional rent" does not matter.

The questions of concern to the tenant are: What expenses are to be passed on? How will the expenses be calculated? What is the proper tenant's share of all the property and building expenses? What controls are there on the expenses? How will the expenses be passed through to the tenant? When do expense increases have to be paid? Many of these concerns are complex because of the various interrelationships between them.

What's the Basis for the Passthrough?

One of the first things a prospective tenant must find out is how much of the operating expenses he or she would be responsible for. The tenant must be sure that all aspects of the building's space are clearly defined (see Chapter 2) in the premises lease clause, which is the initial basis on which the tenant's expenses are calculated. Each tenant in a multitenanted building will be responsible for some portion of all the appropriate operating expenses. A fairly standard method of apportioning the operating expenses is by proration, or giving each tenant a pro rata share. That is, the proportion of the building's total applicable space (e.g., rentable space) the tenant is leasing is the same proportion of the operating expenses for which the tenant will be responsible.

For this reason, the tenant must make sure that the premises are properly and accurately measured and defined in the lease. It is equally important to define the basis for establishing the tenant's percentage use of the total building space.

Creating More Space from Thin Air

What the tenant must always be on guard against is the chance that the use of a building space will change and thereby affect total applicable building space to be used in prorating expenses. Such a change may occur when common area space (e.g., a lobby area) is converted to retail space or when storage areas are rented as office space. In addition, over time, as different tenants rent the same premises, the exact amount of space being leased can be altered through continued rounding of the square footage, or a few square feet might be added each time a space is re-leased. As a result, a landlord could well be reimbursed for operating expenses in excess of 100 percent of the actual building's space. Because each tenant deals with the landlord separately, this proration factor is often difficult to isolate.

The tenant should also be sure that the total applicable space basis is some function of a realistic and measurable total of the building's space and not a function of a variable amount of space. Using the total occupied square footage as a basis is quite unacceptable to a tenant. If a tenant has 10,000 rentable square feet in a building with 100,000 rentable square feet, the tenant has 10 percent of the building forever, or until the total number of rentable square feet changes. But what if the base were total occupied square feet? If the building were fully occupied, the tenant would still have 10 percent of the space. But what if half the building were empty? The tenant would have 20 percent (10,000 sq ft of 50,000 sq ft occupied) of the space and thus that same percentage of prorated operating expenses. (The tenant must be sure this is not incorrectly worded in the applicable lease provision.)

Are the Expenses Included in the Rent?

A tenant can pay for operating expenses in at least three ways. First, the tenant can hire and pay directly for janitorial and utilities services. In these situations the tenant negotiates his or her own separate contract. This situation will not be of concern in this book.

The second method arises when basic rent is paid to the landlord and there is an "additional rent" for all the operating expenses. This type of rent is known as an absolute net rent (see Chapter 6). The tenant is responsible for paying all of the operating expenses and any increases. Since this additional rent will be paid to the landlord, the tenant will be concerned with some, but not all, of the subject areas and provisions of this lease clause.

In the third case the tenant has a full-service lease in which at least initial operating expenses are included in the base rent. The tenant is then responsible for any increases in these operating expenses. It is in this area that the tenant must be wary, because there are significant opportunities for landlord abuse.

There are two common methods for establishing an operating expense base above which the tenant is responsible for the operating expenses. These are known as the expense stop, or fixed landlord contribution, and the base year.

The Expense Stop (Fixed Landlord Contribution)

The expense stop, or fixed landlord contribution, is a fixed dollar amount of the initial base rent that the landlord specifies as his or her maximum contribution to the operating expenses that are to be passed through to the tenant. This fixed dollar amount can be expressed either as one amount covering all the possible operating expenses or as individual maximum amounts specified for a variety of listed expenses such as cleaning and janitorial services or real estate taxes. However specified, once fixed, the landlord's contribution remains the same throughout the full term of the lease. However, the amount of this stop is negotiable with the landlord and can have important implications for the tenant, depending on whether it is specified as one total amount or broken out into individual pieces.

It is important for the tenant to fully understand the expense stop. He or she will be paying all the operating expenses (or those portions of individual items) above the landlord's contribution. These above-stop expenses are in addition to the base rent and any rent escalator.

In this chapter we will continue to use the standard annual $10 psf base rent multiplier (used in Chapter 6). In addition, we will establish a standard annual $1 psf base operating expense multiplier. In this way, the reader can multiply all calculations by whichever factor is appropriate in order to represent specific regional examples. For example, for a rent of $30 psf, the standard base rent would be multiplied by 3. For a total operating expense of $9 psf, the standard operating expense is multiplied by 9.

How much of the base rent is contributed to operating expenses will have different effects in different situations. A base rent is really made up of two components. For example, if the standard base rent is $10 psf, $9 psf can cover the landlord's debt service costs and profit, and $1 psf can be defined as the expense stop (landlord's contribution to operating expenses). If the tenant's pro rata share of total operating expenses is $2 psf for the year, then the tenant will pay not only the $10 psf base rent, but also the additional rent of $1 psf. (The other $1 psf is the landlord's contribution from the $10 psf total rent, leaving the landlord $9 psf.) If another tenant has the same $10 psf base rent but has negotiated for a $1.50 psf expense stop, that tenant will only have to pay an additional $0.50 psf for the extra operating expenses. (The other $1.50 psf is the landlord's contribution from the $10 psf total rent, leaving the landlord $8.50 psf.)

What happens in the above example if the tenant's pro rata share of operating expenses for the year is $0.75 psf? Because the typical lease stipulates the "maximum landlord contribution," the tenant still pays the $10 psf rent, and the landlord has an extra $0.25 psf profit for the year.

An alternative is for the tenant to work in a lease provision that allows for the tenant to receive a rent credit for any portion of the operating expense stop not specifically utilized for operating expenses. Alternatively, any nonutilized portion of the expense stop might be carried over from year to year and counted toward the following year's expenses.

Because different landlords offer not only different rents but also different magnitudes of expense stops, evaluating buildings and premises becomes that much more complex and difficult.

What about Rent Escalators?

An interesting but complex subject pertaining to base rent with a specified expense stop, one that confuses tenants and PREBs alike, is the rent escalator and how it is applied. If the base rent is $10 psf, including a $1 psf expense stop, and the base rent is to be escalated 5 percent, how much does the rent increase? The "normal" answer is that a rent of $10 psf escalated by 5 percent results in a rent of $10.50 psf. But what about the expense stop? That, too, has been escalated. But isn't the tenant already responsible for, and in fact paying for, all of the operating expenses over the expense stop? What then, is the rationale for also increasing the expense stop by 5 percent? (Ask the landlord.) Remember, it does not matter if these initial expenses increased. The tenant pays for all the increases, so there is no inflation or economic erosion factor associated with this initial amount.

A rent escalator of 5 percent applied to the standard $1 psf expense stop results in an additional and unnecessary tenant rent of $0.05 psf. This is an extra $50 per year per 1000 sq ft—for just the first year. In each additional year, the increase in the expense stop is compounded.

Exempting the Expense Stop

The tenant needs to be sure there is a lease provision exempting the expense stop from any rent escalation.

A workable compromise is to have the landlord's contribution to the operating expenses (the expense stop) increased each year by the amount of the rent escalation. Therefore, in this example, the $1 psf landlord contribution to operating expenses (expense stop) in year one would, with a 5 percent rent escalator, increase to $1.05 psf in the second year, and so on throughout the term of the lease.

Separately Listed Expenses

What happens when the landlord contribution to operating expenses is broken down into different amounts for different items? For example:

Item	Landlord's contribution (psf) in dollars
Real estate taxes	0.75
Cleaning and janitorial services	0.50
Utilities and services	0.25
Total	1.50

There is no reason why a landlord could not do this for a whole array of items. Of course, it does tend to make things a bit more complicated both for computational and reporting purposes. But how the expense stops are specified is important—as maximum landlord contributions per expense item or as maximum landlord contributions for the total amount of all items.

If the expense stop is taken to be all items netted together, up to the total dollar amount of the individual items, the tenant avoids the difficulties that can occur when different items go up by different amounts. Further complications can develop when the cost of an expense item goes down, as is possible when certain utilities are bought in bulk.

Consider what happens when not all of the individual expense items increase beyond the stop and the landlord contribution is pegged at a maximum per item, not based on a netted total (Table 7-1). Even though the landlord's total maximum contribution has not been reached in Table 7-1, the tenant still owes $0.25 psf in above-stop expenses just for the real estate taxes. If that weren't bad enough, the landlord is also making an additional "profit" of $0.35 psf because the total for two of the operating expenses did not go above their individual expense stops.

Table 7-1. Separate Landlord Contributions for Operating Expenses (in Dollars)

Item	Landlord's maximum contribution (psf)	Actual expense (psf)	Tenant above-stop cost (psf)
Real estate tax	0.75	1.00	0.25
Cleaning and janitorial services	0.50	0.25	0
Utilities and services	0.25	0.15	0
Total	1.50	1.40	0.25

Where Does the Expense Stop Come From?

A realistic expense stop is supposed to be a landlord's best estimate of actual first-year operating expenses in the building. If the stop is accurate, a tenant should not have any unexpected first-year expenses. However, the expense stop is only an estimate, and there is no incentive for landlord accuracy. Rather, just the opposite is the case.

Older Buildings

In older buildings it is in the landlord's interest to persuade a tenant to accept an underestimate of actual expenses when setting an expense stop. To the extent that the stop is less than the actual expenses, the less the landlord will have to pay, and the sooner the tenant will begin paying for the above-stop expenses.

Although it would not seem too difficult for the landlord to increase the previous year's actual operating expenses in an older building by some average percentage to get a reasonable estimate of current expenses, this is not necessarily in the best interests of the landlord. Before signing any lease in an older building, the tenant should insist on seeing the actual expenses for the building that were prorated to the tenants in the preceding three to five years. In addition, the tenant may need to have his or her PREB check on the operating costs for comparable buildings nearby (see "A Legal Aside" in Chapter 1).

Reducing Artificial Expenses

To attract a tenant or to become more competitive, a landlord will often reduce the total rent by artificially reducing the magnitude of the expense stop. For example, rather than having a rent of $10 psf with a realistic $1 psf expense stop, the landlord may offer a rent of $9.50 psf with an artificially low expense stop of $0.50 psf. Of course, there is still going to be a minimum of $1 psf in expenses. Unless the tenant carefully checks, he or she will incur the extra $0.50 psf as above-stop expenses at the end of the year and wind up paying the $10 psf the landlord originally wanted.

Limiting the Tenant's Exposure

To help keep the landlord "honest," a tenant-preferred lease would provide for a maximum dollar (or percentage) amount over the landlord's estimated expense stop above which the tenant would become responsible for the increased operating expenses. In addition, the tenant and landlord could agree on some percentage (e.g., 20 percent) above the stated expense stop for which the tenant would not be responsible for expenses; there would instead be an upward readjustment of the expense stop in the first year of the lease.

Therefore, using the $10 psf (and the included $1 psf expense stop) standard multiplier rent, the tenant would require that there be no expense passthroughs until the operating expenses in the first year exceeded 5 percent of the standard expense stop (i.e., $1.05 psf), stipulating that the tenant would not be responsible for any operating expense in excess of a 20 percent increase over the stop ($1.20 psf). Furthermore, the operating expense stop would be adjusted in the second year of the lease and would automatically increase to exclude the first-year amount over the stop up to the first 5 percent, as well as the dollar amount by which the expenses exceeded the 20 percent maximum limit of the stop.

Extending this example, if the actual expenses for the first year were $1.40 psf, the tenant would be exempt from the first 5 percent of the expenses over the $1 psf expense stop ($0.05 psf) and all amounts greater than 20 percent of the expense stop ($0.20 psf). The tenant would wind up paying $0.15 psf for above-stop expenses in the first year (the difference between $1.20 psf, the maximum amount, and $1.05 psf, the initial exclusionary amount). In the second year the expense stop (landlord's contribution) would automatically be increased to $1.35 psf ($1.05 psf + $0.20 psf, 20 percent of the original stop).

How a landlord reacts to this type of adjustment will often provide the tenant with valuable insight into the accuracy of the initial expense stop. What the tenant is trying to avoid is having an expense stop of $1 psf and finding out at the end of the first year that the actual expenses are $2 psf, which would leave the tenant owing additional rent of $1 psf.

Newer Buildings

This same kind of adjustment can be considered for a newer building. The difficulty in a new building is that no one knows what the actual expenses will be. Here the tenant's PREB should be able to provide reasonably accurate comparisons of operating expenses in similar buildings.

In new buildings the tenant must be on guard against either too high or too low an estimate. The problems regarding operating expenses in a new building are especially acute. For example, until the building is fully occupied and operating, the extent of service costs may not be fully known, especially if special additional tenant services are to be offered, such as valet parking, concierge services, and a sauna or exercise club. Similarly, until a building is fully leased and operating, the landlord will not incur all expenses (and possible savings) that would otherwise occur. For example, there may be a premium or higher expense for using smaller amounts of a utility such as gas or electric. On the other hand, until they are needed, the landlord will not be incurring or paying for certain expenses such as cleaning and janitorial services or extra utility services.

Therefore, the landlord estimate can be fairly realistic when a building is fully occupied. When it is not, the landlord may be making a windfall profit. If the expense stop is $1 psf but the expenses are only $0.40 psf, the landlord will make a profit of $0.60 psf until the building fills up.

The tenant should put in a limitation provision, as described earlier, so that he or she will pay only the dollar amount of operating expenses incurred, if they are less than the expense stop.

On the other hand, if the estimate is too low, as the building fills up, the tenant may begin receiving operating expense bills, and these could become high in a few years.

Using a Base Year

Instead of using a fixed dollar amount to represent the landlord's contribution to operating expenses, it is possible to establish a baseline expense amount above which the tenant is responsible for operating expenses. The method most often used is called the base year operating expense.

Under this method the tenant and landlord agree upon a base year and state that whatever the total dollar amount of operating expenses incurred in that base year, that dollar amount establishes a baseline value, or the contribution (the expense stop) for which the landlord would be responsible. In all years after the base year, the tenant would be responsible for all operating expenses in excess of the total dollar amount of actual incurred expenses in the base year.

The base year method can work quite well for both new and previously occupied premises. In older buildings the actual operating expenses incurred in the first year of the lease would become the base year amount; the tenant would then become responsible for the additional operating expenses above the base year amount in the second through succeeding years of the lease term.

Even here, however, the tenant must be cautious. One problem that could arise depends on how operating expenses are defined (see "What Should Operating Expenses Include or Exclude?" later in this chapter). If certain capital expenditures, even if they are capitalized, are included as operating expenses, it is possible, especially in older buildings, for a major expense to crop up and create a large increase in the building's total operating expenses. Similarly, the level of various available services for which each tenant is responsible may be significantly increased (e.g., a health club or concierge service may be introduced) or even reduced, against certain tenants' wishes, in a later year (e.g., security services might be reduced or the concierge service eliminated). Unless the lease clearly defines what constitutes allowed expenses and what service levels are to be considered standard (see Chapter 21), the tenant's expenses could rise dramatically in the former case, or the landlord could realize a windfall profit in the latter.

Special Problems with
New Buildings

In a new building, using a base year to calculate operating expenses can create serious problems. Consider a building in which the tenant is one of the first occupants and it will be a year or two before the building is 75 percent leased. How can a base year be established?

Until the building is actually occupied (or close to being so), the expenses incurred will be both unrealistically low for certain items and high for others. For example, cleaning and janitorial services are usually bid and contracted on the basis of the total number of square feet to be cleaned. The larger the building, the less may be charged per square foot (because of a quantity discount). However, with fewer square feet occupied relative to the total size of the building, the cleaning services on a per-square-foot basis will cost more until full occupancy occurs. Similarly, bulk savings for utility services may not be realized. On the other hand, there can be savings from fewer operating elevators, reduced guard services, and limited general building services.

From a tenant's perspective it is not in his or her best interests to pick a base year too early. As the building fills up, the tenant's expenses will continually increase. The ideal situation for the tenant is to have the base year established at that point when the building becomes fully occupied (for commercial real estate purposes, the generally acceptable norm is to consider 90 or 95 percent occupancy as fully occupied).

The landlord will want to be sure that he or she is properly reimbursed for the increase that will occur in operating expenses over the base year as other tenants move into the building and for additional services that may be provided to all tenants.

Grossing Up Base Year
Operating Expenses

The acceptable middle ground is to allow the landlord to extrapolate or project ("gross up") the expenses of a less than full building up to an estimate of the expenses for the building at 90 or 95 percent occupancy. The difficulty for a tenant is that not all expenses can be increased through some simple percentage of space formula, such as the aforementioned utility costs or cleaning and janitorial expenses. Rather, grossing-up requires some agreement between the tenant and the landlord as to what gets increased, and how.

For the tenant's peace of mind, the lease should stipulate that the computations made to establish the grossed-up base year expenses are to be recalculated each year. Furthermore, this provision would require that at the point the building would in fact be 90 to 95 percent leased, each year for which a grossed-up base year estimate had been used would be recalculated, and appropriate credit would be given to the tenant. The tenant must be sure the provision includes a year-for-year reduction of the actual operating expenses for a full building to account for inflation (i.e., to avoid reversed economic erosion) when recalculating operating expenses back to a base year.

The Importance of Establishing the Right Base

Many landlords will not want to use a base year to calculate their contribution to operating expenses. They think this method is too complex and unwieldy because all the different base years must be maintained when the landlord has many projects or when a building has many tenants. Granted, the base year method is more complicated than the landlord contribution method; however, it seems no more complicated than using an economic index to escalate rents—and may be less so.

The importance of establishing the right operating expense base amount is best shown with a simple calculation. If the standard annual $1 psf operating expense is used as the base multiplier (assuming an actual starting base year operating expense of $1.25 psf for the first year and a 10,000-sq-ft premises), the results of a simple 6 percent increase in actual expense each year for 10 years are as shown in Table 7-2. The tenant in this example immediately owes a significant amount for the above-stop operating expenses. This amount then doubles by the fifth year and then doubles again five years later.

If this expense stop were set equal to the actual expenses, using

Table 7-2. Simple 6-Percent Operating Expense Increase
(in Dollars)

Year	Expense stop (psf)	Actual expenses increased at 6% per year (psf)	Cost to tenant (psf)	Total annual cost to tenant (× 10,000 sq ft)
1	1.00	1.25	0.25	2,500
2	1.00	1.33	0.33	3,300
3	1.00	1.41	0.41	4,100
4	1.00	1.49	0.49	4,900
5	1.00	1.58	0.58	5,800
6	1.00	1.67	0.67	6,700
7	1.00	1.77	0.77	7,700
8	1.00	1.88	0.88	8,800
9	1.00	1.99	0.99	9,900
10	1.00	2.11	1.11	11,100

NOTE: Assumes actual starting operating expenses of $1.25 psf.

the same example, the results would be as shown in Table 7-3. Although the cost to the tenant is no less significant than that in Table 7-2, there are considerable savings because of the more realistic expense stop base that will occur through the use of a base year to calculate operating expenses.

What Should Operating Expenses Include or Exclude?

It is virtually impossible to provide an exhaustive list of operating expenses that would be accurate for all jurisdictions. Most lease clauses pertaining to operating expenses have regional variations that continue to develop and evolve over time to meet the particular needs of the tenant and the landlord. For example, things

Table 7-3. Simple 6-Percent Operating Expense Increase, with Landlord's Expense Stop Set at Assumed Actual Expense of $1.25 psf (in Dollars)

Year	Expense stop (psf)	Actual expenses increased at 6% per year (psf)	Cost to tenant (psf)	Total annual cost to tenant (× 10,000 sq ft)
1	1.25	1.25	0	0
2	1.25	1.33	0.08	800
3	1.25	1.41	0.16	1600
4	1.25	1.49	0.24	2400
5	1.25	1.58	0.33	3300
6	1.25	1.67	0.42	4200
7	1.25	1.77	0.52	5200
8	1.25	1.88	0.63	6300
9	1.25	1.99	0.74	7400
10	1.25	2.11	0.86	8600

that would be acceptable as operating expenses in New York City might well be considered outlandish in Oshkosh, Wisconsin.

In general, however, operating expenses include everything that is generally associated with the management, repair, maintenance, and operation of a property, building, or premises. Therefore, the tenant must be wary when it comes to the items included under operating expenses in a lease.

The tenant must be sure that a detailed listing of operating expenses is included in this lease clause. It is up to the tenant or the tenant's PREB to check the list carefully for anything that seems out of the ordinary or is not clearly understood. The tenant's PREB should also be able to supply a half-dozen or more lists from other leases from a variety of landlords and buildings to provide a sample of what would be considered representational and acceptable for the region.

Exclusions

It is important for the tenant to make sure that certain things that may reflect regional variations are excluded from the definition of operating expenses. Here are a number of things that are accepted preferred exclusions for the tenant's benefit.

Leasing Commissions and Related Expenses. This is clearly a landlord expense associated with finding a tenant and avoiding vacant space in a building. This item should be excluded especially if a PREB claims that his or her services are "free" and "don't cost the tenant anything."

In addition, all related costs and expenses for creating and executing a lease between the landlord and the tenant should be excluded from the operating expenses distributed to all tenants.

Accounting and Legal Fees and Related Costs and Expenses Associated with Actions against Specific Tenants or Governmental or Jurisdictional Disputes Regarding Laws, Regulations, or Taxes Unless They Directly Affect All Tenants Equally. The tenant wants to be sure the lease excludes things like a tenant dispute that ended in legal action through eviction notices or lease defaults (especially to the extent that the costs are paid for or reimbursed to the landlord by the tenant). If not excluded, an excess profit results for the landlord. He or she is paid twice for the same thing, once by the affected tenant and again when the expense is passed through to all tenants for payment.

Similarly, a landlord dispute with a government entity should not be charged as an operating expense unless it is for the benefit of the tenant and then only to the extent that the cost does not exceed the benefits gained.

Advertising and Promotional Costs and Expenses for the Property, Building, or Premises. Advertising and promotional expense for any purpose, whether to lease vacant space, promote an area as a good place to do business, or foster general public relations, are unrelated to the tenant's occupancy and should be excluded from operating expenses passed on to tenants.

Depreciation and Amortization Charges for the Property and for Capital Equipment. Depreciation is an expense item the landlord is permitted to offset against income in accordance with various Internal Revenue Services tax requirements. Depreciation is a method that takes the value of an expenditure and expenses it in regular amounts over time, usually representing its supposed useful life, rather than taking the whole cost of the item as one large expense at the time it was incurred. For example, a piece of equipment costing $1 million, with a useful life of 10 years, would be depreciated (or expensed) at $100,000 per year.

The basic commercial real estate assumption is that the cost of the building, and its operating systems and other capital equipment are all placed under one mortgage. The cost of the mortgage principal and its interest is covered by the fixed-cost portion of the basic rent paid by the tenant.

Because the tenant is already paying for the cost of the building and all capital expenditures through the rent and the landlord gets to depreciate and take an annual expense against his or her taxes each year, it would create unreasonable profit if the landlord also received payment from tenants by being able to pass through these items as operating expenses.

Capital Expenditures, Improvements, or Structural Changes Made to the Property or Building. To the extent that a capital expenditure, improvement, or structural change is original to the building and in the mortgage, it should not be included as a tenant operating expense.

There are three related factors to this concept that tend to complicate this area.

New Mortgage Expenses. These include major structural reconstruction and capital improvements, including new equipment for which the current landlord (or new landlord) has refinanced the building and has a new mortgage and associated interest. The assumption is that the landlord will be getting base rents, a fixed amount of which covers the mortgage principal and interest. Therefore, this item should not be included as an operating expense.

What about tenants with older leases? This is a gray area. In general, however, all these leases will be turning over and need to be renewed at some point (presumably at a rent sufficient to cover any landlord costs). Traditionally, when a landlord refinances a building, the refinancing is not only for improvements or capital expenditures. The landlord also takes out any available appreciation in cash for use in other investments. Therefore, even for those with older leases, these additional amounts should not be included in operating costs.

The general rule of thumb is that no capital expenditures, improvements, or structural changes to the building, even if they are made after the original building work, are included as operating expense passed through to the tenants. The exceptions are noted below.

Costs of Compliance with Laws and Regulations.   What happens when capital expenditures, improvements, or structural changes have to be made because some governmental entity has ordered them or because the landlord has to comply with laws and regulations that were not in effect when the building was built? A good example of this is a retroactive requirement to fit a building with a fire suppression system such as sprinklers.

The general rule is that these expenditures should be amortized over the life of the improvement or change (not over the remaining artificial accounting book life of a building, which is strictly a function of depreciation costs). These amortized costs would then be an acceptable addition to the operating expenses passed through to the tenant (to the extent they are not paid for through a refinancing of the property).

Expenses for Increased Efficiencies.   What about capital expenditures, improvements, or structural changes that improve the building systems and increase operating efficiencies and thus help to reduce overall operating expenses?

This expenditure is, again, a gray area, but it is one that traditionally has been amortized over its useful life and charged as part of the operating expenses passed through to the tenant. However, the tenant should make sure that the amortization being paid as part of the operating expenses each year is not larger than the savings (the reduction of cost for the specific operating system) because of the improvement. That is, the amount of the savings should act as a maximum cap for the amount of the improvement that may be passed on to the tenants.

Interest Payments or Financing Charges on Mortgage or Capital Equipment and Improvement. As previously discussed, it is inappropriate to pass mortgage interest through as an operating expense, and the practice should not be accepted by tenants. Similarly, financing charges on all the capital equipment that comes with the building or is not included in the building's refinancing should be excluded from operating expenses.

An interesting related topic comes about when market and economic conditions makes investment capital hard to come by. To continue construction activity and build new buildings, a landlord not only may have to pay premium interest rates but also may have to give up some ownership rights to a money partner. Often the mortgage money can only be obtained at an adjustable interest rate (an ARM) rather then the traditional fixed interest rate. Therefore, the interest rate on the mortgage can vary annually (or monthly or quarterly).

To the extent that an ARM exists on a building, what portion of the interest, if any, should be added to operating expenses and passed on to tenants?

The answer lies in the negotiations between the landlord and tenant. Whether a tenant accepts this anomaly will depend on market conditions, on how much competitive space exists, and on tenant needs and requirements for relocating.

The tenant who agrees to the passing through of variable mortgage interest rates as operating expenses must be sure the provision establishes a base percentage interest rate on an established building mortgage for a fixed and maximum amount of money. The amount of interest that can be passed on to the tenant is only that amount that exceeds a specified percentage interest rate.

In addition, the tenant must be sure also to receive any benefits from a reduction in the interest rate. The tenant must not agree to having a variable interest rate passed through unless there are both upside and downside potentials.

Finally, the tenant should not have to be concerned with a terrible mortgage arrangement made by the landlord. This provision should stipulate the maximum percentage interest increase that can be passed on to the tenant in any one year (e.g., 1 percent).

The Cost for Ground Leases or Property Rent on Which the Building Is Constructed.   Often a building is constructed on land that the landlord does not own; the landlord rents the property through a ground lease. To the extent that a ground lease exists at the time a tenant signs a lease for space, the costs for the lease either will be included as part of the base rent or should be disclosed in the operating expenses passed through to the tenant.

However, if a ground lease does not exist at the tenant's lease signing, this item should specifically be excluded as an operating cost. Why? The tenant wants to be sure that the land under a building is not sold by the landlord at some later period (for example, to a family-related interest or trust). A land sale and subsequent ground rent could significantly increase the operating expenses paid by the tenants.

Any Costs or Expenses Incurred by the Landlord on Behalf of Another Tenant, Any Services Reimbursed by Another Tenant, and Any Services or Operations Not Performed Equitably or on a Regular Basis for All Tenants.   There are a number of services a landlord may perform for a tenant that should not be included as operating expenses passed through to all other tenants:

- Any costs (including licensing and permits) for any alterations, renovations, modifications, or decorating incurred for the benefit of only one tenant or for the preparation of vacant space.

- Any cost or expenses for services provided exclusively for the benefit of one or a few tenants, whether reimbursed or not. Examples would be additional cleaning services for special areas such as private baths or kitchens or excess electric usage for special equipment.

- Any cost or service provided by the landlord for which he or she is entitled to be reimbursed whether or not reimbursement occurs.

Obviously, the tenant does not want to pay for operating expenses that do not benefit his or her occupancy or to pay double for those that the landlord is already being paid for.

All Costs and Expenses Related to the Operation of Any Commercial Concession on the Property or in the Building (e.g., Parking Concession). This exclusion must include any wages, salaries, and related benefits paid to any employees associated with the concession, whether operated by the landlord or not.

This exclusion is made because the operating concession receives a fee for the services performed (such as parking fees) from someone such as a tenant's guest, a customer, or any visitor to the property. This becomes a reimbursable service or a pay-as-used fee-based service. It is not properly included as part of the operating expenses passed through to tenants.

Those Costs and Expenses Related to the Landlord's Operating as a Business, Whether a Partnership, Corporate Entity, or Other Arrangement. These types of expenses are difficult to ferret out and often even more difficult to define properly as an exclusion. The idea is to avoid having the landlord profit unreasonably from being able to charge whatever he or she wants for overseeing and supervising the property and the building. It is equally important to watch that a landlord does not charge as operating expenses those costs related to the operation of the landlord's business rather than to the operation of the building. Items to watch for and exclude are:

- Legal and accounting fees for preparation of landlord business documents, including the preparation of any and all tax returns

- Payment of the landlord's business-related taxes such as corporate income taxes, real property taxes, or gross revenue (or excess profits) tax

- Wages, salaries, and related benefits paid to administration personnel employed by a landlord's business

- Wages, salaries, and related benefits paid to executives and other top officials related to the landlord's business

In regard to the last two items, these individuals may be providing valuable services to the landlord's properties. When that is the situation, there is often an additional caveat that permits these payments, as long as they are made in an amount equivalent to what would be paid under a competitive situation to another company for the same individual performing the same work.

The fact is, there is no way to determine accurately how competitive the wages and salaries are. More important, there is no way to know whether these people are needed to do the work they are said to be doing.

The inclusion of these wages and salaries as operating expenses to tenants gives landlords a subsidy for their business staff. There is no way for a tenant, no matter what the lease provision language, to protect him- or herself properly against this kind of landlord abuse except to exclude totally any payments to employees, officers, and executives related to any landlord business. (Note: This is a different concept from the traditional property management function described in the next section.)

Any Cost or Expense Related to Needed Property or Building Repair, Alteration, Addition, Replacement, or Change, Regardless of Whether It Is Made by the Landlord or Reimbursed by a Third Party. This is a broad category of items that must be specifically excluded from being passed through as operating expenses:

- The costs or expenses for any repair, alteration, addition, replacement, or change that is reimbursed by insurance, by a tenant, or by any third party.

- The costs or expenses for any work related to condemnation or to damage and destruction (see Chapters 27 and 28).

- The costs or expenses for any repair, alteration, addition, replacement, or change that are not the result of normal wear and tear or part of normal property and building maintenance. Rather, these items should be classified as capital expenditures, improvements, or structural changes to the property or building and thus excluded from operating expenses.

- The costs and expenses associated with any work necessary to repair original construction defects on the property, on the building, or to the building's equipment and operating systems.

Property Management and Related Fees

Property must be properly managed if an office building project is to succeed. Property management covers all those areas that affect the building's ambience and environment, as well as tenant satisfaction, such as rent collection, building and premises repairs, general maintenance, cleaning and janitorial services, security services, and concession operations. Property management is properly included as an operating expense that will be passed on to the tenants. However, it is discussed under exclusions in order to catch the tenant's attention.

Often an operating expense exclusion will specify that no payments for overhead, management, or supplies or other services may be paid to an affiliated landlord business or company in excess of what otherwise would be paid if the services or items were performed or supplied on a competitive basis. This exclusion is made because the property management company is often owned either directly or indirectly by the landlord, or the general supervision is performed by a directly or indirectly owned company. When it comes to property management, the rule is "Tenant, watch out!" This is one area in which landlords are known to abuse tenants through excessive operating expenses. Unless there is some way to limit the charges, anything can be charged and be considered an acceptable operating expense.

Because tenant satisfaction greatly depends on the management company, the wise tenant will find out which property management company is responsible for the property and the building, who owns it, and what other buildings it manages. (And then the wise tenant will check out those buildings!)

To avoid excessive property management fees, a tenant may be able to add a provision that puts a maximum percentage cap on how much will be paid to a property management company. This percentage cap can be an average of the fees charged by other management companies for similar-sized buildings and will usually be expressed either on a per-square-foot basis or as a percentage of the annual gross net revenues collected. Therefore, a limiting provision would provide that the annual management fee (specifying the services to be provided) included in the total of operating expenses should not be greater than 1.5 percent (or whatever percentage) of the total annual gross rent dollars collected for the building.

What's Included and Excluded

As a general rule, market and economic conditions are what control the items that are included in or excluded from operating expenses. The more restrictive the space available options for the tenant, the more the landlord dictates what is acceptable as an operating expense to be passed through to a tenant. Likewise, the more vacant space available and the poorer the economic conditions, the more items the tenant can have excluded from total operating expenses.

How Can a Tenant Be Sure about What Is Being Included? Have the Right to Audit the Books!

After a tenant has spent time on defining exactly what is included and excluded from operating expenses, then what? How does a tenant make sure that the bill he or she receives each year accurately reflects what is in the lease? Put another way, how much of the element called trust does the tenant want to put into the landlord?

If the tenant fully trusts the landlord to follow the operating expense inclusions and exclusions as specified in the lease, there is nothing more to worry about. But what happens if, for some unknown reason, the current operating expense passthrough bill is double the one for the previous year, without any explanation or with an explanation that includes an item you thought excluded from operating expenses?

Be Sure to Put Audit Rights into the Lease

The tenant needs to add a provision that give him or her the right to audit the operating expense books and records of the landlord and that guarantees all financial records and tenant statements shall be prepared in accordance with generally accepted accounting principles (GAAP). This will give the tenant the right, but not the obligation, to look over the landlord's books and records on a regular or an irregular basis and determine how accurately the expense passthroughs are being calculated.

As a common example of landlord "error," the cost for a special service, renovation, or repair done exclusively for the benefit of one tenant—and reimbursed by that tenant—will "accidentally" find its way into the total operating expenses passed through to all tenants. This is especially likely to happen when the cost for the item and the tenant reimbursement occur over two different fiscal or calender years.

Who Pays for the Audit?

Normally, the tenant will have to cover the expense of auditing the books and records. However, the tenant should add a provision that provides for the landlord to pay for the costs of the audit if the operating expense passthroughs are found to be inaccurate or if the tenant is being overcharged. Usually, this provision will provide for some dollar range or percentage error factor before the landlord would be required to pay for the audit.

Unless there is a potential penalty to the landlord for making a mistake, the landlord will have no incentive to get it exactly right.

Where Are the Books and Records?

One additional provision a tenant will want to be sure to include is related to the fact that many commercial real estate projects are owned by national or international corporations or by foreign interests (e.g., British, Canadian, Dutch, German, Japanese, and Middle Eastern). When the tenant has the right to audit the books, this provision stipulates that the books and records for the tenant audit will be provided, when needed, at a location in the same or nearby local jurisdiction as the one in which the property is located. Otherwise, the books and records could reside clear across the United States or in another country! In such a situation, the related additional costs would make the audit impractical and prohibitively expensive for the tenant—and for any potential gains.

How and When Passthroughs Are Paid by the Tenant

The tenant should pay particular attention to the lease provision that stipulates how and when the tenant will be required to pay for his or her pro rata share of the operating expenses.

The tenant should ascertain when the expense statements are submitted by the landlord for payment. Are they submitted at the same time for everyone in the building? Are the expense statements calculated using actual or estimated costs and expenses? If estimates are used, when is an adjustment for actual expenses made? When is an operating statement of actual building expenses submitted to the tenant?

Depending on when the statement comes out and how the calculations are made, a new tenant in a building must be sure to have his or her pro rata share of expenses prorated for a less-than-full-year occupancy that does not properly correspond to the operating expense reporting period.

How Are They Paid?

There are at least four different ways that a landlord may expect a tenant to pay for the operating expenses:

1. The tenant owes a lump-sum amount payable in a specified time period (e.g., 30 days, 60 days) from the time the landlord's invoice is submitted.

2. The tenant receives the landlord's invoice, and the total amount is divided into 12 equal payments and added to an adjusted monthly base rent for payment.

3. The tenant receives an invoice that is strictly an estimate of the next year's expenses and is to be paid as a lump sum.

4. The tenant receives an estimate of what the next year's expenses will be, and the amount is divided into 12 equal

payments and added to an adjusted monthly base rent for payment.

The tenant-preferred alternative is the second, because the tenant will be paying the actual operating expenses (in equal monthly installments). The landlord will prefer either the third or the fourth, receiving help with paying for expenses as they occur instead of putting up all the money on his or her own and collecting it later from the tenant.

Most tenants will want to avoid having to make a lump-sum payment for operating expenses. The tenant must also be sure that a time frame is included, specifying when estimated expenses are to be adjusted based on actual expenses.

In addition, there needs to be a provision explaining how any tenant overpayment (or additional tenant lump-sum payments made necessary because the landlord's estimate was too small) will be returned (or paid). For refunds, the landlord will want to provide a credit against future tenant payments rather than a lump-sum payment to the tenant. The tenant can reasonably require the same consideration he or she has had regarding any amounts he or she owes to the landlord (i.e., if the tenant must make lump-sum payments, then so, too, should the landlord be required to make them to the tenant).

If the tenant owes an additional amount after the reconciliation of estimated and actual operating expenses and has paid operating expenses in advance, how the payment is required to be made by the tenant should be clearly specified.

The Right to Contest

An additional tenant-oriented provision would include a means of contesting any portion or all of a landlord-submitted operating expense statement. The ideal tenant provision would stipulate that the related payments for the contested areas should be set aside, or not be due, until the landlord provided supporting materials. There would, of course, be time limitations for the tenant both to claim the dispute and to hold off payment after the materials had been supplied by the landlord. Likewise, the landlord would have a specific period in which to provide the necessary materials.

The tenant wants to be sure that tenant-landlord differences can be reconciled with a minimum of hassle and expense and without the possibility of the tenant's being in default of the lease.

And the Expense Goes On . . .

Depending on the provisions included in the operating expenses clause and the type of rent, the tenant is likely to continue to be liable for operating expenses. The tenant agrees to pay for all operating expenses (net lease), those above a base year, or a fixed amount and will continue to pay the additional increases each year. Sometimes, however, the difference between what the tenant is paying in an adjusted base rent and the actual expenses is not known until a year after the fact (especially when real estate taxes are included). This aspect of the operating expenses lease clause is what a tenant should be particularly cautious about. He or she may still owe the payment for operating expenses in a building previously occupied. Not only will a tenant be paying a higher rent and be facing additional rent charges for operating expenses in the current building—but he or she will now receive an invoice from previously occupied premises demanding a lump-sum payment for the previous year's operating expenses.

For this reason, many tenants, after being hit with such a payment, prefer having the landlord estimate the next year's operating expenses and add the amount to the current year's rent. Landlords also prefer the estimated expense route. The landlord knows how difficult it can be to collect anything from a tenant who has moved out. Even though the tenant may rightfully owe the money, the only course for collection open to a landlord may be court action, which often is not worth the time, money, effort, or hassle.

What Happens During Rent Abatement?

Another important point to mention concerning operating expenses owed by a tenant is what happens during a rent-abatement period. The lease should clearly state what is included or excluded as rent during the rent-abatement period. The tenant would prefer a provision that excludes not only basic rent but also all possible additional rent during the rent-abatement period.

Otherwise, the tenant will often find out, too late, that only the basic rent is included during the abatement period. There is nothing more annoying than finishing up a one-year rent-abatement period and receiving an invoice for a large, lump-sum payment for the excess operating expenses over the base year amount or fixed landlord contribution base. In such a case the abatement includes the full service rent but not the additional rent on operating expenses.

Even more disheartening is to receive a huge bill for the base operating expenses for the full abatement period. In this case, the abatement only includes the basic rent and not the base year expenses or the fixed landlord contribution amount. Although these bases are the point from which increases in operating expenses are measured, they are also included as part of the total rent. Unless the provision states that the total rent is to be abated, the tenant still owes for the operating expense portion. Depending on how this is stated, the amount can be due either as a monthly payment from the moment the tenant moves in (so much for not paying any rent during a rent-abatement period) or as a lump sum at the end of the abatement period.

What Happens If a Lease Is Renewed?

Lease renewals are covered in Chapter 11, but at this point we can touch on the effect of a renewal on operating expenses. The operating expense portion of total rent is, to the tenant's detriment, often overlooked by a PREB or attorney in a lease renewal clause. The tenant wants to be sure that either the operating expenses clause or the renewal clause contains a provision allowing the operating expense base to be adjusted.

If a new market renewal rent is to be determined, a new base for calculating the market operating expenses should also be established. Similarly, if there is a formula basis for the renewal rent, the operating expense base should also be determined anew. In the case of a formula rent increase, the operating base fixed amount can be the same percentage of the total renewal

rent as it is of the total rent. For example, if the landlord's contribution to the operating expenses is 10 percent of the total original base rent, it can also be 10 percent of the renewal rent.

What happens if this provision is not adequately adjusted? The
amount of the landlord's contribution to operating expenses
might stay the same. Using the standard annual base rent of $10
psf and the standard annual $1 psf expense stop, if the rent were
to increase to $20 psf, the landlord contribution would stay at $1
psf if this provision was not adjusted.

Because the tenant will have had some experience at renewal
time with the operating expenses for the building, one option,
when an expense stop is used, is to make the expense stop an estimated increased amount of the last year's actual operating expenses paid by the tenant. However, this may not be acceptable to
a landlord if the negotiated renewal rent is less than the market
rent.

Similarly, when the increase in operating expenses is based on
the actual expenses of a base year, the tenant should be sure that
the base year is changed to reflect the date of the renewal rent.

Who Gets Refunds?
What Happens When
There Is a Refund?

Refunds may be given for electric or gas services because of a rate
adjustment or a change in an operational classification, for water
and sewer service when a utility's estimated bills based on prior
usage or other building averages are adjusted after an actual
meter reading, or for taxes when a governmental jurisdiction adjusts a tax rate because the basis for a building's real estate tax
assessment has changed or in response to a landlord's challenge
to an assessment.

The problem with refunds is that they may not automatically be
passed on to the tenant, because not all refunds are made as adjustments to future service bills. Often a refund may be a check
paid directly to the landlord.

There should not be any question about who gets refunds received directly by a landlord. Both the tenant and landlord

should share the refund according to the percentage each paid. If the full amount of the operating expenses was passed through to the tenants, the tenants should get the full benefit of the refund. Will they, however? Will the tenants even know about the refund?

The tenant must first be sure that an appropriate provision exists to cover refunds. Then the tenant needs to go back and reread the section on the right to audit the landlord's books.

What is the landlord's incentive to pass on the refund to the tenant? There is no landlord incentive. But the tenant should not have any problems if the lease contains the proper refund provision and a provision concerning the right to audit the books. As an added precaution, the tenant should have the right to any operating expenses refund that is made after the tenant leaves the building. This provision (which is similar to the landlord's right to collect operating expense increases after a tenant leaves the building) could be very important for real estate tax refunds, which may not be made for two or more years after being challenged.

8

Real Estate Taxes and Assessments

A lease typically handles real estate taxes and property tax assessments in one of two ways. Either the taxes are considered an operating expense and are included in the general definition of operating expenses, or they have their own lease clause.

A Separate Taxes Lease Clause

When real estate taxes are put into a separate lease clause, the necessary provisions will be much the same as those in the operating expenses lease clause (see Chapter 7). The main items of concern to a tenant are:

1. The landlord can pass on real estate taxes (except for the flat fixed rent, which covers all expenses, including real estate taxes) in three basic ways:
   a. The rent can be net of all expenses (a net lease), so any and all taxes are passed through to the tenant.
   b. The landlord can provide a fixed contribution amount, or landlord tax expense stop. All tax amounts above the tax expense stop amount, including all tax increases, are passed on to the tenant.
   c. There can be a base year for real estate taxes. All in-

creases in the taxes above the taxes paid by the landlord in the base year are passed on to the tenant.

2. When real estate taxes are put into a separate clause and the landlord's contribution is based on either a fixed amount (tax expense stop) or an amount fixed by the taxes incurred in a base year, the landlord's contribution, along with operating expenses, must be netted out from the total base rent, so that only the net rent is used in calculating rent escalations. If this is not done, the tenant will pay a rent escalation on the real estate tax portion of the rent. This is an extra profit to the landlord, since the tenant is already responsible for paying any increases in the taxes.

3. What building attribute (e.g., total amount of rentable square feet) will be used to establish the tenant's pro rata share of real estate taxes?

4. If the building is new and has no tax history, the taxes must be grossed up, or extrapolated, in order to establish a reasonable estimate of the landlord's contribution. However, when the landlord's contribution is the tax expense of a base year for a new building, the tenant will have additional concerns, as explained in the next section.

5. How and when are real estate tax increases to be paid—on an actual or an estimated basis, as a lump sum or in equal increments added to a monthly adjusted base rent?

6. The lease should contain a provision allowing the tenant to audit the landlord's financial books and records. Landlord claims for payment should be backed up by tax assessments and tax bills.

7. During a rent-abatement period, will real estate taxes also be abated? If so, will a new expense base be calculated when the tenant starts to pay the taxes? If not, will the tenant be required to pay a monthly fee from the lease commencement date, or will the payment be in the form of a lump sum?

8. When a lease renewal occurs, is the real estate tax base year or the fixed landlord contribution amount adjusted?

9. How will subsequent tax refunds or reductions in assessed value be passed on to the tenant? Will refunds be made to the tenant as a future rent credit, a credit against future real estate tax passthroughs, or a lump-sum payment? Will tax sav-

ings and refunds that are applicable during the term of the
lease and any tenant overpayment still be in effect after the
tenant has left the building?
10. The tenant will still be liable for increases in real estate taxes
after the lease has expired. Therefore, additional money may
be owed by the tenant, even if he or she is no longer an occupant of the building.

Special Interest Items
Regarding Taxes

Whether real estate taxes are specified in a separate lease clause
or as part of operating expenses, they raise a number of special
concerns for the tenant. These concerns require additional lease
provisions and additional negotiation by the tenant or the
tenant's PREB.

Reduced Property Assessments
and Real Estate Tax Savings

Real estate taxes are different from most other operating expenses. Real estate assessments on commercial property are often
successfully challenged as being too high, and future taxes may
be lowered and refunds provided for overpayment. An initial
fixed landlord contribution amount may turn out to be higher
than necessary because of some unique circumstances or perhaps
because an assessment is lower than expected.

A landlord-oriented lease provision will state that any savings
realized will reduce the amount owed by the tenant but in no
event will the total base rent be less than the initial total base rent
stated in the lease. With this provision, the landlord gets to keep
any part of the fixed landlord contribution of the total base rent
that does not actually go toward taxes. This is clearly a windfall
profit for the landlord. The tenant will continue to pay this
amount until the assessment and taxes catch up with the contribution base amount.

Although the situation resembles that for operating expenses,
real estate taxes and property assessments should be viewed dif-

ferently. When real estate taxes are relegated to a separate lease clause and the landlord's fixed contribution amount is stated separately, the tenant would prefer to have that portion of the total base rent designated as the base real estate tax amount or fixed landlord contribution, reduced penny-for-penny by any savings in the actual taxes to be paid, so that the total base rent would be likewise reduced, but in no event should the total base rent be reduced in excess of the portion stated as the real estate tax base.

Grossing Up Real Estate Taxes—Unique Concerns

A new building that has never been fully assessed for tax purposes presents some interesting problems for the tenant. The assessment of a property is affected by the time factor involved in the construction of a building. In addition, there is usually a built-in lag between the time the property is assessed and the time the corresponding accurate tax is submitted to the landlord.

Depending on when property assessments take place in a jurisdiction and on whether an updated assessment can be generated at any time or more frequently than once a year, if construction will not start on a property until after the assessment date, that property will be assessed as vacant commercial land or as improved vacant commercial land if some site work has been completed. By the next assessment, the building may be only a skeleton, but, depending on the jurisdiction, the assessment may go up some amount to reflect improvements made to the land. By the next assessment the building may still be incomplete and vacant; again, there is a slight assessment increase. By the next assessment, the building may have tenants (e.g., 25 percent occupancy); the property is now assessed to reflect the completed improvement and the fully changed nature of the property to a functioning commercial office building. By the next assessment, the building may be fully occupied; an assessment is made reflecting the fully occupied and improved building and its true value. An adjusted tax bill is sent to the landlord approximately six to seven months after each new assessment.

Depending on where in the construction and assessment process the tenant enters into a lease and moves into a building, the time lag between a realistic assessment and the receipt of a realistic tax amount could be two to three years. This is a very long time. Depending on the economic pressure that exists on the jurisdiction to increase tax assessments or tax rates, the tenant is likely to have an unrealistically low fixed landlord contribution amount (tax expense stop) or a low grossed-up base year amount. In the second or third year of occupancy, the tenant could well be hit with an extremely large passthrough covering the first two or three years of the increased real estate tax expense. Even when the PREB warns the tenant of such a possibility during the lease signing, the tenant will probably have forgotten the warning by the time the increase arrives.

Some tenant protection can be incorporated into a lease provision that may also include more realistic grossing-up of a base year amount (or fixed landlord contribution amount). This provision would stipulate that the real estate tax expense passthrough that may be charged to a tenant may not exceed some specified increase (e.g., 25 to 50 percent) over the previous year's tenant payment. Because property assessments are known to generally increase fairly steadily, in the event of an extraordinary increase the cost to the tenant would be spread out over a number of years. If the tenant wished, another provision could stipulate that any excess tax expense charge would be amortized for payment over the remaining lease term.

Increased Assessments Related to Improvements or Sale

How will a tenant be affected if there is a significant increase in a property's taxes because of a significant increase in the property's assessment? Even when there is no governmental tax increase, assessments usually go up because of major capital expenditures, improvements or structural changes to a property or building, or the sale of the property or building.

In other words, property assessments go up when property increases in value. Obviously, certain improvements and the sale or transfer of property can significantly increase a building's value. Although it depends on market conditions and economic considerations, a property, especially a building, will sell for more, sometimes considerably more, than the property's assessed value. If a straight sale and property transfer have occurred, the high sale price could well form the basis for an immediate reassessment and reevaluation that increases the property's taxes. On the other hand, an increased valuation can sometimes be avoided if the partnership or corporation that owns the building is sold, rather than the property. In that instance, there is no actual sale price for the property or building.

Just as specific items can be excluded from what may be considered an operating expense to be passed through to the tenant, certain exclusions can apply in the case of increased property taxes:

1. Any increased tax expense related to any capital expenditures, improvements, or structural changes to the property or to the building that do not directly benefit the tenant or the tenant's occupancy of the building or the premises or that are made for the benefit of the landlord or that of another tenant, whether or not it is reimbursed to the landlord

2. Any sale of the property or the building (or other financial event) for which the tenant receives no direct benefit, economic or otherwise

Any additional exclusions the tenant might include will be similar to those included under operating expenses, in the preceding chapter.

Contesting an Assessment

Regardless of how outrageous an increased property assessment may be, the landlord may not see any economic benefit or any other reason for contesting the increase. This is especially so if the landlord's tax expense is relatively constant and most of the tax increase is passed on to and paid by the tenants. If an assessment will affect the landlord's pocketbook (as it will when vacancy is high) or if challenging an assessment is otherwise in the landlord's best interest (since higher assessments mean a greater tax expense and higher rents, they may make the landlord's building less competitive with other available space), the landlord may be more likely to make the challenge.

For the tenant's protection, the lease should provide for the right to contest an increased property assessment in the event the landlord does not. Although a small space user is unlikely to implement this type of provision because of the legal expenses involved, it is of significant value nevertheless to all space users, large or small. In a multitenanted building, this provision would permit a group of tenants to band together to challenge an assessment.

The tenant should make sure the right-to-contest provision stipulates the following:

1. The tenant must be notified of an increased assessment. Often a landlord will want to modify this clause to require notification only for excessive increases or as a compromise for some percentage increases over a previous year's assessment (e.g., 25 percent). This provision must be included, because only the landlord, as the property owner, is notified of the property assessment.

2. The tenant has the right to contest an increased assessment.

3. The landlord will do the actual contesting, but the landlord and tenant will cooperate in this matter, and all parties concerned will act in good faith. It is important for the landlord to do the actual contesting, since the landlord is the property owner. Whether or not a tenant can become involved in a property assessment or take the place of the landlord will depend on the laws and regulations in the jurisdiction.

4. A specific person (or specific people) will be responsible for legal fees and related costs and expenses. This provision will state that the legal expenses will either be borne by the tenant insisting on the contesting if there is not a mutual agreement with the landlord to do the contesting or be allocated in the same pro rata way (to tenants and landlord) that total tax expenses are distributed. A tenant-oriented adjustment to this provision would have the landlord pay all the legal fees and other related expenses up to the limits of any savings or refunds generated by a successful assessment challenge, with any refunded overage collected to be distributed among all the parties on a pro rata basis. The important aspect of this provision is that it establishes the detailed procedure that is to be followed if a tenant wishes to contest an assessment.

9
Landlord
Concessions

No lease clause specifically describes or defines the concessions a landlord makes to a tenant. Rather, concessions may be woven into every part of the lease document. However, to fully understand the nature of the various concessions and their interrelationships and financial impact on both the landlord and the tenant, each concession should be examined separately. Some of the following discussion will therefore overlap with material covered elsewhere in the book.

Landlord concessions are inducements to the tenant; they hold out the prospect of getting something for nothing. They are designed to emotionally charge and thus pressure a tenant to enter into a lease for particular premises or a particular building. Landlord concessions and inducements create the atmosphere of an auction; the tenant can be carried away by the hope of getting something at a bargain price.

A properly structured leasing transaction usually carries few financial implications for the landlord. A tenant can become emotionally entangled in a transaction without fully understanding the financial wizardry used to create a monetary illusion.

The landlord is not in the real estate business for sheer enjoyment; he or she expects to make a profit. A tenant must not be naive enough to believe that the landlord concessions and inducements are "free." Somewhere along the way the transaction will be paid for, and a profit made.

Concession: Rent Abatement

Tenants are encouraged to call rent abatement free rent. Rent abatement is the period between the time that a tenant takes possession of the premises, or the date the lease commences (whichever comes first), and the date on which the tenant begins to pay the landlord rent.

Rent-abatement periods can run for any length of time, from one month or less to one year or more. The actual abatement period is affected by the real estate market and economic conditions, for example, whether competitive space is available in other buildings, the space vacancy rates, the length of the lease term, the rent, and other landlord-granted concessions.

The concession, free rent, gives the tenant the feeling that he or she is getting something for nothing. It translates into free use and occupancy of office space without having to pay rent. Or does it?

Free Rent—No Space?

Tenants are sometimes told they can have a period of free rent and yet are asked to start paying rent from the day they move into the new space. This situation commonly occurs in a new building when premises need to be constructed to the tenant's plans and specifications.

A rent-abatement period will usually start on the lease commencement date, not on the tenant's actual occupancy date. For new construction, these two dates are not always the same.

The lease will specify various tenant and landlord response dates for approving plans and specifications and approving any construction pricing. However, the landlord will also insist on not being responsible for any delays caused by the tenant, such as a delay in approving pricing or approving the final construction plans. Construction delays are usually due to special office build-outs the tenant wants, such as executive washrooms, kitchens, computer wiring, and supplemental HVAC. They quickly add up and can push the occupancy date several months behind the lease commencement date. During this delay, the rent-abatement period can be used up. The tenant moves in only to discover that the year of free rent has dwindled to a month or two, or the tenant moves in and has to start paying rent immediately. Worst of all, because of excessive construction delays, the tenant may have to start paying rent before the new space can be occupied.

Is All the Rent Free?

As discussed in the context of other lease clauses, a rent-abatement period may not be free of payments. "Additional rent" may still have to be paid. The extent of additional rent expense during a rent-abatement period will depend on whether the total base rent is being abated or only the net base rent.

The tenant needs to consider the following questions:

- Will he or she still be responsible for a pro rata share of operating expense during the rent-abatement period? (See Chapter 7.)

- Will he or she still be responsible for a pro rata share of real estate taxes during the rent-abatement period? (See Chapter 7.)

- Is the rent escalator in effect during the rent-abatement period?

Services—What Services?

Until a tenant has gone through the experience, he or she is often unaware of the pioneering aspects of moving into a newly constructed building. The worst problems seem to arise when the tenant is one of the first occupants or the only one for six months or more.

Of course, the tenant has the advantage of one year of free rent to fall back on!

If there are only a few tenants in the building and nobody is paying any rent in the rent-abatement period, how realistic is it to expect a landlord to commit any significant resources to the building, especially in a period of economic stress?

To conserve cash, the landlord may reduce the number of days for cleaning and janitorial services (regardless of what the lease says about cleaning every day); reduce the number of general maintenance personnel (so the tenant has no one to call on to handle immediate problems); or not have the building's windows washed for the first year. The landlord may also save money by curtailing security services (guards only at night); by providing heat in winter (and cooling in summer) only to the occupied floors, leaving the lobby, elevators, and corridors cold in the winter (and hot in the summer); and by putting only one elevator out of four in service to reduce maintenance expenses (the one elevator has to be shared by the tenant's employees, guests, construction workers, and delivery people).

It is difficult for a tenant to savor the effects of free rent in an inhospitable building environment. The tenant is in the unenviable position of having to wait until more tenants show up before the landlord increases building services. Otherwise, what can a tenant do—move?

Free Rent?

How free is free rent? It is not! In fact, rent abatement can mean more money in a landlord's pocket. In addition, a tenant could wind up with a higher rent at the end of the lease term. Rent abatement responds to the emotional needs of a tenant and still provides financial stability for a landlord. (Note: The standard annual $10 psf base rent multiplier is again used in the examples in this chapter.)

Consider a landlord who would like to achieve a $10.50 psf net effective rent for a five-year lease for 10,000 sq ft (assuming a 3 percent annual rent escalator). Without any rent abatement, the five-year rent analysis is as shown in Table 9-1. A similar net effective rent can be achieved by giving a rent abatement of six months at a beginning rent of $11.20 psf (Table 9-2). Does it matter whether the rent is the standard $10 psf or $11.20 psf to the landlord? Not really. The landlord still achieves the annual net effective rent of $10.50 psf. However, the landlord is better off with an annual $11.20 psf in beginning rent. This is because the rent at the end of five years will be higher. In addition, with the rent

Table 9-1. Five-Year Rent Analysis without Rent Abatement
(in Dollars)

Year	Base rent plus 3 percent per year increase (psf)	Annual rent (× 10,000 sq ft)
1	10.00	100,000
2	10.30	103,000
3	10.61	106,100
4	10.93	109,300
5	11.26	112,600
Total aggregate rent	=	531,000
Net present value at 8 percent	=	422,096
Net effective rent (annual) (constant payment)	=	10.57 psf

Table 9-2. Five-Year Rent Analysis with Six Months' Rent
Abatement in Year One (in Dollars)

Year	Base rent plus 3 percent per year increase (psf)	Annual rent (× 10,000 sq ft)
1	11.20	56,000*
2	11.54	115,400
3	11.89	118,900
4	12.25	122,500
5	12.62	126,200
Total aggregate rent	=	539,000
Net present value at 8 percent	=	421,106
Net effective rent (annual) (constant payment)	=	10.55 psf

*Total five-year rent equals $112,000, less six-month rent abatement of $56,000.

abatement, the landlord collects a larger total aggregate rent over the five-year period.

The tenant should not expect to get an annual rent of $10 psf and six months of rent abatement. The landlord is in the market on a daily basis. He or she knows the competition and the current emotional expectations of the tenants in the market. The annual rent of $11.20 psf will be the "base rent," and from there the landlord can offer up to six months of rent abatement. If the full rent abatement is not negotiated by the tenant, the landlord does even better.

An annual rent of $10 psf will never enter into the negotiations. It is shown here for illustrative purposes only so that the reader is made fully aware that rent abatement carries a price tag—for the tenant.

Why Landlords Do It

Would the landlord accept a lower rent then the annual $11.20 psf and still give six months of rent abatement? Quite possibly. At $11 psf, even though the annual net effective rent is only $10.35 psf, the transaction is still valuable to the landlord. The total aggregate rent will be $529,000, with rent of $12.38 psf in the fifth year.

The landlord, in terms of total aggregate rent, is not as well off as he or she would be at the annual rent of $10 psf without an abatement. However, the ending rent is significantly higher.

The landlord might accept this transaction, depending on the relocation history of the tenant. Although the landlord would be taking a gamble, if the tenant is typical, the odds are in the landlord's favor. Based on prior experience, the tenant will renew his or her lease for an additional five years in the building. The renewal rent would be no less than the fifth-year rate and more likely be a higher market rent, if appropriate at that time.

Why does a tenant stay? A building doesn't age much in five years. If the building was new to begin with, it will still have a new feel to it in five years. The tenant's space will be built out to his or her plans and specifications. The rent will be competitive with that in other buildings and space because landlords respond to the market.

Perhaps most important, five years is not long enough to erase the tenant's memories of the hassles associated with moving to the current location (working on weekends, packing, unpacking, trying to get phones working, and lost or broken possessions), and the tenant will not want to go through it again quite so soon.

One of the main reasons that tenants do move after five years is growth: The current premises become too small, and there is no space to expand to in the building. But even when a tenant moves in five years, the landlord can still come out ahead. Assuming the five-year lease with six months of rent abatement was considered an aggressive transaction at the time, it would be typical of lease transactions made under declining market conditions, as evidenced by increased building vacancy rates and tightening financial conditions. However, the landlord was able to lease the space and at a total aggregate value within tolerable limits of the preferred annual net effective rent of $10.57 psf. In fact, if it was a declining market, by not having the space vacant for an extra three or six months, the landlord has done well.

Tenant Implications

Rent abatement, at least for the period it lasts, does help an organization's cash flow. Not paying rent for three, six, or twelve months has a luxurious feeling about it. However, reality has a way of intruding on the enjoyment of rent abatement. It can be especially troublesome if the tenant forgets to budget four or five months of rent payment one year because the free rent has become habit forming. Suddenly having to pay a rent of $20,000 a month can be a rude awakening.

Accounting practices can also reduce a tenant's enjoyment of rent abatement. A tenant will find that his or her accountant, in order to follow GAAP, is required to amortize the rent-abatement period over the full life of the lease (i.e., taken in equal increments over the term of the lease). A simplified example is a five-year lease with five months of rent abatement. For amortization purposes, this will be considered to be eleven months of rent expense each year. The five months of abatement is spread out, with one month's rent abatement taken each year. Therefore, in the first year (assuming the whole abatement is in the first five months of the term of the lease), the tenant will pay for only seven months of rent, but the financial records will show eleven months of rent expense. In succeeding years, the tenant must pay for twelve months of rent; however, the financial records continue to show only eleven months of rent expense.

Although this may be in line with normal accounting practices, it is definitely confusing to mere mortals. It is complicated enough to try to balance cash income with ongoing expense payments, much less trying to figure out why twelve months of cash is paid out, with only eleven months of rent expense recorded.

Rent Abatement—An Option

When a tenant or landlord considers rent abatement, all too often it is thought of as being used in consecutive months, at the beginning of the lease term. However, there is no reason why rent abatement needs to be taken all at once, or in its entirety at the beginning of a lease.

The landlord's traditionalist view of having a tenant take the entire rent abatement immediately may make the least sense, because it could have the lowest economic benefit for the landlord. Depending on economic conditions such as inflation and on rent escalators, the landlord might be giving away more valuable dollars at the beginning of a lease term than at the end. This can easily be seen using Table 9-3, which compares six months of rent abatement occurring in year one with the rent abatement occurring in year five. The net effective rent is higher if the landlord puts off the abatement until year five. Even though the total aggregate rent collected is less, its net present value, because of the time value of money, is higher when the abatement is put off (see "Net Present Value Explained" in Chapter 6).

Conversely, the tenant should do better, from an economic standpoint, by taking the rent abatement as soon as possible. In fact, the more variable the rent escalation relative to inflation factors, the better the tenant does. However, with the wrong rent escalator (see Chapter 6) and a lower inflation rate, the tenant may do better by taking the rent abatement at a later point. Repeating the example of Table 9-3 in Table 9-4, the rent increase is changed to 6 percent, and the percentage value of money for the NPV is set at 5 percent. The tenant does much better by having the rent abatement occur at a later period. The net effective rent,

Table 9-3. Five-Year Rent Analysis Comparing Six Months of Rent Abatement in Year One and Six Months of Rent Abatement in Year Five (in Dollars)

Year	Base rent plus 3 percent per year increase (psf)	Annual rent with year one abatement (× 10,000 sq ft)	Annual rent with year five abatement (× 10,000 sq ft)
1	10.00	50,000	100,000
2	10.30	103,000	103,000
3	10.61	106,100	106,100
4	10.93	109,300	109,300
5	11.26	112,500	56,300
Total aggregate rent =		481,000	474,700
Net present value at 8 percent =		375,800	383,780
Net effective rent (annual) (constant payment) =		9.41 psf	9.61 psf

Table 9-4. Five-Year Rent Analysis Comparing Six Months of Rent Abatement in Year One and Six Months of Rent Abatement in Year Five (in Dollars)

Year	Base rent plus 6 percent per year increase (psf)	Annual rent with year one abatement (× 10,000 sq ft)	Annual rent with year five abatement (× 10,000 sq ft)
1	10.00	50,000	100,000
2	10.60	106,000	106,000
3	11.24	112,400	112,400
4	11.91	119,100	119,100
5	12.62	126,200	63,100
Total aggregate rent =		513,700	500,600
Net present value at 5 percent =		437,724	435,903
Net effective rent (annual) (constant payment) =		10.11 psf	10.07 psf

the NPV, and the total aggregate rent collected by the landlord from the tenant are all less. The tenant saves money.

There should be no limit to how a tenant thinks about taking a rent abatement. Alternatives include taking one month's abatement each year, splitting the abatement equally between the beginning and the end of the lease term, and taking the entire abatement at the end of the lease period.

A tenant must also consider whether to increase the lease term to account for the abatement period or leave the length of the lease term the same but have it start after the abatement period. If the terms and conditions of the lease were advantageous, this could provide a longer occupancy period and thereby increase the tenant's benefit from the lease.

Leasing Inducement: Lower Initial Rent

A lower initial rent for space can be considered an inducement for the tenant who has just come into the market to look for space, having had a long-term low-rent lease with minimal rent escalations, and is experiencing rent sticker shock. This sort of tenant often finds that rents are double or triple the rent in their current but ending lease, or even more. These rent increases, moreover, are not only for space in other buildings, but are similar to rent being quoted by their current landlord for staying in the same space. For some organizations, a doubling of the rent would be a budget buster, and without financial alternatives, they could not cope with the strain.

The solution is a landlord rent concession that provides a lease with lower initial rent but subsequent rent bumps at specific times. Depending on market and economic factors, the landlord will usually do better in the long run with such an arrangement.

For the tenant, the concession is needed, the relief greatly appreciated. It allows the tenant to ease into a current or untested market and to lease new office space tailored to his or her needs. However, unless the PREB shows a full financial spreadsheet, the tenant will be unprepared for the rent sticker shock yet to come. Continuing with the example in Table 9-1, in Table 9-5 the lease term is increased to 10 years, but the annual rent increase is kept at 3 percent a year. In Table 9-6 the example in Table 9-5 is extended by adding $1 rent bumps in the third, fifth, seventh, and ninth years. For the sake of simplicity, rent abatement is excluded from the examples. The standard annual base rent multiplier of $10 psf is continued, assuming that this is an initial rent representing a reasonable increase over the tenant's rent for the expiring lease. (Note: The reader is cautioned that, to use the results in these examples as a multiplier, exact comparability between rent and rent bumps is required. Therefore, a $20 rent, or a multiplier of 2, automatically increases the bumps to $2 in the result. It is not possible to use the multiplier results for different rent and rent bump multipliers.)

Table 9-5. Standard Annual $10-PSF Base Rent Multiplier Increased 3 Percent Per Year for Ten Years, without Rent Bumps (in Dollars)

Year	Base rent plus 3 percent per year increase (psf)	Annual rent (× 10,000 sq ft)
1	10.00	100,000
2	10.30	103,000
3	10.61	106,100
4	10.93	109,300
5	11.26	112,600
6	11.60	116,000
7	11.95	119,500
8	12.31	123,100
9	12.68	126,800
10	13.06	130,100
Total aggregate rent	=	1,147,000
Net present value at 8 percent	=	755,355
Net effective rent (annual) (constant payment)	=	11.26 psf

Table 9-6. Standard Annual $10-PSF Base Rent Multiplier with Rent Bumps (in Dollars)

Year	Base rent (psf)	3 percent annual increase	Rent bump	Total annual rent (psf)	Total annual rent (× 10,000 sq ft)
1	10.00	—	—	10.00	100,000
2	10.00	0.30	—	10.30	103,000
3	10.30	0.31	1.00	11.61	116,100
4	11.61	0.35	—	11.96	119,600
5	11.96	0.36	1.00	13.32	133,200
6	13.32	0.40	—	13.72	137,200
7	13.72	0.41	1.00	15.13	151,300
8	15.13	0.45	—	15.58	155,800
9	15.58	0.47	1.00	17.05	170,500
10	17.05	0.51	—	17.56	175,600
Total aggregate rent				=	1,362,300
Net present value at 8 percent				=	877,170
Net effective rent (annual) (constant payment)				=	13.07 psf

There's sticker shock for the tenant in Table 9-6: The annual rent per square foot almost doubles by the end of 10 years (from $10 psf to $17.56 psf). If a $2 psf rent bump were used, the rent would more than double in the 10 years. Without the rent bumps, as Table 9-5 shows, the rent would have increased more moderately by the end of 10 years (from $10 psf to $13.06 psf). In 10 years' time, at any rate, it is reasonable to expect rent sticker shock for tenants with older leases. However, with a graduated type of rent increase, the magnitude of sticker shock in future periods is reduced.

Although this landlord concession costs a tenant more in total dollars over the 10-year period, it allows a tenant to enter the market at an initial level of rent reasonableness. It should be seen as beneficial because it gives the tenant time to prepare for future increases instead of having to cope with them all at once.

Concession: Above-Building-Standard Allowance

All too often tenants exhibit an unbelievably high level of naiveté, expecting premises to be built out "automatically" to the precise office sizes, storage spaces, and conference rooms called for. These tenants expect only to pick out some wallpaper and carpet and bring in the furnishings and furniture. Tenants need to be educated about how the building standard allowance is used to construct an office environment to a tenant's plans and specifications.

An above-building-standard allowance is a landlord concession designed to help a tenant realize his or her ideal office environment. This concession encompasses three broad concepts; each concept could have a variety of components.

Unlimited Building Standard

The first concept is that of the unlimited building standard, a tenant's right to use unlimited quantities of the building standard materials, as specified in the building standard workletter. The items included in this unlimited allowance are nothing more than the basic building materials that provide a minimal office environment, such as basic walls, electric outlets and switches, lights, doors, and floor covering.

Although "unlimited" sounds good, this concession does not allow a tenant to upgrade an office environment above the basic institutional level. Anything not on the building standard list, such as half-height partitions or dedicated electrical outlets for computers, costs extra.

The trend in tenant use of building standard items can be expressed as "use it or lose it." Because landlords offer additional inducements to the tenant for construction of his or her premises, no credit is returned to the tenant for not using building standard items. However, an unlimited building standard still has considerable value to the tenant.

An Allowance

The second concept is that of an above-building-standard allowance. This is a per-square-foot dollar amount the landlord offers to help the tenant upgrade an office environment above the building's standard institutional look. The concept is straightforward. If the building standard workletter allowance provides, for example, a concession worth $10 psf and can create a basic institutional look, the landlord would give an additional amount, say, another $10 psf, of construction and materials to enhance or upgrade the office environment. If the actual costs to create this office environment are more than the dollar allowance, the tenant owes the landlord the additional amount. If the actual costs are less than the allowance, depending on tenant-landlord negotiations, the tenant may lose the unused amount, have a credit applied to future construction and alterations, or take the difference as an offset to future rent.

Turnkey

The third concept, the "turnkey" buildout, is often mistakenly thought to represent unlimited building standard buildout. By *turnkey buildout* it is supposed that the tenant, on the first day of the lease term, turning the key and opening the office door, will find the premises ready to use exactly as specified by the tenant and including every imaginable enhancement thought up by the tenant. However, there is no standard definition of *turnkey buildout:* The landlord may be thinking in terms of fairly standard construction methods and building materials, whereas the tenant has been planning for hand-built wood cabinetry, brass hardware, executive washrooms, employee cafeterias, and marble floors.

Which to Use?

The unlimited building standard leaves much to be desired as a concession package when compared with the other concepts. However, it is often the best available alternative, given the market and economic conditions of the day. For the tenant, a true turnkey buildout is the best option for creating an office environment; however, it can be difficult to agree on what is expected and to translate a tenant's wants and desires into a set of architectural plans in any reasonable amount of time.

To build a tenant's emotional attachment to premises, nothing beats a landlord's offer of a $10 psf above-building-standard allowance. (Tenant beware, however: Is that allowance based on rentable or usable square feet? See Chapter 10.) A tenant with 10,000 sq ft of space can easily become emotionally attached to a $100,000 above-building-standard allowance. Just the thought of having that much money to spend sends most tenants back to the "kid in the candy store" stage. Too late, the tenant will find out that the $100,000 does not go very far, however; rather than having an ideal office environment at no cost, the tenant winds up having to pay an additional $50,000 or $100,000 to get everything wanted—or else go without.

Concession: Relocation Allowance

A relocation allowance is an offshoot of the above-building-standard allowance. It is an additional landlord inducement that elicits an even greater emotional response. The landlord offers to provide a relocation allowance of so many dollars per square foot that the tenant can use in any way he or she sees fit, including taking it in cash or rent credit. (The maximum tenant benefit will be obtained if the allowance is based on rentable square feet and not on usable square feet.)

Imagine what the 10,000-sq-ft tenant must feel when offered a $10 psf allowance totaling $100,000 in cash from the landlord! Often a landlord will even provide a variety of suggested uses designed to whet the appetite of the most jaded tenant. Suggested items might include additional office environment enhancements, paying for moving expenses, purchasing a new telephone system, buying a new computer system, or buying all-new office furnishings and furniture. But nothing beats the good old landlord standby, "You can take it all in cash."

However, cash payments have additional implications.

Take the Cash and Run?

Not taking the cash or its equivalent (e.g., a gift) can often be the best course of action for a tenant. The tenant should never rely on a PREB to suggest the best alternative regarding cash payments. The PREB wants to encourage a tenant to commit to a lease and does everything possible to keep the tenant's emotional commitment high. A PREB is not an attorney or a tax expert. The tenant should be sure to get the proper professional help to avoid making the wrong choice.

As a rule of thumb, any cash or cash equivalents received by the tenant are considered income. All income that a tenant receives is taxable to the tenant. Anything that is an expense to one party, in this case the cash paid as an inducement to the tenant by the landlord, is income to another party, in this case the tenant taking the cash.

The same problem arises for cash equivalents or gifts. For example, having the landlord buy a telephone system, computer equipment, or new furniture is great, but if the benefit and ownership is passed on to the tenant, the tenant has received a cash equivalent, a gift, and it is again considered part of the tenant's taxable income.

To avoid this problem, the tenant should have the landlord not only pay for everything with the relocation allowance, but also retain ownership rights. The general principle that the tenant should follow is that the items the landlord provides for the tenant should be related to the landlord's cost for having the tenant occupy the premises. In this way the expenditure is a valid expense of the landlord for getting the tenant to occupy otherwise vacant space. It is a cost of doing business. Whatever is included, whether telephone or computer systems, built-in cabinetry, modular furniture, or furnishings, the tenant must remember that all improvements remain with the landlord when the tenant leaves the space at the end of the lease term. They all belong to the landlord.

An alternative is to have an unused or untaken relocation allowance applied as a credit against future rent payments, that is, as additional rent abatement.

Who Said It Was Free?

The reader needs to be reminded that the landlord is working in the vacant-space market every day. The landlord knows what competitors are offering both in rent and in concession packages. The rent a landlord offers has a built-in expectation regarding the concession package necessary to attract a tenant. That expectation is what leads the landlord to assign a particular total dollar value to the concession package. It is up to the tenant, when negotiating with the landlord, to win the best possible transaction, which will, in effect, be the lowest net effective rent acceptable to the landlord. Whether the tenant will get it all is a different matter.

The Basic Concession Package

The landlord concessions of rent abatement and initial years of low rent may determine the financial suitability of the premises and thus the tenant's economic commitment. To secure the tenant's emotional commitment, the landlord may have to use other concessions, such as an above-building-standard allowance or a relocation allowance.

In examining the financial impact of a landlord concession package, Table 9-7 and Table 9-8 use the standard annual base rent multiplier of $10 psf with a 3-percent-per-year rent escalator and rent bumps. The lease will be for a 10,000-sq-ft premises. To enhance the package, the landlord is willing to offer an above-building-standard allowance of $3 psf (which may only be used to enhance the office space), an additional $1.50 psf as a relocation allowance (which may be used in any way the tenant wants), and a rent-abatement period. The tenant's objective is to create a reasonable transaction that meets the landlord's goal of a net effective rent of $10.50 psf (staying in line with the original Table 9-1 rent example) and achieves a substantial concessions package, building the tenant's emotional commitment.

The difference between the examples in Tables 9-7 and 9-8 is not large. Surprisingly, although the concessions package in Table 9-8 has a higher dollar value, it gives the landlord a higher total aggregate rent, even though it has a slightly lower net effective rent. The offset is provided by the extra $0.50 psf rent in the first year in Table 9-8, as well as the switch to rent bumps in years two and three. Although these items may seem insignificant, the time value of money has proved otherwise, despite the extra three months of rent abatement.

Table 9-7. Basic Concession Package with Three Months of Rent Abatement (in Dollars)

Year	Adjusted base rent with 3 percent per year increase (psf)	Rent bump (psf)	Annual base rent (psf)	Total annual rent (× 10,000 sq ft)
1	10.00	—	10.00	100,000
				−25,000*
				−30,000†
				−20,000‡
				25,000§
2	10.30	1.00	11.30	113,000
3	11.64	1.50	13.14	131,400
4	13.53	—	13.53	135,300
5	13.94	—	13.94	139,400
Total aggregate rent			=	544,100
Net present value at 8 percent			=	418,650
Net effective rent (annual) (constant payment)			=	10.49 psf

*3-month abatement
†$3 psf above-building-standard allowance
‡$2 psf relocation allowance
§Year-one rent; total concession package value = $75,000

(Note: The standard annual base rent multiplier of $10 psf is used in both tables. To increase the value of the rent to reflect the rents and credits of those actually found in a jurisdiction, multiply by the appropriate amount. For a $30 psf rent, for example, multiply the result by 3. However, the reader is cautioned that each additional element of the concession package will automatically be increased by the same multiplier and will result in an above-building-standard allowance of $9 psf, for example, for a multiplier of 3. The multiplier given as an example cannot be used if there are different increments between the base rent and the values of the concessions.)

Table 9-8. Basic Concession Package with Six Months of Rent Abatement (in Dollars)

Year	Adjusted base rent with 3 percent per year increase (psf)	Rent bump (psf)	Annual base rent (psf)	Total annual rent (× 10,000 sq ft)
1	10.50	—	10.50	105,000
				−55,000*
				−30,000[†]
				−20,000[‡]
				0[§]
2	10.82	1.50	12.32	123,200
3	12.69	1.00	13.69	136,900
4	14.10	—	14.10	141,000
5	14.52	—	14.52	145,200
Total aggregate rent			=	546,300
Net present value at 8 percent			=	416,760
Net effective rent (annual) (constant payment)			=	10.44 psf

*6-month abatement
[†]$3 psf above-building-standard allowance
[‡]$2 psf relocation allowance
[§]Year-one rent; total concession package value = $105,000

It's Never Really Free

Each landlord concession or inducement to a tenant has a value relative to all the others that creates a complex financial interrelationship. There is a way to structure a concession package that will meet the needs of almost any tenant, as well as those of the landlord. No matter how it is structured, however, the elements of a concession package have value and cost money. Somehow, somewhere, somebody has to pay. Nothing is really free.

10

Premises Buildout and Workletters

Every aspect of a tenant's business operations is affected by the overall environment of the premises. Space configuration, space utilization, and furnishings will project an image about the business—successful or struggling, lavish or frugal, productive or not.

How space is configured and constructed is important. Space in an older building may need extensive renovation or reconstruction, or it may just need some cosmetic changes or minor alterations. In a building that is about to be constructed, the tenant leases a void that must be envisioned and transformed into the usable and desirable.

Depending on the exact amount of work required, the lease will contain either clauses or attachments or an addendum describing what has to be done. These lease elements can range from the relatively simple to the quite complex.

If work is to be performed on a space, the tenant and landlord will in effect be entering into a construction contract, and this contract will become part of the lease document. Theoretically, this lease clause should be unique for every tenant. In fact, certain elements invariably creep in that need not be there (i.e., they do not provide for the needs of different-sized space users) and require tenant vigilance.

Who Creates the Buildout Lease Clause?

The first point to note about this clause and its provisions is that, unlike most other clauses, which are in force throughout the term of a lease, these are designed to be used only once. Second, this clause normally affects the tenant before possession or occupancy of the premises. That is, the work specified in the clause usually has to be finished before the tenant moves into the space. Third, this clause will often include the conditions that must be met to put the lease document into effect (i.e., lease commencement date).

A PREB and an attorney generally formulate the various clauses making up the lease document. Because of their intimate knowledge of the law and the commercial real estate marketplace, these professionals can handle the majority of lease clauses. For the buildout lease clause, however, knowledge of the construction industry is also needed. The tenant must have an architect or a construction contractor prepare or review the provisions and elements that affect construction work. They should cover the following points: Who will do the work? What materials will be used? How long will the work take? How much will it cost? Mistakes or omissions in composing the relevant provisions will end up costing the tenant time, money, and work quality.

The Elements of the Clause

Thus, depending on the tenant's needs, the complexity of the work to be done, and whether the space is in a newly constructed building or has been previously occupied, the tenant must be prepared to examine (or have someone else examine) a number of standard provisions and lease elements to protect his or her interests. Because of regional and landlord differences, each provision will have its own quirks. The tenant must be on guard against those elements that favor the landlord exclusively or that will waste the tenant's time, effort, and money.

The lease clause or addendum that includes the specifications necessary to build the space to meet the tenant's requirements is traditionally called the workletter. The term *workletter* suggests that this is a complete document or clause covering all aspects of the landlord-tenant relationship regarding the work that will be done on behalf of the tenant. Actually, there are no standards defining the elements that go into a workletter. Furthermore, the clause may have some other title, such as Tenant Allowances, Building Standard Workletter, Building Standard Allowance, Tenant Improvements, Buildout, Work Agreement, Tenant Finishes, or Completion of Finished Premises. In keeping with the more common and traditional practice, however, the pertinent lease clause will be referred to here either as a workletter or a work agreement.

From the tenant's perspective, the workletter must include at least the following elements:

- Tenant plans and specifications
- Timetables for plans, approvals, and construction
- Construction work by the tenant
- Construction work by the landlord and the building standard
- Cost
- Payment
- Work acceptance—possession or occupancy

(Note: The discussion that follows focuses on new space construction, on the assumption that this will cover the vital elements of both new space and the reconstruction of previously occupied premises. The reader can select the aspects relevant to his or her requirements.)

Tenant Plans and Specifications

To build (or reconstruct) a space, a tenant must provide or have prepared detailed plans and specifications describing exactly what is wanted. This task is done by a space planner or architect, who can be hired by either the tenant or the landlord. The tenant needs to be concerned with a number of plans and specifications.

Basic Space Plans and Specifications (Also Known as the Space Layout). These plans and specifications define the size or amount of space that will be utilized for various staff or functions, for example, the standard size of the space the tenant will want for a secretary or office worker, for a certain number of people in a conference room (in various configurations), and for the number and amount of storage areas.

In addition, specifications must take into account work flow patterns of the staff and their functions, and how they interact. The ideal space arrangement is one that permits maximum work efficiency when people and things are placed together. The term *departmental adjacencies* is often used to refer to configurations that place certain employees, work stations, or departments near others to improve work flow or productivity.

Once standards are established, a space layout or initial space plan can be created. (Often the space standards are established by a tenant's architect or space planner at the beginning of the relocation process, in order to arrive at a realistic estimate of the amount of space the tenant needs.) A space plan takes into account the physical constraints of the space being leased (or being considered if the lease has not yet been signed) and lays out all of the space allotments for the employees and their functions. Depending on the stage of the plan, the drawings will show the placement of dividing walls, door openings, the location of environmental systems (electric and telephone outlets, exhaust fans), and possibly the placement of furniture and furnishings.

Detailed Space Plans or Working Drawings. After the initial space plans are approved by the tenant, detailed space plans (or initial working drawings) with operational standards can be prepared. These are the plans and specifications the contractor (or landlord) will use to estimate the cost of the various building materials and other furnishings (e.g., doors, glass, floor covering, sinks, and cabinetry) needed to build the space as designed. These plans also permit the landlord (or architect) to establish the amount of work and materials to be paid for by the landlord (known as the building standard allowance and the above-building-standard allowance) or that will be supplied or paid for by the tenant.

Working Drawings or Construction Documents.   The final plans and specifications that need to be prepared are often referred to as working drawings or, more accurately, as construction documents. These are the drawings and documents that will permit the parties involved to order the materials to construct the space. A wide range of construction documents will be required. Here are the basic ones the tenant should know about:

- *Architecturals.* These drawings specify exactly where and how the space will be divided and built. They are the blueprints for the placement of walls, doors, windows, and other space-related structural elements (not to be confused with the building's structural elements).

- *Mechanicals.* These are the plans and specifications used for the placement of the mechanical and operating systems pertaining to the environment of the space (e.g., HVAC duct outlets and intakes, exhaust fans, water lines, and plumbing).

- *Electricals.* These are wiring diagrams showing the placement of all wiring and outlets in the space, including electrical outlets and lighting switches, telephone cables and outlets, and computer cables and outlets.

- *Schedules.* Each type of plan is accompanied by a schedule defining and describing the terms and codes used in the plans. For example, a door schedule will describe all the different doors (office, storage), their materials (wood, metal), and other characteristics (size, weight). There will also be a lighting schedule, a floor covering schedule, and so on, each listing all the necessary materials.

- *Elevations.* Elevations are additional drawings showing the special details needed for accurate construction. For example, kitchen cabinet elevations would show detailed views of the front, sides, and back of the cabinets for door and drawer placement, hardware detail and placement, and wall-attachment points.

The tenant is responsible for providing the necessary plans and specifications for the premises. However, who prepares them and who pays for their preparation is open to tenant-land-lord negotiations.

The options range from having the tenant control and pay for everything to the tenant's controlling the process and the landlord's paying for everything. The latter choice is the one preferred by tenants. However, there are many variations between the two extremes. Whatever the arrangement, the tenant needs to know exactly what he or she is (or is not) getting.

Space Planning Allowance

Often a landlord will want to use a particular architect for the tenant's plans and specifications. The tenant should be aware that many architects will (with the full knowledge of the landlord) quote an extremely low fee to the landlord for the building's design, plans, and specification work, on the understanding that they will be the "official" building architects. As they and the landlord know, most tenants will settle for these official architects—and will wind up paying top dollar for their services. Tenants are led to believe that the official building architects are the only ones fully knowledgeable about the building's mechanical and operating systems and thus the only ones truly able to provide accurate and proper plans and specifications for the tenant's space. These official architects may return (or kick back) some of the fees or "design concessions" they receive from the tenant to the landlord. Tenants, beware!

Whether the tenant uses a building's official architect should be strictly the tenant's decision. Whatever architect is used, the landlord often provides a dollar credit or allowance for architectural services. How this allowance is given and its size are important to the tenant.

Typically, this allowance is quoted in dollars per square foot. The tenant needs to be sure the dollar amount specified is to be based on the total *rentable* square feet, not the total usable square feet. Even though the landlord will probably argue that the design services will only be applied to the usable square feet, the tenant must remember that he or she is paying rent on the basis of rentable—not of usable—square feet. All dollar (or other) allowances that are based on the number of square feet should be established in the same way.

The difference to the tenant can be substantial. For each $1 psf of allowance, the difference between rentable and usable square feet is $130 of allowance per 1000 rentable sq ft, with a 15 percent core factor providing 870 usable sq ft (1000 rentable sq ft − 870 usable sq ft = 130 sq ft net difference; see Chapter 2). That is a hefty $1300 for 10,000 rentable sq ft and $13,000 for 100,000 rentable sq ft.

The landlord will provide the bare minimum allowance he or she can get away with. This may be an amount specified in dollars per square foot or a requirement that the landlord's architect provides the initial space plan drawings (this will not include the space allocations needed by the tenant or the standards specifications). Typically, the per-square-foot dollar amount specified will only pay for supplying the initial space plan drawings. The tenant should be aware that initial space plan drawings are the least expensive to produce. The costly items are the working drawings and, afterward, the architectural, mechanical, and electrical plans, specifications, schedules, and elevations.

The landlord's problem in providing a space-planning allowance is how to determine what should be part of the design plan for a space. In the landlord's view the proper items to include are only those used to divide and utilize the space (e.g., walls, windows, doors), as opposed to the tenant's desired options, such as executive washrooms and kitchens. In other words, the landlord accepts as necessary only the plans that specify the standard construction materials and work rather than above-standard building materials and work. To the tenant, however, the space includes everything that needs to be done to create the environment needed to operate the business as desired.

The tenant has two basic options:

1. Check with a number of other sources to determine the realistic per-square-foot dollar amount cost of constructing the space to meet the tenant's requirements, and have that amount specified as the landlord's provided allowance in the lease.

2. In the workletter, clearly specify, in detail, what the tenant will provide and what plans and specifications the landlord's architect will be obligated to provide—regardless of the cost.

A third alternative that blends these options and also works well for the tenant (and often saves money for the landlord) is to have the workletter clearly specify that the tenant is responsible only for providing detailed space plans (original working drawings) for which the landlord will provide a specified per-square-foot dollar allowance. (The tenant would thus be assured that the amount was realistic and have the option to decide which architect to use.) The landlord and his or her preferred architect would then, at the landlord's sole cost, be responsible for providing all the work drawings and construction documents necessary to complete the premises to the tenant's satisfaction.

Who Pays for Changes?

Plans and specifications invariably run into an additional high-cost item that must be clearly specified in the workletter. That is, the workletter must state who is responsible for paying for any changes to the plans and specifications.

For example, what happens after all the plans have been prepared and the tenant finds that other related costs will eat up the relocation budget and therefore a special item that would enhance the space can no longer be afforded? It could be separate air-conditioning units for every conference room, for example. To change and issue revised plans and specifications is a complex task involving detailed mechanical and electrical alterations, and it is, of course, expensive. Who pays?

Or suppose that after construction begins, the tenant finds a particular divided space will not be large enough or will be too large, and a wall needs to be moved (and all the electrical work needs redoing). Again, changes and revised plans need to be prepared and issued to the workers. Who pays?

The landlord's answer is straightforward and logical: Whoever makes the changes should be responsible for the associated costs. (To be fair to landlords, tenants can drive landlords and architects crazy with constant changes—necessary or not.) The tenant, however, would obviously prefer not to pay for any changes, regardless of why they were made or who ordered them. As a compromise, there should be either a drop-dead date, beyond which the costs for any changes will be borne by the responsible party, or a clause making the tenant responsible only for the changes to plans and specifications for work already under construction or for materials already ordered (not for work not yet started) and where the change is not the result of, or required because of, any building-related structural, mechanical, or electrical operation or system or any previous building construction or work unrelated to the tenant's premises (e.g., the construction of another tenant's office).

Timetables for Plans, Approvals, and Construction

A landlord wants a tenant to begin paying rent as soon as possible. Therefore, the landlord needs to have the lease start as early as possible. But the lease usually cannot begin to take effect until the tenant's space construction has been completed. Going backward, this means the plans and specifications necessary to perform construction must be completed as soon as possible, and there should be no delay in the actual construction. It is in the landlord's best interests to include a timetable or schedule in the workletter, providing for the earliest possible dates for the tenant's delivery of plans and specifications and any required approvals for things such as construction pricing or construction documents.

Tenant-Caused Delay Provision

Depending on individual needs, it is often in the tenant's best interests to have a timetable or schedule specifying when things will be accomplished. This is especially important when the landlord insists on a provision stating that the landlord will not be responsible for any delays in readying the premises caused by, or being the responsibility of, the tenant. Such delays might include those due to tenant-requested changes in construction; tenant-requested special materials or work; the tenant's failure to approve the pricing of material and work, the plans and specifications, or the construction documents in a timely manner; the tenant's failure to make required payments; the failure of the tenant's hired contractor to perform; and tenant-approved design flaws.

Lease Commencement Date—Construction Completion Date

The purpose of a timetable is to establish when things are due and when things are to be completed and to provide some criteria for establishing whether a delay has occurred or is likely to occur. A timetable or schedule can be in the best interests of both the tenant and the landlord, as long as it fair to both.

For the tenant, one of the most important dates to include is the lease commencement date, which will usually be tied to the construction completion date, which in turn is tied to other items in the timetable. A tenant needs to know approximately when the new premises will be ready for occupancy or possession. For some tenants, this date can be critical because of an expiring lease in another building. Every relocation process hinges on this date.

Not only must the tenant have a timetable for submitting plans and various approvals, but the landlord should likewise have a schedule for construction times and an estimated completion date. The landlord should be required to give the tenant regular updates on the construction timetable. They should be provided on a monthly basis at a minimum. Furthermore, the landlord should be required to give 30 days' notice of the actual (or strongly anticipated) completion date of construction (the tenant would prefer 60 days' notice; the landlord will want to give only 10 days' notice).

Drop-Dead Date

In addition, there should be a drop-dead completion date, beyond which the tenant has the option of accepting the premises or terminating the lease document. The usefulness of this provision depends on available tenant alternatives or options and the expiration dates and terms of other tenant leases. The landlord will want a drop-dead date as far out as possible (usually specified to be one year after the estimated scheduled date), as well as an act-of-God clause (excusing any construction delays beyond the control of the landlord), which could delay completion indefinitely—to the tenant's detriment.

The tenant's position on the construction completion date will obviously depend on the individual's needs and circumstances, but it is well to remember how much additional time, effort, and hassle will be involved in terminating a lease and starting the whole space-finding process and subsequent construction all over again.

Landlord Estimate of Completion Date

The tenant must be wary of any landlord-inspired provision that is based on a landlord's estimate of what the completion date or lease commencement date will be because of tenant-incurred delays to plans, materials, or construction. The landlord will want to be the judge of how much delay the tenant caused. This estimate is bound to include the various schedules of people who could not get to or complete other work on time.

It therefore becomes vital that any tenant-required timetable or schedule be realistic. This is easier said than done. How long does it take to review plans and construction documents? How long does it take to approve landlord prices and make sure the business can afford the expenses? How long does it take to make a "small" change to a set of construction documents? There are no exact answers. Even though the wise tenant will have professional help (and this does not mean the PREB) in establishing reasonable timetables, there will be as many different estimates as there are professionals.

The Domino Effect

A case of the domino effect that can occur is often not taken into account in a timetable; by default, the tenant will be blamed for any delay related to tenant construction. For example, suppose the tenant approves certain extra space enhancements but because of budget constraints cancels some things. Suppose, moreover, that because of a tight schedule, all this is done from a set of completed construction documents. Even though the tenant met the timetable, the necessary changes and revisions in the construction documents could seriously delay the start or completion of construction since it takes time to complete and issue revised construction documents. One small change could mean changing all the documents—architectural, mechanical, and electrical.

Similarly, if the tenant is merely a day late in meeting the timetable, the landlord may translate this into a delay of a week or even a month because it will affect the schedules of all the required professionals.

Often a tenant delay will have no serious repercussions other than starting the clock ticking earlier for using up a landlord concession such as rent abatement or, at the worst, forcing the tenant to start paying rent before the space can actually be used. More seriously, the tenant may be faced with an expiring lease that will run over if the anticipated construction date is not met. Even though the new lease may contain provisions offering some tenant relief if the landlord is unable to deliver the space in a timely manner, the tenant must watch for an overriding provision tucked away in the workletter that might actually put the tenant at the mercy of the landlord. It might give the landlord the right, depending on the reason for the delay, to put off the construction commencement date or lease commencement date (and therefore any associated landlord-incurred expenses or penalties) by an amount equal to the time associated with the delay, real or landlord estimated, regardless of who is responsible for it.

Not an Exact Date: A Range of Dates

Any timetable or schedule that the tenant is required to follow should always include either a range of dates or a second, later drop-dead date (it is assumed that the tenant will have professional advice in setting the initial dates or timetable). Therefore, when the tenant has 30 days to approve and return a set of plans, the provision will state that on or approximately 30 days after the tenant receives final plans and specifications, but in no event later than 60 days after receipt, the tenant will either approve or disapprove, in writing, the plans and specifications. Similarly, a specified date will always have a second backup date, for example, "on or before April 22, but in no event later than May 21."

As further protection for the tenant, every item included in a timetable or schedule should be accompanied by a statement of the possible effects of a delay. First, there should be some indication of the importance of each item to the overall schedule or timetable and the potential impact of any delay on any other timetable item and on the estimated construction completion date. Second, if an item is important and a potential cause of a completion delay, the schedule should include an estimate of the range of time of the potential delay related to the actual amount of time delay that is incurred. That is, if plans are submitted two days late, is that only a two-day delay for something else, such as construction, or a possible two-week delay?

Allowance for Slippage

As additional protection, the timetable or schedule should automatically provide for some slippage in the schedule or adjustment of dates or time frames for any items that are dependent on each other. The tenant may be responsible for one delay, but he or she certainly does not want any delay compounded because of total scheduling inflexibility. Suppose the tenant has to submit plans by April 22 and to approve pricing by May 21. If the tenant does not submit plans until April 24, the other date should automatically be changed to May 23. Otherwise, the tenant could be held responsible and accountable for an additional two-day delay.

(Note: The circumstances surrounding the buildout and construction of space are similar to renovations and alterations, which are covered in Chapter 17.)

Construction Work by the Tenant

A tenant should have the right to hire and use his or her own contractor rather than the landlord's. Pressure will be put on the tenant to use the landlord's building contractor, who will be described as having the most knowledge about the building's structural, mechanical, and electrical operations and systems and as being the most qualified to perform the work. Although the tenant should always allow the contractor specified by the landlord to submit a bid to perform the tenant's construction work, the tenant must retain the right to choose someone else (see "How Much Will It Cost?").

Depending on the details of the landlord's concession package, because of building standard allowance work and access to building structural elements, the landlord may insist that certain work be done strictly by the landlord's contractor. If there is a plain dollar construction allowance without reference to a building standard allowance, the tenant may not have to use the landlord's contractor for any part of the work. However, if tenants take on the responsibility of doing their own construction, they may have to live by certain landlord requirements.

To avoid the possibility of any misunderstandings and to clearly define responsibilities, any landlord-imposed conditions for permitting the tenant to have his or her own contractor should be specified in the workletter (see Chapter 17). The landlord is likely to insist on the following conditions, and a tenant should be prepared to include them:

1. All plans and specifications and construction work require the prior written approval of the landlord. Tenant should be sure to include a landlord time requirement for response (e.g., "Landlord will respond within 30 days").

The tenant should also include a provision covering non-response or negative acceptance. That is, if the landlord does not respond within the allotted time, the plans and specifications will be considered acceptable to the landlord.

In addition, the tenant should specify that the landlord's consent will not be withheld unreasonably.

2. The landlord should be notified of the name and address of the tenant's contractors before the beginning of any construction work. This requirement protects both the landlord and the tenant. Landlords often know who the unscrupulous or unreasonable contractors are and can warn the tenant in advance. Of course, the tenant will have checked the references and personally visited construction work done for other tenants before hiring a contractor.

3. The tenant's contractors (or the tenant) must have a certificate of insurance in a form and with an insurance company acceptable to the landlord. The landlord will require specific types of insurance and minimum levels of coverage. Typical insurance coverage includes liability, casualty, and property damage, as well as workman's compensation (to protect the landlord from construction workers' claims).

The landlord will want to receive certificates of insurance and to be named an additional insured.

4. The landlord will want to make sure the tenant's contractors and work persons cannot put a mechanic's lien on the landlord's property if the tenant is unable to pay for construction materials and services. Depending on the laws and regulations of the jurisdiction, the landlord may ask for each contractor or an independent tradesperson (e.g., electrician, plumber) to present a signed waiver before the start of construction. When a waiver is not appropriate, the landlord will require that a notice be posted attesting that the landlord is not responsible for such payments.

As further protection, the landlord will require the tenant to post a bond for the full amount of the work. The landlord will include an appropriate provision stating that the landlord has the right to use the bond to remove any mechanic's liens against the landlord's property (see Chapter 17).

5. The tenant will be required to abide by all the laws, rules, and regulations of any governmental agency or body claiming jurisdiction over the property. This means the tenant will have to obtain all applicable zoning approvals, permits, and licenses. Furthermore, the landlord will have to be reimbursed by the tenant for any expense incurred by the landlord to correct or remove any unacceptable work (see Chapter 17).

6. The tenant will also have to reimburse the landlord for any landlord-incurred expenses related to the use of the premises by the tenant's contractors. This will include delays of other construction work, cleanup or removal of trash not properly completed by the tenant's contractor, and any building operations or systems used by the tenant's contractor above those supplied for normal building operations (e.g., after-hours or overtime use of elevators or the HVAC).

7. The tenant's contractors will have limited access to the building or the premises before the lease commencement date or the completion of certain building operations and systems.

Unless provided for elsewhere or in the workletter, the tenant has no right of access to the building or the premises before the lease commencement date. Although it is rarely done, the landlord can prohibit a tenant from having access before the actual lease commencement date. However, because of practical and market needs, landlords do allow early entry subject to whatever rules, regulations, and conditions the landlord feels are appropriate to protect his or her interest or what the landlord can get away with. Typically, such regulations include hold-harmless liability waivers by both the tenant and contractors for any damage, destruction, or loss of work, materials, or tools; the requirement that everyone abide by the landlord's safety and construction rules and regulations; and the requirement that the landlord be notified of and approve all contractors entering the building and premises and all material deliveries.

8. If the landlord can get away with it, the tenant will be required to pay a minimum specified rent for early access to the premises and all of the building's mechanical and electrical operations and systems. In lieu of a minimum rent or sometimes in addition to it, the landlord may try to exact a service fee of some percentage (e.g., 5 percent) of the tenant's construction costs and related expenses as payment for the landlord's coordination of the tenant's construction work in the building.

9. The tenant will be responsible for all costs and related expenses (including permits, fees, and licenses) for any design revisions or construction changes to the base building structural elements or mechanical, electrical, and plumbing operations and systems or any plans, specifications, or construction documents as a result of the tenant's construction work.

10. The tenant will be responsible for all costs and related expenses incurred by the landlord for any design revisions or construction changes affecting the landlord's work on the tenant's space or any plans, specifications, or construction documents as a result of any tenant actions or decisions. In addition, any delays incurred in the completion of the tenant's space under the

tenant's revised or changed plans shall be chargeable to the tenant and will not affect the estimated construction completion date or the lease commencement date as set by the landlord.

Construction Work by the Landlord and the Building Standard

Depending on the landlord's concession package to the tenant and whether the tenant engages professionals to perform the required space construction, the landlord can become involved in the tenant's construction processes in many ways and many degrees, from performing all of the tenant's construction to performing none. There are two other options as well: (1) The landlord could be responsible for the structural work of the base building and for the mechanical, plumbing, and electrical operations and systems that will be used in the tenant's premises; (2) the landlord could construct all standard building items incorporated within the tenant's construction documents.

What Is a Building Standard?

Building standard refers to the construction materials, work, and finish items that a landlord offers tenants as part of the concession package for leasing space in a given building. Building standard items are detailed and listed in a separate building standard workletter or work allowance that is incorporated into the lease document.

The typical building standard workletter is supposed to be capable of providing a bare-bones office environment for a standard tenant. The basic standard provides painted walls, doors, lights, electrical switches and outlets, and floor covering.

The basic institutional look achieved under a building standard workletter is not an acceptable environment for the majority of tenants, whose basic office equipment will include copy machines, computers, and specialized telecommunication devices (e.g., facsimile machines). Some of these machines require a high-voltage outlet or possibly a dedicated electrical outlet or circuit to reduce electrical interference from other machines and equipment. However, the building standard workletter provides only standard electrical outlets; anything else is considered extra and costs the tenant an additional fee. Similarly, any tenant-preferred environmental enhancements, such as plush pile rugs, bookcases, wall coverings, or special paint or paint colors, are considered extra items for the tenant—and they are usually expensive.

What Is Provided?

There are no standards for what a landlord will provide in the workletter. Because no two landlords will provide the same standard items, the tenant's first problem is trying to compare leasing transactions in two different buildings to establish a value for each building's workletter. A landlord will be happy to provide a dollar-per-square-foot estimate for the value of the materials and work being provided. However, no two landlords will use the same basis for evaluating labor and materials. To complicate matters, the quality of construction materials varies greatly.

The only reasonable way to establish the value of a workletter is to consult an independent architect, space planner, or other qualified individual. Architects can evaluate a workletter according to the quantities of materials to be received based on the tenant's space plans and standardized labor costs. They can also evaluate the quality of the materials provided on the basis of land-lord-supplied manufacturer and item numbers. In this way the architect or space planner can provide a tenant with a dollar-per-square-foot estimate of the tenant's exact needs, as specified in the workletter.

The building standard workletter lists the type of materials that will be provided for constructing the space, as well as some basis for the amount that will be provided. For example:

- One linear foot of interior partition to be provided for each x sq ft of (rentable/usable) area (an actual workletter will specify the type of wall to be built, for example, "Interior partitions shall be constructed of ½″ gypsum wallboard, floor to ceiling, taped and spackled and mounted on 2½″ metal studs")

- One interior door for each x sq ft of (rentable/usable) area (with description)

- One single-pole light switch for each x sq ft of (rentable/usable) area

- One 120-volt duplex wall receptacle outlet for each x sq ft of (rentable/usable) area

- One standard wall-mounted telephone outlet for each x sq ft of (rentable/usable) area

For some standard items, the landlord may provide an allowance for an alternative dollar amount per square foot in lieu of, or in conjunction with, a particular manufacturer's items. This is usually done for floor covering. A landlord will indicate what basic covering will be provided at no charge or will specify that the tenant can use the alternative dollar-per-square-foot allowance toward the purchase of the floor covering of his or her choice.

How Is It Counted?

As mentioned earlier, the various standard construction materials and work are based on the amount of square feet the tenant will lease. However, the tenant must watch out for the wording concerning the kind of square feet used—rentable or usable. The landlord prefers usable square feet because that is the actual space the tenant will need to construct and use for business operations. But in the tenant's view the basis should be nothing less than the one the rent is calculated on. That is, any square-foot-based product or service to be received by the tenant in the lease should be specified in terms of rentable square feet.

Another important and negotiable area is that concerning the quantities of building materials a tenant receives; they are related to the basis amount. For example, the tenant may receive one electrical outlet per x rentable square feet. The x square feet is the basis amount.

(Note: All amounts and quantities used will be calculated on $1 or $10 psf amounts and in multiples of 10 or 100 sq ft. This creates a standardized dollar and size multiplier the reader can use and increase to meet specific requirements. For example, if the reader's typical office space is 200 sq ft, then a 100-sq-ft example need only be multiplied by 2. The reader is cautioned that when there are both dollar and square-foot standardized multipliers in an example, both must be increased by the same amount if the multiple is to accurately reflect the increase.)

The basis amount for the quantity to be received can have important cost implications for the tenant. Consider a divided space or employee office that measures 100 sq ft. If the standard allowance for quantity is one outlet per 100 sq ft, the tenant is allowed one outlet for the 100-sq-ft space. But what if this area needs a lot of electrical equipment, and two electrical outlets are required? The tenant can either hope that the extra outlets will be available from other areas that will not need outlets (highly unlikely) or pay for the extra. If the size of the divided space is doubled (200 sq ft) and the standard allowance remains the same, the problem is compounded.

How sacred is the standard allowance? Not very. The tenant must remember that this is a concession used by landlords to attract tenants and thus must be equal to or better than what the competition in the marketplace offers. Changing the basis amount to reflect one outlet per 50 or 75 sq ft increases the building standard quantity.

Whether the specified building standard allowance is based on rentable or usable square feet will affect the value of the allowance to the tenant. If a workletter is valued at a total of $10 psf, the dollar difference between rentable and usable square feet is significant. A space of 10,000 rentable sq ft in a building with a 15 percent core space or common area factor nets 8696 usable sq ft to the tenant. At $10 psf, the cost of constructing a space can range from $86,960 to $100,000—a difference of $13,040. This is a significant difference in what can be built to meet the tenant's needs.

Similarly, if the standard allowance is 1 linear ft of interior partition per 100 sq ft of space, the difference between the use of a rentable versus usable square-foot standard is 1000 linear ft of partition versus 870 linear ft. Again, this is a significant difference, depending on how heavily a tenant divides a space, using walls.

Building Standard Value
Versus Real Value

When a building standard allowance is expressed in dollars, the tenant must determine whether the value expressed is realistic. For example, a floor covering allowance of $1 psf in lieu of the stated building standard material is worth $9 per yard for a carpet (or other) floor covering. Is this a realistic amount for the tenant to purchase his or her choice of carpeting and have it installed? The typical answer is "Of course not!"

Determining the value of standard allowance items is important. What happens to any item that the tenant does not use? Does the tenant get a credit? If so, how much?

What if the tenant makes a substitution? What is it worth? Can the tenant swap a door for lights or for more walls?

The landlord may respond to questions about the credit value of allowance items with a combination of arm waving, double-talk, and hocus-pocus. The best way to find out the value is to look at specific items. For example, how much would it cost to install one electrical outlet if the tenant were to pay for it? Let's say it would cost $10. Now, how much credit would the tenant get for not using any of the building standard items (in this case, one electrical outlet), either in the form of a cash credit or a substitute? A typical response, using the $10 price, would be a $5 per outlet credit. What happened to the other $5? The basic answer is that it would cost $10 to install an electrical outlet, but if the outlet were not installed, there would be no labor charge, so the value of the outlet—the materials alone—would be only $5. In the landlord's view, the value of the savings lies only in the material not bought. If some standard material (such as doors and lights) has been bought, the credit savings is calculated as the resale or reuse value of the now unneeded materials.

A landlord might offer some other credit substitution explanation. It does not matter whether the explanation actually makes any sense—only that a tenant accepts it.

Does It Say What It Means?

Because there are no standards for the workletter, the description of what is actually being provided is often open to interpretation, just as it is with the concept of materials credit. That is, a building standard means exactly what the landlord wants it to mean.

Even more frustrating to a tenant is the fact that what is perfectly obvious to some is not necessarily obvious to others. Vague terminology is the culprit here. The most overused word in workletters is *adequate*. But what is an "adequate" amount of light or air or doors? No two people, much less the tenant and the landlord, will agree on what an "adequate" amount of anything is.

The most overused statement in workletters is "in accordance with the base building plans and specifications." This means that at some time someone drew up a floor plan showing the way the space on a floor might be divided up and used. Then a base building standard was developed for the placing of lighting fixtures for this imaginary use of the space, for HVAC ducts and outlets, and even for fire safety devices such as sprinklers and exit signs. Now along comes a tenant who designs the space quite differently. What happens if the tenant's light placement differs from the landlord's base building light placement? Does the tenant have to pay for relocating all the light fixtures, even though they were never placed in the first place? Or does the tenant only get the number of originally estimated light fixtures and have to pay for any extra ones that the tenant feels are absolutely necessary to provide adequate light for the work spaces?

There are hundreds of building standard items, big and small, and they will frustrate a tenant because they will seem altogether illogical. It is up to the tenant's architect to warn the tenant about all the problem areas in a building standard workletter (often a PREB can help, as he or she will know what happened to other tenants leasing space from a particular landlord). Here are some of the more common problems:

1. The amount of illumination to be provided has not been spelled out. As tenants know, different work spaces need different types and intensity of lighting. Artists need more light and different kinds and amounts of light than personnel entering computer data. An architect or lighting expert establishes illumination levels for different work areas at the level of the work surface.

The illumination level is the kind of standard the tenant will want to include in a workletter. On the other hand, the landlord will want to include a standard that specifies the quantity of a particular type of lighting fixture rather than have to meet some illumination level.

2. The amount of HVAC that will be provided is not clear. As every tenant quickly finds out, ventilation and air temperature are the most difficult items to control to meet the needs of employees. It can be very expensive to change HVAC building standards. The tenant must be sure that what is provided in this area is satisfactory and that the quantity of the various controls, duct work, and air outlets will meet the tenant's needs and be located in the work spaces as determined by the tenant, not be an imaginary "base building standard."

3. Electrical specifications are incomplete or inaccurate. The usual electrical specifications are for standard outlets and standard wall switches. Thought is seldom given to how people use these basic items or how much electrical power will be needed.

If a space is to have a long corridor with exit doors at either end and it should be possible to turn the light off at either doorway, is that a standard electrical switch? Of course not!

If the cleaning and janitorial staff need to have a hallway and corridor electrical outlet for their equipment (e.g., vacuum cleaners), who is responsible for having these outlets installed?

How many electrical outlets will be placed on one circuit, and at what amperage or power level? Can the electrical outlets only be used by normal business machines and equipment, and can all the outlets be used at the same time? It is very frustrating to have to shut off two or three computers because someone turns on a coffee maker.

What is the landlord's definition of *nonstandard business machines and equipment*? And how much power is available for the given space? Many normal heavy-duty business machines require 220 to 250 volts, whereas what the landlord considers normal may be 120 volts. Although 220 volts will be available from most electrical circuit panels serving a space, it will be limited. It is expensive to provide additional electrical circuits and panel boxes.

4. The building standard may not be required to meet fire safety codes for a tenant's premises. This is a particularly annoying point for most tenants. Rarely does a building standard even

bother to address the fire safety codes the tenant will need to observe when occupying the premises. At best, the standard workletter may indicate fire safety materials as provided in the base building plans and specifications.

Local building codes and ordinances will require a certain
number of fire exits for the number of people who will be working on the premises and for the size and complexity of the construction.

What does the building standard workletter supply? Unless it
clearly specifies that it will supply everything necessary to meet all
the codes for the space as designed and constructed by the tenant, the tenant will end up paying for whatever is needed to meet
the codes. It is expensive to put in emergency lighting systems in
the event of electrical power failure. It is expensive to relocate or
add sprinkler heads for out-of-the-way closets, work areas, or
kitchens. It is expensive to add fire and smoke detectors that must
be wired into a central control system. It is expensive to add signs
to mark emergency exits and evacuation routes. It is expensive to
add fire extinguishers at all exits, storage rooms, and other specially designed areas. (There will be local rules and regulations
for the number, type, and location of fire and safety equipment.)
The tenant is required to meet all the codes and ordinances necessary to occupy and conduct business from the premises. The
landlord is responsible only for meeting the codes and ordinances that apply to the building itself.

How Much Will It Cost?

The materials and labor needed to build out a tenant's space are
expensive. The tenant can reduce his or her contribution to the
buildout expenditure either by reducing his or her expectations
and thus reducing or eliminating the quantity or quality of what is
constructed or by getting the landlord to pay for all or some of
the work. Obviously, the building standard workletter is the first
step in getting the landlord to bear the costs of the tenant's construction of space. However, the value of the building standard
allowance is extremely limited, able to provide only barely ade-

quate and minimal construction quantity and quality, and open to the whims of the landlord where interpretation is concerned.

The next stage for transferring additional expenses from the tenant to the landlord is a landlord concession of an unlimited building standard workletter. As was shown in Chapter 9, although *unlimited* sounds good, only the bare necessities for constructing a tenant's space are being offered—but more of them. The unlimited building standard removes the limits to the tenant's use of any of the listed standard materials and construction work. This does help. It allows for extra electrical outlets, lights, walls, and doors that a tenant might need, without any cost to the tenant. But what about other standard enhancements, such as high-voltage electrical outlets, dedicated electrical outlets, half-high partitions, upgraded wall covering (e.g., wood paneling, wallpaper), upgraded doors and hardware, upgraded floor covering, glass walls, and special plumbing and fixtures for executive washrooms, kitchens, and exercise or sauna rooms? None of these last areas is covered by a building standard workletter. The tenant needs to be careful that "unlimited" means truly that and not some hidden quantity.

Above-Building-Standard Allowance

The above-building-standard allowance, or a dollar allowance over the building standard workletter, is a landlord concession typically expressed in dollars per square foot (e.g., $10 psf, $20 psf).

The concept is simple. Depending on the tenant-landlord negotiations, the tenant will receive from the landlord a dollar credit against any tenant-caused buildout expenses incurred by the landlord and for which the tenant owes the landlord, a dollar credit against future rent or additional rent as on offset for any tenant-incurred expenses related to building out the tenant's space, or a check from the landlord in the amount of the dollar credit, which the tenant will be expected to apply against any incurred related buildout expenses (although the tenant can do whatever he or she wants to do with it). (For additional information, see Chapter 9.)

The above-building-standard allowance supposedly pays for all the tenant buildout enhancements not covered in the building standard workletter. Depending on how realistic the dollar allowance is, it does perform its intended purpose, which is to transfer some or all of the costs and expenses related to building out a space from the tenant to the landlord. Here, again, the tenant must be sure that the per-square-foot basis for computing the dollar allowance is based on rentable, not usable, square feet.

Tenant Buildout-Construction Allowance

The tenant buildout-construction allowance is simply a blending of a building standard workletter and an above-building-standard allowance into one landlord concession item. The landlord offers a per-square-foot dollar allowance to the tenant for all the buildout that is required (the tenant must be sure the basis is rentable, not usable, square feet). The allowance can be in the form of cash or a credit, depending on who actually purchases the materials and does the construction work (with this allowance, the landlord will often require that the tenant use the landlord's contractor for the construction work).

A per-square-foot dollar allowance supposedly simplifies things. There is just one pot of money that the tenant gets to use for any and all of the materials and labor necessary to construct the space, without any concern for whether a particular item, such as an electrical outlet, was standard or cost extra.

The most frequent problem with this alternative is that the tenant and landlord fail to have a clear understanding of what buildout or construction work is to be included under the allowance. The fault lies with the base building structural, mechanical, plumbing, and electrical operations and systems (the conduit, pipes, connectors, ducts, wires, diffusers, dampers, hangers, hooks, machinery, and equipment) that are normally found in the ceiling, walls, and floor of a completed space.

The tenant must ascertain the starting point of the space from which he or she will be required to pay for the buildout or construction, since it will have a direct bearing on the amount of dollar allowance needed. The most basic possible starting point is a building shell, also known as slab-to-slab responsibility. Here, the tenant starts with an empty space. There is nothing there. It is up to the tenant to pay (out of the allowance) for all of the base building systems that will have to be installed. This is usually done through the landlord's contractor in order to maintain building consistency and system integrity. When this is the situation, the tenants must be doubly sure that the per-square-foot dollar allowance offered will be enough to cover not only the base building work, but everything that is needed (in most cases it will not be).

Except for extremely large space users or those tenants requiring specialized environmental operating systems, a tenant is better off having the landlord responsible for all the base building operating systems.

Turnkey Buildout

Theoretically, turnkey buildout transfers all buildout or construction costs for a tenant's space from the tenant to the landlord. In its purest sense, turnkey means that when a tenant turns his or her key in the front door on move-in day, the premises will contain everything needed, ready and waiting, at no cost to the tenant. Because of the potential prohibitive cost to a landlord (e.g., a tenant might want solid brass door hardware, built-in wood bookcases everywhere, marble floors, and wood paneling), the term *turnkey buildout* must be clearly defined by the tenant and the landlord during negotiations.

The two most common meanings for turnkey buildout today are:

- An unlimited building standard workletter allowance
- The tenant's buildout requirements that will be at the landlord's expense

Unreasonable Fees

Without knowing it, the majority of tenants who pay for some aspect of the buildout or construction of their space are paying too much. They are being overcharged by the landlord. The tenant needs to be sure that any fees he or she is to pay for construction material or labor are clearly spelled out in a work agreement. The amount and nature of these fees are both negotiable items. A tenant who ignores these fees is virtually assured of paying more and receiving less.

Landlords and their contractors usually have strong business ties and relationships. Landlords are relatively large users of construction materials and labor and thus are valued clients. Over time, close working relationships develop between landlords and contractors. As a result, a landlord can usually buy a contractor's services at discount prices.

It is not unreasonable (from a landlord's perspective) for a landlord to make a little money, or profit, from being the middle person and facilitating the relationship and work between the tenant and the contractor. The landlord can monetarily benefit in a number of ways:

1. A landlord may hire a contractor to construct a building on the understanding that this will be the contractor of choice for the majority of tenant buildout or construction work. For this "right," the contractor will typically offer a low bid for the building work on the understanding that the landlord will "make it up" on the tenant-paid work.

2. The landlord's building contractor will be the contractor of choice for all tenant work, whether paid for by the landlord or by the tenant. The landlord and contractor then work out a monetary relationship, such as special landlord discounts or fee rebates to the landlord that pay the landlord back for choosing and using the contractor.

Depending on the total building financial package, even when landlords are paying for the tenant's work, they may still be getting special discounts or fee rebates from the contractor. A fairly typical approach is to show the total charged cost for the tenant's work on the books and thus draw down construction money or build up the total building value for permanent financing purposes. The fee rebate belongs to the landlord, of course.

3. The landlord's contractor is permitted to charge extra or higher-than-normal fees for the work done. The landlord and contractor split the overpayment.

4. The contractor adds an additional markup that goes directly back to the landlord for the goodwill of the relationship.

5. The landlord imposes an additional fee for supervision, beyond the contractor's charges, whether or not any other rebate is in effect.

6. The tenant pays the full original invoice price. However, the landlord receives a bulk purchaser's discount for materials and labor from the contractor. The landlord gets to keep the difference.

This last item seems clever because the tenant can be made to feel good. As an attempt to help the tenant save money, the PREB admonishes that the tenant pay only for work and materials from the contractor's invoice to the landlord. The tenant pays from the contractor's invoice and therefore knows that he or she was not charged a landlord markup—or so it seems.

The Great Dollars Giveaway

When a tenant puts all the possible combinations together, the total cost to the tenant, or the lack of actual work received, can be significant.

A contractor starts off with the basic costs for materials and labor. Supposedly these are at contractor cost prices; the contractor will mark them up to obtain a fee and profit. The tenant should realize that there may be similar contractor-supplier relationships offering various discounts on material and labor or fee arrangements to the contractor.

How much should or will the contractor mark up the base prices? The answer depends on regional practices, competition, and market and economic considerations. In general, the markups a contractor would like to get are overhead, general conditions, and profit. Overhead is the contractor's fee for overseeing the work, making sure everything is completed properly, paying the bills, and providing general administrative services, with a little extra thrown in for whatever is considered reasonable—or whatever the contractor can get. The general conditions fee is supposed to cover miscellaneous materials, labor, and services that are not otherwise directly charged for. These may entail more difficult than anticipated cleanup conditions or trash removal, the wearing out of a broom during cleaning, or the use of trash bags. Profit is just that—profit margin for the contractor.

On top of these contractor charges, a landlord will often impose his or her own additional fee, generally classified under "landlord supervision and coordination."

If being charged all these fees were not enough, all these fees are compounded against each other rather than being applied against a standard base amount. Using a basic 10 percent amount for each fee structure and considering a standard multiplier amount of $10,000, the excess tenant costs are easily computed as follows:

	Compounding effects ($)	Applied against standard base ($)
Standardized base amount	10,000	10,000
Overhead (10 percent)	1,000	1,000
Subtotal	11,000	11,000
General conditions (10 percent)	1,100	1,000
Subtotal	12,100	12,000
Profit (10 percent)	1,210	1,000
Subtotal	13,310	13,000
Landlord supervision (10 percent)	1,331	1,000
Total	14,641	14,000

By compounding the fees, an additional $640 (4 percent) is added to the total for absolutely no practical reason. The results can be analyzed in two ways. On the one hand, the tenant received $10,000 worth of construction but had to pay $14,640 for it. On the other hand, the tenant paid $14,640 for the buildout or construction of his or her space but got only $10,000 worth of materials and labor.

The tenant must be sure that there is a provision in either the lease or the workletter specifying exactly what fees will be charged, the percentage of each of the permitted fees, and how the fees will be applied to the base buildout or construction costs.

It is impossible to state what fees are the proper ones or what the right percentage for each fee should be. However, fee structure percentages tend to be in the range of 5 to 10 percent, applied against a base amount only (i.e., with no compounding), with a maximum of two fee structures being charged. This means the percentage increase over the base buildout or construction costs will range from 10 to 20 percent.

In the example above, this will amount to a minimum saving of $2000 on each $10,000 of base cost. Better yet, rather than getting only $10,000 worth of buildout or construction for $14,000, the tenant can now have between $12,700 and $11,700 worth of work for the same $14,000. For a user of 50,000 sq ft of space, the amount of additional space enhancements available would be five times greater, or approximately $60,000 worth of such items.

Comparing What Is Offered

As the reader has by now determined, it is virtually impossible to accurately compare the value of buildout or construction packages between different landlords and buildings. There is no way to accurately assess what will be constructed, given the fact that different landlords have different concepts of building standard construction materials and labor. Nor is there any way to make simple comparisons between the per-square-foot dollar allowance offered by different landlords. To make matters worse, the total costs for doing essentially the same work will be different, depending on the contractor's markup to a particular landlord.

However, all of the pertinent information can be correlated and a calculation made to establish a reasonable per-square-foot dollar value being offered by a particular landlord. All it takes is a professional—in this case, an architect, a space planner, or a construction consultant. A tenant should not expect a PREB to be able to compute these values properly or accurately. Nor should a PREB even try to do so; it would be a disservice to the tenant. From reasonable estimates of the landlord's buildout or construction concession package, as well as the landlord's total concession and inducements package, a true comparison can be made between landlords and buildings.

Payment

After taking into account all the building standard items and the above-building-standard allowance; after reviewing construction plans and specifications and the related costs and contractor's pricing; after reevaluating the need for kitchens, executive washrooms, marble floors, built-in bookcases, rosewood wall paneling, glass doors and partitions, private interior stairways, brass hardware, special lighting fixtures, and all the other special touches that create the aura of success and prestige; after getting the landlord to pay for as much of the space enhancements as is possible, there will often remain some cost the tenant will be responsible for.

In the business world, the normal practice is to pay for goods and services when, or some reasonable time after, they are received. In the buildout or construction of tenant space, this practice does not prevail. For a host of reasons, landlords require that tenants pay up front, before actually receiving any benefit from the work done. The landlord can request advance payment in various ways. To avoid any misunderstanding, the landlord will include a provision in a lease or a workletter specifying exactly how much and when tenant payments are due.

Although the landlord would like all of the tenant's payment as soon as possible, the usual practice is to break the payment down into two or three parts. This way, the tenant sees, or believes, that construction is progressing as expected and the established timetable is being met.

The landlord will require an initial payment at the time the tenant submits final plans and specifications or at the time the tenant approves final buildout or construction costs and pricing, but in no event later then the start of the buildout or construction or the ordering of the materials and goods for which the tenant is responsible.

The normal practice is to accept an initial 50 percent of the tenant amount due, with the remaining 50 percent due when the work is half completed. There are various alternatives, including one-third at the start, one-third at the halfway point, and the last third due just before the tenant takes possession; in the same vein, 35 percent can be due at the start, with 35 percent due at the halfway point and 30 percent due before occupancy.

Why Payment Up Front?

There are numerous reasons why a landlord will want payment up front. First and foremost, the creed of the building landlord, developer, or owner is to always use someone else's money whenever possible. Although these entrepreneurs do take some big risks and put up much of their own money, it is not until a project fails that everyone finds out that most of the money and risk were someone else's. Because each project is maintained as an independent entity, except in severe market and economic downturns, the majority of landlords, developers, and owners are isolated from huge losses when one or two projects fail. A friend once told me, "If you borrow one hundred thousand dollars from a bank for a project, and the project fails, you're in trouble. On the other hand, if you borrow ten million dollars from the bank for a project and the project fails, the bank is in trouble."

- As a nonpractical reason for asking for the money up front, the landlord wants to be sure the tenant is truly committed to his or her plans and specifications. All too often, tenants have been known to have a change of heart and decide that something that sounded great is really beyond what they can afford. The landlord does not want to get stuck holding the bag—in this case, the goods and services. Except for use in a particular tenant's space, the landlord has no need or use for special-order items such as marble sinks, cabinetry work, or glass room dividers.

- The landlord also wants the money up front because of the nature of the workletter. As mentioned earlier, the workletter is really a construction contract between the tenant and landlord. Although it is included in the lease, it is not the same as the other lease clauses. Typically, everything in the lease document, except for the workletter, is in effect throughout the term of the lease. But some areas can only be used at certain, later times (e.g., lease renewal rights). The workletter requires that work be completed before occupancy and usually helps define the lease commencement date.

If a dispute occurred between the landlord and the tenant, for example, over the quality of work or material, the tenant could, in the normal, time-honored business tradition, withhold payment. The landlord's recourse for payment would not be through the lease document. Even a tenant who has moved in and is paying rent might not be in default of the lease in not paying for the landlord's goods and services prior to the lease commencement date. The dispute would need to be settled by the landlord and the tenant, in or out of court, just as any other business dispute would be settled.

The tenant-preferred alternative for paying the landlord is to be sure the final payment due is not made until the tenant (as well as the tenant's architect, if applicable) has thoroughly examined the work and finds it acceptable. The biggest difficulty here can arise over special work requested by the tenant that is not necessary for occupancy and yet remains incomplete (e.g., an executive washroom or employee exercise room). The lease commencement date will begin. The tenant can move in. However, the tenant should not make a final payment until all the work is completed, even if it is done after the tenant has occupied the space. The tenant must also make sure that any buildout or construction money owed to the landlord for construction is kept separate from the money owed under the lease document.

Work Acceptance—
Possession or Occupancy

The acceptance of the buildout or construction work and subsequent possession or occupancy of the space by the tenant often proves to be a catch-22 proposition to a tenant.

Depending on the situation, when the landlord's basic work is completed so that the premises are in the condition specified in the workletter, whether actually ready for tenant's occupancy or not, the tenant will be required to take possession, and the lease commencement date will be established. Therefore, for example, when a tenant hires his or her own contractor to do the finishing work on the premises, all the landlord may be obligated to deliver is a bare building shell or a concrete slab-to-slab emptiness. Even when the landlord is doing all the finish work, the premises will typically only need to be in occupiable condition. That is, the enhanced work may be incomplete (built-in bookcases or the kitchen may be missing), but as long as the basic business needs are met, such as walls, windows, HVAC, electricity, and the telephone, the premises are ready for business operations.

The tenant may choose not to occupy the premises. But the tenant may have little or no choice in having possession and thus a lease commencement date.

When Are Premises Deemed to Be Ready?

The landlord and tenant (or their representatives) will jointly inspect the premises to determine whether they are ready. A checklist of incomplete or unacceptable items will be prepared (the punch list—see Chapter 5, pages 57–59). However, if the premises are deemed to be in an occupiable condition so that business operations can commence, or if the tenant's contractors or tradespersons can enter and install equipment and special finishes, the premises are considered to be in the possession of the tenant. Unless the items on the punch list are considered a significant impairment to possession or occupancy, they will be completed as soon as possible.

Who Decides Readiness?

The landlord's preferred—and usually only acceptable—provision calls on the landlord's architect to evaluate the punch list and determine whether the premises are ready for possession or occupancy. The tenant should request that the decision be acceptable to both the landlord's and the tenant's architects. Any disagreement would require landlord and tenant negotiation and agreement. In the event of a severe disagreement, it would also be possible for the two to hire a third-party architect to make a final decision that would be binding on both the landlord and the tenant.

However, nobody likes disputes. Nobody wins with acrimony and arguments. The best course for both landlord and tenant is to have regular progress meetings and on-premises reviews to examine and evaluate the ongoing buildout or construction work.

Landlords don't like this process. There is, of course, the question of liability and insurance when people are walking around a construction site. There is also the annoyance of the tenant construction amateur, who does not fully understand what is going on and is constantly asking questions, often silly ones at that. In addition, construction is not always very neat, and some strange-looking assemblies wind up hidden behind walls. These have absolutely no effect on the look and usefulness of the finished product, but they may upset the sensibilities of a tenant looking for perfection.

However, the landlord should recognize that this buildout or construction period is an important element to a tenant's taking possession of the premises. It works to the landlord's advantage to get the tenant into the space as quickly as possible. Although it is annoying and time-consuming, educating the tenant in construction techniques and processes provides a fantastic opportunity to build a trusting rather than an adversarial relationship; in addition, the tenant begins to feel the pride of "ownership." The ongoing visitation process works best for both the landlord and the tenant.

Final Premises Inspection

One additional tenant-preferred option is to have two final walkthrough inspections 10 to 30 or more days apart (the larger the space or the greater the amount of work done, the longer the time should be between the two inspections). The first walkthrough and inspection would prepare a full punch list of incomplete and unacceptable items. This walkthrough should be required by the tenant and should be done when the landlord believes the premises are almost ready for possession. But on no account would this walkthrough have any effect on readiness to possess.

During this preview inspection, the landlord is given a time frame (between 10 and 30 or more days) for fixing defects; the final inspection should produce at worst a punch list of minor incomplete and unacceptable items that would not interfere with the tenant's possession. To ensure that defects on the first punch list will be corrected between the two inspections, some quantitative specification should be included (e.g., at least 50 percent of the items on the initial preview inspection punch list must be satisfactorily completed by the second inspection of the premises, and not more than x percent additional or new defects may be added to the revised punch list). If there is no measurable improvement by the time of final inspection, a provision would permit a day-by-day delay until the measurable improvement specification has been met and the landlord can pronounce the premises ready for possession.

11
Renewals, Options, and First Rights

Landlords consider renewals, options, and first right of refusal to be of greater benefit to the tenant than to themselves. Depending on the wording of the lease provisions and on certain unpredictable factors such as market and economic conditions at the time the options or renewals were agreed to or when they are due, this view has some validity.

An option, renewal, or first right of refusal given to a tenant limits what a landlord can do with his or her property subject to the tenant's rights. For example, the landlord's ability to sell a property can be limited by a tenant's option to purchase the building or a first right of refusal. The ability to lease certain space in a building can be restricted by a tenant's right to expand or an option to renew a lease.

On the other hand, the landlord is freely giving these rights to the tenant. Although market or economic conditions may force a landlord to make these types of concessions in order to attract tenants, the right to give and the magnitude of the concessions are still the landlord's decision.

Because there is nothing standard about options, renewals, and first right of refusal, the tenant starts negotiating with a clean slate. The only limits are the creativity and negotiating skills of the tenant or the PREB.

Lease Renewals and Options to Extend the Lease

If any lease clause could be made simple, it would be a renewal or option to extend a lease. Both the landlord's and the tenant's needs can be met through a lease extension or renewal process. The tenant would be able to continue to occupy the premises and conduct business without interruption, while the landlord would continue to collect rent and have the premises occupied.

Technically, there is a significant difference between a lease renewal and an option to extend the lease. Under a true lease renewal, the lease would actually end on the expiration date and then renew itself in entirety, beginning again as it did on the original lease execution date. The option to extend a lease means that, subject to certain conditions, the lease remains in force or extends beyond the initially stated expiration date without any interruption or changes.

A technically correct renewal clause would repeat all of the landlord's original concessions, as originally specified. Therefore, theoretically, a tenant would, for example, have the right to have the premises reconstructed according to submitted plans and specifications and have initial rent abatement concessions repeated for the beginning of the "new" lease term. Even more interesting to contemplate, because of a renewal clause, a lease document that is renewed also has the same renewal clause. This, of course, could theoretically provide a tenant with perpetual possession or occupancy of the premises. However, a theoretically correct lease renewal is rarely the intention of either landlord or tenant.

Rather, in practice, the terms *lease renewal* and *option to extend the lease* have become synonymous. The intention is that the landlord and tenant agree that the tenant, subject to certain stated conditions, will have the right to extend the lease for some specified period of time beyond the stated expiration date of the original term of the lease. Exactly what those conditions are requires some tenant or PREB ingenuity or creativity. For the purpose of consistency, in this book the term *lease renewal or extension* will denote a single concept.

Both Landlord and Tenant Benefit

Logically, both tenants and landlords would prefer a lease renewal or extension, as there are benefits for both. The tenant's considerations would include the following:

- Relocating to new premises is, at the best of times, both costly and traumatic. Many tenants prefer renewing or extending a lease to moving to new premises.

- A lease renewal or extension protects an organization to some extent from uncontrolled future rent increases.

- The assurance that a lease can be renewed or extended provides some comfort regarding the tenant's investment in the premises. Many tenants have, over time, either upgraded their premises with items such as wall coverings, floor coverings, or special cabinetry or woodwork or made significant expenditures for special areas such as kitchens, executive washrooms, storage rooms, computer rooms, or conference rooms. To the tenant, this investment is an important and visible aspect of the current premises. Relocating to new premises would mean duplicating expenses in order to attain the same minimum comforts of the current space. (This perception tends to prevail even when the landlord at a different building offers a concession package that would provide equal or better premises at virtually no additional tenant cost.)

For the landlord, the granting of a lease renewal or extension depends on his or her expectations regarding future rentability, market conditions, and economic stability. As history teaches us, of course, market and economic conditions are impossible to predict. Nonetheless, the landlord will consider these and several other expectations:

- What will be a reasonable projection of rents for the general area, the particular property and building, and the specific premises at the end of the proposed initial lease term?

- What will the future market be like with respect to the number of tenants looking for space and the availability of space? How the landlord answers this question will affect the costs incurred in order to attract a new tenant if a current tenant does not renew or extend or a lease renewal or extension clause is not provided by the landlord. These costs will cover items such as advertising, marketing, brokerage fees, and the very expensive possibility that the premises will remain vacant for an unknown period of time.

- What additional costs and expenses will be associated with signing up a new tenant? Tenant signing costs include attorney fees for writing or creating a new lease, credit and reference checks, refurbishing or renovation expenses, special tenant alterations and improvements, rent abatement, and other necessary and competitive concessions or inducements.

- What additional qualitative factors are there to consider regarding an unknown tenant in comparison with the current tenant? What will be a new tenant's use of the premises? How intensely will the space be utilized or worn out? Will a new tenant be prompt in observing monetary obligations? How will a new tenant's business operation affect the stability of the building's operations? What type of employees, visitors, and clients will be associated with a new tenant?

Regardless of the specific lease clause negotiated between the landlord and the tenant, it is not until the time the renewal or extension is due that either party actually knows how much, or even if, it will be affected by this clause. Depending on the initial conditions and agreements, it is assumed that one party will do better, or at least feel more satisfied, if and when the renewal or extension occurs. For example, a provision that provides for a fixed formula rent increase for the renewal or extension term may benefit either party. If economic conditions are good, there is a tight market for space and the renewal or extension rent is less than other current market rents, so a fixed formula rent benefits the tenant. However, if there is an economic decline or an abundance of vacant space available, the fixed formula rent may benefit the landlord in that it may well be higher than what the space would otherwise bring if it were placed on the open market—if it could be leased at all.

What's Included

Because a lease renewal or extension clause is based on the ingenuity, creativity, and negotiating skills of the landlord and the tenant, it cannot be said to have any standard or normal components. There will undoubtedly be a lot of give-and-take in the negotiating between the landlord and tenant. Perhaps the most important word of caution to offer concerning these lease provisions is this: The language must be clear as to its intent.

Therefore, attention should focus on being specific and on providing exact definitions of the terms in the clause. Avoid vague phrasing such as "The tenant shall have the right to renew the lease." Such a sentence is virtually meaningless. It says nothing about the agreed-upon responsibilities or obligations associated with or conferred by "the right." Does "right to renew," moreover, allow the tenant the same lease, starting over again? If so, when? Whenever the tenant wants?

Restrictions

The tenant's first concern will be to find out whether there are restrictions that could affect the right to renew or extend the lease. The most common restrictions have to do with tenant default, the subletting of any portion of the premises, or the assignment of the lease to another party.

The default restrictions should be examined carefully to make sure that the only basis for not being able to renew or extend the lease would be a current, ongoing, or continuing tenant default. Even better from the tenant's perspective, defaults should be limited to monetary tenant defaults that are current or ongoing at the time of the renewal or extension. The tenant must not agree to a refusal to grant a renewal or an extension because of a tenant default in the past. The tenant must also avoid broad statements that provide for a renewal or extension as long as the tenant has met all of his or her obligations under the lease. Obviously, it is all too easy for a landlord who does not want to renew or extend a lease to dig up a long-forgotten and possibly minor default or some vague, obscure tenant responsibility or obligation that was never met. Although the tenant can sue for his or her rights, think of the time, the hassles, and the money that would be involved.

The tenant should resist any provision stating that the right to renew or extend will be terminated because of an assignment of the lease. The only exception might be a specific landlord objection. In general, however, if the tenant has the right to assign the lease or the landlord gives permission, everything in the lease should also transfer.

A restriction on a lease assignment can be a problem for the tenant whose business is failing and who has only a year or two left on the lease. The renewal or extension provision may be the only means for a tenant to get someone to take over the lease liability. It would also be a problem for a business that has merged with or been taken over by another firm, since a lease assignment would normally occur in such an instance.

In the landlord's view, this provision is necessary because the lease renewal or extension is given to the original tenant as a concession or because of some other special reason. Because such a provision is not normal and the original tenant will no longer be occupying the premises, it should not be transferable.

The restrictions regarding the subletting of any or all of the premises are slightly more complex. Landlords will usually argue that, to be able to renew or extend the lease, a tenant should be occupying all of the leased premises. It is a basic landlord precept that the landlord is in the business of leasing space; the tenant is in whatever business he or she is expert at and, by extension, should not expect to be subsidized or supported by the landlord by subleasing space in competition with the landlord. This concept originated when large, economically powerful space users would get excellent rents and then be able to sublease unneeded space immediately at a higher rent and thus make a profit that landlords saw as being at their expense. Alternatively, a tenant would purposely rent more space than needed, with the idea, depending on economic and market conditions, of leasing the excess and making some money. This practice is especially common among tenants whose business depends on the vagaries of government contracts, since the amount of space they need can change regularly, depending on the business environment. Of course, landlords will not mention the fact that usually, unless it is in their absolute best interests, they will not take back unneeded or unwanted tenant space without the tenant paying a penalty or being responsible for the full, original rent for the leased premises.

In any case, the tenant should follow the same guidelines for a subleasing restriction as for a lease assignment. That is, the landlord has made the economic and market decision to lease the premises at the stated rent to the tenant. To the extent that the tenant also has the right to sublease part (or all) of the premises, whether with or without prior landlord approval, the right to renew or extend the lease should be unaffected.

In our constantly changing economic environment, businesses are faced with many kinds of operational and monetary difficulties. The entrepreneur's goal is to survive, but to do so depends on having the maximum flexibility to make business decisions. Therefore, the ability to sublease unneeded or unwanted space is one option that a tenant needs to keep open.

The right to renew or extend a lease should not be lost because the tenant has sublet any space (assuming it is done properly and in accordance with other lease provisions). However, the tenant is, as a landlord says, *not* in the business of leasing space (with certain understandable exceptions, such as a temporary or small business office center). Therefore, a landlord will often want to include a sublease restriction regarding renewal or extension. The landlord will specify that if some percentage (such as 50 or 60 percent) of the leased space is sublet, the renewal or extension provision will be terminated.

Before accepting this landlord compromise, the tenant needs to be sure that there is a clearly specified time period for considering what percentage of the space is under sublease. That is, it is relevant only at the time that the renewal or extension is due whether the space is 50 percent or more under sublease; the concern should not be whether it was ever previously at or above that level.

In addition, the tenant should make sure not to lose the renewal or extension right if, for example, the space was ever offered back to the landlord and refused. Such a past offer should not permit the landlord, who may now see the chance for a profit that was not evident before, to override the rights of the tenant.

Number of Renewal Options and Length of Term for Each

The tenant will also want to know how many times a renewal or extension option will be available, and what length of lease term will each renewal or extension be limited to.

The basic landlord-oriented provision permits only one renewal or extension and typically for a time period equal to the original lease term. If the initial lease was for a long term, the renewal or extension will often be for one-half the original period (e.g., a five-year renewal for an original ten-year term).

It would be in the tenant's best interest to have the right, but not the obligation, to renew or extend a lease for two or preferably more time periods, with each being equal to the original lease term. Tenants should never be obligated to renew or extend the lease because changing business conditions may force them to relocate to larger or smaller premises. Under such circumstances, they will not want to lease more space than is necessary or have more than one office from which to conduct business.

Ideally, the tenant should have multiple renewal or extension options, each for a "reasonable" amount of time (e.g., four renewal or extension options, each for a five-year term). Depending on other lease provisions, this gives the tenant maximum flexibility and allows the lease to expire at the convenience the tenant.

Notice

Since the tenant will have the right but not the obligation to renew or extend a lease, there must be some provision for a notice of intent to give both the landlord and the tenant time to react. Depending on the needs and preferences of either the landlord or the tenant, these time frames will often be in conflict. There is no ideal notification time period. Often it depends on other related lease provisions. For example, if the renewal is based on a market rent rather than a formula rent, the landlord will want the tenant to provide notice of the intent not to renew early enough for the landlord to find a new tenant. Notice should not be so late that the tenant's options, such as finding other space, are limited, putting pressure on the tenant to accept a rent more to the landlord's preference. Since insufficient notice time can leave the landlord with vacant space or the task of finding a new tenant, however, the landlord will reasonably want notice time based on the amount of space involved as a percentage of the total space available in the building.

A tenant who has a fixed-formula rent for the renewal will prefer a notice date as late as possible so that he or she can go out and examine the market to see if a better transaction is available. Under a market rent clause, the best course of action for a tenant is to look at market conditions as early as possible (such as one or two years) before the lease expiration date. This will allow the tenant to engage in reasonable and unpressured rent negotiations with the landlord and still give the tenant enough time to seek new premises if it becomes necessary (if for no other reason than to force the landlord to negotiate competitively).

Both tenant and landlord should insist that the renewal or extension option notice be in writing. Furthermore, any details required for giving the notice should be spelled out in this provision. The ideal situation for the tenant is to have the required notice prepared in advance and appended to the lease document. This saves time and helps avoid any future misunderstandings, since the form of the renewal or extension notice is accepted in advance.

Whose responsibility is it to give advance notification or the actual notice of the due date for the renewal or extension? The landlord will argue that the tenant gets the benefits and therefore the tenant should give notice on time. If the tenant does not, too bad (unless of course, it is in the landlord's best interest to remind the tenant that the notice is due).

Depending on the length of the lease, a tenant is often at a disadvantage when it comes to notices or similar provisions in a lease. Often the individual who did the negotiating for the business, the one most familiar with the lease, will not be with the business when the notice dates become due. Because of the complexity of most leases, this provision is generally one of the last things the employee taking over this responsibility will bother to look at, if at all. Obviously, important dates can easily slip through the cracks.

The solution is simple but requires finesse by the tenant. The landlord has a staff or employs a management company whose job is to be thoroughly familiar with every lease document and tenant. Therefore, the landlord should bear some responsibility for notifying the tenant of various due or notification dates with enough advance notice to allow the tenant to meet his or her lease obligations.

The landlord may give many reasons why this is not possible and certainly not his or her responsibility, or the landlord may argue that such a responsibility would increase management costs or overhead, but the fact remains that the landlord is in the best position to provide notification. Landlords usually try to fall back on language indicating they will use their "best efforts" to notify (or remind) the tenant of vital or important dates. This position is acceptable to the tenant. If the landlord is later found not to have truly used his or her "best efforts," the landlord will have defaulted on that provision, and the tenant can argue that the appropriate tenant notice to renew or extend the lease, even if given extremely late, was valid.

The Terms of the Lease

When a lease is extended or renewed, what happens to all of its terms and conditions? The tenant would like to see as few changes as possible, perhaps only an increase in rent and a new expiration date. Surprisingly enough, these are often the only changes, usually because the PREB has neglected to pay attention to the terms. In fact, PREBs and attorneys have been known to leave out even specified rents or other renewal or extension terms.

The landlord is likely to go through the lease with a fine-tooth comb and provide detailed specifications as to what carries forward with a lease renewal or extension and what changes. The tenant, of course, must do the same thing. This means that every lease clause must be reexamined and alternative language provided for the renewal or extension period.

The tenant must see to it that any terms that are a function of, or related to, the original lease expiration date survive the original expiration date and are automatically extended to any new expiration date or an extended term. This is important, regardless of how obvious it seems; never think that it would be "ridiculous to assume otherwise" or that the matter is "too simple to worry about." It is better to avoid any possibility of a future misunderstanding. For example, if the alterations lease clause permits the tenant to remove certain items or make improvements before the expiration date, is this right automatically extended when there is a renewal? Seems obvious? Do not assume it is.

Important Clause Consideration

You, the tenant, must examine everything in the lease document. Better yet, make sure there is a "negative exception" providing for the automatic extension of every item in every lease clause. The negative exception provision will state that, unless otherwise specifically provided for, all terms, conditions, covenants, responsibilities, and obligations of both the landlord and the tenant are automatically extended to any adjusted or changed lease expiration date or extended lease term as the result of any renewal or extension of the lease.

Condition of the Premises

Virtually all premises suffer some wear and tear over the term of the lease. This is true not only for previously occupied space that was re-leased with minimal alterations or improvements but also for the newest buildings and those that provided improvements to a tenant's exact plans and specifications. Even when buildings or new premises start out with up-to-date features, it is not too long before they become tired looking and outmoded. Possibly except for their lower rents, they are no longer competitive with the newest and latest construction.

The alterations or improvements initially provided for in a lease are seldom completely repeated in a renewal or extension. However, some level of renovation and refurbishing should be offered. It depends on the size of the premises, economic and market conditions, and the original lease benefits, but at a minimum, a tenant should expect a thorough cleaning and new paint and floor covering, all the way up to a per-square-foot dollar allowance comparable (except for the construction portion) to the original allowance, increased and adjusted for inflation.

In addition, the tenant needs to look at the electrical, mechanical, and other building systems to determine whether high-quality services will be provided for the premises. Quantitative and qualitative standards must be specified for the building system operations and service levels that are to be provided for the premises.

Rental Rates

The deciding factor as to whether a tenant will renew or extend a lease is the rent. Tenants must evaluate their needs just as they did to determine whether the rent in the initial lease document was acceptable. Three general methods are used to establish renewal or extension rent.

Method 1. Whatever rent is in effect at the time of the renewal or extension is continued without interruption. This rent remains subject to any increases or escalations that also prevailed in the original lease. This is the best of all the alternatives as it provides an uninterrupted extension.

Why isn't this the alternative tenants prefer? Because it is possible that, as a result of carelessness or a poorly worded or understood rent escalation clause, the rent at the end of the initial lease expiration date is considerably higher than market rent.

Method 2. A fixed formula may be used to increase the rent over either the original base rent or the prevailing rent at the time of the renewal or extension. The fixed-formula concept is the method acceptable to both the landlord and the tenant for determining what the rent will be for a lease renewal or extension.

This concept can be applied in many ways:

- A fixed dollar amount that includes any annual increases or escalators can be added to the prevailing rent.

- The prevailing rent can be increased by a specified percentage.

- The rent increase can be based on an index that reflects the effects of inflation. The most common index used is one of the available CPIs. Even here there are alternatives: The increase in the CPI applied may be the one in effect from the lease commencement date to the lease expiration date, or the increase may be applied to the original base rent or to the prevailing rent, which may already include increases and escalations (see Chapter 6 for a description of rent escalators).

Method 3. The rent may be based on the market rent (what the premises, if vacant, in the then-current economic and market conditions, would otherwise rent for) at the time of the lease renewal or extension. Tenants are usually wary of a renewal or extension clause that is based on a market rent. The difficulty is defining market rent and establishing how it will be determined and by whom.

Market rent determined by the landlord obviously puts the tenant at the mercy of the landlord. Even if there is to be mutual agreement by the landlord and the tenant, there is usually no agreement on what the rent will be, only on the expectation that it will somehow be determined when it is needed.

However, a market rent renewal can be beneficial to a tenant, considering tangibles such as the improvements the tenant has made to the premises and intangibles such as the fact that the tenant's customers will identify the tenant with the building or area currently occupied. In these cases market rent is better than nothing, and under the right circumstances it can be quite fair (or, as mentioned earlier, even less than an excessively escalated original rent). The tenant needs only to provide some specific detail concerning the concept of market rent being applied, for example:

1. The market rent can be a maximum percentage or fixed dollar amount over the rent currently being paid. This gives at least some upside limit and, although minor, some protection to the tenant.

2. The timing of how and when the new rate will be determined can be spelled out. For example, after the tenant's written notification of intent to renew or extend, the landlord would have *x* number of days in which to provide a proposed market rent. The tenant would then have *y* number of days to agree to a fair market rent for the premises. If they are unable to agree, some specified third process would be used to determine the rent.

3. A specified third party could be asked to determine the market rent. To begin with, each party would choose and pay for an appropriate and experienced appraiser. If, after a certain period of time, the two appraisers could not agree, then the two appraisers would chose a third appraiser (or employ some alternative means of having one chosen) that both parties would pay for equally. The majority opinion of the three appraisers would rule; lacking a majority, the three appraisers' valuations would be averaged. (This is just the bare outline of how this option works; many specifics would have to be put into a lease provision.)

Whatever third-party method is used to determine market rent, both the landlord and the tenant must agree to be bound by the decision. Although there are good reasons for both parties to avoid being bound by the results, without such agreement the market rent determination will be a waste of time and money.

4. The tenant should make sure that the factors used in determining the market rent will be detailed, sufficient, and favorable to him or her. Some of the factors that should be included are the length of time for the renewal or extension; the size of the premises; the estimated vacancy period and lost income; costs and expenses not incurred, for example, the absence of designer or architect fees for tenant construction and no or limited brokerage fees; and savings attributable to a lease renewal or extension compared to a new tenant relocation, such as rent abatement, tenant alterations and improvements, a relocation allowance, and other concessions or inducements.

Another possibility that would offer the tenant an extra benefit—but would depend on economic and market conditions, as well as on the landlord's disposition at the time—would be to provide an either-or alternative to the market rent. This provision would state that the agreed-to rent would be the lesser of the determined market rent or one of the other alternatives for determining the rent (the one best meeting the tenant's needs). As an example, the agreed-to rent would be the lower of the market rent or the then-prevailing rent being paid escalated by a fixed percentage increase.

Rent Increases and Escalations

Just as a new base rent must be determined for a lease renewal or extension, so, too, must any rent increase or escalation provisions be appropriately adjusted. If the rent increases and escalators in the original lease were acceptable to both the landlord and tenant, there may be no reason to change the arrangement. However, the tenant must be sure that formulas, computations, indexes, and the starting base for calculations are appropriately adjusted to reflect both the adjusted lease renewal or extension and expiration dates. For example, a new base year would need to be specified for a proper CPI escalation calculation using the new starting rent.

Operating Expense Base, Passthroughs, and Taxes

The specifications for any original lease calculation will also have to be adjusted for expense passthroughs and real estate taxes. What is done here should mirror an original lease provision that continues to have landlord and tenant agreement.

As with the original rent (see Chapter 6), the concept of an operating expense base—a full-service lease, a net rent, or whatever basis is used—is still valid and should be adapted to the renewal or extension lease date and the renewal base rent.

The Right, but No Obligation

As general protection, the tenant should have the right but not the obligation to renew or extend the lease. However, when the tenant gives written notice to the landlord of the intent to renew or extend, is the tenant forced to renew? If everything regarding the renewal or extension is spelled out in the lease, both the landlord and tenant may want to include a lease provision calling on both parties to consummate the renewal or extension.

If any items require some final determination, as in the case of market rent, the tenant should try to get a one-way no-obligation provision. That is, if, in the opinion of the tenant, the final determined market rent does not reflect the proper value for the premises, the tenant will have no obligation to complete the renewal or extension transaction or will have the right to terminate it.

Option to Terminate and Landlord Takeback of Premises

Tenants seldom have the right to cancel or terminate a lease voluntarily. A tenant is normally responsible for a lease until it expires. However, other lease clauses often provide a tenant some outlets if business conditions become extremely unfavorable. In times of normal economic and market conditions, sublease and assignment clauses help tenants shed excess space and the associated costs.

There is always the possibility that tenants will just default on the lease and sneak away into the night, but then they will still be liable for the lease, and they will have added the landlord to their business problems. Of course, bankruptcy is another solution. But either of these solutions would put a black mark on the credit record of the business.

The tenant might negotiate for an option to terminate a lease or to have the landlord take back the premises, but he or she would have to present a strong case for the landlord to agree to such a provision. Many a landlord, when informed of what the tenant is facing, if also assured of being adequately reimbursed for his or her costs and expenses, may be more than willing to gamble on the tenant. Usually tenants requesting this type of provision fall into two broad categories.

The first includes those tenants starting a new venture, who, because they do not know whether they will succeed, want to be able to have some control over the loss that could occur, including being able to rid themselves of the lease liability. This category includes not only new start-up small businesses but also medium-sized businesses attempting a major expansion and large corporations starting new divisions or product lines.

The second category consists of businesses that are in the midst of an expansion or tremendous growth but have no idea of how far the business will expand. Such tenants would be wise to increase their space in increments. However, they may need the flexibility to continue expanding even if a cost would be incurred in getting rid of a lease for outgrown premises.

Depending on the landlord involved, the extent of his or her property holdings, and the tenant's intentions regarding staying in business, a tenant can often suggest an option that provides some mutual benefit. At a minimum, the provision should state that, subject to certain specified conditions (such as levels of business income), the landlord would take back the too-small or too-large premises on the proviso that the landlord would be able to provide either smaller or larger premises in the same or another building and the tenant would enter into a new, mutually agreeable lease.

Because an option to terminate or have the landlord take the space back is out of the ordinary, the landlord will control most of this provision. The tenant should therefore be prepared for the provision to include the following items:

1. A condition of no tenant default or the requirement that the tenant cure any defaults before lease termination is permitted.

2. Reimbursement to the landlord for any costs and expenses associated with the implementation of the lease. This provision will usually call for the return of any unrecovered costs and expenses by taking the total amount and amortizing it as equal monthly amounts over the original term of the lease. The tenant would owe the specified monthly amount (or amount to be provided by the landlord with the tenant's termination notice) times the number of months the tenant is canceling.

These costs and expenses include brokerage fees, space design or architect fees, and advertising and marketing costs.

3. Reimbursement on a similarly amortized basis of any costs and expenses associated with the tenant's occupancy. These costs

222

and expenses include alterations and improvements to the premises (done when the landlord is preparing the premises either because of the wear and tear of a vacating tenant or to satisfy the tenant's plans and specifications), licensing and permit fees, and any landlord-granted concessions or inducements.

A major expense the tenant might face is having to return rent abatement (in effect, having to pay the rent for an earlier "free-rent" period) for any period originally provided by the landlord. Obviously, the landlord will not be inclined to provide a 5-year lease, give 6 or 12 months of up-front rent abatement, and then let the tenant walk away from the lease after the first 12 months, without getting paid for the period of possession and occupancy.

4. With the landlord's agreement, and acceptable repayments, the mutual termination of responsibilities and obligations under the lease. This will be especially important to the landlord if the lease includes any renewal options, options to purchase, or right to expand the space.

Going Through the Back Door
for the Same Result

Another option to consider, one that is acceptable to most landlords, is the structuring of a landlord takeback provision so that it hinges on the sublease provision. Here, the tenant would be permitted to sublease 100 percent of the premises. He or she would be responsible for finding a subtenant and paying any associated costs for getting the space leased. The sublease document would be subject to landlord approval.

With all these conditions met, at the tenant's request, the landlord would then agree to take back the premises (as it would now continue to be leased and occupied) and relieve the tenant of any further lease responsibilities and obligations as long as the subtenant agrees to have the sublease assigned to the landlord.

Options and First Rights of
Refusal—They're Different

The main difference between an option and a first right of refusal is the degree of specific details. Consider an option to purchase property versus the first right of refusal to purchase property.

A good option to purchase will specify that at a certain time or within a certain time period the option holder can purchase the property at the price and conditions already specified in the option. A less preferred option would provide for a purchase price to be determined and would specify the method by which the price would be determined (in a manner similar to the determination of the market rent, discussed under Rental Rates, Method 3, page 217).

The general concept behind a first right of refusal is that if the property owner decides to sell (or the time period when the sale is to take place is specified), whatever written and bona fide offer to purchase is received, the holder of the right has the first right of refusal to buy the property by matching the price and conditions of the purchase offer.

The first right of refusal should not be confused with a right of first offer, where, continuing with the purchase example, at a time of the owner's choosing (or a specified time period), the owner offers the property for sale to the holder of the right. The main problem with this "right" is that unless specific details are given regarding the purchase price, the way it will be determined, and the purchase conditions, the property owner can ask any price and put on any conditions. If the holder of the right refuses the property, the owner is free to go out and find another purchaser, without any requirement that the price and conditions remain the same as those offered to the holder of the right. The holder of a right of first offer should always be sure to couple that right with a backup right to match any bona fide written purchase offer received after the initial refusal to buy at the owner's stated conditions. This, of course, is similar to the first right of refusal, but it must be made a separate provision so that the original right holder will have an opportunity to match an actual competitive market condition purchase offer rather than be shut out by an owner's unrealistic initial offer.

It is obvious that specific details are absolutely necessary in any clause pertaining to options or first rights. The more details, the more a right is in fact an option.

Whatever the terminology, the option or right holder must ensure that a provision specifies when the option or right may be invoked and further that the holder is not obligated to exercise the option or right.

Expansion Space Options

Many a tenant will prefer an option to expand into additional
space, thus avoiding the need for renting a space larger than immediately required—and having to worry about subleasing the
excess—so as to have the extra space available should it be
needed. This type of provision is for businesses that expect substantial growth.

This option is closely related to the renewal or extension of a
lease option and requires similar provisions:

- *Restrictions.* Can the option be invoked if the tenant is in default, has sublet most of the premises, or has assigned the lease?

- *Timing.* On what specific dates will the option be invocable?

- *Notice.* Who is required to give notice? How much notice is
  required?

- *Delivery.* When must the landlord deliver the premises to the
  tenant?

- *Number of options.* Is the option only available once, or will
  there be different dates for different amounts of space, with
  each covered as a separate or ongoing expansion option?

- *Terms.* Are all the basic terms of the lease specified? Are they
  to be the same as those in the original lease for the base
  premises? Or are additional negotiations required for each
  expansion space?

- *Rent.* Is the amount of rent for the expansion space specified?
  If not, how is it to be determined?

- *Condition of premises.* Will the expansion space be subject to
  any alterations, improvements, or construction allowance? Will
  the landlord provide any renovation or refurbishing of the
  space? Or is the expansion space to be taken on an as-is basis?

- *Amount of space.* What is the total amount of expansion space
  that will be made available to the tenant? Must it all be taken at
  once? If not, are there any minimum increments? Must all the
  expansion space be contiguous to the original base premises?

Except for its intent and the fact that it is slightly more complicated, the expansion space option is much like the renewal or

extension option. The big difference is how the landlord is affected. Depending on the strength of the option, the landlord may well be subjected to restrictions regarding how the expansion space for one tenant can be leased until needed by another tenant. The landlord may have to offer lower than market rates, additional concessions, and tenant inducements to attract a tenant to a premises with a lease term less than normal for a given area (for example, a three-year term when the norm is five or more years). Because of the short lease period, there may be no opportunity to provide special tenant alterations or improvements, and there may be only an outside chance that the tenant will be able to extend the lease or stay for a longer period in the space, regardless of what rent he or she is willing to pay.

In effect, the tenant with an expansion option has severely limited the control and alternatives available to a landlord; this will understandably be reflected in the price and conditions for the base premises and the expansion space.

It should be obvious to the tenant that the landlord will, to the extent he or she is able, avoid expansion options. The "true" option is usually based on market conditions and the economic leverage of the tenant. Otherwise, the landlord will provide an alternative to, or additional conditions on, an expansion option.

Space Availability and First Options

A tenant must avoid any expansion option that is conditioned on whether the space is in fact available. Here the option is invoked in an either-or situation. It can be invoked either on a certain date if the space is vacant or when the space becomes vacant, whichever is later.

Instead of an option, the landlord is more likely to offer the tenant a first right of refusal to lease space or, even worse, a first right of offer to lease space. As in the purchase example, a first right of refusal to lease space means that when space becomes available, the landlord will give the tenant the right to match the terms and conditions that another tenant might be willing to commit to. This situation is not ideal for either the landlord or the tenant. It prevents the landlord from closing the transaction with a potential tenant at the time desired (thus risking the loss of a tenant), and it may keep the current tenant from using badly needed space, as the mutual agreement regarding price and conditions hinges on a competitive offer being available.

The first right of offer is just that. The landlord tells a tenant first when space is available. The terms and conditions will be whatever the landlord wants them to be. Unless the tenant modifies the provision with a backup right to match another outside offer, what the tenant is initially offered will often bear no relationship to what the landlord may actually be willing to accept under competitive conditions.

Contiguous Space

When a lease includes expansion options and rights, the tenant must be sure that, at a minimum, the term of the lease for each expansion space fits within or is contiguous to the term of the original lease for the base premises. Nothing is more frustrating to a tenant than to have a ten-year lease and then in the sixth year get an expansion of space only for a three-year term that may or may not be extended for the last year. Even worse, the tenant may be forced to take the additional space for two or three years beyond the term of the original lease and base premises, without a corresponding increase in the length of the term for the original lease.

Tenants often settle for inequitable terms because they figure it is better to get what is needed when it is available and to figure out the consequences later. Of course, this practice is beneficial for the landlord. Convoluted as it is, it gives the landlord power and control over the tenant. On the other hand, a landlord does not always create inequalities on purpose. Sometimes the inequalities are a function of conditions, demand, and availability.

12
Subletting and Assignments

The subject of subleasing all or part of the tenant's premises, or the rights of the tenant to assign his or her total rights in a lease to another tenant, can quickly become mired in legal minutiae and jargon. One must be wary of terms such as *reversion* (the right to repossess the property at the end of the lease period) or *operation of law* (despite what a lease may say, applicable laws take precedence) and the quagmire of regional differences in laws and ordinances. The tenant must rely on his or her attorney and PREB to take care of any legal requirements or restrictions that need to be included (or excluded) from this lease clause.

For example, it is generally in the tenant's best interests not to have a clause regarding subleasing or assignments in the lease. If there is nothing contrary in the lease, the tenant is free to sublease or assign the lease to whomever and whenever he or she chooses (subject, of course, to any other appropriate lease clauses; also, some local laws and statutory regulations may restrict a tenant's right to sublease or assign a lease). Therefore, when it is in the tenant's best interests, these clauses should be left out of a lease. When they are included in a lease, it is best to have the tenant's sublease or assign rights clearly stated.

The tenant should have a clear understanding of what an assignment and sublease lease clause actually accomplishes. An assignment transfers all the rights and interests of one individual (the tenant) in the leased premises to another individual (another, or the replacement, tenant). An assignment can apply to the entire premises or to some portion thereof.

A sublease transfers something less than all the rights and interests of one individual (the tenant) in the leased premises to another individual (another, or the additional, tenant). A sublease may apply to the entire premises or to some portion thereof.

Whatever a tenant thinks he or she may have done (for example, assigned all his or her rights and interests to another tenant), the tenant who signed the original lease still retains full liability for that lease, even when the landlord has fully approved the assignment or subleasing. This often confuses a tenant who thinks he or she is off the hook for the lease after assigning it to another tenant. Unless the lease clearly provides that an assignment will terminate the lease between the tenant and the landlord and cancel all rights, responsibilities, and obligations toward each other, the tenant remains liable for the lease. When an assignment is made, the tenant needs to have a separate agreement with the landlord (or have a provision included in the assignment document that the landlord also signs) that relieves the tenant completely of any liability and obligations with respect to the original lease document (the release of the original tenant is often in the landlord's best interests as well).

A tenant who assigns his or her rights and interests in a lease wants out from the lease document. Subleasing is different. When subleasing, the tenant is not trying to get out of any lease responsibility or obligation, but rather trying to shed unneeded or excess space, either permanently or until it is needed again at a later time. Although the excess space could be left vacant, few businesses could afford such an extravagance, and even if they could afford to do so, it would be a waste of resources.

The Tenant as Landlord

The sublease concept allows the tenant to become a landlord. In real estate jargon, the tenant now becomes a sublandlord with respect to the sublease, and the subleasing tenant becomes the subtenant. The tenant now needs to find a tenant and must go through the same advertising, marketing, brokerage, and other processes that any other landlord does, also incurring the related costs. Once another tenant is found, the original tenant must create and enter into a lease with the subtenant. However, that arrangement is quite separate from the subleasing clause that is covered here. The sublease clause in the original lease only permits the tenant to proceed; it does not do the work.

The point to remember is that the tenant must not give away all the rights and interests he or she has in the original lease. In fact, the tenant cannot give the subtenant any rights or responsibilities regarding the premises and the building other than, or additional to, those the tenant has in the original lease. For example, if the building is to be locked at 6:00 p.m. every night, the tenant cannot offer to leave the building open until 7:00 p.m. for a subtenant unless the tenant can get the landlord to make the change. Similarly, the tenant cannot offer to leave the building open on a holiday when it is normally closed, offer after-hours HVAC if it is not already available, or provide for a sublease term in excess of the original lease's expiration date. Nor can the tenant offer to do major renovations or alterations for the subtenant unless permitted to do so under the original lease (which will be known as the master lease in the tenant's, or sublandlord's, and subtenant's lease document).

Sublease = Assignment?

If the tenant subleases the entire premises, has he or she in effect actually created a lease assignment? Can a landlord make that claim? It may or may not matter, depending on what is included in the lease. For example, the lease clause may not always cover both assignments and subleases, but only specify one or the other. The exclusion of one does not exclude the right of the tenant to do the other. However, the laws of the jurisdiction will prevail. But if it looks like a duck, waddles like a duck, and quacks like a duck—is it a duck?

A sublease is not an assignment as long as the tenant keeps to him or herself at least one right that is not given to a subtenant. The easiest way around the sublease-equals-an-assignment problem is to be sure that the expiration date of a sublease for the entire premises is one day short of the lease expiration date for the master lease. In this way, the original tenant takes back the space for one day (has reversion, that is, repossesses the space). However, to keep a sublease from becoming an assignment (if that's what is required), the tenant should ask a local attorney to construct the provision using the proper language.

The landlord would want to see a subleasing and assignment clause in the lease (subleasing and assignment will be considered together, as though they made up one lease clause) in order to retain absolute control over his or her property. To that extent, the landlord would like a nice, simple clause that prohibits the tenant from subletting or assigning the lease. But the tenant will want no prohibitions whatsoever.

Admittedly, the landlord does have significantly more interest in the premises, building, and property than the tenant. The landlord's responsibility extends not only to protecting the property as an investment but also (when applicable) to protecting other tenants. The landlord will want to exercise at least some control to avoid undesirable tenants or business operations that would either annoy other tenants or otherwise affect the landlord's investment.

Tenants Need Flexibility

The tenant enters into a lease with the best of intentions but needs a certain degree of flexibility in order to respond to continually changing economic and business conditions. A tenant who experiences explosive or extraordinary growth, expects to do so in the near future, or is just optimistic may want to bank extra space and thus rent larger premises than immediately needed (especially if contiguous space coupled with an expansion option is not possible). There is also the case of the tenant who may want to get rid of the overhead expenses of rent for vacant space (just like the landlord) because he or she has suffered business losses or is experiencing a downturn that is forcing a reduction of staff or other expenses.

If landlords were willing or even able to allow businesses to add or reduce space as needed, there would be no space problems for tenants. Further, if landlords were willing to take back unneeded space from a tenant or to reduce the tenant's lease liability, tenant problems would be reduced. But they are not; nor should they be. At the same time, the tenant must have some means of getting rid of unneeded space, either by subleasing it or, in the case of a fast-growing company, by giving up or assigning a lease so that the firm can move on to larger premises. Therefore, while retaining adequate controls, landlords need to be more understanding and cooperative regarding the subleasing and assignment of space by the tenant.

Suppose that a business undergoes any one of the massive changes it must endure to survive or grow: It might be taken over by another company, merge with another business, become a corporation, become a subsidiary of a larger corporation, lose partners or bring on new partners (e.g., in the case of a law firm), or sell all its stock. Unless the tenant properly prepares the assignment lease provision in advance, these lease transfers or assignments might well be excluded. As any prudent business person knows, it is the assets of a business taken as a whole that effectively "sells" a business. A lease is really nothing more than another asset—or liability.

Ideally for the tenant, there would be no prohibitions against lease assignment. However, if prohibitions are unavoidable, the tenant must be sure to exclude transfers or assignments due to business changes. The provision must contain enough specific details to include this type of assignment or to delineate clearly the assignments that are prohibited, for example, with respect to unrelated business entities and disinterested third parties.

The wording of a lease clause or a provision often reveals a great deal about how the landlord in general views the tenant and about future landlord-tenant relationships. Consider, for example, the following two lease provisions, each producing the same result:

1. Tenant will not sublet all or any portion of the premises nor assign, transfer, mortgage or encumber the lease, nor shall any assignment or transfer of this lease be effectuated by operation of law or otherwise without the prior written consent of landlord, such consent not to be unreasonably withheld.

2. Tenant shall have the right to assign or encumber his or her interest in this lease or in the premises, or sublease all or any part of the premises, or allow any other person or entity to occupy or use all or any part of the premises, after first obtaining landlord's prior written consent, which consent shall not be unreasonably withheld, delayed, or conditioned.

Although both lease provisions will accomplish the same end, the second one reflects a more positive tenant-landlord relationship.

Maintaining Landlord Control

Once a subleasing and assignment clause has been formulated, the landlord will want to add a number of other provisions that will enable him or her to maintain control. Although there is no reason for the landlord not to have enough control to protect his or her interests and investments, the tenant should also be able to exercise considerable flexibility regarding the premises for which he or she has taken on the responsibility.

As with many of the tenant options and rights clauses, the landlord will base assignment and subleasing on a condition of no tenant default. The tenant should be sure this is modified to reflect the precise nature of the default. That is, the only tenant default that should be considered is that of significant monetary default. Furthermore, the monetary default should exclude any money that the tenant has disputed, in writing to the landlord, and for which tenant-landlord discussions are still continuing. In addition, the tenant must be sure that any default affecting the subleasing or assignment right is an ongoing or current one. The tenant does not want to lose the right to sublet because of some long-forgotten minor (or even major) default that has been taken care of.

Landlord's Prior Approval

Typically the tenant is required to notify the landlord in writing, asking for prior approval of a sublease or assignment. Although the landlord's consent will probably not be unreasonably delayed, withheld, or conditioned, it is in the tenant's best interests to have this consent provision spelled out in detail. It should state a specific time limit by which the landlord must respond and allow no response to be interpreted as an indication of approval. Therefore, the landlord would have perhaps 30 days in which to provide a written response to the tenant's consent request. If written consent were not received within the agreed-to time period, the landlord's consent would be considered as given. In addition, the tenant should insist that any landlord denial for a sublease or assignment be stated in writing and the reasons for it be clearly detailed.

Subtenant Identification

Before consenting, the landlord usually insists that the tenant identify the proposed subtenant by name and address, giving the nature of the business and the proposed use of the premises; usually the landlord also requires a credit report, financial statement, or other tangible evidence of financial responsibility. The landlord is trying to assess the character of the proposed subtenant and anticipate any potential negative impact on the premises, such as excessive employee, guest, or tradesperson traffic (e.g., as with a temporary employment agency or a courier service); extraordinary strain on the building's services, utilities, and mechanical and electrical systems; and the extent of possible disruption to other tenants' businesses. The landlord will also require a copy of the lease document between the tenant and the subtenant. The landlord will want to be certain that the document references the master lease of the tenant and that the subtenant is subject to the same covenants and conditions as the tenant.

Although the landlord has a right to be concerned about the subtenant, the tenant needs to supply only whatever information conforms to the contents of the assignment or sublease and has bearing on the tenant's continuing responsibilities for the master lease. Therefore, the smaller the amount of space being subleased, the less information a landlord should receive. If the entire premises are being subleased or the tenant wants to assign the lease, however, the landlord would have a larger concern, and the tenant would have to provide considerably more information.

Landlord Takeback, or Recapture, of Space

The tenant is not supposed to be in the business of leasing space. Therefore, a landlord-preferred provision will state that the landlord has the right to take back, or recapture, any space the tenant wants to sublease and to reduce the tenant's lease responsibilities and obligations accordingly. Or it may state that the landlord will have the first right to sublease the tenant's space, matching any price, terms, and conditions of a potential subtenant. In addition, the landlord will want to be sure any takeback, or recapture, provision gives him or her the right but not the obligation to invoke the takeback, or recapture.

For the tenant's protection, this provision should distinguish between subleases made for space that is considered (by the tenant) to be excess or temporarily unneeded and space that the tenant would be glad to get rid of permanently. It is for the latter that the tenant would, or should, not object to a clause giving the landlord the right to take back, or recapture, the space. Otherwise, a tenant's business strategies, operations, and future flexibility could be adversely affected.

Conditioning the Takeback

The landlord's takeback, or recapture, right would be conditioned, first, on the tenant's written intentions regarding the space. Unless the tenant declares the intended sublease space is excess space and of no further interest to the tenant, a landlord's takeback, or recapture, right could not be invoked. An alternative or compromise is to condition the takeback on the amount of space being offered for sublet (e.g., 50 percent or more of the premises) or to the length of term of the sublease (e.g., for the remainder of the tenant's original lease).

The tenant must include a specification regarding timing. The tenant would notify the landlord in advance of his or her intention to sublease space, stating whether the space was excess and unwanted. The landlord would then have, say, 30 days to declare his or her intention to invoke the takeback, or recapture, right. Should the landlord not invoke this right or not respond in the specified time, the tenant would be free to begin subleasing the space.

All too often the provision concerning the landlord's takeback, or recapture, right provision is structured (by the landlord) so that it can be invoked after the tenant has had the space vacant for a long period of time and finally subleased it. The tenant may have spent considerable money and time getting a subtenant, while the landlord reaps the benefits. To cover this situation, the provision should state that after a subtenant has been found (and not only is acceptable to the landlord but also remains in the space), the tenant will be reimbursed for any marketing and advertising expenses, brokerage fees, and other costs incurred in finding a subtenant.

Landlord Profit Sharing

Instead of giving the landlord the right to take back, or recapture, the space, some provision can be made to share the income from the tenant sublease with the landlord. Such a response is designed to keep the tenant out of the business of leasing space. The landlord consents to the subleasing of space for virtually any reason, so long as the tenant does not do it as a business venture or make an intentional profit. If the tenant will make a profit, the landlord believes that he or she deserves at least a share of that profit. In the landlord's view, the tenant should have no right to profit from space that the landlord could otherwise have leased, especially if it is for more money than the tenant is paying.

A tenant's ability to make a profit on a sublease is strictly a function of economic and market conditions. Landlords have managed to talk many tenants into these profit-sharing provisions. The tenant should resist such a provision unless the landlord is willing to agree to equal tenant-landlord treatment regarding any and all monetary obligations toward the subleased space. Specifically, the landlord would share not only in the subleasing profits, but also in the downside risks, that is, any related subleasing losses that might be incurred by the tenant. The landlord will not want to do this, of course. The landlord wants the profit merely to keep the tenant from making any money at his or her expense.

The arguments for the landlord in this case are specious, capricious, convoluted, and bullying. Nobody twisted the landlord's arm to lease the space to the tenant at the particular terms and under the particular conditions that apply, regardless of the economic and market conditions at the time. A lease is an agreement between two parties. It is a business decision of the tenant, similar to any other business decision that creates income and expenses. The business person is in the business to make money. If, for whatever reasons, be it shrewd negotiating, farsightedness, or plain luck, the business person makes a profit on space that he or she has leased with a landlord, why should that profit not belong to the business person?

The landlord will no doubt justify profit sharing by comparing it to the percentage rents that retail operations pay. The argument is patently ridiculous. Retail spaces are not office, storage, or manufacturing space. Retailers require visibility and volume traffic; that is what they pay for in the percentage rent. If this argument were extended, the landlord should be getting a percentage of the income from every tenant's business operations, not just the profit on a subleased space.

Perhaps the landlord wants to share in the subleasing profits out of embarrassment over not being able to lease the space for more money in the first place or because the tenant has proven to be a better business person.

Consider, too, that not every subleasing of space creates a profit for the tenant. The tenant may need to reduce overhead expenses and, depending on market and economic conditions, would be willing to sublease space for something less than the actual rent being paid, thereby incurring a loss. In addition to the rent loss, there will be the associated costs and expenses of subleasing, including those incurred in finding and getting a subtenant into the space. Unless a landlord were willing to share in the risks by taking space back or sharing in subleasing losses, that landlord would have no right to share in the sublease profits.

What Are Subleasing Profits?

When tenants do agree to profit-share, they must clearly define the subleasing profit in the lease provision. *Sublease profit* is the difference between the sublease rent and the tenant's rent payment (the then-current rent, including all rent escalators) minus a pro rata share (based on the sublease space as a percentage of the total premises) of operating expenses and real estate taxes (unless these items are passthrough expense items to the subtenant), minus all costs and expenses to the tenant for subleasing the space (often these costs and expenses would be deducted on an amortized basis over the term of the sublease). The tenant must be sure that all related costs and expenses are clearly specified, including advertising; marketing; brokerage fees; legal, accounting, and administrative fees; rent abatement; other concessions and inducements; any subpremises alterations, improvements, and construction; vacancy period; and any other related costs and expenses.

In a profit-sharing provision, the tenant should be sure to have the landlord release, in a manner similar to that for a landlord's takeback or recapture, the tenant from any further liability, responsibility, or obligations for the sublease space for the period of time that the sublease profit sharing is in effect.

Subtenant Attornment

A landlord may wish to include a number of additional provisions to further control or protect his or her rights and interests. To protect against a serious monetary loss, the landlord will often insist that the tenant-subtenant lease document include an attornment provision (see Chapter 34). This provision works the same as the tenant's attornment provision, which protects the mortgage lender in the event of a landlord default or bankruptcy (the tenant agrees to continue to pay rent to the mortgage lender). The subtenant agrees to continue paying rent to the landlord in the event of a tenant default or bankruptcy.

Limitation of Subtenant Rights

In addition, the landlord will often insist that any tenant options and rights, for example, lease renewal, extension options, or expansion options, are personal and unique to the tenant and may not be transferred to a subtenant or be made part of a lease assignment. Although this view is easy to understand and even justify for small parts of rented space, it will place severe restrictions on the tenant. The tenant must closely consider the value of the options and rights in being able to find a subtenant or to get a lease to be taken over by another business. Such restrictions on transfer rights would significantly reduce the value of the lease and create an undue economic sanction against the tenant (see Chapter 11).

If a sublease or lease assignment is acceptable to a landlord, the master lease provisions should also pertain to any sublease.

13
Security and Rent Deposits

Virtually every commercial landlord's version of the lease document includes a security deposit lease clause. Depending on the negotiating abilities of the PREB and the tenant or on the economic power and leverage of the tenant, the requirement for a security deposit and the accompanying clause may be dropped.

In theory, the security deposit belongs to the tenant. It is given to a landlord at his or her insistence, with the basic provision stating: "The security deposit shall be security for the performance by the tenant of all tenant's obligations, covenants, conditions, and agreements under the lease."

In addition, a provision will give examples of what the landlord might use the money for, for example:

> In the event of tenant default, the landlord shall have the right, but not the obligation, to use, apply, or retain all or any portion of the security deposit for the payment of any base rent or additional rent or any other monetary sum for which the tenant is in default; the payment of any amount that landlord may spend or become obligated to spend to repair damages to the premises or the building (as specified elsewhere in the lease); or the payment of any amount the landlord may spend or become obligated to spend, or to compensate the landlord for any losses incurred, by reason of the tenant's default under the lease.

For whatever reason, then, the landlord insists and the tenant acquiesces to the request for a security deposit. Yet this money provides no benefits for the tenant. The tenant has no access to or use of it, and so it will no longer be a producing asset as far as the tenant is concerned.

It is one thing for a landlord to request some assurance that the tenant will be responsible for monetary obligations under the lease. It is quite another for a landlord to have free use of a tenant's money until the expiration of the lease.

At the same time, different leasing situations do require landlords and tenants to make certain adjustments. For example, the landlord will often have to make a significant investment in an extensive and expensive buildout done expressly for a tenant going into a new building. Similarly, an older space may require significant landlord investment in renovations. The tenant, too, may be making a significant investment in alterations, renovations, or new equipment for the premises, well in excess of what any deposit may be. Or the lease may be backed by a separate guarantor (see Chapter 45).

Whatever the situation, the tenant or the PREB on the tenant's behalf should, to the extent possible, have the deposit security lease clause tilted as much as possible in the tenant's favor.

The tenant's first preference is to have no security deposit. Barring that, to the extent possible, the purpose of the security deposit should be set out in detail in the lease clause. It is not in the landlord's best interests for the security deposit to be treated as advanced rent, for example, to cover the rent for the last month of the lease. Any designation of the deposit as a monetary payment of any kind to the landlord will convert the deposit to taxable income to the landlord. On the other hand, to the extent a security deposit is designated as advanced rent or some other specified advanced payment, the landlord may not be able to use the specified deposit legally for anything other than its intended purpose. For example, it could not be used to repair damaged premises.

Size of Deposit

If there is to be a security deposit, the first detail that needs to be established is how large it should be. Landlords usually ask for an

amount that is some multiple of the monthly rent. However, there
is no magic formula. Monthly rent is simply a convenient amount.
Any amount that meets the needs of both the tenant and the
landlord would be just as acceptable. Obviously the tenant will
want as low a deposit as possible, while the landlord would like
one as high as possible. The only real reason for basing the deposit on the rent is to give the landlord the equivalent of a
month's rent if the tenant should default and not pay the rent on
time.

Interest on Deposits

If the tenant has a long-term lease or if the lease attaches an annual (or other regular) escalator to the rent, a month's rent paid
at the beginning of the lease term, with no increases or changes
during the term of the lease, works to the tenant's benefit in the
later years of the lease. As the rent goes up, the deposit amount
remains constant and thus has indirectly earned a return for the
tenant, in that the tenant has not had to increase the base deposit
amount each year to keep up with increases in the rent. Also, because money loses value over time unless it is earning interest or
some investment return, the base deposit amount has much less
value to the landlord in being able to cover, as an example, a
tenant's default of a month's rent in the later years. On the one
hand, then, the tenant gains because the base deposit amount
stays the same and there is no increasing cost to the tenant; on
the other hand, however, the deposit money languishes and produces no return or value to the tenant.

The tenant wants to earn interest on the money left on deposit
with a landlord. Unless required by the laws in the jurisdiction or
because of a tenant's economic power and leverage, the landlord
will not acquiesce to this request. Although it is not necessary for
the tenant to earn a return on the deposit (depending on some
of the other aspects related to the deposit), the tenant or PREB
should not easily give in on this point. A good intermediate fallback position is to request a discounted deposit based on whatever interest or monetary return the tenant is giving up over the
length of time the landlord will be holding the deposit. That is,
the tenant gives an amount of money today that, if it were earning

interest or a return, would be the amount needed to cover the deposit at some future time. The difficulty for the landlord is that unless the money is deposited to earn a return in the early years of the lease, in the later years the deposit amount will never equal an amount that would cover a month's rent.

Keeping Track of a Deposit

The ideal situation for the tenant is to have the deposit money placed in its own special trust or escrow account. Landlords will not want to do this. Not only does this complicate the bookkeeping, but the landlord will not have free and immediate use of the money to supplement his or her cash flow. This situation should be of considerable concern to the tenant (and the tenant's PREB).

Unless the deposit money is kept in a separate escrow account for the tenant's benefit, the tenant in effect loses the deposit and becomes like any other general creditor to whom money is owed if the landlord goes bankrupt. The question of deposits is also of some concern to mortgage lenders. If a landlord should go bankrupt, the first place a tenant turns to get his or her deposit money back is the lender. The lender has nothing to do with the deposit, however, and, as the new "owner," may now require an additional deposit from the tenant. The tenant's broker or attorney, or the lender's attorney, will often put a provision in this lease clause stating that the tenant's only recourse for the deposit is to the landlord. This should be unacceptable to the tenant; after all, it is the tenant's money. The money may be held (and even used interest free) by the landlord, but it does not belong to him or her.

The tenant's best position is to insist on an escrow account. Otherwise, in the event of the landlord's bankruptcy or the foreclosure on the property by the mortgage lender(s), the tenant must trust to luck (or perhaps to some astute business judgements) that the mortgage lender(s) will recognize the existence of the deposit and permit the amount to be credited toward any additional deposit requirements of the lender or toward a future rent payment. Obtaining an escrow account, however, will be difficult, even for the tenant with considerable economic leverage— but it never hurts to try.

A similar problem can occur when the landlord voluntarily sells the property. What happens to the deposit? If the money is in an escrow account, there must be some provision to have the account transferred to the new landlord. Otherwise, at the end of the lease, who gives back the tenant's deposit?

What the landlord will not want (and will undoubtedly protect against) is the responsibility for any deposits in the event of a sale. This does little to help the tenant secure a separate escrow account. The tenant must insist that a provision be included requiring the current landlord to transfer any deposit to the new landlord. Furthermore, this provision must make the current landlord responsible for having the new landlord provide the tenant with certification that the deposit has been transferred or with a credit for the deposit made on behalf of the tenant. The new landlord must then accept all the responsibility and obligations regarding the deposit that the original landlord had (including its return to the tenant). Otherwise, the lease must clearly stipulate that the original landlord will remain liable for the deposit or, better yet, that upon a sale or transfer of the property, the deposit will be returned to the tenant.

In a related situation, the tenant must clarify for the landlord what will happen to a deposit if the tenant should assign the lease to another company or tenant (for example, in a merger or a corporate takeover). Who gets the deposit? Because the lease is with the tenant, the tenant will still be entitled to the return of the deposit at the end of the lease, even if the business no longer exists. The tenant must provide (if it is in the tenant's best interests) for the deposit to follow the lease, that is, must transfer its ownership and obligations to an assignee. It will be the tenant's responsibility to provide the necessary documentation to the landlord and ensure that a lease provision exists permitting the transfer and prior acceptance of the landlord.

Furthermore, the tenant needs take into account any area of the lease in which the transfer, moving, changing, or return of the deposit may be affected. For example, what happens to the deposit if and when the lease is renewed or extended for an additional term or period? Is the deposit returned because the tenant has exhibited consistent economic stability during the initial term of the lease? Is there a provision in the renewal or extension clause to provide for carrying the deposit forward with continu-

ing landlord responsibilities and obligations? Is the landlord able
to override the request for an escrow deposit account? Is the requirement for a new, larger deposit consistent with a new renewal
or extension rent? (Surprisingly, this last item is rarely provided
in a landlord-favorable lease. For some reason, this concept is
often overlooked by drafters of the lease document. And there is
no need for the tenant to bring up the subject.)

When Is a Deposit Returned?

Perhaps a more important question regarding the deposit is when
it will be returned to the tenant. A tenant-oriented provision will
state that the deposit must be returned on the lease expiration
date. Depending on his or her prior experiences, however, the
landlord may have some specific provisions to protect his or her
interests. For example, the wary landlord will want some time period after the lease expiration date to return the deposit, such as
30, 60, or 90 days. The obvious reason is to make sure that the
tenant has moved out properly; has removed all the required furnishings and alterations; has not left extensive rubble, debris, or
trash; and has not damaged the premises (especially during the
move-out process).

The landlord may not want to return some tenants' deposits
until all their responsibilities and obligations under the lease
have ceased. For example, the tenant who is obligated to pay for
increased real estate taxes or operating expenses each year may
not know the final increases until six months or more after moving out. The landlord wants some way of ensuring that the money
due will be paid in a timely manner; hence, the keeping of the
deposit.

Yes, the tenant will have, because of the lease, a legal obligation
to pay these increases. However, many tenants tend to "forget"
these amounts owed and will ignore the landlord's invoices. After
all, they are no longer in the building, so they do not feel obligated to pay any more money to that landlord. The landlord can
collect, but using a collection agency or going to court costs
money and is bothersome. From the landlord's perspective, it is

better to hold the deposit, especially if the deposit is greater than the estimated amount owed. The tenant must make sure that, if the deposit is being held for specific purposes after the lease expiration date, the amount held is not excessive and any estimated "overage" amount will be returned to the tenant.

The tenant must also recognize that the deposit is not to be used as, or be part of, the last month's rent unless there is a specification to this effect in the lease. The purpose for which the deposit can be used should be clearly spelled out in the lease. All too often a tenant moves out and does not pay the last month's rent, under the impression that the deposit will take care of it. The landlord knows this will happen; hence, one month's rent is the basis for the security deposit. Although this use of the deposit is not really legal, many tenants, especially the smaller ones, get away with it. As long as there is nothing else the landlord will need to use the deposit for and the tenant does not owe any other money or leave extensive damage, it is much less trouble to take the deposit and not stand on legal principles.

Deposit = Money?

The tenant must remember that a deposit does not and should not automatically be equated with money. Keeping in mind that the landlord should be required to specify the exact purposes for which a deposit will be used, the tenant's responsibility should be limited to meeting any monetary obligations when due. The deposit, although it gives the landlord peace of mind, costs the tenant money through the loss of alternative economic strategies and options.

Therefore, the tenant should talk to his or her accountant, attorney, and PREB and be prepared to negotiate a deposit in some form other than money that will meet both the landlord's and tenant's needs. The basic idea is to put forward a monetary or banking instrument that the landlord can collect on if it becomes necessary, while at the same time allowing the tenant to earn a return or interest on unused or unneeded money and still retain certain ownership rights. Exactly what instrument will work will depend on the landlord's expertise and regional standards. Some examples to consider include a letter of credit; jointly held inter-est-bearing escrow accounts; money market certificates; certifi-cates of deposit; federal, state, or local government notes, bonds, or bills; and corporate stock or bonds. A special provision will have to be incorporated into the lease document to cover items such as the continuing value of the security deposit, the way and with whom it is to be kept on deposit, and details concerning the way the landlord will collect the money when needed.

Use of the Security Deposit

An additional provision of the security deposit lease clause will state that the landlord has the right but not the obligation to use the deposit to cure a tenant's default. In other words, depending on the extent of the provision, a landlord may be able to ignore the security deposit and begin eviction proceedings against the tenant. The landlord would have ultimate control if the lease gave him or her cumulative rights, permitting the use of the secu-rity deposit and allowing the landlord to pursue any other reme-dies available in the lease.

The tenant must safeguard against ambiguities in the lease and against landlord vindictiveness. The preferred tenant provision would require the landlord to use the security deposit as a first and continuing measure to cure any tenant defaults. Subject to the default lease clause permitting the tenant the right to cure any and all defaults prior to any other landlord action, if the ten-ant were unable to satisfy a monetary default either through addi-tional payments or through increased security deposit, the land-lord would be able to pursue other specified remedies in the lease or under the laws of the jurisdiction.

What happens if the landlord actually uses the security deposit? The tenant will have three concerns:

1. *When a security deposit is used, is there any requirement that it be replenished?* Many a lease neglects to specify what might hap-pen if the deposit were used. The tenant has no obligation to remind the landlord that a deposit needs to be replenished. If the lease does specify that a deposit is to be replenished, will this apply only once or on a regular basis if the deposit is used?

2. *If a security deposit is used and is to be replenished, how much has to be replaced?* From the tenant's perspective, the deposit should be replenished up to the original deposit amount. Alternative landlord considerations will be replenishment based on the updating of the original deposit basis (e.g., a replenished deposit equal to the then-current one month's rent); replenishment that increases the original base amount using a time factor to account for inflation, because the original deposit had to be used; or replenishment of the higher of either of the above, or the amount of the default, if greater than the original deposit amount.

3. *When the deposit is to be replenished, how soon must replenishment be accomplished?* This point can be particularly important to a tenant. If the tenant defaults, it is often because of a business setback or cash-flow problems. The deposit will then become a useful prepaid cash hoard that can help a business through a rough period. An immediate (e.g., three-day) replenishment could create an undue burden on the tenant's business. As a practical matter, the tenant should strive for a replenishment cycle of a minimum of 30 days, with a tenant-preferred 90-day requirement.

Rent Deposit

A rent deposit is used when the premises are leased before the tenant is able to take possession or move in. Depending on a number of factors (such as the length of the lease or its economic value), a fairly standard rent deposit is equal to the first month's rent, with the deposit credited to the rent payment when it is due and payable (as may be specified in another lease clause). On occasion, especially for tenants with short-term leases and for smaller-sized space users, both the first and the last months' rents may constitute the required deposit.

A rent deposit is, and should remain, distinctly different from a security deposit. It should be considered usable only for its stated purpose—as a rent payment. It is not generally considered to be usable for other tenant breaches or lease defaults unless specifically stated in the lease document. This deposit is not to be used for liquidation or compensatory damages, say, for any other tenant monetary default that may occur or as a default consideration (or compensation) for the landlord's having signed the lease, even if the tenant is unable to take possession or occupancy (as may otherwise be permitted within the lease).

The importance of keeping the rent deposit as a separate entity from the security deposit cannot be stressed enough. Suppose there is a lengthy (six-month or one-year) rent-abatement concession period, during which the tenant has occupancy and possession of the premises, and some type of tenant default occurs. The advanced rent deposit (not actually due to the landlord until the first rent payment is due after the abatement period) should not be used to cure the default. That is what the security deposit (if there is one) is for (as well as any other landlord remedies specified in the lease).

Although the rent deposit is distinct from a security deposit, virtually everything previously said about the security deposit will pertain to the rent deposit, but it must be spelled out separately, of course. The following example shows why. A tenant pays a rent deposit well in advance of being able to take possession because new building construction or extensive tenant renovations are being provided by the landlord. Before the tenant takes possession, however, the landlord sells the building or the bank forecloses on the property. What happens to the rent deposit? Exactly what a tenant might imagine, if every possible safeguard is not provided to keep the money safe.

14
Signs and Directory Listings

A signs and directory listings clause will not be found in lease documents in every region of the country. Many leases include signs in the rules and regulations clause. In some areas there will be a separate lease clause devoted to signs, and the subject will also be included in the rules and regulations clause. Keeping the signs clause separate helps establish its importance for the landlord.

The signs clause is indeed important to the landlord. Without it, there is nothing to prevent a space user from erecting a sign on the building wall (or roof) right outside his or her premises. The tenant could also paint a sign on a wall (outside wall signs would, of course, be subject to national, state, and local laws and ordinances) or put signs in an adjacent hallway, on doors, or, horror of horrors, in a window (subject to other possible lease clauses, such as building rules and regulations).

Even without a specific sign clause, the tenant should have the lease document carefully scrutinized regarding this point. Often the language specifying the premises will not mention the walls and the roof. This limits the tenant's access to those areas so that signs cannot be installed.

The issue of a signs clause boils down to the landlord wanting

249

to control the "look" of the building and protect the building's prestige. The landlord has "eyesore" rights in this regard, as well as the support of a majority of the tenants. Tenants choose a building for its looks and how it "feels," that is, the overall ambience of the building and how it contributes to their own conception of the type of environment in which they want to conduct business. A building with signs tacked all over the outside or clustered on the roof will repel many space users. If a few tenants were allowed to put up signs, they would, of course, have a significant advertising or publicity advantage, but with a proliferation of signs, none would be readable, and the clutter would be a visual blight on the environment.

For a single building user, the issue is a little more complicated. The user's negotiating power will be great enough to easily gain the right to put a sign on the building or the roof. In many cases, it may be possible even to name the building. For many landlords, this will not be a problem, even though over time a building might become associated with one tenant alone. At some later time, when that tenant relocates, the landlord may not be able to find another single building user willing to move in. A stigma will be connected with the building because the previous user occupied it for so long. The building is known as the XYZ building, and the name may be virtually impossible to change in the mind of the public.

What is true for a single building user is often true for a large and dominant space user concerning the right to put a sign on the building. Regardless of any other name the building has been given by the landlord, this often attaches a particular name to the building, sometimes with negative consequences for the landlord. Often, middle-sized space users and even small space users do not want to move into a building that is known by some other company's or organization's name. Of course, the opposite may also be true. An organization may be so large and well known that other space users have no aversion to being in "that" building. A certain status may even be associated with being in the building, especially if the smaller user is in a related business field.

By and large, the signs clause provides the landlord with the absolute right to name the building and to change the name whenever it may suit the landlord. In addition, the landlord will retain the right to select (to the extent practical) the address for the building. Furthermore, the clause may specifically prohibit tenants from using the building's name for anything other than address purposes (without prior landlord approval). This prevents any tenant from creating an advertising or publicity campaign that instantly associates a company's identity with the building's name.

This lease clause states that signs (often defined to include awnings and any visible notice, display, or advertising, whether affixed, inscribed, or painted) may not be affixed without prior landlord approval. The landlord also retains the right to specify size, color, and placement. This clause gives the landlord the right to set sign specifications and approve the sign before placement.

When a landlord has verbally approved a tenant's placing of a sign (including special signs for entrance doors or in hallways or lobbies) before the lease has actually been signed, the lease clause should be modified immediately to reflect that approval has already been granted. The wise tenant will also have placement, color, size, and any other relevant item preapproved and specified in the lease document.

For most space users, the landlord's answer to a sign request is a quick no. But not always, especially when the sign is for an elevator lobby or a modified entrance door. Whatever response the tenant is expecting from the landlord, this clause should specify a time frame for both the initial request and the final approval of a sign. For example, a reasonable time frame for the landlord's response to the tenant's (written) sign request is within 30 days of its receipt. That is, the landlord should approve or return modified and approved sign plans and specifications to the tenant within 30 days of receiving them.

Under this clause, the tenant will be fully responsible for obtaining necessary permits or licenses and governmental approvals for the erection of the sign. The tenant will also be responsible for all the costs associated with the sign, including installation, maintenance, and repair, and for all costs associated with the removal of the sign at the conclusion of the lease term.

An interesting variation to this clause allows the landlord—at any time and at his or her sole discretion—to order any previously approved signs or advertisements removed because such items are said to "impair the reputation or desirability" of the building.

This problem could easily come about because a potential tenant, especially a large space user, has objected to a tenant's sign and will not consider relocating to that building unless the sign(s) are removed. Likewise, the building may be sold, and the new landlord may have a different set of standards regarding signs: All signs become prohibited and must be removed. In accordance with this clause, the sign owner is, of course, required to pay all costs of removal, even if it is done by the landlord.

The tenant with approved signs and advertisements will find it useful to have the lease clearly state that they are approved for the full length of the lease term (and for any lease renewals or lease extensions that may occur).

A tenant must also watch for sign clauses that require an additional payment beyond the actual costs for sign removal by the landlord. These additional payments will fall under a landlord's lease provision for his or her "time and effort."

Directory Listings

If directories are not specified in a separate lease clause or a separate agreement between the landlord and the tenant, the sign clause will include references to whatever tenant directories are available in the building (in any common areas in which the tenant might be able to place a small sign and at the door to the entrance of the premises).

Depending on landlord and regional differences, there are at least three places to put tenant directories in a building: in the main entrance lobby, inside the elevator cabs, and in the elevator lobby area on each individual floor. Although there is limited space on a building's tenant directory boards, this is an area in which the tenant has considerable leeway during negotiations with the landlord.

The directory in the main entrance lobby is the most obvious place for a tenant's name to get some exposure. The listings on a directory board will be made up of standard-sized letters, and each line in the listing will have a uniform appearance. Directory board space tends to be allocated on the basis of the number of square feet being leased. Larger space users will tend to get the most listings, but only if they ask. A landlord will usually want a single directory board that simply lists each company or organization name and the location, either by floor or by suite number. Usually, the landlord's provision will state that an initial one-line listing is the standard and provided at no charge. After that, every time a listing is changed, the tenant will be charged accordingly.

A tenant must negotiate three main points concerning the directory board, beginning with the total number of directory lines. The more lines, the more name listings the tenant will be able to show. With more lines, individual staff names can be put into the directory beside the name of the firm. This can be important to an organization whose clients identify more with individuals, such as a law firm or an accounting firm.

The second negotiating item is the number of lines a tenant gets in the directory at no charge. This means not only the number of lines in the directory, but also the number of lines given at no charge over the lease term. This is an important area. A business will have employee turnover, departmental name changes, and sometimes an organizational name change (as in a partnership). The tenant would prefer a provision for a total of directory lines (a tenant-supplied number, e.g., 30) over the lease term at no charge, allowing a number of line listings (a tenant-supplied number, e.g., 10) on the building directory board at any one time. (In this example, each line in the listing could be changed three times at no charge.)

The third negotiating point is to fix the cost for changing a directory line. Without predetermined guidelines, theoretically the landlord can change whatever he or she wants. The tenant's only choice is to accept the cost and pay gracefully or reject it and not change the directory listing.

Two additional areas that should also be covered in the lease clause are how often directory changes may be made and, even more important, how long a directory change will take. In regard to the first point, there should be no limit: The tenant should be able to change the directory listing as many times as he or she wants. After all, after the first directory listings are used up, the tenant will be paying for them, so there really should be no problem. The second point is important because, all too often, changing a directory board listing is a low priority for a building's management, so it may take months to delete or add a name.

Individual floor directories are a different problem. Tenants

will usually have more leeway with any directory board that may
be present (subject to the same cost and listing limitations attached to a main lobby directory). The main difference is that a
whole floor user will, or should, get the right to put a sign in the
floor elevator lobby. What the sign looks like (e.g., a tastefully
small brass plaque or foot-high stainless steel letters) is up to the
negotiating prowess of the individual—anything goes.

For multitenanted floors, most directories can only accommodate each firm's name and location (suite number). The reader
should refer to the points discussed regarding the main lobby
directory.

Directories in elevator cabs seem to be disappearing thanks to
new, high-tech elevators. However, change begets even more
change, and as technology advances, there will be new elevator directory options available. Two possibilities in the near term are a flat
screen monitor showing a directory listing as each floor is ap-
proached and a voice directory announcing the tenants on each
floor. The tenant should ask for access to any newly installed directories or technically advanced substitute systems on the same basis as
has been negotiated for the main lobby directory. The tenant must
check whether a building being considered has an elevator cab directory. The tenant's provision should also include the possibility of
future changes, upgrading, or renovation of the elevators.

Entrance Door Signs
(Suite Entry Signs)

Provisions for signs near entrance doors have a standard format
similar to that found in a building's tenant directory lease provision. Landlords want to control the interior "look" of their building. Although they may give the tenant some choice in the type of
entry door to the suite (e.g., glass, metal, painted or stained
wood), the size of the letters, material used, and format for the
sign on the door usually have to follow a specified standard. The
landlord may also specify size, color, and typeface. However, because of the great proliferation of corporate logos, many landlords will permit a logo design and logo typeface to be utilized as
an entrance door sign—as long as it meets the other required criteria, such as size or color.

The sign on the entrance door can also be negotiated. A landlord will often agree to pay for the door signage. Of course, the landlord will start by saying that the tenant is responsible for paying for the sign; after all, it is the tenant who wants it. Otherwise, the landlord will reason, the door should be left blank. The tenant needs to be sure that any information concerning location, such as the suite number, is coordinated with the door signage. Otherwise, the mismatch could be visually abhorrent—and correctable only at the tenant's cost.

Unseen Signs

One additional provision that is often found in this clause (or in the building rules and regulations clause) is that there may be no posting of signs or advertisements anywhere within the space being leased. Tenants, beware of this little add-on. Understandably, no signs, advertising, or publicity should be visible from outside the suite, but the tenant should not permit the landlord to control what may be displayed to staff and clients within the tenant's premises. Obviously, areas with glass doors, windows, and walls that can be seem from outside the enclosed space present special problems (or opportunities).

Landlord Signs

A tenant should have the same concerns about landlord-generated signs that the landlord has about tenant signs.

Because of the potential negative impact on a tenant's business operations, customer relationships, and the general appeal of the property, a tenant should try to gain some control over the size, type, and placement of any signs, placards, banners, or the like that will be used by a landlord and placed on, in, or around a building or property to advertise or market either the sale of the building and property or the availability of space. For the tenant, small, nicely lettered, unobtrusively placed signs would be preferred. The landlord is more likely to want a large banner strung across the outside of the building, if local ordinance permits it.

15
Tenant Equipment

Tenant equipment is not always covered in a separate lease clause; it is likely to be included under the building's rules and regulations. However, for many landlords this area does rate its own lease clause. It may then be repeated or summarized within the overall rules and regulations of the lease.

The equipment clause specifically prohibits the tenant from installing or operating any electrical equipment or machinery other than "normal business machines" (a listing of which may include typewriters, adding machines, calculators, standard-size copying machines that do not use more than a 115-volt line, radios, televisions, and clocks) unless first obtaining the written approval of the landlord. The clause may also state that landlord approval is subject to certain conditions. For example, the tenant may be required to pay additional rent or compensation for the estimated "excess" consumption of electricity (or water, if appropriate).

In addition, a lease provision may state: "The tenant will not install equipment or machinery of any kind that may require changes, replacement, or additions to any of the building's water, plumbing, heating, air-conditioning, or electrical systems, without first obtaining the landlord's written permission."

The general purpose of this clause is to protect the integrity of the building and the investment of the landlord. The clause may also give the landlord greater control over the tenant—enabling the landlord to charge for whatever he or she perceives to be excess water, electricity, or other utility consumption.

The tenant must be aware of his or her business needs and have any requirements included within the lease, added to the list of permitted equipment and machinery, or have a lease addendum that automatically provides any required prior written landlord consent.

What is "normal or standard" business equipment or machinery? What is normal for one business may not be so for another, especially when it comes to computers and telecommunications technology. Fiber optics, lasers, and other enhanced light technologies, not to mention the equipment and machines utilizing superconductivity, promise to create future needs not being considered in today's lease.

Commonly, the lease clause provides for "landlord approval." A tenant-preferred provision would have all tenant needs included in a listing of equipment and machinery acceptable for, or necessary for, his or her business environment. As an important tenant addition, the clause would reflect an automatic acceptance of all equipment and machinery, existing now or in the future, considered to be normal and standard for a general business environment, as well as specifically related, unique to, or required for the tenant's type of business.

When the lease document is being formulated (or negotiated), that is the time to include language specifying that the landlord's approval is understood for any item specified, noted, or shown on any layout plans provided by the tenant. It is then up to the tenant to provide a clear space plan so there will be no landlord surprises and no unexpected extra tenant expenses. These details are especially important for tenants who intend to have or need kitchen areas, private bathrooms, internal staircases, special security areas, centralized computer facilities, large-capacity copying machines or printing equipment, microwave transmission facilities, enhanced telecommunications capability, or even such mundane things as small refrigerators, water coolers, copy machines, storage rooms, mini-kitchens, vending machines, and the like.

It is particularly important to include enhanced HVAC systems for conference rooms or work areas, because the items may need to be hooked into the existing building systems or may utilize existing mechanical areas of the building. Anything that requires extra utility usage (of any type) or access to a building's internal systems needs to be given careful thought by the tenant. Tenant equipment and related lease clauses have been known to create intense animosity between tenants and landlords. These difficulties stem from slight misunderstandings or the landlord's failure to forewarn a tenant properly about the potentially onerous nature of this clause.

A landlord-preferred provision in this clause will, depending on his or her experience, specify that the tenant must provide and maintain, at his or her expense, noise reduction systems and vibration eliminators for equipment and machinery as the landlord solely deems necessary. Depending on the tenant, the landlord may in addition require that certain equipment or machinery (e.g., x-ray equipment, microwave transmission equipment, high-voltage equipment) have whatever shielding or other protection the landlord deems necessary.

For a space user who needs a great deal of equipment, it is far better to be sure this clause is included in a lease document and meets his or her needs than to hope there will be no problems with a landlord. The tenant does not want to rely on the landlord's goodwill and vaguely worded building rules and regulations.

16
Furnishings and Use Restrictions

Like the tenant equipment clause, the furnishings use clause is often tucked away in the building's rules and regulations section of the lease. It may be in a separate clause either because of regional variations or because of prior landlord experience. Since there are no lease clause standards, the exact title and contents of this clause vary greatly. Often the title may be "Furnishings," for example, but the clause will include prohibitions on floor loading or elevator use.

Weight and Placement Restrictions

This clause permits the landlord some measure of control over the safe use of the building by tenants and establishes uniform usage for all tenants. As with a building regulation, the intent of the clause is to prevent one tenant and his or her guests, clients, or customers from inconveniencing or annoying other tenants.

This clause usually has two parts. The first part will give the landlord the absolute right to proscribe the allowable weight and position for all "heavy" furniture, fixtures, equipment, and machinery within any premises and on any floor of the building. As a building safety feature, this provides the landlord with control

261

over furnishings that would otherwise exceed the floor-load capacity of the building.

In placing heavy furnishings, the weight should be evenly distributed over as much of the floor area as possible. Because there are a number of ways to do this, it is in the tenant's best interests to work with the landlord, since it affords protection for all parties. The tenant must be aware of his or her needs. Items that create the most difficulty are library shelves (especially law libraries), which, when loaded with books, can create enough downward force to significantly weaken a building floor or even cause it to collapse; storage shelving; heavy machinery (e.g., a printing press); large banks of file cabinets; safes; and special fixtures (e.g., showroom cases). Naturally, there will be a provision specifying that any damages caused to the premises because of heavy furnishings will be the responsibility of the tenant and must be repaired at his or her cost.

Delivery Restrictions

A second major restriction often included in this clause is the prohibition against any furnishings, fixtures, equipment, or other bulky matter being delivered to or received at the building or carried in any elevator without the prior approval of the landlord. (The tenant must be sure to include a provision specifying that the approval will be issued in a timely manner and will not be withheld unreasonably.) Furthermore, the clause will state that all such bulky materials must only be delivered through certain entrances and at certain times and may use only certain elevators, as designated by the landlord. The tenant will also be required to remove promptly any delivered furnishings, equipment, or materials from any sidewalks or other areas adjacent to the building. This clause does help a tenant to avoid having employees, guests, and clients or customers sharing elevators or building entrances with another tenant's deliveries or furniture.

However, depending on the exact wording of this clause, a particular tenant may be severely inconvenienced to the extent that material needed to operate the business (e.g., printed matter) may be considered "bulky material." Building management employees may stop a delivery or neglect to notify a tenant immediately about a delivery at a loading dock. How is *bulky* to be defined, and how restrictive will the building's management be? It is not uncommon for tenants to complain that they could not get a delivery of sodas to replenish vending machines except during certain hours, that deliveries of food stuff for replenishment of vending machines were restricted, that the delivery of a business's annual report was delayed because it was packed in "bulky boxes," that the delivery of a business's publication was restricted to one- or two-carton quantities, or that the delivery of "normal" business machines (e.g., copiers, computers) was limited to special times in the afternoon.

The tenant must never assume that, because certain materials were delivered to the premises at a former building, the same will be true for a new building. All too often the landlord's "Don't worry about it" or "No problem" leads to a major exercise in frustration for the tenant. Again, it is up to the tenant to have his or her special needs listed as exceptions within this clause or in a lease addendum.

Moving Restrictions

A third item that can be buried in this clause is a restriction on the moving of all materials, furniture, equipment, machinery, or any other item into, out of, or within the building, unless the landlord has given prior written approval and it is done under the landlord's supervision (although the landlord will have no responsibility for damages or any charges). This adjunct to the clause provides added restrictions regarding the delivery of bulky furnishings, equipment, and materials. As such, it provides protection for all tenants. It supposedly avoids the "surprise" of having to share an elevator with a piece of furniture being moved, even by a business's employees from one floor to another, or of having guests and clients sharing elevators with boxes of materials being moved from one place to another.

On the other hand, this clause does severely restrict a tenant's ability to move things around. Theoretically, this provision prohibits the moving of items even within the user's own space and absolutely restricts the tenant from moving things from space on one floor to space on another floor, such as basement storage areas to the business premises.

Again, the tenant must be aware of this potential limitation and have included in the lease clause any waivers or specific details regarding his or her needs.

Tenants, Be Aware

When lawyers examine a lease document, they are looking for legal difficulties or problems. In contrast, real estate brokers are trying to make a "deal." They dote on the dollars they save you. Only you, the tenant, are really watching out for your interests. Even the most innocuous-sounding lease clause can cause a tenant much anguish and frustration. Tenants must take care.

17
Alterations

In a lease the tenant agrees to keep the premises in good repair and condition except for ordinary wear and tear. Depending on the length of the lease or because of heavy usage, good maintenance and repair may involve repainting, changing the wall covering, or changing the floor covering. Even for a tenant with a short-term lease, ever-changing business operations and advancing technology will make it necessary to purchase new equipment and new business systems, which will in turn require better ventilation, more lighting, or greater electrical capacity.

After a tenant has taken possession or is occupying the premises, any changes, modifications, improvements, or construction, whether it be painting a wall or tearing it down, is an alteration of the premises. Landlords do not want tenants to be able to alter the premises without their knowledge and approval. Depending on the laws and ordinances in the jurisdiction, the length of the lease, and even the kind of change or improvement, tenants generally will have no real rights to change, modify, or alter the landlord's property without permission.

The purpose of the alterations lease clause is to avoid disagreeable tenant-landlord relations. The essence of this clause is stated in the opening provision: "The tenant shall not make or permit anyone to make any alterations, decorations, installations, changes, additions, improvements, or any construction of any kind (structural or otherwise), in or to the premises or the building, without the prior written consent of the landlord." As an initial statement, this provision is not unreasonable. However, the tenant should be sure to add that the landlord will not unreasonably withhold, condition, or unduly delay his or her consent in this matter. Actually, the "no unreasonable delay" concept is the fallback for the tenant. The tenant should start out by requesting that within 30 days after the landlord has received the tenant's written request to perform alterations, which should include all necessary plans and construction documents, if applicable, the landlord will issue his or her written consent, provide written details concerning the deficiencies that need correcting, or state why consent is being withheld. In no event, however, shall the landlord unreasonably withhold his or her consent. If the landlord has not responded in writing within 30 days to the contrary, landlord approval and consent to the alterations will be deemed to have been given.

"No unreasonable delay" by the landlord becomes a fallback compromise, for one reason, because, often in response to the tenant-preferred 30-day "no response means approval granted" provision, the landlord will want to add a statement like "When granting his or her consent, the landlord may impose any condition he or she deems appropriate, including, without limitation, the approval of plans and specifications, approval of the contractor or other persons who will perform the work, and the obtaining of specified insurance, and any completion, indemnity, or other specified bonds."

Structural Versus Nonstructural

A tenant-oriented variation to the consent provision states that landlord consent is required only for structural alterations, whereas no landlord consent is required for nonstructural alterations. Of course, what constitutes structural versus nonstructural alterations would have to be clearly defined. Given the fact that no two commercial real estate landlords are likely to provide the same definition of *structural* and *nonstructural,* it is usually better to include examples of what is meant by each rather than trying to define them.

This alternative consent provision might state:

The tenant shall have the right to make minor, nonstructural alterations, decorations, additions, or improvements to the premises, such as the painting of walls, the changing of wall coverings, the changing of floor coverings, the hanging of pictures or other fixtures, and the constructing and installing of built-in cabinetry (e.g., bookcases), without the prior consent of the landlord, as long as such alterations are done in a careful, attractive manner and the tenant agrees to provide landlord with notice (including any plans, blueprints, or other specifications) of all such alterations within 30 days after the alterations are completed. The tenant shall make no structural alterations, constructions, or improvements to the premises without the landlord's prior written consent, which consent shall not be unreasonably withheld, conditioned, or unduly delayed. Structural alterations, construction, and improvements shall include, without limitation, any changes, replacement, addition to, or use of, the water or waste system, heating system, ventilation system, air-conditioning system, plumbing system, or any electrical or mechanical system of the building, or any activity that would involve the change, removal, relocation, or addition of any windows, walls, or ceilings or that may include any through penetrations of any building walls, ceilings, or floors.

Prior Consent

Many landlords will object to giving a tenant alteration rights without prior consent. Otherwise, the landlord will have no way to exercise that all-important element of control over the process. An alternative for the tenant is to propose specific and known alterations that will be considered in the future with a fixed time frame for doing the alteration. In this way, the landlord would be given the right to exercise prior approval or consent and would know exactly what to expect. For example, the tenant could have the right to change the wall covering, paint the walls, or change the floor coverings every fourth or fifth year of the lease (at the tenant's option). As another alternative, generally better for the tenant, the lease can specify a fixed dollar amount, usually a per-square-foot dollar amount (preferably adjusted for inflation each year), of nonstructural alternatives that the tenant may make without prior landlord approval but with full notification (including plans and specifications).

Quality Work?
At What Price?

Both the tenant and the landlord will want the work to be performed properly and in accordance with all laws and ordinances. A typical provision will state:

> All alterations and improvements made by the tenant, with or without prior written landlord consent or otherwise permitted by landlord, shall be performed in a good, first-class, and workmanlike manner, by reputable contractors licensed to do business in [the jurisdiction] and shall be in full compliance with all laws, rules, orders, ordinances, directives, regulations, and requirements of all government agencies, offices, departments, and bureaus, as well as other public or quasi-public authority having jurisdiction over the premises.

To ensure first-class work and compliance with all the laws, the tenant may be required to use either the landlord as the contractor or a contractor of the landlord's choice. For the uninformed tenant and inexperienced PREB, this is tantamount to giving a blank check to the landlord. This is not to imply that all landlords are dishonest. Far from it. However, it would be foolish for a landlord to pass up a little extra profit for doing virtually nothing.

As the contractor, the landlord is not likely to charge the most reasonable and competitive rates for the work to be done. After all, there is no competition. The tenant should expect a minimum of 10 percent greater costs than in a competitive situation— and possibly as much as 50 percent greater—just for the base construction and material prices.

The lease document should put a cap on the percentage markups allowed by both the contractor or the landlord. Markups that a landlord will try to exact from the tenant are for overhead, profit, general conditions, and supervision.

The Markup

As an extreme but reasonable example, consider that the base construction costs and prices of materials are marked up by 10 percent for contractor overhead, 10 percent for general tasks (for things like cleanup and unforeseen and unpriced quirks of the job), 10 percent for contractor profit, and, depending on the situation, an additional 10 percent for landlord supervision. If the number of markups is not daunting enough, the next major question is how will the markup be applied—only against a standard base or compounded against each other? That is, should the 10 percent profit be applied not just to the construction and materials but also to the overhead? Will the same hold for the supervision?

How this works is straightforward. Consider a standard base construction and materials amount of $1000 (this way, the results can be multiplied by multiples of $1000 to find out how much overcharging occurs). If the four different markups are used, with each being 10 percent, the results are as follows:

	Markup applied against base only ($)	Markup compounded against base plus previous markup ($)
Base construction and materials	1000	1000
Overhead @ 10 percent	100	100
Subtotal	1100	1100
General conditions @ 10 percent	100	110
Subtotal	1200	1210
Contractor profit @ 10 percent	100	121
Subtotal	1300	1331
Landlord supervision @ 10 percent	100	133
Total	1400	1464

As can be seen, the extra amount from the compounding of costs is "only" 4.6 percent of the total $1400, or an extra $64 for each

$1000 of the base cost. That's $640 extra for each $10,000 of materials and construction work and $6,400 extra for each $100,000 of materials and work! Considering that the markups should only be the first two 10 percents noncompounded, the extras can be presumed, in this example, to be $264 per $1000 of the cost of the job ($1464 for the four items at 10 percent compounded versus $1200 for the first two items only without the compounding). That's $2,640 extra for every $10,000 of job cost and $26,400 extra for every $100,000 of job cost!

Obviously, it is in the tenant's interests to limit the size of the markups (e.g., 5 percent is more than sufficient for things like general conditions and supervision), to limit the number of markups (e.g., overhead and profit are more than adequate at 10 percent and 5 percent, respectively), and to be sure that each markup applies only against the base and is not compounded against the others.

Bid the Work Out

There is no law, written or unwritten, that tenants are supposed to allow themselves to be charged more than reasonable or generally acceptable amounts for alterations, construction, or improvements simply because they are tenants. It is up to the tenant to insist that all alteration work be put out to bid. Either the tenant can do this or the landlord can be required to supply a minimum of three bids. In some instances, a minimum total estimated dollar value of work could be established before the landlord or tenant would be required to get three bids; for example, "All alteration material and construction work estimated to be in excess of $10,000 shall require a minimum of three bids before a contractor may be selected." The tenant should *always* retain the right to get his or her own contractor or be allowed to choose from those submitting bids to the landlord.

The landlord will use the old tactic: "Our contractors must be used because they know the base building best and will therefore not only do the best job but be less likely to damage any of the base building electrical or mechanical systems. Furthermore, if your [the tenant's] contractors damaged the base building systems, you [the tenant] would be responsible for the costs of repairing them. Furthermore," and this is always good for a tenant scare, "if you [the tenant] use your own contractors you will be required to post additional bonds and get special insurance before the contractors are allowed in the building." (No one tells the tenant, of course, that most reputable contractors already provide or have the necessary bonds and insurance.)

As a face-saving negotiating point for the landlord, the tenant can "understand" the landlord's concern about the base building and then "give in" to the extent that the landlord's contractor will be used as long as the bid does not exceed 5 percent (or whatever percentage the tenant prefers) of any bids by contractors the tenant has contacted and the markups are specified and capped.

If the tenant is permitted to hire his or her own contractor, the landlord will require a provision stating that the tenant (or the hired contractor) will post various bonds (such as a completion bond) and obtain special risk insurance, as well as obtain and present to the landlord, before any work starts, all required governmental (this may involve local, county, state, and federal jurisdictions) licenses and permits.

Indemnification of the Landlord and the Mechanics' Lien

The basic indemnification provision that a landlord will request will state:

> The tenant shall indemnify and hold the landlord harmless from and against all expenses, liens [where applicable for the jurisdiction], claims, liabilities, or damages to person or property based on, or arising directly or indirectly by reason of the making of any alterations, decorations, changes, modifications, additions, improvements, or construction to the premises.

This provision gives the landlord broad indemnification. An additional liability concern of the landlord arises from the nature of the construction industry. Despite differences in the various jurisdictions, statutes governing mechanics' liens ensure that sup-

pliers and contractors in the construction industry will be paid
for providing labor and materials. However, as there are no established national standards, the tenant must look to an attorney or
a PREB for guidance regarding this issue.

Consider the following provision, which supplements the
tenant's indemnification of the landlord, especially as it pertains
to alterations, improvements, or construction on the premises:

> The tenant covenants and agrees that any alterations, modifi-
> cations, changes, improvements, or construction made to the
> premises shall be conducted on behalf of the tenant and not
> on behalf of landlord. Tenant further covenants and agrees
> that in the event the landlord shall give his or her written con-
> sent to the making of any alteration or improvement to the
> premises, such written consent shall not be deemed to be an
> agreement or consent by landlord to subject his or her inter-
> est in the premises, the building, or the adjacent real property
> to any mechanics' or materialmen's liens that may be filed for
> alterations, modifications, or improvements made on behalf
> of the tenant. Landlord shall have the right to post notices, in
> and around the building and property, as well as on the
> tenant's premises, of nonresponsibility of the landlord for any
> and all work performed on behalf of the tenant, in order to
> protect the property, the building, and the premises from any
> liens. [The following may be in addition to, or in place of, the
> previous sentence, subject to what is permitted in the jurisdic-
> tion.] As a condition precedent to performing any alterations,
> modifications, or improvements to the premises, the tenant
> agrees to obtain and deliver to landlord written and uncondi-
> tional waivers of mechanics' and materialmen's liens upon the
> real property and building of which the premises are a part,
> for all work, labor, and services to be performed, and materi-
> als to be furnished by them in connection with such work,
> signed by all contractors, subcontractors, materialmen, and la-
> borers to be involved in the premises work. If, regardless, any
> mechanics' or materialmen's lien is filed against the premises,
> the building, or the associated real property for work claimed
> to have been done for, or materials claimed to have been fur-
> nished to, the tenant, such lien shall be discharged by the ten-
> ant within ten (10) days thereafter, at the tenant's sole cost
> and expense, by full payment of owed amounts or the filing
> and posting of a bond. If the tenant shall fail to discharge any
> such mechanics' or materialmen's lien, the landlord may, at
> his or her option, discharge the same and treat the costs (in-

cluding any and all attorney's fees and other associated expenses) incurred in connection with the discharging of the lien as additional rent, immediately payable to the landlord. The tenant covenants and agrees that such discharge by the landlord shall not be deemed to waive, or release, the default of the tenant in not discharging the lien.

One drawback of the mechanics' lien lease provision (or separate clause) is that in indemnifying the landlord, the tenant loses any leverage he or she might otherwise possess in the event of a contractor dispute. Any holdback of payment by the tenant to a contractor that results in a lien being placed on the property can, and will be, immediately discharged by the landlord. The tenant will then owe the landlord rather than the contractor—end of any dispute. The tenant should modify any mechanics' lien provision to provide for the contesting of a mechanics' lien. This will involve the posting of a security or surety bond with the landlord, as well as the possible additional requirement of special risk and property title insurance.

Who Owns What

Tenant expectations concerning what they own in the premises often conflict with the realities specified in a lease document. From a practical standpoint, it is easy to understand the tenant's confusion. A tenant who paints the walls of the premises or puts up new wall coverings expects to leave these alterations in place when the premises are vacated. Imagine a tenant's confusion when the landlord insists that fancy wall paneling, wallpaper, or other special wall treatments must be removed in accordance with the lease and the walls put back in their original condition, as they were on the date the lease began, ordinary wear and tear excepted.

The opposite situation can also lead to intense confrontations between landlord and tenant, for example, when the tenant has installed specially constructed bookcases, has purchased special kitchen cabinets, installed expensive lighting fixtures, or had conference room furniture specially built. The tenant expects to be able to remove these items and take them on to other premises, with every intention of repairing any damages and leaving the premises in the same original leased condition. However, given the nature of a landlord and how easily a provision is slipped into the alterations lease clause, the tenant may be in for an abrupt and unpleasant surprise. After all, the landlord also knows the value of certain alterations and improvements and their ability to help attract a new tenant and re-lease the premises as quickly as possible.

The basic landlord provision states:

> If any alterations, decorations, or improvements are made without the prior written consent of the landlord, the landlord shall have the right in his or her sole discretion to remove and correct such alterations and restore the premises to their original condition and configuration, ordinary wear and tear excepted, as of the lease commencement date. All alterations, decorations, or improvements to the premises or the building made by either party shall immediately become the property of the landlord and shall be surrendered with the premises either with the expiration or termination of the lease. The landlord may, by giving written notice at least thirty (30) days prior to the expiration or termination of the lease, require the tenant, at tenant's sole cost and expense, to remove all alterations, decorations, or improvements, including all fixtures and equipment installed by the tenant. The tenant will be responsible for any repair and damages to the premises arising from their removal, or if tenant fails to remove and properly repair the premises, the landlord, at the landlord's option, may remove all alterations, decorations, modifications, or improvements made to the premises and repair any damage incurred, and the tenant covenants and agrees to reimburse the landlord for the costs and expense of such removal and repair and in addition for any and all damages and related expenses the landlord may sustain by reason of default by the tenant.

For this lease provision, the tenant should consider at least one obvious modification for his or her benefit, although it may not be easy to achieve. The tenant should have no responsibility for removing any alterations, decorations, or improvements that were made with the prior written consent of the landlord.

This provision will obviously not sit well with many landlords. They will argue that they permitted certain alterations or improvements at the tenant's request and that these alterations made the premises a better place for the tenant. The permission was given in the spirit of cooperation and better business relations. The tenant must not now expect to walk away and leave the landlord stuck with an alteration or improvement made especially for the tenant's purposes.

The tenant's point of view must also, however, be succinct. That is, the landlord knew what was to be done in advance and approved the change. It is presumed that the landlord would not permit any alterations that were going to be detrimental to the premises and thus the property.

The general point of reconciliation is to recognize that certain alterations do improve the premises, and upon departure, the tenant will have no responsibility to remove or change any that had prior consent. For other alterations, the landlord and tenant should, at the time that landlord consent is granted, agree on whether the alteration or improvement is to be removed and the premises placed back in near-original condition and configuration upon the tenant's departure.

Under this compromise, both parties must now consider each alteration separately and weigh its merits and any other possible options. But it is a favorable compromise for the tenant.

Effects of Tenant Default

An additional aspect of the alterations clause can cause the unwary tenant much grief. This provision is often tacked on to the preceding provision, which would continue as follows:

> If tenant is not in default under the lease, the tenant shall have the right to remove, prior to the expiration of the lease term, all furniture, furnishings, and equipment installed in the premises solely at the expense of the tenant that can be removed without any substantial damage to the premises or the building. All damage and injury to the premises or the building caused by such removal shall be repaired by the tenant, at the tenant's sole cost and expense. If the tenant shall fail to remove all of the tenant's effects and property from the premises upon the expiration or termination of the lease, then all effects and property shall become the property of the landlord and shall be surrendered with the premises at the ex-

piration or termination of the lease. The landlord, at his or her option, may remove the tenant's property in any manner the landlord chooses and store the effects and property without any liability to the tenant for any losses that may occur. The tenant agrees to pay the landlord on demand any and all costs and expenses in such removal, including court costs, attorney and any other related fees, and storage charges for the time the effects and property are in the landlord's possession. The landlord may, at his or her option and without notice to the tenant, sell the effects and property at private sale and without additional legal process for whatever price the landlord can obtain and may apply the sale proceeds to any amounts due and owing under the lease from the tenant to the landlord or to satisfy any costs or expenses incurred for the removal and sale of effects and property.

This additional provision can be pretty heady and serious-sounding stuff to a tenant. Whether it is included as stated, is modified, or is even included at all depends on the laws and ordinances of the jurisdiction. But whatever version is included, the tenant must make sure that his or her needs are also met.

The tenant must recognize that the intent of this provision is to cover any alterations made during the tenant's occupancy. Unless stated elsewhere in the lease, this may also be the only place where initial alterations paid for and owned by the tenant are addressed.

First and foremost, the generalized statement about "as long as tenant is not in default" should be modified to specify exactly what type of default or the extent of default required before a tenant would be prohibited from removing his or her own furniture and equipment. Although it may seem obvious, the nature of a serious default, such as the tenant's being 30 days or more late with rent or other money, must be specified. The tenant does not want to encounter difficulty with a landlord because of some long-forgotten landlord-tenant disagreement or an infraction of some minor rule putting the tenant in technical default. (This is an example of why defaults during a lease term must not be allowed to linger and carry over throughout a lease term; see Chapter 23.)

By and large, however, this provision does not cause that much difficulty between landlords and tenants. It is only occasionally that a tenant finds that certain furniture, furnishings, equipment, or fixtures cannot be moved to new premises. Still, tenants find it hard to understand how something they paid a great deal for does not belong to them.

Put in Writing
What Is to Be Taken

Whenever a tenant makes an alteration or installs a fixture in the premises, the tenant's intent to remove and take the item at the end of the lease should be clearly stated in writing to the landlord. A provision that would be tenant-oriented would state:

> All effects, personal property, and all business and trade fixtures, machinery and equipment, raised flooring installed for the operation of computer systems, additional air-conditioning systems, furniture, and movable partitions owned by tenant or installed by tenant at his or her expense in the premises shall be and remain the property of the tenant and may be removed by the tenant at any time during the lease term, provided the tenant is not in any serious monetary default under the lease and that the tenant shall repair any injury or damage to the premises or the building caused by such removal, including any and all holes in floors, walls, ceilings, and floor slabs.

How specific a tenant needs to be regarding property is a function of how expensive or important the items are to the tenant and how easily they can be removed. Although it may be obvious to a tenant that a certain item or system is intended to be removed and taken, the landlord may not see it that way. Therefore, a tenant should, to the extent possible, provide a detailed listing of the less obvious systems to be removed.

The following items have caused tenant difficulties:

- Security systems, including card readers, code entry devices, power transformers, power and control wires, special door latches and door strikes, and special door handles and mechanisms

- Computer room equipment, including air-conditioning equipment; raised floor construction along with structural members and floor tile covering; fire suppression systems and all associated equipment and materials; and backup power equipment such as motor generators, batteries, switching gear, and all associated equipment and materials

- Telecommunication equipment, including all antennas, antenna and other equipment support beams and structures, power and other wiring, and all associated equipment and materials

- Kitchen or cafeteria equipment, including freezers, refrigerators, ice makers, ovens, grills, serving units, dishwashers, trash compactors, counters, cabinets, and all associated equipment, and materials

- Private bath, shower, or exercise room equipment, including commodes, sinks, showers, lockers, cabinets, counters, exercise equipment (both free-standing or affixed to walls, floors, or ceilings), mats, sound absorbing material, and all associated fixtures, equipment, and materials

- General equipment and systems, including additional HVAC units in conference rooms, computer rooms, classrooms, training areas, or any other area; tenant-installed mechanical and electrical equipment and systems above base building items, such as power transformers; tenant-installed fire suppression systems above base building system; communication and sound system speakers and speaker wiring; telephone equipment and all associated wires and materials; computer or word processing wires and hookups; tenant-installed supplemental lighting, including wall sconces and chandeliers; tenant-installed built-in cabinetry, including bookcases, credenzas, cabinets, counters, tables, and seating areas; all modular furniture equipment and materials, including hanging wall strips and power strips

To the extent that the tenant's property is expensive, was specially produced or constructed, and is related to either the general business environment or general business operations, the tenant should be sure there will be no confusion or misunderstandings with the landlord as to when the tenant wants to, or will attempt to, take the property with him or her.

Increased Costs from
Increased Property Value

Certain alterations can increase the overall value of the building or the associated property or create a different general or fire insurance rating and thus make it necessary to purchase additional insurance or increase the building or property insurance.

From the perspective of a tenant who is not responsible for any of the increased costs or expenses, the question is whether he or she will wind up paying for any portion of the increase. From the perspective of a landlord, especially in a multitenanted building, the question is whether the increased costs will be passed on in a general way to everyone in the building.

When certain costs increase, the difficulty lies in determining what part, if any, of the increase may be due to an alteration or improvement for a tenant. For the single-tenanted building, this is not a problem since the tenant will be paying for the increased costs anyway or can be directly charged (assuming it is in the lease) for the increased amount.

This is not as easy in a multitenanted structure. In fairness to all other tenants, the landlord is obliged to try to isolate any increased costs resulting from the actions of only one tenant and have that tenant made responsible for the increase. Isolating these cost increases can be difficult and complex, however, and will be more trouble than it is worth to the landlord. After all, it is far easier to pass on the increases to everyone regardless of the reason for the increase—and who is to really know?

If for no other reason than to soothe the troubled conscience of the tenant creating an increased cost because of an improvement, or to satisfy all other tenants, whose interests the landlord will seem to be looking out for, a simple provision should be included requiring that any increases in property taxes or insurance expense as the result of a tenant alteration, modification, or improvement must be paid by the tenant responsible for the increase.

All the tenants need to do is figure out how to be sure that the landlord is not collecting the increased cost from the responsible tenant and also including it as an expense passthrough assignable to every tenant.

18
Maintenance and Repairs

Has your professional real estate broker (PREB) explained that the purpose of a lease clause on maintenance and repairs is not simply to clarify who is responsible for what? This lease clause is actually critical to the landlord and can be equally so to the tenant. Without it, neither the tenant nor the landlord has any obligation to maintain or repair the premises during the term of the lease.

This lease clause affects the tenant's premises only. It does not refer to the property, building, or common areas—unless there is a single building user, in which case the tenant's lease may include everything connected with the building and property (the tenant would operate much the same as an owner of the property and would be responsible and liable for all maintenance and repair).

In multitenanted buildings, the landlord will be responsible for maintaining and repairing the property, the building, and the building's common areas. Attached to this responsibility is the liability for any injuries that may occur because maintenance or repair has been neglected.

But the landlord's concern goes beyond the responsibility and liability issues. For the landlord, the property and building are an investment, and as long as the investment remains sound, the landlord will be concerned with every aspect of the property, including the tenant's premises. It is not in the landlord's best interests to allow the property to become neglected or misused.

The landlord wants the tenant to take care of, repair, and maintain the premises. The landlord encourages tenants to tell him or her when something is not right, and if given notice (even though the responsibility may be the tenant's), the landlord will arrange for the necessary maintenance or repair work, expecting the tenant to pay for the work.

A tenant's perspective changes over time. Early in a lease cycle, a tenant will be more concerned about the premises. Even old space will look nice to a new tenant. But with time and use, look deteriorates; the premises become old, tired, and worn looking—whether or not they are actually run down. Near the end of the lease term, especially if the tenant will be relocating, the tenant does not want to be concerned about the space. Maintenance and repair of a former space is the last thing a departing tenant cares about.

In the normal course of business, there are no reasons for a tenant to misuse or destroy the premises. Although the premises may become worn, old, and tired looking over time, with shabby, worn floor coverings and dirty, dingy wall coverings, the walls will usually still be standing, doors will still be attached, and windows will be intact. Over time, mechanical, electrical, and other building systems that feed the premises may wear out or become outmoded; these are building operations, the responsibility of the landlord, who expects them to wear out over time. The premises themselves, however, need only some renovation and refurbishing to make them look clean, hospitable, and new.

The landlord expects the tenant not to abuse the premises. Therefore, the lease will state, either in this clause or perhaps under the surrender of possession clause, the simple concept that the tenant shall return the premises in the same order and condition as on the lease commencement date: broom-clean and debris-free, with ordinary and reasonable wear and tear, and any unavoidable damage by the elements excepted.

The majority of tenants will not have any problem with this basic statement, nor should they. It is a straightforward acceptance of normal business practices. However, difficulties do occur. Some tenants do not want to be responsible for, or have anything to do with, keeping up the premises. Their attitude is "Use the premises as hard as possible, wear them out, and move on." To these tenants, compounded wear and tear from year to year is acceptable, and they believe the space should be returned to the landlord in that final condition.

We should be thankful that this is a minority view, in no way consistent with good business practices. There is no reason why a tenant should not agree to the usual opening statement of this lease clause: "The tenant will keep the premises and any included fixtures and equipment in clean, safe, and sanitary condition, will take good care of same, and will suffer no waste or injury."

Up to this point, a repair and maintenance clause is relatively straightforward and simple. In fact, it probably should not become any more complicated, except that both tenants and landlords will have some specific concerns based on past experiences that each will want to have addressed in the clause.

The tenant must watch for and avoid the hard-nosed landlord approach, taken because of previous tenant difficulties, that specifies the tenant will make all repairs necessary to keep the premises from deteriorating in value or condition, and that exempts the landlord from making any repairs to the premises during the term of the lease. This type of provision should be unacceptable to the tenant. There is no way a tenant can guarantee or should have any reason to be responsible for the reduced value of the premises. While worn-out carpet and peeling paint are deteriorating conditions, they are part of normal use and wear. The tenant should be concerned about the amount of repair that will be required at the end of the lease period. The tenant only wants to be responsible for having to perform the normal wear-and-tear repair work, as was done in the previous years of the lease.

The tenant will also be concerned with what happens at the end of the lease term to any alterations and improvements made to the premises (and approved by the landlord). Unless a provision is made to the contrary, either here or in the alterations clause, it is possible for the landlord to demand that all improvements or changes be removed and the premises put back the way they were at the lease commencement date. It therefore becomes critical for this clause to be modified to state "ordinary wear and tear and landlord-approved alterations, modifications, changes, and improvements to the premises excepted." This, of course, assumes the tenant does not want to take the improvement with him or her to new premises. Otherwise, the provision will need to take removal into account (see Chapter 17).

What happens if the premises have been damaged by fire or other casualty and the tenant and his or her employees, agents, representatives, guests, and customers were not responsible for the damage? From the tenant's perspective, it would be nice to include some wording that exempts the tenant from having to repair any damage by fire or casualty that was not the responsibility of, or due to the neglect of, the tenant. This simple phraseology however, may be in serious conflict with other lease clauses covering casualty damage, insurance, or subrogation. If these other lease clauses exist, they are the proper places to take care of this type of special tenant concern. It is best to avoid cluttering up the "ordinary wear and tear" phrase.

Who Is Responsible for What

The job of a lease clause is to specify the responsibilities and obligations of the tenant or the landlord. Nothing can be more frustrating, from a tenant's perspective, than not knowing who is responsible for fixing, repairing, or maintaining something in the premises or the building. To avoid any misunderstandings and possible future lawsuits, it behooves the tenant to make sure that any landlord responsibilities concerning the premises are spelled out. Here, again, some other lease clauses may indicate what services the landlord will provide (see Chapter 21), and this is where the majority of these items will go. On occasion, however, some specific items of concern can go into this lease clause without causing excessive clutter.

For example, a provision may specify that all replacement bulbs or tubes for the building standard lighting shall be provided and installed by the landlord at the landlord's cost and expense. All other bulbs, tubes, and installed fixtures in the premises will be provided and installed either by the tenant at the tenant's cost and expense or by the landlord at the tenant's cost and expense (here is an example of a case where there is often a tenant or landlord choice). Similarly, if certain alterations and improvements are provided for the tenant and the items involved must remain with the premises, is it the landlord's responsibility or the tenant's to repair and maintain them?

It can be either one, but whose it is should be made clear. For example, the maintenance and repair of fixtures and equipment such as kitchen fixtures, executive washrooms, shower and sauna rooms, specially installed HVAC equipment separate from the base building units, or any other type of special equipment or fixtures, whether installed by the tenant or by the landlord on behalf of the tenant, will either be the sole responsibility of the tenant (the landlord shall have no obligation for its repair or maintenance) or be repaired and maintained by the landlord with all associated expenses the responsibility of the tenant.

What both the tenant and the landlord want to avoid is the omitting of any mention of their respective responsibilities. If an issue is not addressed, each party will expect the other to take responsibility should any problem occur.

Consider these situations. If a specially installed conference room air-conditioning system breaks down and no one is responsible, who repairs it? The landlord can sit back and enjoy the discomfort of the tenant; when the tenant becomes uncomfortable enough, he or she will be forced to arrange for and bear the costs of the repair (which might have been avoided if the unit had been properly maintained—but by whom?). However, the breakdown may cause not only some discomfort to the tenant, but also flooding and damage to the premises of another tenant (adjacent or below). Can the tenant now sit back and enjoy the discomfort and mad scrambling of the landlord? Or is the tenant equally concerned? Consider the tenant who suffers the damages turning around and suing both the tenant and the landlord for neglect!

19

Rules and Regulations

Landlords establish many rules and regulations for multi-tenanted buildings. Yet the lease document may only briefly refer either to the right of the landlord to create building rules and regulations or to an invisible set of rules and regulations. Although these rules and regulations may not be listed in a specific lease clause or provision, they are no less important than the items covered in other parts of the lease.

The basic lease clause refers to the tenant's invitees, guests, agents, employees, licensees, visitors, and clients or customers (some or all of these may be included) and requires that all abide by and strictly observe the rules and regulations, either those attached to the lease document or those as may be created, changed, or promulgated from time to time by the landlord. The clause will also relieve the landlord of any responsibility or obligation to enforce the rules and regulations, its terms, and conditions against any other tenant. The landlord will also take no responsibility or liability for violation of the rules and regulations by any other tenant or his or her employees, agents, guests, licensees, and customers. This clause also provides that, in the event of conflict between a rule or regulation and the lease document, the lease document will take precedence.

This lease clause is considered innocuous by the majority of tenants, who underestimate its importance to the landlord. Rules

and regulations give the landlord control over the tenant's utilization of the building and often over the tenant's own space. Violat-
ing the rules and regulations technically puts a tenant in default
of the lease. Being in default can have grave consequences for
lease renewals, subleasing, expansion options, and a host of other
issues directly affecting the tenant.

Under no circumstances should a tenant sign a lease that does
not spell out the rules and regulations or have them attached to
the lease document. Even though the lease clause usually permits
the landlord to make whatever changes he or she wants whenever
he or she wants to, the tenant must carefully review the starting
document that will be affecting the tenant's conduct of business
within and around the building.

The tenant must never assume that the same rules and regulations apply in all buildings. They do not. In many instances they
may not even be consistent in different buildings under the same
landlord. Therefore, the new tenant will have a new set of rules
and regulations to abide by, and these new rules and regulations
may possibly be contrary to what the tenant has been used to.

What a tenant can insist on regarding a landlord's rules and
regulations is usually subject to the market power (e.g., size) of
the user. However, there are a few items that every tenant should
have incorporated into the basic rules and regulations clause.
This is especially important when the landlord retains the right to
make rule and regulation changes at his or her sole discretion.

In particular, the tenant must be notified of any contemplated
rule changes within some reasonable period (e.g., 30 days) in
advance of the changes taking effect. Having advance notice
won't necessarily allow the tenant to do anything about a new or
changed regulation, but it does give the tenant an opportunity
at least to try to do something if the regulation is disliked or
onerous.

The tenant should also insist that any changes in the rules and
regulations will not incur an additional cost, an administrative
burden, or compliance difficulties over the rules and regulations
in effect at the time the tenant signs the lease. This tenant-preferred lease provision should not be unacceptable to the ethical
landlord. In addition, the tenant should include a provision stating that any changes from the original set of rules and regulations

will have no new or additional effects on the tenant's business operations or premises. Rule or regulation changes or additions should only affect the building's general common spaces and adjacent property areas (e.g., parking lots).

The actual number of items included in a list of rules and regulations varies significantly from building to building, from landlord to landlord, and from region to region. However, the tenant should be aware of a number of themes common to most lists of rules and regulations. The tenant must carefully read (and understand) every rule and regulation that he or she will be agreeing to abide by. The tenant should insist on the landlord's written clarification or adjustments regarding anything that he or she does not understand, finds confusing or objectionable, or expects to have an effect on business operations or the office environment.

It is the wise tenant who remembers that in the world of negotiations and the signing of leases and contracts, "after" is too late. After the lease is signed is not the time to raise objections to things agreed to.

What to Watch Out For

Tenants must watch out for several kinds of regulation problems.

General Right of Waiver by the Landlord

This lease provision gives the landlord the right to provide the tenant with a written waiver regarding compliance to one or all of the rules and regulations for a specified or unspecified time period. The waiver, however, does not apply to the tenant's future obligation to comply with the rules and regulations. Furthermore, any waiver granted to one tenant does not relieve any or all other tenants from having to comply with the rules and regulations.

A waiver granted by the landlord to a tenant does not relieve the tenant of any liabilities or damages that may occur whether or not the tenant has complied with the rules and regulations.

No Open Suite Doors

Usually the restriction pertaining to open suite doors is so well buried that it is easy to miss. Its intent is to achieve uniformity on multitenanted floors with respect to containing a tenant's business operations, noise, and personal decorating preferences within the confines of the premises. If the rule is taken literally, however, especially by building maintenance or janitorial staff, any suite with open doors may lead to an unpleasant confrontation.

Consider, for example, a large, multifloor tenant with a number of different entrances to the premises on each floor or a smaller tenant who, through growth, has acquired a number of small spaces on different floors. Suppose there is an "open house" for customers to visit the premises and meet the staff, or suppose a group of visitors arrives for a special meeting that requires access to different spaces on different floors. Normally, for security purposes, all but the main entrance to the premises would be locked; access to the auxiliary entrances would require a key. However, for an open house or a special meeting, all the doors are unlocked or propped open to facilitate the movement of people.

Now picture overachieving building employees constantly moving from floor to floor, entrance to entrance, closing all the open doors because they violate the rules of the building. There is no way those doors will be allowed to stay open. Sounds far-fetched? This actually happened. In desperation, the tenant stationed employees at each open door to stare down the building employees, much to the distaste of all concerned.

No Signs in Hallways or Other Common Spaces

With this prohibition, a tenant is unable to display any directional or informational signs to guide visitors or guests, regardless of the occasion—a party, a meeting, or a client open house. One tenant's solution was to station employees with every sign, to keep the building employees from removing them. The staff might just as well have provided the directions and information.

Deliveries

Depending on how this provision is worded, it may prohibit virtually all deliveries, general or specific, from going directly to a tenant's space, except at specified times that are usually inconvenient for everybody concerned. The definition of what constitutes a delivery can be extended to include everything from the tenant's own goods and products to office supplies and vending machine supplies (sodas, candy) to copiers and letter and parcel courier services (both pickups and deliveries).

The intent of these rules and regulations is to control the use of elevators, avoid inconveniencing and annoying the other tenants, minimize the wandering of uninvited people, and generally maintain a "quality" atmosphere. The result is often inconvenience for tenants, lost goods and materials, and unhappy suppliers—but no landlord liability or responsibility.

Suppose that every package, no matter what size, must enter or leave the building through a particular loading dock or delivery area. Tenants are required to take their outgoing packages there and leave them to be picked up by the delivery service. There should be numerous tenant concerns. Is the area fully staffed? Who is in control? Who is responsible for lost or stolen goods or packages? Who watches valuables? What are the security arrangements?

The same would be true for deliveries to tenants. Every package to the building would be dropped off at this central area, but the tenant's employees would not be allowed to come down to get anything (no deliveries through the building, thank you). Rather, the building's employees would have to deliver everything to the tenant's premises. Is this really the quality touch a landlord would lead you to believe it is? When will the deliveries be made? (When there are enough packages?) When will the building staff be available for deliveries? (During off-hours for elevator use?)

Obviously, many businesses could not possibly live with this kind of pickup and delivery system. Imagine a diamond dealer leaving and receiving products at an unsecured loading dock or a law or accounting firm leaving private papers unattended by its own staff! Yet a landlord can require this and not be liable for untoward consequences.

Unquestionably, some kind of trade-off is needed in relation to the magnitude of the delivery (or pickup).

Vending Machines Prohibited

This rule prohibits the installation of vending machines of any type anywhere in the building without prior landlord approval. Tenants are often surprised to find that the prohibition also includes their business premises.

This restriction is designed to keep any tenant from establishing, under the guise of providing food and drink for his or her own employees, an annoying and trash-producing vending machine business in the building. The tenant needs to be sure this restriction does not extend to a limited number of vending machines provided and maintained within the premises for his or her own employees. These machines are often an employee benefit, the food and drink subsidized by the tenant and sold at or below cost.

Most landlords are likely to waive the prohibition within a tenant's premises. However, the tenant must also be sure that there are no other restrictions, such as the delivery prohibition, that would keep the machines from being stocked by a supplier.

No Bicycles on the Premises

This rule prohibits mopeds, motorcycles, and bicycles from being on the tenant's premises. Regulations will require that these items be left in a garage area, on a special parking area adjacent to the building, or on a lower basement or storage floor of the building. The storage of these vehicles in a tenant's space is not the real concern. Rather, the intent is to keep these vehicles from entering the building, where they may create traffic and cleaning problems and cause annoyance and inconvenience to other tenants (do you want to ride in an elevator with a bicycle, especially one lifted vertically to fit into the cab?) and damage to elevator cab interiors and hallway walls.

There is nothing wrong with this rule as long as everyone knows about, understands, and agrees to it. For a tenant, difficulties come about when employees change their habits or new employees arrive who are used to different building standards. Before a tenant knows what is happening, bicycles are being brought into the space. Why? Security. Where else can you put one of these vehicles and be sure it will be safe from theft and vandalism? In a bike rack in a parking lot? Not likely. At any rate, no matter where they are put, the landlord will accept no responsibility or liability for such vehicles.

People become very attached to their bikes. For peace of mind, they want them nearby, physically and visually present. Even if the tenant is unaware that an employee is bringing a bicycle onto the premises, he or she is still responsible for the acts of the employees. Welcome to default.

No Cooking, No Odors

There are a hundred different variations on this rule, but what it boils down to is that no cooking by the tenant is permitted on the premises. In addition, no odors objectionable to other tenants or the landlord are permitted to emanate from the tenant's premises.

This rule is violated virtually every day by a tenant somewhere. Using microwave ovens, employees daily prepare quick lunches and snacks. The odor of cooking popcorn wafts through the halls of many buildings in the late afternoon. Theoretically, this rule could be extended to coffee machines.

The intent of the restriction is to limit extensive food preparation unrelated to a tenant's actual business operations. Even with the best ventilation and air-conditioning systems, certain food odors tend to linger and be offensive to other tenants, as well as turn off visitors, guests, and customers coming into the building.

Normally the rule is not intended to restrict a tenant's employees from limited food preparation for personal consumption. However, without some modification or explicit statement recognizing such personal food preparation, the tenant can technically be considered in default of his or her lease the moment anyone microwaves a lunch (not to mention being in default for having on the premises a nonstandard business machine utilizing building electricity). And what about the businesses that may have to hold certain events in their premises, such as a Christmas party, a business anniversary party, or an annual open house? The business or employee party can cause a great deal of hostility, especially when the landlord may be looking for a reason to find the tenant in default, to prevent the tenant from executing an option or right (e.g., expansion right) provided for in his or her lease.

It is in the tenant's best interests to have this rule adjusted to reflect reality and the needs and requirements of a business. Because the rules and regulations can be changed by landlord decree, any tenant-preferred changes are best made with an explicit lease provision or an addendum to the lease.

No Heating or Cooling Except as Provided by the Landlord

This restriction is established to protect the base building systems. The prohibition is directed at tenant connections to the electric, water, HVAC, and other utility and operating systems in the building and at nonstandard office equipment and machines.

Few buildings have ideal HVAC systems. Because of the way space is utilized, be it a total open space plan or one with floor-to-ceiling partitions, there will always be areas that are warmer or colder than others or that have drafts (especially busy reception areas where the main suite door is continually opening and closing). Even when the HVAC systems are 100 percent efficient and in perfect working order, someone is bound to be too warm or too cold and ready to plug in a cooling fan or personal mini-heater (or space heater). This rule specifically prohibits these items for reasons of safety. All too often, staff will forget to turn off or unplug fans and space heaters. Not only do these items consume excessive electrical power, but they are subject to overheating, and the resulting burned-out motors or hot coils can cause fires. In many buildings maintenance and janitorial service staff are instructed to unplug such prohibited appliances and to remove them from the premises.

The tenant is caught in the middle, between an employee who is cold and wants supplemental heating and the rules—the building's HVAC system probably provides adequate heating but not enough to satisfy this particular employee. The landlord is most likely providing the amount of heat specified or required under the lease document and is concerned for the safety of the building and all the other tenants.

There is no easy answer here. If the tenant wants supplemental HVAC for the premises or a particular area of the premises (such as increased ventilation for a smoking lounge or extra heating for a reception area), in most instances the landlord can authorize it or actually provide it with supplemental air-handling units—as long as the tenant is willing to pay for the equipment, installation, maintenance, and operations. The best solution is to learn from previous experiences and have the additional HVAC system installed where needed before moving into a new space. When planned in advance, the costs for supplying the additional needs are at least subject to tenant-landlord negotiation before a lease is signed.

And the List Goes On

The rules and regulations given above are those that cause the most difficulties for tenants and landlords. However, a great number of other restrictions and prohibitions lie buried in the rules and regulations of a building. Here are some other potential sources of tenant problems:

- *Restrictions on the use of freight elevators.* Such restrictions usually apply to certain times of the day.

- *Limitations on the moving of furniture, fixtures, machinery, and equipment within the building.* This can sorely limit the tenant's ability to reorganize operations without considerable planning.

- *No pets or animals.* This rule actually makes good sense, except for the employee who wants to bring a dog or cat in on a weekend so that he or she can have company while finishing up important work.

- *No curtains, drapes, or any window treatment without landlord approval.* This regulation provides a building with a consistent façade.

- *Nothing placed on windowsills or ledges that is visible from outside the building.* This is another regulation designed to provide for a consistent image outside the building.

- *No signs or advertising that can be seen from outside the tenant's premises.*
- *No tenant-supplied door locks or other security locks.* The landlord retains the right to provide all door locks and to retain a key for access.
- *Limited or no quantities of flammable or combustible fluids or materials permitted on the premises unless they are required to maintain office equipment.* This is an obvious building safety measure, but it can create difficulties for a tenant whose printing press, say, requires inks and solvents (usually highly flammable). If you think that this situation is an automatic exception, think again. It is not.
- *The requirement that a tenant carry certain types of insurance, which is individually listed and has specified dollar limits.*
- *Restrictions on building access for nonbusiness hours (such as weekends and holidays).* Similarly, the landlord may institute a separate set of rules regulating building security before and after normal business hours.
- *No use of the premises for any immoral or illegal business activities.* Depending on the landlord, this provision will also tend to limit certain additional types of activities, particularly those that are likely to create heavy customer or supplemental employee traffic that could be an annoyance or inconvenience to other tenants. For example, the landlord may prohibit the premises from being used as a central payment point for a large number of off-site employees (e.g., as would be the case in a construction office or a temporary employment agency).

The list of landlord restrictions and prohibitions goes on. These rules are intended to provide the landlord with as much control as possible, on the assumption that such control will benefit all of the building's tenants.

Rules and Regulations Do Matter

The tenant should not and cannot afford to rely on a third party (e.g., a PREB) to inform him or her of the difficulties that *might* be encountered because of a particular building's rules and regulations. As this chapter points out, various rules or regulations can have a profound impact on the operation and employees of a business. It is up to the tenant to read carefully every line, every word, of a building's rules and regulations before signing a lease and to determine how they will affect the organization.

There should be no doubt in the tenant's mind that the rules and regulations will have an impact. The questions are how great the impact will be and whether it will lead to future difficulties or hostilities with the landlord.

For example, somewhere the lease document will contain a separate provision or an addendum specifying the operating hours and days of the building and the legal holidays for which the building will be closed. These items can have great impact on a tenant's business. These are the times the building is generally accessible to the public and for which building services such as HVAC will be provided. Although the subject is often covered elsewhere in the lease document, a listing of when the building will be closed for certain holidays may be appended to the building's rules and regulations and should not be overlooked by the tenant.

To evaluate the impact of a building's rules and regulations, the tenant might solicit employee comments. Pass the rules and regulations list around. Ask the staff what operational difficulties they anticipate and, because they are the backbone of the organization, what limitations they feel would be placed on the business by the regulations. The response from the employees will give management a new perspective on what can affect the business.

20

Landlord Entry for Repairs and Inspection

The repairs and inspection clause provides the landlord with the right to enter the tenant's premises to perform general inspection, repair, maintenance, and alteration of the property. Without this clause, under certain circumstances a landlord's entry into a tenant's premises would be in clear violation of the lease (the right to quiet enjoyment of the premises) and possibly even local laws and ordinances (trespass and nonauthorized or forced entry).

Therefore, the landlord is likely to add this clause automatically to the lease document or the general "boilerplate" (the standard legal parts of a contract or agreement that fill up a page, make the lawyers happy, make a contract a legally binding document, and are rarely paid any attention) provided by the landlord's attorney. This clause provides necessary protection for the landlord.

For the tenant, the clause can seem both restrictive and permissive. It almost gives the landlord carte blanche to enter into the tenant's premises at the landlord's discretion or whim. The basic clause states: "The tenant shall permit the landlord, or his or her employees, agents, and representatives to enter the premises at any time in response to an emergency. . . . "

On the other hand, the clause can be viewed as protecting the tenant's interests. The intention of the clause is as follows:

1. It allows the landlord to inspect and repair any building operating system used by the premises or passing through the premises for the benefit of others, including but not limited to pipes, water and waste lines, conduits, ducts, vents, plumbing, cables, and wires.

2. It allows a landlord to repair a premises neglected by a tenant.

3. It permits the landlord to enter the premises in order to have access to building systems for alterations, construction, or repair for an adjoining tenant's premises.

4. It provides for the repair and alteration of the premises as the landlord, in his or her sole discretion, deems necessary, proper, or desirable for the proper operation and maintenance of the building and property.

5. It permits the landlord to make any changes or improvements to the building or property as required by governmental laws or regulations, mortgage lenders, and the landlord's or tenant's insurance company.

In addition, this clause will often state that the landlord will also be able to do the following:

- Show the premises to existing or potential mortgage lenders, ground lessor, insurance companies, and prospective tenants.

- Provide janitorial or other services and materials as required under the lease.

- Inspect the premises to determine tenant compliance with all lease obligations.

- Remove, without landlord responsibility or liability, any obvious lease violation, such as placards, signs, or window or door coverings.

Even though there will be a no-landlord-liability or tenant-recourse lease clause elsewhere in the lease document, the landlord may also want to put a specific provision here, as well. This provision would waive any tenant claims against the landlord in the event that the landlord's entry interfered with, caused inconvenience to, or in any way disturbed the tenant's business operations.

Entry as Eviction

More important to the landlord is a provision that states:

> The conduct of the landlord does not constitute an eviction of the tenant, actual or constructive, from the premises or any part of the premises, nor shall such entry be in any way construed to be forced or unlawful. Furthermore, the landlord's entry shall be without any charge to the landlord, and the tenant shall not be entitled to any abatement or reduction of rent or other monetary obligations.

The importance of the no-eviction provision may not be obvious to all tenants. Without this protection, a tenant could, depending on how often the landlord entered the premises or how long and disruptive a particular repair or maintenance service was, claim that business operations were severely disrupted, that he or she was unable to conduct business because of the landlord's actions, and that this situation in turn forced him or her to seek new premises and was therefore a constructive eviction by the landlord.

For the landlord, the provision is vital. But would a tenant really do something like this? The answer is an obvious yes. Tenants have attempted to do this and more. Some have tried to withhold a portion of the rent on the grounds that the landlord's entry interfered with their use, enjoyment, and possession of the premises. Some tenants will use any excuse to avoid paying rent or to try to break a lease.

The Landlord's Early Entry

There is at least one case, however, in which a landlord's use of a tenant's premises provides justification for a rent reduction. When a tenant has moved out before the lease expiration but continues to fully honor all monetary obligations of the lease, the landlord has no right to enter the vacant premises before the end of the lease term to begin alterations and construction to meet the requirements of the next tenant.

The tenant clearly has specific obligations until the end of the lease term, but so does the landlord, and entry for purposes other than inspection and repair is not proper. Without worrying about the legalities of the situation, it is obvious that the landlord is receiving beneficial use of the premises, so it would be nice, for a change, for a landlord who wishes to modify the premises to provide a rent credit or a rent reduction during this period.

Instead, the landlord is more likely to try to put in a provision that permits the unrestricted right to enter the premises after the tenant has departed and before the lease expires in order to begin preparations for a successor tenant or for some other purpose without affecting the tenant's continuing obligations under the lease. The fact is, there is no obligation for a tenant to give this right away. This item can be worth one or more month's rent to the tenant.

Additional Tenant Rights

A tenant has an obligation to conduct business operations as efficiently as possible. In the extreme, having the landlord's employees or agents enter the premises can be disruptive and annoying. Although the landlord needs certain rights, so do the tenants.

Here are some additional lease provisions a tenant should consider including:

1. Any repairs, changes, or improvements the landlord makes to the premises, for whatever approved reason, will not detract from the general business appearance of the premises or materially interfere with ongoing business operations.

2. The landlord and his or her employees, agents, and representatives, except in times of emergency or to provide janitorial or other related services or materials as specified in the lease, is required to provide written notification to the tenant a minimum of 24 hours in advance of any need or expectation to enter the tenant's premises. The notification will state the reason for the entry, specify the day (or days) and a reasonable

approximate entry time, and note any potential disruptions to the tenant's business operations. To the extent possible, this provision should stipulate that the tenant must provide written consent before the landlord can gain entry.

3. To ensure the confidentiality of the tenant's operations and to safeguard proprietary information, the tenant has the right to require that all landlord employees, agents, and representatives present or be required to wear adequate identification while on the tenant's premises. Furthermore, the tenant shall have the right to require that the landlord's employees, agents, representatives, or guests be escorted by a tenant's employee, agent, or representative, who shall be made available by the tenant for all prior-approved entry.

The Landlord's Showing of Premises

An area of entry right that many landlords take for granted is the showing of premises to a prospective tenant near the end of a tenant's lease term. Depending on market conditions, a landlord will want to begin advertising or marketing space as soon as possible in order to avoid vacant and thus unproductive space. In the landlord's view, six months or more in advance of a lease expiration date may be a reasonable time to start showing space, whereas 60 days may be extreme from a tenant's point of view. After all, it is the tenant who will need to put up with the disruption and hassle of nonemployees and noncustomers walking through and poking around every area of the premises.

The tenant should be sure to put an upper limit on when a landlord can begin showing the premises to prospective tenants. Depending on the market, a reasonable compromise is 90 to 120 days before the date the lease expires. In addition, inasmuch as prospective tenants rarely walk in off the street, but rather make appointments and often go through a PREB, it should not be unreasonable to expect the landlord's employee, agent, or representative to call the tenant—in cases involving larger spaces, at least 24 hours ahead (even providing written notice). The tenant should always retain the right to have a tenant's employee, agent, or representative accompany the visitors.

Keys to Locks

Given that this lease clause provides the right of entry to the land-lord, and because the landlord may be responsible for providing janitorial and other services and materials to the premises, it is usually understood that the landlord will have the means to enter, meaning the necessary keys or security codes. The landlord's right to keys may also be stated elsewhere in the lease, because the landlord's employees or agents may be the only individuals permitted to change locks or make duplicate keys.

Since it is never wise to assume anything, it is usually best to have the landlord's rights (if any) to keys and security codes clearly spelled out in a lease provision, along with any tenant-required restrictions.

This provision will state:

> The landlord shall at all times have and retain the necessary key or keys and security and password or number codes with which to unlock all doors and entrances in, upon, and about the premises and the property, excluding any tenant-specified vaults, safes, or other secure areas. In the event of an emergency, the landlord shall have the right to use any and all means that the landlord and his or her employees, agents, or representatives may deem proper to open any and all doors and entrances to gain entrance to all areas of the premises or property.

21
Services and Utilities

Building services and building utilities can either be dealt with in separate clauses in a lease document or, depending on how long and complex they are, be combined into one clause that specifies the services or utilities the landlord will provide (if any) for the tenant and for which payment is included in the rent. In its simplest form, the services and utilities clause specifies only that the landlord will provide services and utilities in accordance with what is provided for similar buildings during generally recognized business days and times. Short and sweet. And vague. Who determines what are "generally recognized business days and times"? What constitutes a "similar" building? For most tenants, there is little comfort in this simple clause. It leaves too much open to interpretation—especially by the landlord.

Services and utilities provided for a tenant encompass a wide variety of items, including HVAC, water and sewage, electricity, other utility services or supplies (such as gas or oil), elevator service, routine maintenance of the premises, char and janitorial services, maintenance of the lavatories and common area, and general building security.

One important concern for the majority of tenants is the building's general business hours and days (i.e., the hours and days the building is open to the public), for which all services and utilities will be provided for the tenant's premises. A related concern is what services (and utilities, if appropriate) are not supplied, are provided in limited quantities, or cost extra for the other hours and days.

What Services Are Supplied, When?

This clause requires careful attention. The tenant must determine whether the services or utilities being supplied and the time periods specified meet the needs of the business. The tenant needs to evaluate the effects of having different services and utilities supplied during different times.

Building Operation Hours

What are the weekday and the weekend hours of operation, and what days will be considered legal holidays?

The hours for a building's operations can greatly affect business operations, especially for firms whose employees arrive early, stay late, or work weekends. For example, although building hours of 7:00 a.m. to 6:00 p.m. may seem normal, for an accounting firm during tax season the 6:00 p.m. closing could be too early and could wind up costing the firm a considerable amount (see After-Hour Services and Utilities Availability, page 310). An 8:00 a.m. to 8:00 p.m. operating day might seem better, but it could prove inconvenient for staff arriving early at a temporary employment service firm.

The time of day that the building's operations close determines when these same services are going to be cut off or stopped. With the air-conditioning turned off, an office can become awfully stuffy and uncomfortably warm on a hot summer day, especially in a modern office building with windows that do not open. Staff productivity will fall dramatically—if staff is even willing to stay.

Weekend Hours. The building will also have different hours of operation and services on the weekend. Most buildings will be officially closed for business on Sundays and will provide services for only half a day on Saturday, for example, from 9:00 a.m. to

1:00 p.m. (However, the hours can vary greatly and are often from 8:00 a.m. to 4:00 p.m.) Because of their greater market power, large space users help determine the building's hours of operation. The multitenanted buildings with the "best" hours (at least in terms of starting and ending times) are usually those containing law and accounting firms (these firms are traditionally known for having long workdays and also requiring weekend work).

Holidays. An additional tenant concern is the days of the year that are to be considered legal (or public) holidays, for which the building will officially be closed or on a Sunday schedule. (Some holidays vary by region of the country.) For firms that take extra days as holidays, there is no real problem. When a building is open, a tenant's business may be closed. (However, security is a potential problem, especially when only one or two businesses are closed in an otherwise open building.)

The opposite situation does cause problems. Some businesses have opted to work on what would otherwise be a legal holiday and then take an alternative day off, for example, the Friday after Thanksgiving, giving employees a four-day weekend, to make up for working during a legal or public holiday such as Veteran's Day or Columbus Day. However, when during a legal holiday the building is in effect closed, getting customers into and out of the building will be inconvenient, and there will be few landlord-provided services.

There is no perfect operation, period. Different tenants have different needs.

Level of Services to Be Supplied

There are no standards for the services or utilities that will be provided for a building. What is provided varies greatly from building to building and especially from region to region. Everything from electricity to heating and cooling to clean bathrooms can be included in the services and utilities a landlord supplies to a tenant. Traditionally, tenants must rely on a landlord for the supply of most services or utilities. Some can be more important or cost more to supply than others. Therefore, different things are often provided at different times.

For example, electrical service to the tenant's premises tends to be supplied as long as the electric service is also provided for the building. But this is not always true, and it depends on the region of the country.

HVAC.   A major service item is heating and cooling. This service tends to revolve around the business hours or days of the building, with different service hours and service standards for weekends and holidays. The tenant who needs these services during nonstandard times must decide whether to pay the landlord for the additional services or utilities or to install supplemental HVAC systems to serve only his or her space.

The landlord will specify that HVAC will be operated and maintained in the most energy-efficient manner possible. Therefore, the landlord may install computerized energy management systems (without accepting liability or responsibility for any local, state, or federal regulations that may affect energy consumption, such as reduced temperature settings and reduced consumption). Computerized energy management systems have broad consequences for a tenant. These systems not only adjust heating and cooling cycles but also perform on-off cycles for a building's energy, including electricity.

HVAC Performance Criteria.   An experienced tenant will add HVAC performance criteria to the lease document to ensure that a specified temperature is maintained in the premises. HVAC performance criteria specify an indoor maximum temperature for the summer months and a minimum temperature for the winter months, measured against a simultaneous outdoor temperature. (Outdoor temperature specifications are vital for establishing acceptable indoor temperatures.) Because employee comfort is affected by humidity, an indoor relative humidity level also needs to be specified and used in conjunction with an actual temperature measurement.

When HVAC performance criteria are included in a lease, the landlord will add language stipulating that the building's HVAC system will provide the specified temperatures subject to the tenant's use of normal and standard business machines and equipment. If the tenant's equipment produces excessive heat, most landlords will offer the option of a supplemental HVAC system for the tenant's premises. However, depending on negotiations, the tenant may be required to bear all, some, or none of the costs of installation, maintenance, and operation.

Elevator Service. A key building service is accessibility to the tenant's space, especially that on an upper floor that can only be reached by elevator. In many buildings the number of elevators in operation and the hours of operation change during evening hours and on weekends and holidays. Evening elevator service tends to be restricted, with a minimum number of cabs on automatic service. This is done to save on energy costs, maintain security, and enable the janitorial staff to use the other cabs. Weekend service may be limited regardless of the operating hours of the other building services.

These limitations can annoy and frustrate the tenant's employees, guests, and customers. Extremely long waits for elevator service are not uncommon, and access to and from upper floors is severely limited.

Other Services to Watch For. Several other building services with different hours or days of operation can also affect a tenant's business operations:

- *No or reduced hot water.* Boilers are shut down except during service hours.

- *Lack of lavatory supplies (e.g., towels, soaps, toilet paper).* This usually happens when employees work late hours or on the weekend and supplies are used up and not replaced for the normal workday until the next evening's cleaning service.

- *Excessive trash, messy conference room tables, dirty kitchens and bathrooms.* This also happens as a result of employees working late hours and on the weekend, after the scheduled char and janitorial services.

The services and utilities clause may contain a provision regarding the landlord's obligation to provide routine maintenance. This provision may be vague in many cases, but often details the replacement of building standard light bulbs or tubes and provides a schedule for repainting or refurbishing the tenant's premise (e.g., every five years).

After-Hours Services and Utilities Availability

What happens if the tenant's employees have to work on a Sunday? How do these employees get heat or cooling in the tenant's space, assuming there are no tenant-installed supplemental units? In most instances, a landlord will provide services after regular hours of usage. However, not all services or utilities will be available at all times (or even some of the time), and the landlord will charge for the service—cost plus a hefty markup.

The tenant needs to consider several factors in connection with after-hours services:

- How much advance notice must the tenant provide the landlord in order to receive a service? This should be specified in the lease provision. For example, for extended nighttime heating or cooling, notification may amount to only a few hours. Weekend service may require two or three days' notification in order to make certain that appropriate building staff will be available.

- How much will the services cost? This is often a function of the type of systems that exist in the building and how much markup the landlord puts on the service. A cost of hundreds of dollars an hour for heat or air-conditioning because a whole building has to be heated or cooled in order to heat or cool the tenant's premises can be unaffordable. If overtime use is contemplated or is a normal aspect of a business operation, the tenant must have a clear understanding of the building's systems before leasing space. The tenant should get professional help (and not just rely on what the landlord or the PREB says) to explain the system and make sure it performs to the tenant's satisfaction and at a reasonable cost.

- By what percentage does the landlord mark up the cost of overtime services or utilities? This should be negotiated in advance and specified in the lease provision.

- What supplemental building services or utilities will not be provided by the landlord? For example, a landlord may not be able to provide daytime or weekend char and janitorial services. This should be clearly stated in the lease provision.

Security and Hours of Building Availability

The lease should specify that the tenant has access to the building 24 hours a day, seven days a week. If the building does not offer 24-hour access, this provision should specify the exact hours and days that access is available. The tenant should make sure the minimum access available is defined in the lease provision. It should not simply be part of the building's rules and regulations, which the landlord may change at any time.

Security.   Building security is one of those areas that cannot be trusted to the general provision "as provided in other similar buildings in the area." Nor can the tenant trust that what appeared to be security during a visit to a building will remain security throughout the term of the lease.

The minimum level of security that the landlord will provide over the term of the tenant's lease should be stated in the lease, with the proviso that the landlord may, from time to time, improve or increase (not decrease) the service standard. The tenant will also want to know what additional or optional security is available, and at what additional cost.

Security measures can become very complex. The simplest security consists of ensuring that all building perimeter and tenant premises doors are locked. Security measures can be expanded to one-way exits and wire mesh (or cage) doors with alarms inside fire stairwells, nighttime or 24-hour on-site security personnel, television monitoring of entrances and hallways, electronic entry, electronic elevator access and usage, and individual alarm systems for the tenant's premises.

A security specialist will have to be contacted to obtain advice on the many possible security alternatives that are available. Security and protection can be expensive, depending on the level of security the tenant wants. The tenant's costs for security are reduced as the level of security the landlord provides increases. The tenant will therefore find it helpful to hook up with the landlord's building systems for protection of the premises.

The Landlord Provides Services and Utilities, Subject to . . .

"Subject to" is the landlord's favorite phrase to get out of doing something. One landlord "out" that no tenant should accept is the stipulation that services or utilities will be provided as long as the tenant is not in default under the lease. This is both ridiculous and unwarranted. As noted throughout this book, a tenant can easily default inadvertently, especially in regard to the building's rules and regulations. But so what! A building's services and utilities are provided as part of the rent. Any other defaults do not, and should not, count. If the landlord cuts off the services or utilities to a tenant's premises, the tenant is virtually being evicted. The lack of services or utilities could make a tenant's space untenantable. A tenant has the right to due legal process before any actual or "enforced" eviction occurs.

The landlord's way out in this lease provision is to state that the specified services or utilities will be supplied to the best of his or her ability. However, the landlord will not be liable or responsible for any interruptions or lack of services or utilities because of acts of God, government decrees, or anything not in the landlord's control (or some future event or action not currently contemplated by the landlord).

A landlord will also try to put in a provision limiting his or her liability and responsibility for the breakdown or malfunction of equipment and machinery and for the conduct or abilities of the landlord's employees. The landlord's limit will be to promise only "reasonable diligence" to repair breakdowns or have services or utilities function properly. Within this "subject to" provision the landlord will also want to specify that, even in the event that services and utilities cannot be provided, the tenant will still be responsible for paying the rent and any other additional rent items. That is, the rent will not be abated even if services or utilities are not supplied.

Is this fair? Who said a landlord had to be fair? From a tenant's perspective, if there are no services or utilities, the tenant should not have to pay rent during that period or, in other words, should get a 100 percent rent abatement. However, this too may be a bit harsh.

As a middle ground, the tenant and landlord can agree on a list of services and utilities that the tenant needs to keep the business operating. This list would incorporate a time frame indicating how long each service or utility would be discontinued before the tenant (and landlord) would consider the space untenantable. The tenant and landlord agreement would specify that "subject to" the lack of services or utilities and until such time as the services or utilities could be provided again to the tenant's premises (or the building), the tenant's rent would be abated (100 percent or another specified and agreed-to percentage).

At some point, even 100 percent rent abatement would be of no use if the tenant's business had to stop operating; if the period were long enough, the tenant could be put out of business. Therefore, in addition to rent abatement, the tenant should include an option in the lease that permits him or her to terminate the lease under certain extreme circumstances related to the time period in which services or utilities are lacking. A tenant must be able to make alternative plans and move without penalty, if absolutely necessary.

More on Utilities

Utilities generally consist of water and sewage, gas, oil, and electricity. The tenant's greatest concern regarding the provision of a utility and the cost of the service is whether the tenant or the landlord is responsible.

Tenant Responsibilities

Tenant responsibilities range from dealing directly with the utility companies and having the appropriate utilities hooked up, installed, and started to merely paying for the service, either directly to the utility or to the landlord.

When the tenant is fully responsible for all aspects of a utility service, the lease must clearly define the responsibilities or liabilities of the landlord, if there are any. The tenant must not take anything for granted because "it seemed obvious at the time."

For example, landlord responsibility for providing building utilities (where it is the responsibility of the tenant to have them hooked up) is not the same as the landlord's providing the utilities to the tenant's premises. For certain utility services (e.g., electricity, gas), the landlord may provide the necessary wiring or piping for the tenant's premises. The tenant would be responsible for contacting the utility to arrange service hookup and would pay for the service. This direct, or individual, tenant metering supposedly takes the landlord out of the tenant-utility loop. However, the landlord may still be responsible for the wiring and piping. The cost for maintenance may also require payment by the tenant to the landlord. In addition, the landlord may state that "in order to control and maintain quality," hookup meters must be purchased through the landlord, obviously with an appropriate (for the landlord) markup.

How to Pay

When the landlord is providing the utility services and the tenant pays for it separately, the tenant will want to know how the payment is to be made.

Tenant payment options vary: making an estimated separate utility payment to the landlord or including it as part of the general operating expense escalation or passthrough expenses, direct submetering on the premises from the building's master meter, or having the costs included in the base rent.

When the utility cost is distributed through a separate lease clause or is included with the operating expense clause, payment tends to be distributed through the tenant's rentable space as a percentage of the building's total rentable square feet (see Chapter 7).

When the utility cost is channeled through submetering to the tenant's premises, the tenant will want to know the following:

- Who (the tenant or the landlord) pays for the cost of hooking up the submeter, and in the case of tenant payment, how much profit markup is there for the landlord?

- Is the landlord going to share with tenants the savings from buying a utility (e.g., electricity) in bulk (for the whole building) or charge each tenant as an individual small purchaser? And how will the landlord distribute the utility costs for common and other general areas of the building to each tenant? A tack-on service charge to the submetering cost? A separate calculation? Also, does the landlord have the right to charge an additional service charge to cover the administration and maintenance of providing the submetering service?

When the utility cost is included in the base rent, any increases to the landlord are not immediately passed on to the tenant. Rather, there will be a general, or specially calculated, annual (or monthly) base rent escalation into which the landlord will incorporate his or her estimates to cover increases for things such as utility services.

The tenant has a number of concerns regarding utility expenses:

- If utility costs are to be separately charged, the tenant needs to be assured that they will not also find their way into the building's operating expenses and end up a double charge to tenants. Unfortunately, few safeguards really work. At a minimum, the tenant should insist on having the right to audit the landlord's books.

- What type of utility user is the tenant in relation to all the other tenants? Are any tenants high-energy or intensive users of a utility? Are these users charged separately for their "excessive" consumption or otherwise held accountable or responsible for higher utility consumption? If not, then all tenants, willingly or not, must bear some of the cost of the heavier utility user in the amount they pay individually as a share of the total cost.

- What are the landlord's incentives for using energy conservation techniques for utility costs for common areas of the building? There are few such incentives. The landlord usually just passes the costs on to all the tenants.

- How and when will the tenant be required to pay for the utility costs? Will it be in arrears, with the landlord sending an allocation billing after he or she has received or paid for the expenses? Will it be in advance, based on averages of previous years, with an end-of-the-year reconciliation for the actual costs? How do tenants get paid back for overpayment? Do tenants share in utility cost reductions as well as increases, or is there some minimum expense?

Electricity Issues

All buildings utilize electricity either for tenant premises or as the building's utility. Even when other utilities are also used, many services and utilities lease clauses include a special provision regarding the use of utilities by tenants, specifically the use of electricity. (This provision is often included, alternatively, as part of the building's rules and regulations.) This type of provision is relatively standard when the utility costs are part of the base rent or part of the passthrough operating expenses.

The provision will state:

> The landlord will provide the tenant premises with electricity [or other utility service] in the quantity necessary for normal and standard business operations [this may be further detailed, listing building standard lighting and standard business machines, among other items, and excluding certain types of equipment and machinery]. In the event that the tenant requires or actually uses electricity in excessive quantities, as determined by the landlord, the landlord will have the right to charge the tenant, and the tenant will pay on demand, the excess electricity charges. In addition, the landlord will have the right to charge the tenant for any additional wiring or electrical feeder lines that, in the landlord's sole judgment, are required to meet the tenant's excessive electric usage.

This provision is significant for the tenant. The tenant must be absolutely sure that an electric use provision reflects or includes both current and future estimated needs. This is especially true for tenants who rely heavily on business machines or must keep up with new technological advances. Otherwise, a proliferation of "normal and standard" business machines can be said to use excessive amounts of electricity. Many "normal and standard" business machines require special electric wiring (such as dedicated electric circuits for computers) or higher-than-standard voltages for operations (such as large copy machines); in these cases, the tenant may be made liable for "excessive" usage charges.

The problem is defining what is really standard and normal, especially when it comes to business operations.

If a tenant is a heavy utility user, the landlord may classify the use as "standard and normal" (after negotiation, of course), passing on the cost of "excessive" use, to be shared by every other tenant. Not a bad deal for the favored tenant. Tenants who are standard and normal users pay a share of the expenses of tenants who are excessive users. Too bad?

A tenant who believes there is an overcharge can always insist on an energy audit of the premises. (Get this into the lease as a tenant's right.) If the building has the capability and the tenant is willing to pay for the associated costs (which can be substantial if the landlord has not set up the building for it in advance), a separate electric meter can be installed on the premises.

Tenants who use "excessive" electricity, at least in comparison with other tenants in the building, probably do not think of themselves as excessive users. Often they see themselves as being merely up-to-date and highly efficient business operations utilizing available normal, standard technology. This perception makes it hard to establish a standard measurement of electric consumption.

Establishing a Standard

One standard many landlords use is known as the 3-watt rule. The landlord specifies that he or she will provide the tenant's premises with a building standard of 110-volt electric power, at the rate of an average 3 watts per rentable square foot. Any electrical use requirements above this amount will be considered excessive, and the tenant will be required to pay for the extra.

Is 3 watts per rentable square foot the correct amount? Someone once determined it was, so, on the basis of whatever was then standard and normal electrical use by a business operation, it eventually became the standard in other regions. Like everything else in the lease, this proposed standard is often negotiable. However, it falls to the tenant to prove, through engineering or business standards that can be located or established through consultants, what a proper required standard would be for the tenant's business.

Landlord Waivers and Double Dipping

Although the following practices are almost impossible to detect or fully guard against, the tenant should be aware of them:

- The landlord may exercise his or her absolute right to waive the electric utilization standard for certain tenants because they are large space users and wield considerable market power.

- The landlord may have charged an excessive energy cost to tenants but not reduced, by the amount collected, the total electric expense that is passed on to all the tenants. Such double dipping is often difficult to detect.

22

Char and
Janitorial Services

Is the landlord to be responsible for providing the tenant with char and janitorial services? For a single-tenanted building, the answer is often no. The tenant is often expected to arrange and be responsible for any and all janitorial services. For the large space user in a multitenanted building, the answer is maybe. Depending on how this lease clause is constructed, the large space user may have some options. For the typical tenant, the landlord will provide the char and janitorial services. These services will include maintenance and cleaning of common areas (including rest rooms) and the cleaning and trash removal of the tenant's premises.

A char and janitorial cleaning schedule should always be included in the lease document, and it should specify what will be cleaned and how often and when the service will occur. The tenant has two main concerns regarding this lease clause.

First, the prospective tenant must make sure the appropriate lease clause does not specify that the char and janitorial services will only be performed "provided the tenant is not in default under the lease." As discussed in Chapter 21, whether a tenant is in default of a lease is often the subject of lawsuits and court actions. If the landlord has the right to determine whether a tenant is in default, a tenant could find him- or herself without these services, in view of the many possible inadvertent default areas running throughout a lease document. The lack of char and janitorial services could lead to an untenantable condition inasmuch as the business could not be operated. If premises become untenantable in such a situation, the tenant would, for all practical purposes, be evicted—without proper legal representation and judicial process. A tenant should not sign (nor should a PREB permit the signing of) a lease document that incorporates this type of offending statement.

Second, this lease clause should specify the alternatives that are available to the tenant in the event that the char and janitorial services are not performed in an adequate and satisfactory manner in the tenant's view. The landlord-provided clause will have no provisions for any tenant alternatives. From the tenant's perspective, the lease clause should, at a minimum, be adjusted to include the following items. They are not written as, or intended to be, actual lease provisions but are provided merely to illustrate the appropriate intent.

- In the event char and janitorial services do not meet the specifications attached to the lease (see example below), the tenant may give written notice to the landlord specifying the deficiencies.

- The landlord will have 10 days from the delivery of tenant notice to meet the specified service standards. In the event that the landlord cannot comply within 10 days, the landlord will notify the tenant in writing specifying the reason for being unable to meet the char and janitorial specifications.

- By mutual agreement, the tenant may extend the time period for which the landlord may correct the deficiencies.

- The tenant may, with a second written notice to the landlord specifying continued deficiencies with regard to the char and janitorial specifications, terminate the landlord's obligation to provide char and janitorial services for the tenant's demised premises.

- The tenant will then be obligated to provide char and janitorial services for his or her own demised premises of a level equal to or better than that originally specified.

- The landlord agrees to cooperate with the tenant and the tenant's agents in providing services for the demised premises.

- The tenant agrees to provide any required bonds and supplemental insurance coverage necessary for tenant's agents to provide char and janitorial services within the building.

- As a result of the termination of the landlord's responsibility for providing char and janitorial services for tenant's demised premises, the landlord agrees that there are actual cost savings to the landlord and that these savings will be passed on to the tenant through the reduction of the annual base rent by \$x per square foot.

This blank dollar area is the most difficult item for the landlord to agree to. It is difficult to place an actual value on the savings achieved by not having char and janitorial services performed for only one tenant. (To complicate matters, the landlord's per-square-foot cleaning costs may go up in the rest of the building. The janitorial service may increase its per-square-foot costs if it no longer has an exclusive contract for the building or if the number of square feet to be cleaned is reduced.) The landlord will not want to reimburse the tenant for the actual service costs, because the tenant could provide a service quality far superior to anything normally provided for other building tenants. The tenant will not want to accept the per-square-foot costs the landlord is actually paying, since in most instances the landlord will have a lower per-square-foot cost than can be purchased by the tenant. This lower cost is achieved by virtue of market power in the case of the cleaning contract that includes the whole building, and there may be an additional quantity discount for cleaning contracts for multiple buildings.

This is a major area for tenant-landlord negotiation. As a practical matter, some agreed-to dollar amount, percentage method, or other formula should be included, specifying exactly how much the landlord will reimburse or provide as an offsetting rent credit if the tenant rightfully terminates the service and provides it for him- or herself.

A Sample Specification

There are no absolute standards for char and janitorial services. They vary from one building to another and from one region to another. What is considered a first-class cleaning standard for one landlord may not be an acceptable standard for another land-lord.

The tenant is, of course, caught in the middle. To help the tenant determine what is adequate, a PREB should provide information on what would be considered a top-quality char and janitorial standard for buildings in the surrounding area that the tenant could compare with the landlord's standard.

An important point to consider is whether certain built-in or decorator items, unique to the tenant's space, will be covered by the landlord's standard or will cost extra. For example, a cleaning specification may often require the tenant to pay extra for things such as the cleaning of glass partitions; wood, linoleum, or marble floors; wainscoted walls; wallpaper; private kitchen areas; and private bathrooms (and especially for the restocking of consumables in the last two areas).

The following char and janitorial schedule, taken from an office lease (with some modifications), is not intended as an all-encompassing specification, but it does provide an example of a reasonable base for tenants, especially if a standard is not provided by a PREB.

**Char and Janitorial
Specifications**

1. General
   a. Bathrooms and restrooms
      (1) Daily:
         - Wash all mirrors.
         - Wash hand basins and hardware.
         - Wash urinals.
         - Wash toilet seats using disinfectant in water.
         - Wash toilet bowls.
         - Damp-wipe, clean, and disinfect all tile surfaces. Spot wipe and clean where necessary.
         - Damp-wipe, using disinfectant, all shelves and booth partitions.
         - Supply and resupply sanitary napkins in coin-operated dispensers, as needed.
         - Replenish toilet tissue, soap, and towel dispensers.

(2) General: Toilet bowl brush will be used on toilet bowls, and care will be given to clean flush holes under rims of bowls and passage traps. Bowl cleaner will be used at least once each month, and more if necessary. The intent of this specification is that bathrooms and restrooms be maintained in a spotlessly clean and odor-free condition at all times.

b. Dusting

(1) Daily, weekly: All furniture, business equipment and appliances, windowsills, and the like will be dusted daily with a chemically treated cloth. This will include all horizontal surfaces daily and enough vertical surfaces daily to complete all vertical surfaces within each week. Desks and tables not cleared of paper and work materials will only be dusted where surface is exposed.

(2) Monthly: Pipes, ledges, ceiling, moldings, picture frames, and anything above hand-high areas will be cleaned.

c. Dust mopping, floors—daily: All noncarpeted floor areas will be dust-mopped with a treated yarn dust mop. Special attention will be given to areas under desks and furniture to prevent the accumulation of dust and dirt. Floor-dusting will be done after furniture has been dusted.

d. Waste paper, ashtrays—daily, monthly: Waste baskets and ashtrays to be emptied daily and wiped clean. Waste baskets will be washed once a month, or as needed. All waste containers are to be lined with a plastic liner. Plastic liners are to be changed as needed.

e. Vacuuming—daily, weekly: All rugs and carpets in office areas, as well as public spaces, are to be vacuumed daily in all traffic areas. Corners, hard-to-reach places, and areas under desks, tables, and chairs will be vacuumed weekly, using accessory tools as required. The intent of this specification is to provide a vacuuming of all needed areas on a daily basis and a complete vacuuming at least once a week.

f. Spot cleaning carpets—daily: All carpeted areas will be inspected daily for spots and stains. All spots and stains will be removed daily. Where difficult spots are encountered, a notation should be left with the building engineer and management. The intent of this specification is to maintain the carpet in a clean condition at all times, with no obvious spots showing.

g. Carpet cleaning—semiannually: All carpeted areas in public corridors will be shampooed once every six months.

h. Stairways and landings—daily, weekly: All stairways and landings will be dust-mopped with a treated yarn dust mop daily. Railings, ledges, and equipment will be dusted weekly. Spot cleaning of walls and doors will be done weekly; these areas will be damp-mopped weekly and scrubbed when necessary. The intent of this specification is that stairways be kept in neat and clean condition at all times.

i. Wet mopping—daily, as needed: Wherever floors require wet mopping, only clean water will be used, and floors will be left in a streak-free condition. Water and other liquids will be transported in a manner that will avoid splashing walls or furniture and prevent spillage over carpeted areas. Floors will be scrubbed or wet-mopped whenever required to prevent a build-up of wax.

j. Tile floors—daily: All tile floors will be kept in a waxed, polished, scuff-free, and spot-free condition at all times. Since some tile areas will require more attention than others, waxing and buffing will only be done on an as-needed basis. Wax and liquid will be transported over carpeted areas in a manner that will avoid spillage. Extreme care will be taken in applying the wax to avoid splashing or damaging furniture and walls. Stripping of waxed floors will include edging. Buffing machines will avoid damaging the walls, baseboards, and furniture.

k. Water coolers or fountains—daily: Water coolers or fountains will be cleaned and polished daily. Sluggishly operating drains and other failures will be reported to the building engineer or management. The intent of this specification is that water coolers and fountains be maintained in a spotlessly clean condition at all times.

l. Spot cleaning of vertical surfaces—daily, weekly: All hand prints, spots, and other dirty areas will be removed from doors and light switches daily. Walls and woodwork will be spot-cleaned weekly.

m. Cigarette urns, ash receivers—daily: Cigarette urns and

ash receivers will be cleaned as necessary and sanitized, and, where required, the sand level will be maintained.

n. Entrance lobby—daily: The entrance lobby will be thoroughly cleaned daily. Lobby glass and metal will be cleaned and dusted daily. During inclement weather, the cleaning contractor will put walk-off mats in place before leaving the premises. The lobby floor and entranceways will be thoroughly cleaned nightly. Directory board glass will be damp-cleaned and wiped.

o. Polishing—daily, monthly: All door plates, kick plates, and brass and metal fixtures within the building will be wiped daily and polished monthly. Door entrances and elevator tracks (car and lobby) will be cleaned or polished daily.

p. Elevators—daily, monthly: The interior surfaces and fixtures of the elevators will be dusted and damp-wiped daily. Carpets in elevator cars will be spot-cleaned as needed and vacuumed daily. All ceilings and light fixtures will be damp-cleaned once a month.

q. Light fixtures—periodically, annually: The exterior of all light fixtures will be dusted as needed. The entire light fixture will be washed annually.

r. Venetian blinds—weekly, annually: Venetian blinds will be dusted weekly and washed annually.

s. Walls, woodwork, and partitions—weekly, quarterly, semiannually: Finger and hand prints, spots, and other grimy areas will be removed weekly using a damp cloth or sponge, and care will be exercised to prevent the streaking of paint. All walls and ceilings will be brushed down with an approved wall duster or a vacuum cleaner every three months. Partitions of wood or steel will be washed with a neutral soap every six months, or on request.

t. Glass partitions and doors—weekly: All glass partitions and doors will be damp-cleaned weekly or as needed.

u. HVAC grills—monthly: All areas around HVAC outlet and return air grills will be cleaned once a month, or more often if necessary.

v. General cleaning—as necessary:
   (1) The cleaning supervisor will report to the building engineer or management any maintenance or repair

conditions, such as leaky faucets, stopped toilets and drains, broken fixtures, and so on. All unusual happenings in the building will also be reported.

(2) All cleaning will be done behind locked doors. When the cleaner(s) enter the premises to perform the required duties, all entrance doors of the premises will be locked and remain locked.

(3) All employees of the contractor will be uniformed or neatly dressed and will be identified by a visible badge or other approved identification containing the employee's picture and name and the name of the contract cleaning/janitorial company.

(4) Employees of the contractor will not disturb papers on desks, tables, open drawers, or cabinets; use telephones, televisions, or radios; or drink or gamble while on duty.

(5) The contractor will be responsible for any loss or damage caused by his or her employees.

(6) The building management agent may call for the dismissal of any employee who is incompetent, careless, insubordinate, or otherwise objectionable or whose continued employment is contrary to consistent good relations with the tenants.

(7) The contractor will submit to the building engineer and management progress reports on all items of cleaning that are specially scheduled or scheduled for less than a daily basis. The projected work is to be conducted by a written schedule and inspected as completed. The building engineer or management will conduct the inspection with the cleaning supervisor and initial his or her acceptance or note his or her rejection of each item.

(8) The contractor will furnish all labor, material, supplies, and equipment needed to perform the described services. The contractor will also maintain his or her equipment in a clean and usable condition and will store equipment in areas designated by the building engineer or management. Equipment will be stored in a neat and clean manner.

(9) Upon completion of the daily work, the contractor will ensure that all slop sinks and equipment storage areas are left in a neat and orderly condition, all lights are extinguished, and all doors locked.

2. Window washing: Inside and outside window washing will be scheduled four times a year (quarterly). However, first-floor windows will be washed outside once a month, unless the space is occupied by retail tenants.

   a. Interior washing will be scheduled through the building engineer or management several days in advance. The building engineer or management will notify the building occupants to determine accessibility for their employees. The window-washing superintendent will cooperate with the building engineer and management in scheduling the interior washing, in accordance with the occupants' wishes.

   b. Special care will be exercised to avoid damaging draperies or venetian blinds during the interior washing operation.

   The intent of this specification is that all windows will be left in a clean and streak-free condition, that the occupants will not be unduly inconvenienced, that the operation will be conducted safely and efficiently, and that the contractor will be responsible for any damage caused by his or her operation.

   After each window-washing operation is completed, the building engineer or management and the window-washing superintendent will conduct a thorough inspection. The job will not be considered complete until it has received the written acceptance of the building engineer or management.

3. Trash removal—daily:

   a. Trash will be removed from the premises daily between the hours of 10:00 p.m. and 7:00 a.m., Monday through Friday.

   b. The contractor is responsible for maintaining the trash room in a clean and odor-free condition at all times.

   c. The contractor is responsible for making sure that any trash spilled inside or outside the building will be promptly removed.

   d. Trash pickup will be scheduled through the building engineer or management so as not to jeopardize the integrity of the building security system.

4. Day porter service: The landlord will provide one uniformed
   day porter eight hours a day, five days a week, Monday
   through Friday, excluding legal holidays. The day porter will
   perform the following duties:

   a. Police and maintain the lobbies to ensure they are kept in
       a neat and clean condition.
   b. Police and maintain all restrooms so that they are kept in a
       neat and clean condition, replenishing lavatory supplies as
       required.
   c. Police public stairwells, removing trash and sweeping and
       washing the stairs and landings as required.
   d. Provide snow removal as allowed by regular staffing and
       equipment provided.
   e. Police exterior plaza, arcades, and surrounding property
       twice daily.
   f. Set out entrance mats during inclement weather and clean
       and return same to storage areas when not in use.
   g. Wipe down all metal trim on entrance doors and building
       metal trim within hand-high reach.
   h. Perform other duties as directed by building engineer or
       management.

23
Events of Tenant Default

The PREB all too often treats the default lease clause as a "so what" matter. This attitude tends to spill over to the PREB's negotiations of the lease, so little attention may be paid to what, for a tenant, is often a vital lease clause.

This clause details exactly what will constitute a default by the tenant. This clause is particularly important when other lease clauses depend on whether the tenant is in default. Lease clauses that may refer to tenant default as a disqualifying criterion before a tenant is able to invoke a tenant's inherent right include lease renewal, space expansion options, the subletting of unneeded space, assignment of the lease, and the building or space (as in a commercial condominium) purchase option.

Because a default can have a severe negative impact on his or her rights, the tenant must carefully review this clause and, to the extent possible, reduce the items or criteria determining tenant default. The items in this clause tend to be taken for granted and show up as regionally based standards in the lease document. Many PREBs glance at this lease clause and, seeing what they expect to see, move on to other clauses. But this is not acceptable tenant representation. Nor should a tenant blithely accept what is written without first evaluating it in conjunction with his or her own needs. This lease clause, like many others, is fully negotiable. When the lease document is a complex one and a number of tenant options and rights depend on there being no default, the tenant will have to monitor all these possibilities throughout the term of the lease. Consequently, the fewer such possibilities, the better.

The landlord and tenant should carefully work out whether this lease clause needs to be short, containing broadly based default criteria, or long, spelling out every possible default situation.

In general, the following would constitute a tenant's default or breach of the lease.

1. *Failure by the tenant to make the due and punctual payment of rent, "additional rent," or any other monetary amounts due (such as real estate taxes, assessments, utility charges, other operating expenses).* A useful tenant-preferred addition, when monetary payments are involved, is to specify what time frame constitutes a late payment. For example, this provision might state: "Default will be considered to have occurred when the tenant's failure to make any payments due continues for a period of 10 or more days after the due date." The tenant's interests would be served even better if the time frame provision were conditioned on landlord notification. The time frame provision would thus be adjusted to state "10 or more days after written notice by the landlord to the tenant."

The landlord will want the default to occur if payment is not made by the due date. The landlord will feel he or she has made a major concession by allowing a time frame beyond the due date to temper the default event and that after the specified time, the tenant should be in default whether or not the demand for payment or notice has been made by the landlord.

Whether landlord demand or notice should be required may well depend on what type of monetary payment is required. For example, landlord notice is required for pro rata shares of real estate taxes or operating expenses. But in the case of regular rent payments or amounts or due dates clearly specified in the lease, a landlord would find it amusing that a tenant would claim not to know whether a payment had been made at the proper time and thus would require notice that the rent was or had been due.

The tenant could argue that the landlord notice provision would pertain to everything, not only to monetary items. Therefore, written notice of the potential for a tenant default should be a requirement before an event actually creates a tenant default.

2. *The neglect or failure of the tenant to observe, perform, or comply with any terms, covenants, conditions, or provisions of the lease that pertain to the tenant.* This provision of the lease is relatively broad but is always insisted upon by the landlord. For the tenant, the addition of a time frame is important, as is a "reasonableness" statement allowing the tenant to cure or eliminate the event of a default.

The tenant-biased provision would therefore state:

> The landlord will provide written notice of the tenant's failure to perform or observe a lease provision. The tenant default will not be deemed to have occurred unless such failure shall continue for a period of 20 days after written notice is received by the tenant. However, the tenant shall not be deemed to be in default if the tenant will, within a 20-day period from the landlord notice, commence a cure for the default event and continues diligently to pursue its completion.

Getting a landlord to accept both the advance-notice and time-frame conditions will take a bit of work. The landlord may well want to put a limit on how much time the tenant will have to cure the default event. For example, a landlord may want the cure for the default to be completed no later than 90 days after the landlord's notice.

The tenant needs to resist vigorously any maximum time frame, especially since there is no way to judge in advance what might be the cause of the potential default. Any time deadline must be tempered with language such as "the tenant will use his or her best efforts to complete the cure for a default within [a specified time period]."

3. *The vacating or abandonment of the premises by the tenant.* Landlords vary in their opinion of what constitutes a tenant's vacating or abandoning of the premises and may not even care about it. Landlords want to continue getting rent whether or not the tenant is actually occupying the premises. However, some landlords are not satisfied simply with rent payments, since they feel that vacant or abandoned premises affect the overall quality of their building or project. Besides being unsightly, abandoned premises can be an open invitation for unwanted guests.

Depending on how strongly he or she feels about empty premises, the landlord may insist that a default event be defined in terms of a specified time frame (for example, the cessation of use of the premises for a period of time in excess of 30 days). He or she may also state that a default will occur whether or not the tenant intends to (or actually does) continue to pay rent or make other monetary payments due under the lease.

A tenant does need to understand the landlord's position regarding vacant premises. However, the clause needs to be tempered so that a default will not occur if rent and other monetary payments continue after the tenant has vacated the premises. The tenant and landlord need to agree on other lease provisions regarding the assignment and subletting of space and perhaps even the takeback of space by the landlord (subject to leasing expenses, achievable rent differentials, etc.).

There is no excuse for a tenant to walk away from a lease and truly abandon the premises. This would give the landlord good grounds for declaring a tenant default.

4. *The failure of the tenant to take possession of the premises within a reasonable period of time after the lease commencement date.* This provision is often included as an adjustment to the vacating and abandonment provision. Obviously, if the tenant does not take possession, the premises will remain empty. Therefore, everything that applies to the vacating provision applies here as well.

5. *The involvement of the tenant, or any guarantor, in financial difficulties as evidenced by the admission, in writing, of the inability to pay debts as they become due or the filing of a petition in bankruptcy or for reorganization or any other arrangement available under the current or any future Bankruptcy Act.* (An actual lease provision would include additional evidence areas, all wrapped in legalese and revolving around the financial ability of the tenant.) This provision is important to the landlord. Any threat to the financial wellbeing of the tenant can affect the tenant's ability to meet the obligations of the lease, especially the payment of rent or other monetary payments. Similarly, financial difficulties incurred by a guarantor affect the ability of the landlord to seek redress from the guarantor for financial difficulties incurred by the tenant. The difficulties may be of such a magnitude that a guarantee of the lease is essentially meaningless. Since the guarantee of a lease is an important element of a landlord's decision to lease the

premises to the tenant, it is understandable if the landlord may want to recapture the premises.

The bankruptcy provision is discussed in detail in Chapter 26. Here it should be recognized that the Bankruptcy Act provides specific protection for an organization, and within the criteria of the law the landlord is not able to terminate the lease or recapture the premises simply because there is an act of bankruptcy or a trustee has been appointed.

6. *The involvement by the tenant in any act that annoys, disturbs, or is objectionable to other tenants in the building and for which the landlord in his or her sole discretion agrees with the other tenants.* Although this provision can be construed as being covered under the covenants concerning the failure to abide by the lease or the rules and regulations pertaining to default, it actually provides a greater degree of latitude to the landlord. With this provision, the landlord can afford to be somewhat less objective in establishing a tenant's defects. This provision will also state: "The tenant will have 30 days from the receipt of written notice from the landlord to cure, repair, eliminate, or cease any and all objectionable acts, after which time the tenant will be deemed to be in default of the lease."

However, the general nature of this provision is also its undoing: It is too subjective. Just because a lease clause or a specific provision exists does not mean that it can automatically be implemented or even supported in a court of law.

7. *The assignment, transfer, mortgaging or encumbering of the lease, or the subletting of all or part of the premises without first obtaining the landlord's written permission.* This provision is often a duplication of the prohibition of these events in other clauses of the lease document. By being repeated, it emphasizes that the landlord wants to have this event of default spelled out clearly. Where the duplicate clauses obviously serve no clear additional purpose, they and all other extraneous material should be removed.

8. *The default by the tenant under any other lease between the tenant (or any affiliate, partner, division, subsidiary, or any individual, partnership, or corporation-controlling tenant) and the landlord for any space (other than the leased premises), either in the same or in any other building owned by the landlord or his or her affiliates.* This provision is an ex-

ample of a landlord-inspired provision that responds to a specific difficulty a landlord has previously experienced. It is not something that shows up often, nor will it necessarily be found in many areas of the country. Whatever the case, this provision is not acceptable to a tenant except under extreme duress or hardship. It punishes the tenant for acts or events that have occurred elsewhere. Separate business dealings with a landlord are just that: separate.

Problems encountered with specific premises or a particular building, and whatever remedy or business decision the tenant feels is justified regarding those problems—legally or morally right or wrong—should not be sufficient grounds to call for the default of a current tenant, nor should they be permitted to spill over and affect another independent business arrangement. This is precisely why landlords often create separate corporations or partnerships for each building they own. The default, bankruptcy, or inability to make a go of one building should not have an effect on any others.

Depending on how specific or general this lease clause is, a tenant can easily come to be in default. Because of all the options available to the landlord and the number of prohibitions restricting the tenant, there are not many alternatives available to a tenant in the event of disagreements, difficulties, or problems with the landlord, short of getting the landlord to agree with the tenant's position or finding some legal relief or remedy. For example, regardless of how strongly a tenant feels about a landlord's actions or inaction (such as not providing heat or air conditioning for some period of time), the tenant has no recourse.

At most, a tenant can withhold rent payments. However, doing this clearly creates a specific default event under the lease. The question is: What can or will the landlord do if default occurs?

24
Landlord Remedies for Tenant Defaults

How the landlord exercises his or her rights when a tenant defaults, what remedies the landlord can invoke, and when the landlord has the right to invoke any or all of the remedies, are extremely important to the tenant. Although these remedies tend to be intimidating, the specification of remedies in the lease document does not mean that the landlord can, will, or even has any legal right to exercise them. The tenant has certain rights to due process of law.

However, even if legal approval is required before a remedy can be imposed by a landlord, the tenant must not be smug or complacent regarding this lease provision. Its mere existence in the lease document indicates that the tenant accepts and implicitly approves the landlord's proposed default remedies. Otherwise, why would they be in a lease document the tenant signed?

The tenant's attention should first focus on the introduction to the remedies lease clause. A landlord-inspired introduction will state:

> Upon the occurrence of a default, the landlord shall have the right, but not the requirement or obligation, at his or her elec-

tion and in his or her sole discretion, at the time of the default or any time thereafter, to invoke or pursue the specified remedies.

This introduction clearly gives broad latitude to the landlord. From the tenant's perspective, the landlord's ability and right to invoke any or all the remedies should be limited to the time the default occurs or to some clearly defined and limited period immediately thereafter. Without any time limits, the landlord supposedly has the right to invoke a remedy long after the default event occurs.

At a minimum, the tenant should add language providing some time limit or state that the remedies are available only at the time of occurrence or as long as the event or condition of default continues. Once a default condition has been cured or no longer exists, the landlord should have no continuing right to seek a remedy.

The landlord will want to include a number of rights and remedies:

1. *The right, at landlord's sole option, to terminate the lease.* This provision will state:

> The landlord has the right to provide the tenant with written notice of his or her intent to terminate the lease on the date of the notice, or any date as specified in the notice. As of the specified date, the tenant will lose any right to possess or occupy the premises, and the lease is considered to be terminated.

This is a good example of the landlord wanting to have his or her cake and to eat it, too. That is, the landlord will want to include other provisions that continue tenant liability even when the lease has terminated (see below).

2. *The right of the landlord to reenter or take possession of all, or some part, of the premises.* This particular provision will state:

> The reentering, or taking possession by the landlord, can be done without demand or notice, and the tenant, or those claiming any rights through the tenant [such as a subtenant], can be expelled and all property and possessions can be removed, either by legal actions or otherwise. This can be done

without the landlord being guilty of trespass and without any prejudice to the landlord for any additional remedies for the payment of rent or other lease covenants.

Often this provision will also state that any property or possessions removed from the premises may be stored, at the landlord's option, at a public warehouse or elsewhere, at the cost and for the account of the tenant.

3. *The right of the landlord to alter locks and other security devices*

4. *The right of the landlord to cease supplying services and utilities for the benefit of the tenant and the premises*

The landlord will also want to include a lease provision that offers additional protection in the event that one of the remedies is exercised. This provision will state:

> The landlord's exercise of one or more of the remedies as provided in the lease, or otherwise available, will not be deemed an acceptance of surrender of the premises by the tenant, such surrender only able to occur with the written agreement between the landlord and the tenant. If the landlord elects to reenter the premises, the landlord may terminate this lease or, from time to time, without terminating this lease, may relet all or any part of the premises as agent for the tenant, for such term and at such rental and other terms and conditions as landlord may deem advisable, with the right to make alterations and repairs to the premises. No such reentry or taking possession of the premises by the landlord shall be construed as an election on the landlord's part to terminate this lease unless a written notice of such intention is given to the tenant or unless the termination be decreed by a court or competent jurisdiction at the insistence of the landlord.

The Threat Provides the Landlord with Clout

Whether or not the landlord can actually terminate the lease will depend on state laws. From a landlord's perspective, it is the threat of terminating the lease that provides the landlord with clout over the tenant. What the landlord wants to avoid is the automatic termination of a lease. The landlord will want the termination to be his or her option. A lease termination, especially if it occurs automatically because of some default, may work against the landlord in that the tenant will have no further liabilities, except for those incurred up to the time of termination.

Likewise, the landlord must also be careful about being able to reenter the premises and relet any portion or all of the space, guarding against the suggestion that the landlord accepts a tenant's surrender of the premises or is terminating the lease. If this action were construed as such, the tenant would have no further lease obligations, and that would affect the amount of compensation the landlord might receive.

From the tenant's perspective, although the lease termination or the reentering or reletting of all or part of the premises is the landlord's option, it should only be possible to trigger these draconian rights through specific and major leasehold defaults.

Because of the punitive aspects of some of these default remedies, the landlord will want to have a specific provision that protects him or her in spite of any actions taken. This provision will state that the tenant gives prior consent and recognizes that any landlord actions are authorized for such things as the removal of property or possessions of the tenant or others from the premises, the alteration of locks or security devices, and the cessation of services and utilities. This provision will also have the tenant waiving any and all claims or payment for any damages resulting from the landlord's actions, and the tenant will agree in advance that no landlord reentry will be considered trespassing.

Some Tenant Rights

Although the landlord may insist on including protection language, the tenant must not lose sight of his or her own rights and needs. None of the aforementioned remedies should be permitted to occur unless the tenant has been notified in advance, within sufficient time (e.g., 90 days) and in writing. Furthermore, the tenant should insist that no default remedies can be pursued until the landlord has given the tenant prior sufficient, written notification of the presence of a default and a sufficient time period has elapsed for the tenant to cure the default, and they can be pursued only if the tenant has made no attempt to cure the default.

Tenant Liabilities

An interesting aspect of the default lease clause is that even if the landlord exercises one of the specified default remedies, such as terminating the lease, there will be additional provisions protecting the landlord and ensuring the continuation of his or her economic benefits. The main provisions will relate to the following items:

- Continuing tenant liability for rent and other monies
- The landlord's right to liquidated damages
- Cumulative rights of the landlord
- Late rent payments
- Accelerated rent payments
- General acts of default

Continuing Tenant Liability for Rent and Other Monies

Even if the landlord exercises his or her right to terminate the lease, this provision ensures that the tenant will continue to be liable for all of the rent and other money anticipated in the lease up to the original lease expiration date. The standard provision states that the tenant will remain liable for rent, "additional rent," and any other monetary amounts provided for in the lease until the lease expiration date, had the lease termination not occurred.

In addition, the tenant is expected to be liable for all costs, fees, and expenses, including but not limited to, attorney's fees, brokerage fees, and other disbursements and expenses incurred by the landlord in reentering and repossessing the premises; in correcting any tenant defaults under the lease; in painting, altering, repairing, or dividing the premises as necessary to place the premises in rentable condition; in protecting and preserving the premises by use of watchpersons or caretakers; in reletting the premises, including any and all expenses the landlord may incur during the occupancy of the new tenant; and any other costs or expenses incurred by the landlord in pursuit of any legal or non-legal remedies associated with the tenant's default or the landlord's termination of the lease. This provision will also enable the landlord to offset any monetary amounts owed by the tenant by any proceeds generated when the premises are relet.

The landlord is trying to protect his or her economic and legal rights in the event a tenant defaults. However, assuming that his or her default would not be on purpose but rather due to circumstances beyond his or her control, the tenant should add or modify this provision to the extent of his or her economic liabilities.

Contrary to expectations, the landlord might not try to relet the premises as quickly as possible. The tenant is at a distinct disadvantage during a default, and there is no way to ensure that a landlord will do everything possible to mitigate the losses incurred by the tenant. For example, if a landlord has reasonable expectation that a defaulted tenant can or will be able to pay the money owed under the lease even if no longer on the premises, that landlord may have no economic incentive to see that the premises are relet. This is especially true if that landlord has other vacant space in the same building or in other building projects.

At a minimum, a tenant-oriented lease will ensure that, if the landlord should terminate the lease (for proper and sufficient default reasons), he or she would be required to make a good faith effort to relet any vacant space in a timely manner and at a rent sufficient to cover any rent, costs, or other expenses that would otherwise be expected to be paid by the tenant.

The only way to ensure that the landlord will abide by this provision is to include an economic or other incentive. The landlord should not be encouraged or rewarded for doing nothing, knowing that there is no recourse for the tenant. In that spirit, the tenant should work hard to have any economic costs to him or her expire as of the date the landlord actually terminates the lease. If there are no further tenant rights under the lease, there should be no expectation of continued tenant liability.

To provide additional incentive for the landlord to relet the premises, this clause should include a provision that gives the tenant the right to relet the premises, without restrictions, if the landlord has been unable to do so after some "reasonable" (specified) period of time.

The Landlord's Right to Liquidated Damages

The liquidated damages provision gives the landlord the right, at his or her sole option, to require the tenant to pay a sufficient and acceptable amount, often specified to be payment as "additional damages" (usually the amount is specified or a detailed method is given to calculate the damages).

For the tenant's benefit, the concept of liquidated damages should be carefully spelled out. From a tenant's perspective, liquidation damages should be payable at the tenant's option, with an agreed-to landlord-tenant amount (or method of calculating it). With the payment of these damages, which are intended to be punitive in nature, any tenant's liability under the lease should immediately cease, and the lease should be considered ended.

Cumulative Rights of the Landlord

This lease provision is legal jargon intended to maintain the landlord's continuing legal rights regardless of what actions a landlord may or may not take in the event of a default. The landlord's exercising any permitted right or remedy will not preclude or prevent him or her from exercising another right at the same or subsequent time; thus, the provision is cumulative.

This provision also states that any delay by the landlord in exercising a right or remedy is not a waiver by the landlord of the tenant's default or a waiver of the landlord's rights to exercise a right or remedy. In addition, language specifies that any landlord waiver of a tenant's default must be in writing and that any such written waiver is not a waiver of any of the covenants or conditions of the lease but only pertains to the specific circumstances described in the waiver.

Late Rent Payments

In the landlord's view, the nonpayment of rent is the greatest default sin; second only to this is the late payment of rent. Landlords need cash to pay bills just like everyone else. For this reason, they can be forgiven for being upset when rent payments are late.

To discourage late rent, the lease document often contains a provision stipulating the monetary damages to be paid by a tenant. Because late rent payments can often stretch into nonpayment of rent and rent disputes are a major factor for a tenant's default, a pertinent late rent payment provision is often included in the default lease clause (or it may reside in the rent lease clause or in the clause pertaining to the landlord's right to cure a default).

This default provision specifies that if the tenant fails to make any payment of rent or "additional rent" or any other money due on or before the date the payment is due and payable, the tenant will pay a specified late charge (for example, 5 percent of the total amount due). There is often an additional statement providing for the tenant to pay interest on the amount due, usually specified as the maximum permitted by state law, computed from the due date to the date paid. Finally, these payments will be specified "additional rent" and liquidated damages rather than penalties; they will be in addition to, not in lieu of, all other rights and remedies given to the landlord in the lease.

It is hard to argue with a landlord's provisions, no matter how onerous, when it is nothing more than backup protection for money that will or should not have to be paid. However, since late payment of money occurs for all kinds of reasons, from a tenant's perspective, this provision, despite what it says, is a monetary punishment. The tenant should not balk at accepting this provision, but he or she should have sufficient language added so that, with valid reasons, a late payment is not automatically considered late.

As discussed throughout this book, the tenant is at a disadvantage regarding the lease, especially when it comes to trying to use the nonpayment of rent as a weapon against the landlord. Not paying rent is a major reason for default for which there is no good excuse, including the landlord's failure to supply services (unless there is lease language to the contrary).

However, the validity of other types of money due from a tenant under a lease is not as clear-cut as the basic rent payment. Examples of this are base rent increases computed by an index (such as the CPI) rather than a set percentage, computations for pro rata shares of a building's increases in utilities and services, and common area services and utilities.

Therefore, although it is almost impossible to get, the tenant should still try to have language added protecting his or her interests in certain circumstances. A tenant's lease provision would clearly define what is not a late payment and what would constitute a valid reason for being late with a monetary payment. For example, if some portion of an "additional rent" demanded by the landlord were disputed by the tenant, the amount in dispute would be exempt from any late payment provision until the dispute had been resolved.

More important, there should be a process within the lease for the proper (or additional) notification of the tenant regarding money owed that is going to be considered "late payment." The landlord will argue that the tenant should know when the basic rent is due since it is detailed in the lease, and any additional payments are specified in the letter or billing submitted by the landlord. The fact is, however, that the landlord's business is to handle commercial real estate and deal with tenants, whereas the tenant has other concerns: He or she must also pay attention to business. Therefore, a tenant who writes a letter of disagreement to the landlord may assume, not hearing anything to the contrary, that the disagreement is under consideration and the disputed amount is on hold until further notice. The landlord often thinks differently and is either ignoring the disagreement or complaint or even, if looking into it, expecting the disputed money to be paid, with a refund or rent credit due in the future.

Whatever the process, since it is the landlord's business, the burden should be on the landlord to maintain contact with the tenant, to provide necessary reminders about payments due or about to be considered late, and especially to follow up on tenant disagreements.

Accelerated Rent Payments

Why this provision is included in the lease document is important for the tenant to know. Often an accelerated rent payment is included as part of the liquidation damages provision and, as such, is patently unfair to the tenant.

Accelerated rent payments are a typical landlord cure for tenants who are consistently late with the rent. It may be found either as a separate provision or as part of the late rent payment provision. Generally, a liquidated damages provision is invoked when a landlord is terminating a lease. However, for this provision, if a tenant is forced to prepay future rent through acceleration and does so, it would seem reasonable for the tenant to continue to have possession of the premises.

The tenant must be sure to carefully relate all payments made to or demanded by the landlord with the continued possession of the premises. If the tenant does not comply with the accelerated rent payment provision, then the landlord should retain the right to terminate the lease.

A reasonable acceleration rent payment provision states:

> If the tenant fails to pay any installment of rent in accordance with the lease, together with any additional rent due under the lease, within [an agreed-to period, say, 20 days] of the date such payment is due, for three consecutive months or three times in any period of six consecutive months, the landlord may, at his or her option and after giving written notice to the tenant:
>
> 1. Declare the rent for the full lease period to be due and payable within 10 days of the written notice. [Note: Additional language is often needed to specify how future rent and "additional rent" amounts subject to economic or financial indexes are to be estimated.]
> 2. Declare the rent and "additional rent" for the next six months (or at the landlord's option, for some lesser period) to be due and payable within 10 days of the written notice.
> 3. Require an additional security or rent deposit to be paid within 10 days of the notice in an amount not to exceed six months' rent.

From the tenant's perspective, an additional provision would specify that the landlord may only invoke one of these options and only during the period that the default event remains uncured by the tenant.

General Acts of Default

A general provision that will often be included in a lease document states:

In the event the tenant defaults in the making of any payment or in the doing of any act required in the lease, the landlord may, but is not required to, make any such payment or do any act for and on behalf of the tenant. If the landlord does act for the tenant, the tenant agrees to pay the landlord, as additional rent, all costs and expenses incurred by the landlord plus interest on the amount paid at a rate of "____" percent [the percentage specified as the maximum interest amount permitted by law] from the date the amount is paid by the landlord to the date the additional rent payment is made by the tenant. If the landlord takes these actions, they should not be considered a cure of the default by the tenant nor prevent the landlord from pursuing any remedy he or she is otherwise entitled to in connection with the default.

25
Events of
Landlord Default

A clause pertaining to landlord default is rarely found in a lease document, and when it is, it is usually so watered down, it is meaningless. That it appears at all in a lease attests to the persuasiveness of the tenant or to the tenant's economic leverage and power.

Only the Tenant Is
Promising to Pay

A lease document defines the relationship between a tenant and a landlord. The tenant agrees to pay the landlord money, and the landlord, in turn, promises to provide the tenant with space in a building and appropriate building services for the comfort and convenience of the tenant.

Only the tenant has promised to pay money. If he or she does not pay, the landlord can claim specific monetary damages. If the landlord does not provide a particular service or is lax about maintenance, it is difficult for the tenant to show specific monetary damages; the tenant can only say that he or she did not get exactly what was promised in return for the money paid.

Without a specific clause providing an incentive for the landlord to do what he or she says will be done (such as one requiring a landlord to pay punitive monetary damages), how can a tenant get what is being paid for? What if the landlord does not provide heat or janitorial services, only keeps one of four elevators in service, or skimps on security services? Although litigation is expensive, the tenant must sue when the landlord is in default under the lease, as the landlord must do when a tenant defaults. However, although the lease often spells out tenant defaults and remedies, it is silent about landlord defaults.

Landlord's Nonperformance

A landlord will not want to be pinned down on any criteria having to do with maintenance, repair, or the provision of services. In any tenant-landlord relationship, there will almost always be disagreements. In most cases, the differences of opinion are judgment calls, and the landlord wants to be the one who controls.

For example, for the safety of the building and the other tenants, the landlord will not want any tenant to have the right to perform structural or major building repairs. The timing, type, and quality of a repair or maintenance problem is the owner's prerogative, at least to the extent that it does not jeopardize lives. On the other hand, the tenant will also have safety concerns and will want to be sure that repair and maintenance work is done.

Tenants will also be concerned when a landlord does not pay taxes or utility bills when due. Tax liens and subsequent foreclosure proceedings or the cancellation of utility services to a building will and do affect tenants directly. But should a tenant become involved in these problems?

The tenant is often powerless to remedy a problem that has not been fixed by the landlord, possibly resulting in the interruption of business operations. The biggest obstacle to tenant involvement is the financial cost, which is usually beyond the capability of tenants who are not very large or single building users.

Getting a Start

If the landlord is desperate to find and sign up tenants or if a tenant has significant economic leverage and power, the landlord may agree to put into a lease document remedies for any of his or her potential defaults. A landlord can "give in" in such a way that the resulting clause will be almost meaningless but will give the tenant some reassurance. Why don't landlords give in more? Because they do not want to start a precedent with such a clause or to give tenants ideas about their rights and what can or cannot be put into a lease document.

An innocuous landlord default lease clause will state:

> In the event of default by the landlord in the performance of any obligation under the lease, the tenant shall give a written notice of default to the landlord. The landlord shall be entitled to have 30 days after receipt of such notice to cure any and all specified defaults, unless any or all of the defaults cannot be cured within the 30-day period. In such event, the landlord will be entitled to a reasonable time to cure the defaults, provided that, within the initial time period, the landlord will promptly commence and thereafter diligently pursue to completion the curing of the specified defaults.

This lease clause does not permit the tenant to take any specific action, such as terminating the lease. But is termination implied in a silent understanding between the landlord and tenant? To answer that question, the tenant will have to seek the advice of a lawyer.

As a start, the clause is better than nothing.

Putting Some Bite into It

As the economic leverage and power of the tenant increases, additional lease provisions, similar to those in the tenant's default lease clause, can be considered, each providing more tenant clout. Two specific provisions that give the tenant significant clout are the following:

1. "The tenant has the right, at his or her option, to cure a landlord's default and to offset any tenant-incurred costs and related expenses with immediate and direct rent credit or rent abatement." This provision should list examples to avoid future conflicts. Examples could include items such as janitorial services, building maintenance, utility services, the payment of taxes,

property repair, and even mortgage payment to avoid foreclosure.

2. "The tenant has the right to terminate the lease after due
and proper notice of defaults to the landlord and after some reasonable time period in which such defaults have not been cured."
This provision, too, should include some examples of a significant landlord default or the cumulative effects of various defaults
resulting in direct and detrimental effects to a tenant's business
operations. One case might be the failure of the landlord to pay
utility bills in a timely manner, with the result that utilities to the
building are cut off and thus the tenant is unable to continue
business operations.

The rights of the mortgage holder must also be addressed in
any termination provision. The mortgage holder will object if tenants have the right to terminate a lease without the holder's right
to cure the default on the landlord's behalf. This will, of course,
clearly be at the option of the mortgage holder and not be an
obligation. Also, the mortgage holder will require written notice
of the default, notice of the failure by the landlord to cure the
default, and an additional reasonable time to cure the default.

These two provisions will give the tenant the clout needed to
persuade a landlord to cure any default. However, the tenant
must be sure, and the provisions must specify, that it is a specific
or willful default of the landlord.

It Doesn't Hurt to Try

Can these provisions be obtained? It will be difficult, but it
doesn't hurt to try. Who knows, the market may favor the tenant
and make it possible to have this tenant-biased clause added to
the lease.

26
Tenant Bankruptcy

Landlords worry, and rightly so, about the possible impact of a tenant bankruptcy. Perhaps most disturbing is the landlord's complete lack of control over the property involved. For a landlord, delayed rent payments, vacant space, assigned leases, and different unapproved tenants are only some of the more serious problems that a bankruptcy can cause.

Interestingly, many landlords continue to put onerous bankruptcy clauses into a lease document with the general warning that bankruptcy will be considered a default of the lease and will give the landlord the right to terminate the lease immediately. Tenants become nervous about the clause because they would not be able to work their way out of bankruptcy if they lost their lease. So tenants spend time haggling over the specific language of this clause and become sidetracked. In the process, they often give up some leverage from other more important areas of the lease document.

The Court Decides, Not the Lease Clause

When a tenant's business goes bankrupt or the tenant seeks bankruptcy protection in the courts, it is usually the court-assigned trustee who decides the outcome of the lease document. The bankruptcy legal process protects the business from its creditors, including landlords.

Landlords cannot terminate a lease for a bankrupt tenant who is under the protection of the court. Therefore, the tenant should stop worrying about specific lease language that seems to provide some options to the landlord. What is important for the tenant to understand is that other parts of the lease document can give the landlord some protection, but only if he or she acts before bankruptcy proceedings begin. It is for this reason that the landlord-inspired lease document tries to define specific actions resulting from lease defaults, the most onerous being those for nonpayment of rent or other money.

The logic behind this is simple. A tenant who cannot keep up with the rent in an ongoing and timely manner is usually having financial problems and may eventually go bankrupt. Since the landlord will have no control during a bankruptcy proceeding, he or she will want to become aware of a troubled business as quickly as possible. Then the landlord can act, he or she hopes, speedily enough to terminate a lease or implement an eviction process and get rid of a potentially troubling tenant before that tenant comes under the protection of the bankruptcy court.

Therefore, to the extent possible, a tenant in financial difficulty should be sure the landlord is the last to know, at least until it will be too late for any landlord action to occur faster than tenant actions that would protect the business.

Providing a Definition

Despite the protection provided by the bankruptcy courts, it is still useful to consider having a bankruptcy lease clause that defines what will be considered an event of bankruptcy. Typical items include the following:

- The tenant becomes insolvent, as defined by the U.S. Bankruptcy Code or under the insolvency laws of the state.

- A receiver or custodian is appointed for any or all of the tenant's property or assets, or a foreclosure action is begun on any of the tenant's real or personal property.

- A voluntary petition is filed under the provisions of the Bankruptcy Code or Insolvency Laws.

- An involuntary petition is filed naming the tenant a debtor under the Bankruptcy Code or Insolvency Laws, and such petition is not dismissed within 30 days or results in the issuance of an order for relief.

- The tenant agrees to or makes an assignment of the tenant's property and assets for the benefit of creditors.

A landlord may want to include many other items and thereby bind the tenant and potential future bankruptcy trustee. Unless the items added fully conform with the Bankruptcy Code, the court-appointed trustee will follow the requirements of the code.

In addition, the landlord may want to include certain language, whether valid or not, that will help sway or guide a trustee. For example, the landlord would like to see statements to the effect that there will be no actions or liquidation sales conducted on the premises; that, in the event of an assignment of the lease, the business use of the premises will remain unchanged and there will be no prohibited use of the premises (if defined in the lease); and that an assignment or assumption of the lease will not disturb, affect, or violate the rights of other tenants on the property.

The Landlord Is Just a Creditor

Often the items a landlord includes in this clause are designed in the hope that the lease document will be enforced and will protect the leasehold and the premises. At other times the items included represent an attempt to influence the trustee with respect to the payment of monetary damages to, or establishing certain rights of, the landlord. In actuality, the U.S. Bankruptcy Code or a state's Insolvency Laws will rule. The landlord will become a creditor and, just like any creditor, will only have the rights afforded to all creditors. The lease document becomes just another asset (or a liability) to be disposed of for the bankrupt business.

27

Casualty Damage or Destruction

Casualty damage refers to the destruction of property by any major natural or environmental cause such as fire, flood, earthquake, or tornado. This lease clause is important to tenants and landlords alike. Casualty damage can occur to a tenant's premises, to a portion of the building, to the entire building, or to another property that affects either the building or the tenant's premises (or business operations). The big question is, will the damage be repaired? If so, by whom and when? The tenant will also want to know what will happen to his or her business operations during these repairs.

Too often, with adverse consequences, the PREB will pay scant attention to this lease clause. If the PREB also ignores the required related lease clauses, such as those pertaining to landlord and tenant insurance provisions, the tenant will find him- or herself covered by limited protection.

The problem in writing this lease clause is finding language that will satisfy the divergent needs of the landlord, the tenants, and the mortgage holder. The landlord's main concerns will be to protect his or her investment, protect an asset, ensure a continuing cash flow, and maintain control. To the extent this clause permits a tenant, for whatever reason, valid or not, to terminate the lease, the landlord feels that control has been lost and thus the investment may be affected.

The Landlord's Concerns

From the landlord's perspective, giving the tenant termination rights without strict guidelines means giving the tenant the right to leave the building for less than satisfactory causes. The tenant could use the excuse of damage to terminate the lease and move to a newer building. Worse yet, the tenant could use casualty damage as an excuse to exact economic benefits from the landlord (for example, the tenant would agree to stay only if the rent were lowered).

Also, the damage to the building could be so great that the landlord would find it more beneficial not to undertake repairs. The landlord does not want to be forced to fix the property; he or she wants the option, not the obligation.

The landlord is also concerned about tenant responsibilities. Will the tenant be required to make repairs to damaged premises beyond those the landlord must make to the building structure and operations? More important, does the lease specify that the tenant must make such repairs and have continued lease obligations?

Landlords are usually wary about tenants and see an unsavory side to every tenant, especially a tenant who has any right to exercise control within the lease.

On the other hand, a landlord may be required to do something that may not be in the best interests of either the landlord or the tenant. Both the landlord and the building's tenants may want to use insurance proceeds to repair a property, for example; however, the mortgage lender may be able to protect the loan by insisting that insurance proceeds be applied to the mortgage balance. In this case, any agreement between the landlord and a given tenant will be superseded by the mortgage lender (unless the tenant signed the lease before the permanent financing agreement and has not otherwise released his or her lease priority over the mortgage). For the tenant who has a significant investment in the premises or is leasing a large amount of space, a separate agreement between the tenant and the mortgage lender is in order.

The Tenant's Concerns

Many tenant concerns will mirror those of the landlord. However, the tenant needs to be sure that his or her concerns are adequately addressed. When it comes to the issue of casualty damage, the tenant needs to expand the focus beyond the premises. Damage to the premises is clearly important, since it can put an end to the tenant's business operations, but damage to a building or the attached surrounding property can also have a serious impact.

This lease provision should stipulate the amount (e.g., the percentage) of damage that needs to occur either to the building or to the premises before the rights of the tenant can be invoked. Often these rights are some combination of rent abatement and the right to terminate the lease.

The tenant's concerns usually involve a multiplicity of complex factors that no one lease provision could possibly cover. The wording of the clause must be such that the tenant has some, if not considerable, control over his or her business destiny. The tenant's main concern will be the extent of interruption to the business because of the unusability of the premises. The tenant will want to make sure the effects on the business can be minimized; of course, the tenant will also want to know who will be responsible for economic losses suffered by the tenant due to damage or destruction.

How much damage or destruction constitutes enough to render premises unusable? Is unusability of the premises the right business measurement? And what is meant by "unusable"?

What if fire destroys only the front entrance of the premises, denying customers easy access to the business—to what extent are the premises unusable? If a computer room is burned out or all the windows of the premises are destroyed in the middle of the coldest winter ever, how much of the tenant's space is unusable? What happens if there is no damage to the tenant's premises but a neighbor's premises on the same building floor are destroyed by fire and the smell permeates the tenant's premises—is the space unusable? What about damage to the main entrance to the building, restricting access to the office? What if the utility closet on the floor is destroyed and all telephone service is knocked out or the elevators in a 20-story building are no longer operational? What if the damage is to the surrounding but attached property?

What happens if an attached parking structure is no longer usable or the roadway or sidewalk leading to and around the building is destroyed?

The number of things that can affect the premises go far beyond the space itself. A related question is how long the effects of any damage or destruction must last before tenant rights can be invoked. Is 10 days too short a time to be concerned about? Is one year too long a period to expect tenant sacrifices? Often the answer depends on the type of damage. Although 10 days without electricity or elevator service can be devastating to a tenant's business, the premises may be perfectly usable. At what point does merely being "put out" escalate to extreme distress? And what remedies are available to the tenant?

In the landlord's view, the lease should state that if some agreed-to percentage of the premises or, in some cases, the building is damaged or destroyed, the landlord has the right, after some period of time (e.g., 30 days) to notify the tenant that he or she will be repairing the damage. A stronger version of this provision would specify a time limit for any repair. However, the tenant's lease obligations would remain in full force, although there might be some rent abatement for the inconvenience.

The tenant needs to adjust this provision to add the percentage of damage, not only for the premises but also for the building and the attached surrounding property, and to stipulate how long such damages will be tolerated. Perhaps most important, this provision should state the percentage of specific business operation interruptions that would be acceptable, the percentage of lost business income that would be tolerable, and the time frame that would be acceptable to the tenant in both cases.

The Tenant's Right to Terminate

When the damage meets or exceeds the agreed-to percentage calculation, then what? Generally, the lease clause provides that the landlord will have the right to terminate the lease and may want this right even if the damage or destruction does not quite meet the necessary percentages.

How much damage is too much—or not enough? Will the landlord be required to repair? Is the tenant required to stay?

The tenant needs to add an acceptable method for determining who is to decide whether the lease is terminated and how this will be done. Otherwise, the landlord with termination rights could use the excuse of damage to pick and choose some tenants over others. Therefore, the tenant must include some provision for equal tenant treatment throughout a property, and it must be related to the approximate levels of damage affecting other tenants.

The tenant will also want termination rights but will first have to allay the landlord's fears regarding these rights and try to avoid a tenant-landlord confrontation. The tenant's termination rights should therefore be carefully related to the percentage of interruption to the business. This will provide a fairer, less biased assessment of whether there is justification for either party to terminate the lease.

One other termination problem that often crops up pertains to damage or destruction for the tenant with only a few years remaining on his or her lease. Often a landlord will want to terminate the lease, since he or she will usually be able to re-lease the premises, after appropriate repairs, for a higher rent than would be paid by the tenant with a long-term lease. Similarly a tenant will often want to terminate a lease when the damage or destruction occurs near the end of the lease term. The tenant may envision having to relocate to new premises or may not relish the time involved in and the business disruptions that are part of the repair process, whether to the tenant's premises, the building, or the surrounding property.

From the tenant's view, it would seem reasonable to permit termination due to damage or destruction to begin when there is less than one or up to three years remaining on a lease. To have this work properly, the termination rights must be evaluated in terms of the estimated (or landlord-guaranteed) time it will take to complete the repairs and the level of disruption to the tenant's business operations or business income.

The landlord will want equal or similar termination rights. In particular, the landlord will want to be sure that the lease language in no way forces the landlord to repair a property that, for investment or cost reasons, he or she does not want to repair. It could be onerous if, for instance, only one tenant of a multi-tenanted building were able to force the landlord to repair a severely damaged building. The landlord must also pay attention to related lease clauses. For example, the tenant's renewal right clause could override the landlord's right to terminate the lease near the end of the tenant's term.

How Much Rent?

Terminating the lease because of the damage or destruction would be the final solution. In most cases, the tenant's business will continue to some extent, although income may be disrupted during the period the landlord is repairing the premises, building, or attached property. During this repair period, the tenant will want to know whether he or she will be required to pay rent, and, if so, how much. Obviously the landlord will want the tenant to continue paying the full rent. The tenant will not want to be paying any rent. Somewhere between these two extremes is a compromise.

From the tenant's perspective, the compromise should relate the amount of damage to the amount of disruption to the business operation or the tenant's income. With that provision firmly established, the amount of rent a tenant should pay during this period can then be directly related to a percentage of the damage incurred. Tenant rent abatement would then occur in a fairly straightforward manner.

However, there are some additional rent-related matters to look at. For example, what happens to a last month's rent deposit or a security deposit, especially in the extreme situation of a tenant-induced lease termination? The tenant needs to be sure there is sufficient lease language to ensure the return of these deposits (rather than their forfeiture). Similarly, what about rent, "additional rent" items, and operating expenses paid for in advance? A provision is required for the return of any prepaid items. Tenants must also be sure that any negotiated abatement items, especially those with a dollar value, are extended rather than used up during damage-induced abatement periods. Otherwise, any rent abatement period given as a lease-signing inducement may be used up if there is severe damage to the building or premises during this period.

Notice Date

The vital question for a tenant is when an actual abatement period starts when there is damage or destruction. The landlord will be required to notify the tenant in writing of any damage or destruction. This provision requiring official notification will usually include the landlord's estimate of the amount of damage that has occurred, as well as a declaration of whether the premises, building, or property are to be repaired and an estimate of the time it will take to do the repairs (or the completion date). The problem for the tenant is that there are no guidelines or requirements in the lease document concerning when this notification must take place; all too often it is given 30, 60, or more days after the damage has occurred. Furthermore, since any rent-abatement period will be tied into this notice, the landlord has little incentive to be informative.

It is up to the tenant to make sure that the language in the lease provides an incentive for the landlord to give timely notice of the damage or destruction—in this case, a negative incentive if the landlord does not do so. At a minimum, a lease provision should require the landlord to notify the tenant in a timely manner, but in no event later than 30 days after the damage or destruction occurred. Failing to do so, the landlord would be considered in default of his or her obligations under the lease, and the tenant, at his or her option, could terminate the lease by giving 30 days' written notice to the landlord.

Inasmuch as any tenant monetary abatement is to be related to disruptions in business or income, the abatements should also be specified to begin (or be retroactive to) the damage or destruction date—*not* the notification date.

Repair Time

The landlord's notification of casualty damage should automatically start the clock ticking for all the appropriate lease provisions, such as the tenant's lease termination right and rent or other abatements. Any notification letter to the tenant should include the amount or percentage of damage that has occurred to the premises, building, and attached property, in accordance with the appropriate lease provision specifying how the amount is to be calculated.

The damage notification letter to the tenant should also specify the extent to which the damage can be repaired and whether the landlord intends to make the required repairs. In addition, the landlord's notification should specify both the exact time the repairs will commence (e.g., within 30 days) and the range of time they will take (e.g., 60 to 90 days).

The provision pertaining to the time for repair of casualty damage should be incorporated in (or related to) the provision for the disruption of business operations and income. The intent, for the tenant, is to introduce an additional benchmark by which the tenant could invoke appropriate rights or remedies.

An important tenant right to consider is that of lease termination. In this lease provision a certain percentage of the damage calculations would be related to the estimated time of repair. In this way, if certain types of damage were only of medium intensity but the landlord was unable or unwilling to repair the damage in a reasonable time, the business operation or income disruption quotient would be intensified, enabling the tenant to invoke the termination provision. Similarly, the landlord would have termination rights depending on the time needed to make the repair and its effect on the damage intensity quotient.

Any tenant termination provision should always be at the tenant's option. This allows the tenant to evaluate the disruption and cost of relocating to new premises in relation to remaining in place (or seeking temporary quarters) during the damage repair.

Repair of Tenant Premises

The last but perhaps most important question for the tenant in regard to casualty damage is the way to decide who pays for the damage to the tenant's premises and property. In a normal casualty damage lease clause, the landlord will only be responsible for bringing the building and attached property to their original standards and operations. This will also apply to the tenant's premises. The landlord will only be responsible for the base building standard and will not cover any tenant improvements or personal property.

For this reason, it is vital for the tenant to have the proper insurance. Without insurance, the tenant may find it impossible to continue business even after the premises or the building has been restored. The tenant should carefully choose a program from the wide variety of business insurance that is available. Everything from furniture, equipment, machinery, rugs, and other improvements to rent payments for temporary space and living expenses can be covered with the right insurance program.

However, the tenant should be sure of the ownership of any improvements made to the premises on his or her behalf. Often, as an inducement to a tenant, the landlord, besides abating rent, will provide additional premises improvements, including glass partition walls, special wall coverings, computer wiring, upgraded floor coverings, built-in wooden bookcases, executive washrooms, and even private kitchen facilities. In many instances, because the landlord built the improvements at his or her cost, the improvements actually belong to the landlord. They are assets of the landlord, not of the tenant, so the landlord's insurance should cover their replacement.

The tenant should be sure the casualty damages clause includes a provision specifying that any damages to the tenant's premises will be repaired to a level equal to or better than their original condition and to the same specifications and buildout as originally provided by the landlord. This can be especially important to tenants who lease space that was specifically built for a previous tenant but that provides the necessary and proper environment for the tenant's business operations.

28
Condemnation

Probably no lease clause is more commonly ignored by tenants and PREBs than the condemnation lease clause—and often with good reason. To most tenants and PREBs, the idea of the local, state, or federal government condemning or taking property by the right of eminent domain seems far-fetched. They have seen buildings being torn down in older neighborhoods or unused and deserted downtown areas, but they cannot imagine such a thing happening to a nice, new office building in a commercially viable downtown area or parklike suburban office campus.

Actually, condemnation can occur almost anytime and anywhere, for a multitude of reasons. The government often takes property to serve the greater good for the greatest number of people. The "good" may be a new highway, a rapid or light rail commuter service, expanded utilities, or a new government office center.

The lease clause covering such action is often viewed as just another of those things a landlord requires. However, tenants and PREBs should pay close attention to this clause—not because they will want to or even be able to make many changes (in general, this clause favors the landlord entirely and offers absolutely no rights or protection for the tenant), but because the clause should include at least a few small items on the tenant's behalf. If it does not, when and if a building is condemned or taken over, the tenant may be in for some nasty surprises.

Perhaps the first point to make is that commercially viable

property is not condemned all that often. Although there are
some items a tenant may want to include in this lease clause, this
is one of those areas in which a tenant can "give in" to a landlord
during negotiations. Rather than pursue strong protection in the
wording of this clause, the tenant can earn concessions or negotiate harder on the lease clauses that have a more immediate effect
on the tenant, such as those on rent abatement and premises
buildout.

The Costs to the Tenant

However, the tenant needs to be aware of the potential effects of
a condemnation. The taking of property can be complete or partial. If complete, the entire property is usually destroyed. This
means every tenant will have to find a new place to conduct business. If partial, only part of a property will be lost—perhaps a
surface parking area will disappear or one of the building's entrances will be closed.

Whatever happens, the effects will often be monetary effects
felt by the tenant, especially when leases are terminated early
without any reimbursement to the tenant for the ensuing costs.
Moving to new premises costs money. Being unable to take built-
in furnishings or improvements (e.g., glass divider walls) translates into lost dollars to a tenant. A long-term lease with favorable
rent is often irreplaceable. The loss of a convenient customer
parking area or the inability to use a particular building entrance
can directly affect a tenant's income stream.

From the condemning authority's point of view, many of these
effects are not pertinent "business losses." What is pertinent is the
cost directly related to the taking of the property, which includes
the cost of the land and the building on it. Consequently, a property owner will be reimbursed for the appropriate value of what
amounts to confiscated property.

All too often, therefore, it is the tenants who feel the brunt of
the condemnation, because they have no ownership position in
the property. They are renters. They can move and relocate their
businesses. They can adjust for lost parking spaces. Although
there may be considerable economic impact on their business, it
is often difficult to show true dollar value when a rented property

is lost, taken, or seized. Therefore, tenants are paid little, if anything, in a condemnation.

The good news is that the taking of property by eminent domain is indeed rare. The bad news is that, when it does occur, it
usually creates terrible hardships and burdens on a tenant.

When Does Title Transfer?

This lease provision will state:

> If the whole or a substantial part of the premises are taken or
> condemned by any governmental authority for any public or
> quasi-public use or purpose, the term of the lease shall cease
> and terminate as of the date when the title vests to the govern-
> mental authority.

The problem for the tenant is to establish when the condemnation will actually take place or be official. The provision says,
"when the title is vested with the condemning authority," but the
tenant may not even know that a condemnation or taking of the
property is under consideration. In addition, it can take quite
some time before condemnation proceedings take place and the
title is transferred. Until that time, the tenant must continue paying rent. As the landlord knows, despite any delaying court actions, the property taking will undoubtedly occur. It is possible
that to save costs, the landlord may reduce services to the building; this results in a less than desirable business environment for a
tenant.

Tenant Notification

The ideal situation for a tenant is a lease provision that calls for
written notification from the landlord of any known or contemplated government condemnation or taking of the property as
soon as he or she is notified. The timing is important because
condemnation proceedings can be such long, drawn-out affairs.

With proper notice, the tenant would have some reasonable
time to find new space. However, the tenant would still be required to pay rent and be bound by the terms of the lease. It
would be advantageous to modify the termination provision so

that, at the tenant's option, the lease could be ended at some earlier period in the condemnation proceedings. For example, there might be a modification allowing the lease to be terminated if the proceedings were to go to court for a judgment on the valuation of the property.

Although the property title may not be vested with the condemning authority for quite some time, the outcome is known, and it is only a matter of time before the tenant will be caught in no-man's-land. He or she must continue to pay rent until the title transfer. If new space is found and the tenant wants to move earlier, he or she will have to pay two rents (or negotiate some arrangement with the new landlord). For the tenant, the preferred situation is to be able to leave when condemnation proceedings have begun.

The landlord will not want this. There is no income from empty space and, given the condemnation proceedings, no ethical way to re-lease any vacant space. The emptier a building, the less commercially viable it is and thus the less valuable. This, in turn, can affect the condemnation value of the building by appraisers or a court.

Selling in Lieu of Condemning

Another difficulty the tenant should be aware of is that an owner, knowing the property is about to be condemned, may negotiate with the governmental authority and sell the building to it. Now the property title has been transferred in a normal property sale. Such a sale can create more difficulties and confusion for the tenant.

The ideal tenant's lease provision will, at the tenant's option, permit the lease to be terminated after the purchase of the property by a governmental authority, when done so in lieu of a condemnation or taking by eminent domain.

No Tenant Claims for Dollars?

This lease clause will also often state:

> The tenant will have no claim against a landlord for any portion of the amount that may be awarded as damages as the result of the governmental condemnation or taking, or for the

value of any unexpired term of the lease, any leasehold improvements, or any business goodwill.

Another provision may also state that the tenant assigns, in advance, all rights regarding any payments to the landlord. The landlord does not want the tenant interfering with any payments he or she gets for the property and does not want any tenant claims for compensation to interfere with the landlord's valuation of the property.

However, the tenant needs to ensure that he or she can at least make a claim against the condemning authority for compensation for leasehold improvements, fixtures, equipment, and relocation expenses. It should not be difficult to have this provision added to this clause. The landlord will, in turn, want to adjust this provision so that it states that any compensation award to the tenant will be in addition to, and stated separately from, any compensation award for the land and the building.

Partial Condemnation

The condemning or taking of only part of a property can be much more complicated than a full condemnation. The tenant needs to be cautious about how the partial taking is to be defined in the lease clause and what the outcome of such a taking will be.

A partial condemnation or taking can involve both internal and external portions of a building, for example, when some land is taken and the amount of space for parking is reduced, a building entrance is closed, a building's delivery alley is no longer available, storage areas are removed, or part of a building is demolished.

Too often, to a tenant's detriment, this lease clause will state: "For a partial taking to be considered substantial and therefore comparable to a full taking, the tenant must lose the use of [some percentage, say, 50 percent] of his or her premises." Although the tenant loses the use of some of his or her premises, the lease remains in full force, and the rent must continue to be paid. (However, this provision will usually call on the landlord to make an "equitable" adjustment of the rent in recognition of the tenant's loss.)

Whether a tenant will want, or even be able, to stay in a building or on a premises is rarely taken into account. Moreover, whether the tenant can continue with normal business operations or might suffer a significant loss of business income is seldom considered.

The tenant should have the lease clause carefully delineate the parts of a property whose loss (and the exact percentage of that loss) to a condemnation or taking would affect the tenant's business operations or ability to generate income. This delineation should distinguish between the land, the building, and the tenant's premises. Since each of these separately can be affected by a condemnation or taking, each should have leasehold implications related to them.

No two properties are exactly the same; therefore, no one lease clause will work for every property, at least not from a tenant's point of view. The significant point is that a partial condemnation or taking should not be conditioned only on the percentage of the tenant's premises that becomes unusable.

By delineating the effects of a partial condemnation or taking on both the landlord's property and the tenant's business, such a clause makes it possible for either the landlord or the tenant to invoke a lease termination. (The more common lease provision merely allows the landlord to decide whether a lease is terminated if enough of a condemnation or taking has occurred.)

The tenant is the only one who can decide how much the loss of a part of a particular property—such as parking, delivery, or customer entrances, or part of a building that does not directly adjoin the tenant's premises—will affect his or her business; therefore, the tenant should be entitled to terminate the lease.

Rent Abatement

The loss of parts of a property, other than a tenant's premises, should be evaluated in relation to the actual rent paid by the tenant. The tenant agreed to lease a particular space in a building on a particular property and agreed to pay a certain rent based on consideration of the property as a whole. After a condemnation or taking, the property is no longer the one that was originally chosen. Therefore, rent reductions should reflect not only the loss of part of a tenant's premises, but also the loss of being able to conduct business in a normal manner and possibly even the loss of business income.

At a minimum, the lease should contain a tenant-preferred provision for total (or partial) rent abatement for the period of time a tenant's business is unable to operate in a normal manner as a result of the condemnation or taking. Suppose for example, that part of a building or a building's original main entrance is taken. Until new entrances are constructed or the building is properly modified to reflect the loss, the tenant should have his or her rent reduced or abated to the extent that business is disrupted.

How Much of the Premises Is Left?

Often a condemnation or taking does affect a tenant's premises. When that occurs, who is to be responsible for the rebuilding of the space and the loss or the moving of fixtures and equipment? Because the landlord will be negotiating with the condemning or taking authority and the landlord determines the effect, partial or full, that the condemnation or taking has on the tenant's premises, any necessary restoration of the premises or the tenant's property should be the responsibility of the landlord, or it should be paid for out of any condemnation compensation.

A partial condemnation or taking can complicate life for a tenant. Although tenant and landlord may suffer alike, in general the condemning authority's obligation of fairness is to the property owner. Often there is no one looking out for the interests of the tenant, especially when the tenant is "just" a small business.

29
Limited Liability of the Landlord

The limitations to a landlord's liability are fully discussed in Chapter 30. However, a brief comment should be made about a second lease clause that places certain limits on a landlord's liability to a tenant. This clause limits the tenant's right to any monetary compensation or awarded judgments against a landlord.

A general limitation clause will state:

> The tenant agrees that in the event the tenant is awarded a money judgment against the landlord, the tenant's sole recourse for satisfaction of such judgment shall be limited to execution against the estate and interest of the landlord in the building and the land of which it is a part. In no event shall any other assets of the landlord, or of any partner of the landlord, or of any other person or entity, be available to satisfy or be subject to such judgment, nor shall any partner of the landlord or any other person or entity be held to have any personal liability for the satisfaction of any claims or judgments that the tenant may have against the landlord.

Often such a provision will protect the landlord and others for any actual or alleged failure, breach, or default of the lease by the landlord. In addition, other provisions may state that no partner of the landlord may be sued or named as a party to any suit or action by the tenant, that no service of process will be made against a partner of the landlord, that no partner of the landlord will be required to answer or otherwise plead to any service or process, and that no writ of execution will ever be levied against the assets of any partner of the landlord.

The intent of this lease clause is obvious. The landlord wants to limit his or her financial liability to a tenant to the specific property the tenant occupies. Furthermore, the landlord wants to limit the liability of any ownership interests to the partnership owning the one building (having a separate partnership for each building is a typical ownership method), as though each building were owned by a separate corporation. If the building were in fact under a separate corporation, it would already have limited liability.

The problem for the tenant, especially a major tenant or the occupant of a whole building, is that if financial damages or a judgment are granted against the landlord, the tenant has no means of collecting. That is, the tenant has no real way, without much research, to determine the true value of a property. If a building is new, it will have little value, because it will be carrying a large amount of debt. As time passes, there is, again, no easy way for the tenant to continually monitor the value of a property or any additional debt or other encumbrances put on the property by the owners.

From the landlord's perspective, this is no worse than, and not much different from, having the tenant dealing with a corporation. To the extent that it can, the ownership of a property wants to protect each individual's personal assets, as well as any separate and unrelated business assets and other investments.

From the tenant's perspective, this is just not good enough. The tenant wants to be sure that there is some way to collect in the event that he or she should win financial damages or a judgment against the landlord.

Depending on the economic leverage and power the tenant possesses relative to the leasing needs of the landlord, some type of compromise can usually be worked out. One possibility would be to drop the clause entirely. This may or may not be acceptable, depending on how the property and any other investments are structured by the owners. In addition, certain limited liabilities may be built into the property's owner partnership that will be difficult to pierce without protracted legal maneuvering—an expensive proposition for the tenant.

Other alternatives may address the tenant's concern directly and provide access to other partnership assets, with appropriate safeguards for the individual owners. For example, the tenant could be given specific rights for rent credit or rent abatement to satisfy any court-ordered monetary damages or judgments. This latter option is often quickly taken by tenants as an equitable and good-faith arrangement by the landlord. However, depending on the tenant's size and actual lease obligations, it is possible for monetary compensation to be well in excess of any continued rent due to a landlord.

30
No Waiver

The no-waiver clause is one that can sneak up and cause a lot of problems for the tenant. It is very simple and, unlike most lease clauses, brief. The gist of a no-waiver clause is as follows: Because some action or behavior, even though specifically prohibited by the lease document, was permitted or ignored by the landlord at some earlier time, it does not mean that the action or behavior is acceptable or the prohibition is being waived; the landlord retains the right to seek satisfaction at some future time. This clause can have far-reaching implications for a tenant, particularly if the implementation of some provisions of the lease, such as a renewal or an expansion option, depends on the tenant's not being in default of the lease.

However, it may not take much for a tenant to be technically in default of the lease. For example, being late with one or more rent payments, being late with the annual payment for the landlord-invoiced pro rata share of the building's operating expenses, ignoring a rule or regulation, such as not using a specific elevator for freight or having a delivery made through the lobby area—any of these actions technically puts the tenant in default. Obviously, they are not serious defaults. Nonetheless, they are tenant defaults of the lease.

The best option for the tenant is to have this clause excluded from the lease document. Without this no-waiver clause, if the landlord said and did nothing about a tenant's default, it could presumably be forgotten. Even in a court of law, the landlord could not garner much sympathy regarding a tenant's past default transgressions about which nothing had been done. Without a say in past default transgressions, the landlord would have no way to invalidate any tenant's rights, such as a purchase option for the building.

The inclusion of this lease clause provides some, albeit limited, protection for the landlord and should serve as notice to the tenant to be continually on guard and aware of what lease defaults he or she may have incurred. This is especially true if the tenant has a significant future right (for example, in purchasing the building) that depends on not being in default.

This lease clause has two basic versions, both of which are fairly simple and brief. The first version will state:

> No consent, express or implied, by either party, to, or of, any breach of any covenant, condition, duty, or agreement of the other party, shall be construed or operate as a waiver to, or of, any other breach of the same or any other covenant, condition, duty, or agreement.

The second version will often contain specific language that clarifies difficulties a landlord has had with past tenants. A generalized version will state:

> If under the provisions of the lease, the landlord shall institute proceedings and a compromise or settlement is made, this shall not constitute a waiver of any covenant contained in the lease nor of any of the landlord's rights under the lease. No waiver by the landlord of any breach of any covenant, condition, duty, or agreement contained in the lease shall be construed or operate as a waiver of such covenant, condition, duty, or agreement itself or of any subsequent breach of them. The landlord's consent to, or approval of, any act by the tenant shall not eliminate the necessity for obtaining the landlord's approval for any subsequent act of the tenant. No payment by the tenant, or receipt by the landlord, of a lesser amount than the monthly installments of rent, shall be other than on account. No endorsement on any check, or accompanying letter, for payment of rent or any other sums owed under the lease, will be deemed an accord and satisfaction. [Note: This endorsement statement is included so that nothing a tenant may write on the back of the check, such as "Pay-

ment in full for June rent," will have validity, despite the
landlord's cashing of the check.] The landlord may accept
such check or payment without prejudice to the landlord's
rights to recover the balance of rent or other sums owed
under the lease, or to pursue any other remedy provided in
the lease. No reentry or any act done by the landlord or
landlord's employees or agents, and no acceptance by the
landlord or landlord's employees or agents of keys from the
tenant or the tenant's employees or agents shall be considered
an acceptance of a surrender of the lease or operate as a termination of the lease.

There are two obvious differences between these versions:

1. The first clause provides for a mutual no-waiver provision.
2. The second clause is specifically oriented toward landlord protection and has included the three most common areas that
   could cause a landlord difficulty regarding a tenant's default:
   a. Nonpayment, late payment, or partial payment of rent
   b. No automatic termination of the lease just because a ten-
       ant turns over the keys of the premises to the landlord
       (and by implication moves out)
   c. No waiver of the landlord's right to a future default claim
       because a landlord does not specifically claim there has
       been a breach or default of the lease or did not do any-
       thing about it at the exact time it occurred

Creating a Paper Trail

If a landlord regularly admonishes the tenant in writing about
late rent payments or the breaking of the building's rules and regulations (e.g., "You are required to keep your entrance doors
closed at all times during building's normal operating hours"),
regardless of how insignificant the infractions may be, they are
technically defaults. The landlord may be creating a paper trail
for some future declaration of tenant default in order to have the
option to deny what would otherwise be a future tenant right
under the lease.

This lease clause is set up so that the paper trail, at least in regard to the tenant, is not absolutely necessary. Therefore, the ten-

ant should keep track of, and follow up on, any action or lack of action that might possibly be perceived as a default. The ideal situation is a landlord-tenant agreement that an actual default did not occur or that whatever happened falls into the gray area of landlord-tenant disagreement.

No Waiver + Tenant Default = No Rights

The tenant's problems occurs near the end of the lease term, when he or she says, "Okay, Landlord, I'm ready to exercise my rights, and I want to buy your building for the originally agreed to ten dollars." And the landlord says, "No way, man. You are, or have been, in default of your lease, and you therefore don't have the right." He or she pulls out a piece of paper (or perhaps a whole file folder of letters written to the tenant) showing that the rent was late five years ago and then points out this lease clause in the lease document.

Big joke? The landlord can't possibly be serious? The landlord is very serious and is not about to let the tenant buy the building or to honor whatever other right may be in question.

The Ultimate Arbitrator— A Court of Law

The result, depending on the importance of the item or right to the tenant, is to go to court to resolve the disagreement. Legal actions have three aspects, of which only two are certain.

First, any court action is going to take time, especially civil cases that may involve millions of dollars. Time can easily stretch into years. The wait can take great patience and stamina, and the end result, even if the case is found in the tenant's favor, can come after any value to the right being pursued has long passed.

Second, legal action takes money. The amount of money a tenant might spend can easily pass the tens of thousands of dollars and, depending on the value of the right and the landlord's obstinacy, may quickly climb into the hundreds of thousands of dollars. Of course, the right may well be worth it, particularly if it means being able to buy a building that has significantly increased in value (and especially if the price was fixed years before in the lease). Compounding the legal costs, however, is the cost of time that must be devoted by nonprofessionals to the action. The owners of the business, major stockholders, and especially top management will be drawn into the legal preparations. Claims and counterclaims will be necessary to pursue the legal actions. The amount of time involved will keep increasing. Owners and management will become enmeshed in the case, spending more and more of their valuable time on it, rather than on running and managing the business. In the end, the business will suffer from the lack of attention; lost business will mean reduced profits and deteriorating employer-employee relations.

The third aspect is perhaps the most important. If anything about a legal action is certain, it is that nothing is certain. There is no way to know in advance the outcome of a legal action. Although the tenant may think that "right" and sympathy are on his or her side, the law may well be weighted in the landlord's favor.

The moral is this: Pay close attention to this lease clause, maintain good landlord-tenant relations, and respond fully and in a timely manner to all lease requirements to avoid any defaults, especially if valuable future rights are at stake.

31

Insurance

The insurance clause in a lease document can be anything from a small paragraph to three or more pages of details specifying the amount and type of insurance coverage that will be required by both tenant and landlord. The number of details in this clause depends on factors such as the past experience of the landlord regarding tenant-caused fire, property, and personal liability damages, the size of the tenant (large space users or a single-building user will be required to carry minimum amounts of coverage), and the advice of legal counsel or a PREB.

From their experience with other tenants, a PREB and attorneys can provide advice on what this clause should contain. They can help fashion the clause so that it protects the tenant's interests. However, none of them is an insurance expert, regardless of how many tenants or leases he or she has worked with.

When this lease clause is kept brief, the tenant needs only to be sure that certain items protecting his or her interests are covered and clearly understood. When the lease clause has many details, the tenant must seek competent professional advice. The best person to give this advice is the tenant's insurance agent. Better yet, the tenant should seek out a qualified risk management consultant. A group of small space users, in particular, can benefit even more from such assistance. A risk management professional is in the best position to evaluate a tenant's insurance needs and to protect his or her interests. (This book will not discuss, except in passing, the various types of insurance that are available. It is left to the tenant to establish the coverage needed.)

The general insurance clause covers three areas: the types (and amounts) of insurance coverage for the tenant and, on occasion, the landlord; the insurance rating of the building; and a waiver of subrogation provision.

Insurance Coverage

The landlord's statement regarding his or her insurance coverage will be relatively brief:

> The landlord shall insure the building of which the premises are a part against damage by fire, including extended coverage, in any amount the landlord in his or her sole discretion shall deem adequate, and shall maintain such insurance throughout the tenant's lease term.

The tenant's insurance provision will be more detailed. The basic provision will state:

> The tenant shall insure all of his or her property in the premises against damage by fire and vandalism, including extended coverage, in an amount determined by the landlord in consultation with the tenant. The tenant will maintain such insurance throughout the lease term. In addition, the tenant will maintain, with respect to the premises, comprehensive public liability insurance and property damage. [The provision may also include limits and amounts for each.]

The fire insurance coverage provision is important to the tenant. Too often a small business, in trying to cut expenses, will cut out insurance premiums, usually with disastrous results.

The insurance that the landlord may require or that is appropriate for a business varies greatly. As a general rule, casualty coverage provides protection for those losses suffered personally by the insured party, whereas liability coverage protects the insured party from the claims of others for pain, suffering, and injury for which the insured is claimed to be responsible. Basic insurance includes the following coverage:

1. *Comprehensive general liability insurance.* This insurance covers personal and bodily injury and can include general property damage, contractual liability, and business operations hazards.

2. *"All-risk" comprehensive or property insurance.* This is also known as hazard insurance and would cover losses both of the tenant's furniture, fixtures, equipment, and machinery and to the building itself within the premises, as well as all leasehold improvements (walls, wiring, etc.). This also covers damage or destruction by fire and vandalism and includes extended coverage for malicious mischief against the building itself, not just against the tenant property within the premises.

3. *Business interruption insurance.* This insurance pays for lost profits in the event that the business is unable to operate because of damage or destruction to premises. This insurance is highly recommended for small businesses that could be closed permanently if they were shut down for even a short period of time.

4. *Leasehold coverage.* This insurance will pay for the loss of the leasehold or the premises. It covers the difference between what was paid in rent and any additional rent costs that are incurred because the tenant, having lost the use of the premises, must relocate to other, more costly space to continue business.

5. *Workmen's compensation and employer's liability insurance.* This coverage is typically mandated by state law and covers work-related pain, injury, and suffering incurred by employees.

There are many other kinds of coverage for the business person to consider. Key-man life insurance, for example, pays for the loss of a vital employee, such as a top salesperson or a business partner, and product liability insurance protects against pain, injury, or suffering to someone because of the purchase or use of the business products or services.

The insurance coverage in a lease document should be arrived at by mutual agreement between the landlord and tenant. However, the landlord (and/or the mortgage lender) will have specific requirements concerning the minimum needed to protect his or her investment, the building. This lease clause will include the following points:

- The tenant will maintain the specified insurance coverage with a responsible and recognized company licensed to do business in the state, a company acceptable to the landlord, its agents, and the mortgage holder.

- All applicable insurance coverage will name as additional insureds the landlord, his or her managing agent(s), and the mortgage holder, as deemed appropriate by the landlord. By being named additional insureds, the landlord is covered by the tenant's insurance for things such as bodily injury, property damage, and possibly personal liability. Depending on the insurance the tenant has, there may be coverage for "consequential losses" for the additional insureds, which in effect covers the landlord's rent payments.

- The tenant will deliver certificates of insurance regarding all the specified insurance coverage at the lease commencement date. He or she will be required to provide evidence of continuing coverage or evidence that policy premiums have been paid on an annual basis or as requested by the landlord.

- Each specified insurance policy will include a provision that the policy cannot be canceled without first providing 30 days' written notice to the landlord. In addition, all policies will include a provision that the landlord be given 15 days' advance notice of any major changes, additions, or alterations to the insurance coverage.

- The landlord and tenant both agree to have a waiver of subrogation (see Chapter 32) included in their respective (and appropriate) insurance policies.

- In the event that the tenant fails to maintain and keep in full force and effect any of the specified insurance policies, the landlord will have the option (but not the obligation), at his or her sole discretion, to procure the necessary insurance coverage on behalf of the tenant and to pay the requisite premiums. These landlord-paid premiums will immediately become obligations of the tenant, and the tenant will pay them to the landlord as "additional rent" with the next monthly installment of rent or on the demand of the landlord.

Some Special Additions

A variety of special provisions can be added to the insurance clause to meet the tenant's or the landlord's needs. Here are two examples:

1. All tenant insurance policies will be written as primary insurance coverage and not as contributing with, in excess of, or in addition to any coverage carried by the landlord. When two policies are working in tandem or are contributory to each other, significant delays may be encountered in receiving insurance proceeds and having damages repaired. Landlords want this provision in the lease clause to ensure that each party will provide his or her own insurance. Of course, coverage will be duplicated, and premium payments will be excessive as a result. Good business practices would have the landlord and the tenant cooperating so that each party's coverage would complement and reinforce that of the other.

2. Tenant-required insurance may be covered under a blanket insurance policy. A blanket policy enables a tenant with multiple business locations to insure all of them under one large policy. This can provide better insurance proceeds for losses incurred at one or two of the locations but might provide inadequate coverage if all the locations were destroyed or damaged at the same time. However, a blanket policy will involve considerable savings on the premium (check with your insurance agent or risk management consultant).

Getting Tenant Equality

All too often the insurance clause is one-sided, affording more than adequate protection to the landlord. It is beneficial for a business to carry the right types and amounts of insurance. However, as in the case of many other lease clauses, the tenant should seek equal treatment with the landlord, who should have to meet certain needs of the tenant.

The lease clause should indicate what insurance coverage the

landlord will provide and in what amounts. Ideally, all the
tenant's provisions in this clause will be adapted to include the
landlord.

The landlord's skimpy initial, one-line statement of the insurance he or she carries may be of concern to the tenant. A mortgage lender often requires specific insurance provisions in the
mortgage document, in many instances similar to what a tenant
must contend with in this lease clause. However, the mortgage
lender is interested in protecting the loan and being assured it
will be paid back, so the bulk of the insurance provisions are limited to that one requirement.

There is, of course, a trust factor that says a landlord will follow
good business practices and maintain the proper types and
amounts of insurance in order to protect his or her investment.
But this may be misplaced, blind trust. What is to stop a landlord
from discontinuing a particular insurance if its costs becomes
prohibitive? And what if this ceased insurance coverage had nothing to do with protecting the mortgage lender's investment, but
rather offered liability insurance for use of the building by, for
example, the tenant's employees, visitors, customers, and other
guests? So the landlord gambles a little bit and does not renew
the insurance. Who is to know? Maybe no one. And maybe there
is no harm done. But what if a tenant's employee is injured in the
building because of landlord negligence and there is no insurance coverage?

It takes a large space user with market clout to get the landlord
to adjust the insurance clause to create mutually acceptable provisions. But it does not hurt for the small space user to try.

Some areas the tenant should explore include the following:

- *The mutual waiver of subrogation clause (see Chapter 32).* This
  clause can often be more important for the tenant than for the
  landlord; however, it should not promise something that may
  well be undeliverable. From both the tenant's and landlord's
  perspective, the more general version of this clause should
  include language that states agreement as long as the waivers
  are obtainable from the insurers. However, from a tenant's
  perspective, this provision should include language stating that
  both parties will require that their respective insurance companies include a provision in each insurance policy regarding the

mutual waiver of subrogation between the insurance companies. Of course, the landlord will want to modify this to say that
he or she will use his or her best efforts to have the provision
included and that the tenant can also have this language adjustment. For the tenant, this may not be good enough. More often
than not, the tenant will have less protection if there is no
mutual waiver provision (see Chapter 32).

- *Being sure what types and amounts of insurance coverage exist for the
  building.* There should be a mutual requirement that each
  party supplies the other with certificates of insurance (in accordance with the requirements specified above).

- *The tenant's right to have his or her risk management consultant review
  the landlord's insurance policies.* In the ideal situation, because
  of the buying power of the landlord's insurance needs and thus
  reduced premium costs, the tenant is able to ride piggyback on
  a landlord's policy and save on premium costs. The landlord
  may strenuously object to this happening. It may create a co-
  insurance situation that complicates, for the landlord, any damage or injury awards by the insurance company.

- *Double-checking the property insurance the landlord carries.* The
  landlord should carry and be responsible for any leasehold
  improvements made at landlord expense, including any within
  the tenant's premises. The tenant should not need, or be required, to duplicate this coverage.

Generally, the tenant should have both his or her business
insurance coverage and the insurance lease clause reviewed by an
insurance agent or risk management consultant. Although legal
counsel or a PREB can write and evaluate the clause in terms of
what other landlords have done or even what other tenants have
accepted, the resulting clause may not be right for the tenant.
Only the tenant's insurance advisers can be certain that the requirements of the clause are achievable and mutually equitable.

Insurance Rating

The basic insurance rating provision of the insurance lease clause
is designed to protect the building and minimize increases in the

landlord's insurance premiums because of misuse by a tenant. The provision is straightforward, and there is little for a tenant to disagree with. The one part of this provision that requires tenant scrutiny is a statement designed to ensure that there is sufficient and factual proof that the tenant is actually responsible for any insurance increases. The burden for such proof should rest with the landlord. In the absence of such proof, the tenant should be presumed innocent.

This provision generally states:

> The tenant will not conduct or permit to be conducted by his or her employees, agents, customers, guests, or invitees any activity, or place any equipment or machinery, or keep, use, sell, or offer for sale any article that may be prohibited by any insurance policy in force, in or about the premises or the building, that will in any way increase the cost of fire insurance on the building.

The tenant's concern is how it will be determined that the tenant is truly at fault and therefore charged for any insurance premium increases. If the lease is to respond to this question, the landlord's basic provision will have to be modified.

The applicable landlord provision will state:

> If the tenant's occupancy or conduct of business in or on the premises or the building, whether or not the landlord has consented to it, results in any increase in the landlord's insurance premiums for the building [or property], or if any part of the increase in the rate of insurance premiums is stated by the insuring company or by the applicable insurance rating bureau to be the result of the tenant's actions, then such statement shall be conclusive evidence that the increase or applicable portion of the increase is due to activity or equipment or other use by the tenant in or about the premises, and the tenant will be liable for the increase and reimburse landlord within 10 days of receiving written notice.

At a minimum, the tenant must make sure that the word *conclusive* is removed from this provision and that he or she can examine any "evidence" and contest it. The additional provision would state:

The landlord will be required to send to the tenant any and all copies of any notices sent by any insuring company or insurance rating agency relating to any increase in the rate of fire or other insurance for the building that states that the tenant is responsible. The tenant will have the right, but not the obligation, to request the landlord's insurance company [or other applicable agency] to review the findings and contest the findings to the full extent of applicable laws and regulations.

Trampling the Tenant's Rights

Although rarely seen, an additional provision to this lease clause attempts to offer some extraordinary protection to a landlord. The problem is that the provision tramples a bit on the rights of the tenant. Because of its rarity, it is not something a tenant needs to be particularly concerned about. It is provided here only so that the reader will be aware of its existence and at least be on the lookout for it in his or her lease. Its appearance in a lease is the result of a bad experience by the landlord due to a tenant's activity. If a landlord has had a serious encounter with a tenant, it will be almost impossible to get the landlord to remove the provision. However, the tenant should have legal counsel modify the provision to suit the tenant's needs and provide the necessary level of comfort for the tenant.

The onerous provision will state:

If any insurance policies carried by the landlord for the building shall actually be canceled, or coverage reduced, or the insuring company shall threaten to cancel or reduce insurance coverage for any reason, due to the use, activity, or general occupation of the premises by the tenant, his or her assignees, any subtenant of the tenant, or anyone permitted in or about the premises or building by the tenant, and if the tenant fails to remedy the stated condition within 48 hours of receiving written notice from the landlord, as well as a copy of the insuring company's notification to the landlord, the landlord, at his or her option, can either terminate this lease or enter the premises and to the extent possible remedy the condition. The landlord shall not be liable for any damage or injury caused to any property of the tenant or others located in or about the premises or the building as result of this entry. The tenant shall be responsible for all costs and expenses associated with the landlord's entry and shall reimburse the landlord for the amount, specified as additional rent, within 30 days of receiving written notice.

Obviously, this provision is quite harsh and the result of some difficult landlord-tenant relationships. The landlord wants and needs to protect his or her investment. However, the landlord has recourses without this provision. Because of the insurance coverage and insurance rating clauses and other clauses within the lease document, including the building's rules and regulations, a tenant who caused this much difficulty could be declared in default of the lease, and the landlord could then pursue the appropriate remedies, including lease termination.

32

Mutual Waiver of Subrogation

This lease provision is often found tucked away in an insurance lease clause. The complex-sounding title is usually enough to keep tenants from reading the provision too closely, but that can be a mistake, because the provision can have important repercussions for a tenant. It has therefore been separated from the insurance lease clause and given its own chapter.

Subrogation Is . . .

The term *subrogation* refers to a situation in which a creditor substitutes its rights for that of another creditor *and* has all the rights of the original creditor. The concept is relatively straightforward. Suppose that a tenant has accidentally damaged something in a building. The landlord fixes the damages and collects from his or her insurance company. Unless there is a waiver of subrogation by the insurance company, not just by the landlord, the landlord's insurance company can then subrogate its rights for the landlord's and sue the tenant to collect for the damages—and it will inevitably win.

Because the landlord and the tenant both have their own insurance and each company will pay for the respective losses, the waiver of subrogation concept is accepted between and by insurance companies. However, the tenant does need to be sure the lease provision provides adequate protection and a proper follow-up procedure.

This provision generally deals with two points: the mutual waiver of subrogation between the landlord and the tenant and the intent for the waiver of subrogation between the landlord's and tenant's insurance companies.

It's Like "No-Fault" Insurance

The typical provision will state:

> Neither the landlord nor the tenant will be liable (by way of subrogation or otherwise) to the other party (or to any insurance company insuring the other party) for any loss or damage to any property of the landlord or the tenant, respectively, that is covered by insurance, even if the loss or damage is due to the negligence of the landlord or the tenant and their respective agents, employees, customers, or guests. This mutual release shall remain in effect only if the applicable insurance policies of the landlord and tenant contain an endorsement stating that this mutual waiver will not affect the right of the insured to recover for any losses or damages under the policy. In addition, both the landlord and tenant will use their best efforts (including the payment of additional premiums) to have their respective insurance polices include a standard insurance company waiver of subrogation provision.

The problem with the mutual waiver of subrogation as it relates to the insurance company is that neither the tenant nor the landlord has any say in getting his or her company to put such a provision into the insurance policy. The promises of the tenant or landlord have no effect when what must occur is not under their control. Therefore, both parties can only use their "best efforts" to get the insurance companies to do what they want.

Make Sure It Exists

It is especially important for the tenant to have the provision in the landlord's insurance policy because the tenant will be the one most likely to suffer if it is missing—it is more likely that some action of the tenant's guests or employees will damage the landlord's property. The landlord also needs to be concerned, however, especially if it can be shown that poor maintenance or landlord negligence contributed to the loss of or damages to a tenant's property.

The tenant must press for an annual review of the landlord's insurance policy or at least for some type of written confirmation that the waiver of subrogation remains in full force and effect. The landlord will want similar assurances. Two additional provisions can accomplish this. The first provision will cause a waiver by either party to be nonoperative if the mutual waiver of subrogation does not exist. The second provision will ensure that both parties receive written notification.

These additions would state:

> In the event that the landlord's or the tenant's insurance company declines to include a standard waiver of subrogation provision, the affected party will immediately notify the other party, which will then no longer be required to have its insurance policies include a waiver of subrogation, and the entire mutual waiver of subrogation provision will have no force or effect. In addition, during the term of the lease, both the landlord and the tenant agree to provide the other party, at least annually, with written confirmation of their respective insurance companies' certifications that a waiver of subrogation provision or endorsement is in full force and effect for the appropriate policy year.

33
Indemnity

The insurance clause usually contains a statement about indemnity. This statement is given a chapter of its own to emphasize its importance. It is considered an extension of the insurance being carried by the tenant. In fact, the combination of all the tenant's insurance policies will act as tenant indemnification for the landlord. Indemnification is insurable by the tenant. Even so, the tenant must be wary of and fully understand any indemnification clause that appears in the lease document.

The basic indemnity clause frees the landlord from any liability resulting from a tenant's actions. At least, that is what it is supposed to do. The tenant can run into problems when the indemnification is made a separate clause in the lease document.

Many times the landlord takes the occasion of a separate clause to expand its intent, stipulating that he or she will not be liable for the tenant's actions and that the tenant will not hold the landlord liable for the landlord's own actions. This is definitely something the tenant must have modified or removed from the lease. The tenant's legal counsel should not allow this addition, but on occasion it slips through. That is why the tenant, who will ultimately be responsible, needs to understand everything in the lease document, legal mumbo-jumbo notwithstanding.

A second item that often finds its way into the indemnification clause is a blanket waiver releasing the landlord of responsibility for virtually any action, including negligence in maintaining the building. This would be an impossible situation for a tenant. The tenant would need to procure insurance for these possibilities or be included as an additional insured under the landlord's insurance policy (the tenant can be made a secondary party achieving insurance coverage by being added to the primary party's insurance policy, usually at no cost to the secondary party). Otherwise, the tenant would be fully responsible for things such as bursting pipes related to the building (not just related to the premises), which should clearly be a landlord responsibility. There is never a good reason for a tenant to accept the addition of a blanket waiver or release provision.

An indemnification provision can be worded in various ways. Basically it will state:

> The tenant shall indemnify and hold harmless the landlord from and against any and all claims arising from tenant's use of the premises, or from the conduct of tenant's business, or from any activity or work permitted or suffered by the tenant or his or her agents, employees, customers, guests, or invitees in or about the premises or the building. The tenant shall also indemnify and hold harmless the landlord from and against any and all claims arising from any breach or default of the tenant's performances or obligations under the lease, or that may arise from the negligence of the tenant or his or her agents, employees, contractors, customers, guests, or invitees, and from any costs, attorney's fees, expenses, and liabilities incurred in the defense of any related claim, action, or proceeding. The tenant, upon written notice from the landlord regarding any claim, action, or proceeding brought against the landlord covered by this indemnification, shall defend the landlord at the tenant's expense by legal counsel acceptable to the landlord.

Two additional small provisions may be included. First, the tenant must be sure that he or she can accept the implied liability and has adequate insurance; second, the landlord should acknowledge the tenant's insurance coverage.

The first additional provision will state:

> The tenant assumes all risks of damage to property or injury to persons, upon or about the premises caused by or resulting from the fault of the tenant.

The tenant must not accept two alternatives or landlord additions to this provision: (1) the inclusion of liability for the building, as well as for the premises, and (2) the statement "resulting from any cause," not limiting the fault of the tenant.

The second additional provision will state:

> The landlord agrees that in the event that the tenant's liability insurance carrier acknowledges coverage and defends for any claim, damage, or loss, then the landlord, to the extent of the limits of such liability insurance, will look to the insurance carrier rather than to the tenant for indemnification and defense.

A General Landlord Waiver—It's Not Necessary

What the tenant must watch out for is a section (or a separate clause) that waives any landlord responsibility, whether or not the fault is the tenant's. This additional provision is not necessarily a problem if both the tenant and the landlord have proper and sufficient insurance, but it is extraneous and should be removed.

This additional lease clause or provision will make fairly broad and generalized statements, for example:

> The tenant agrees that the landlord shall not be liable for injury or any loss of income to the tenant's business, for any damages or loss to the tenant's goods, merchandise, or other property of the tenant and his or her employees, customers, guests, or invitees, or for any personal injury or loss of tenant's employees, customers, guests or invitees in or about the premises. The tenant further agrees that the landlord will not be liable for any injury, damages, or loss to the tenant and his or her employees, agents, contractors, customers, guests, or invitees from any cause, whether in or upon the premises or the building, or any other source or place, including that caused as a result of fire, steam, electricity, gas, water, rain, or from the breakage, leakage, obstruction, or other defects of pipes, sprinklers, wires, appliances, plumbing, air-conditioning fixtures, lighting fixtures, equipment, or machinery [this list can include anything else the landlord can think of, such as elevators, windows, and doors], regardless of whether the cause of the damage, injury, or loss, or the ability or means to repair the cause, is inaccessible to the tenant. Furthermore, the landlord shall not be liable for any damages arising from any act or

neglect of any other tenant and his or her employees, agents, contractors, customers, guests, or invitees in the building.

How fair are these broad and generalized indemnification lease clauses or even those relating specifically to tenant negligence? There is really nothing unfair about them. The landlord is merely trying to protect him- or herself.

Mutual Indemnification

However, the tenant should also have the right to some protection. The easiest way for the tenant to judge the fairness of an indemnification clause and to garner some of the same protection for him- or herself is to take the full clause and duplicate it, substituting the term *tenant* for *landlord,* and vice versa, throughout.

In effect, the tenant is seeking mutual indemnification. The tenant wants the same protection and sense of comfort given to the landlord. Will the landlord give it? Probably not without a lot of negotiation and soothing of the landlord's ruffled feathers. After all, this will be a new concept to the landlord. At a minimum, however, the landlord should be willing to offer some version of tenant indemnification, subject to the landlord's insurance coverage.

More important, with a properly structured, nonthreatening tenant challenge, the tenant will have a better understanding of what the landlord is trying to achieve. The landlord will then be more likely to be amenable to some mutual tenant-landlord language within the indemnification clause.

34

Subordination
and Attornment

Subordination and attornment are two separate but related subjects that are usually treated in the same lease clause. These two items are included for legal purposes on behalf of the financial institution providing the mortgage for the building.

Subordination

Subordination refers to the priority of two documents and means simply that one document shall be less important, or junior, to the other document. In a lease document this clause means that the lease and the rights of the tenant will be subject and subordinate to all mortgages, deeds of trust, ground leases, and the like, that now exist or may exist at some future period.

Furthermore, the lease clause will make the clause and the subordination "self-operative." That is, no further action on the part of the tenant or landlord will be required. However, there will often be a provision requiring that, at the landlord's request, the tenant will execute a certificate reiterating this subordination, and if it is not executed by the tenant within some stated period of time, the landlord will automatically be appointed the tenant's attorney-in-fact to execute such a certificate on behalf of the tenant.

401

The tenant may well wonder what the subordination issue is all about. In simple terms, the order in which documents are created often determines their rank in relationship to each other. For example, a lease document that is signed by the tenant for premises in a new building before the final permanent mortgage is secured will outrank the mortgage. Therefore, the mortgage will be subordinate to the lease.

Is this really an important issue? It may be to a lender if a foreclosure ever takes place. If the landlord defaults and is unable to pay the mortgage payments, the lender can foreclose and take over the property. However, if a mortgage were subordinate to any lease in the building, those leases would—or could (depending on the appropriate state law)—remain in force. And regardless of how economically unsound those leases might be, the lender could not end the leases before the end of the lease term.

But this lease provision subordinates the leases to the mortgage. Therefore, if and when the lender takes over a property through foreclosure, because of certain past legal proceedings (and subject to state laws), the lender may have complete control over what happens with respect to the subordinate leases. In other instances, when the lender forecloses, the lease will be terminated by the act of foreclosure.

Whether it is in the best interests of the lender to have a building's leases terminate will depend on the market and the economy. In a strong market, where space is leasing well, a lender will be happy to get rid of older, cheaper rent leases. In a weak market the lender might be glad to have anything leased and even be willing to accept a negative cash flow rather than have no income from an empty building.

Attornment

If a foreclosure can automatically terminate a lease, what keeps tenants from leaving (if they want) or immediately trying to renegotiate their leases (if market conditions favor the tenant)?

The reason is the attornment provision of this lease clause. Attorning is the tenant's automatic acceptance of and paying rent (and any other money) to a new landlord or owner. Obviously, this clause is also very important to a lender, as it prevents the tenant from terminating a lease under a foreclosure.

Like the subordination provision, this one calls on the tenant, upon landlord request, to execute an appropriate certificate acknowledging the attornment provision. Otherwise, the landlord will automatically be appointed attorney-in-fact to execute one on behalf of the tenant.

How important is all this to the tenant? It is quite important to both large and small tenants. Small tenants are often at a greater risk of having their leases terminated under a foreclosure. They have little market power, and a new owner may want to clean out the building in the expectation of attracting a larger space user or getting higher market rents from different small space users.

For the large tenant the importance may be one of degree. Because of the monetary difficulties of the original landlord, the tenant may not feel the building is any longer suitable for a quality business environment. Regardless of who the new landlord will be, the larger space user may want to move to a new location to find what he or she perceives to be higher-quality space. Alternatively, the large tenant may not wish to have anything changed in the lease. The large tenant may have such a financially beneficial lease that it was the tenant, and others like him or her, who contributed to the economic difficulties of the original landlord.

What about Tenant Hardships?

The subordination and attornment provisions give the lender or new owner the final say in what will happen to the continued leasing and occupancy of the premises. However, all tenants have an investment in their premises, be it economic or a matter of general convenience or customer recognition. To have a lender terminate a lease under foreclosure can create hardships. A nondisturbance provision is needed to ensure the premises will remain stable and to relieve the tenant of any anxiety over the possibility of lease termination through foreclosure (see Chapter 35).

35
Quiet Enjoyment and Nondisturbance

The quiet enjoyment and the nondisturbance lease clauses are designed, each in its own way, to protect the rights of the tenant for the peaceful and uninterrupted use of the tenant's premises. They are completely separate clauses and should not be confused. Often the nondisturbance clause (when it is included), is an additional provision of the subordination and attornment clause.

In any case, it takes an experienced commercial PREB or legal counsel to explain the difference to the tenant. All too often an inexperienced PREB will incorrectly give a tenant the impression that with the quiet enjoyment lease clause, nothing will or can disturb the tenant's occupancy of the space. This is not true.

Quiet Enjoyment

The quiet enjoyment lease clause is a covenant of the landlord's. That is, it is a promise made by the landlord and no one else. The landlord cannot make any promises regarding the conduct of other parties over which the landlord has no control.

The clause will simply state:

> As long as the tenant pays his or her rent and any other money due under the lease and observes and performs the terms, covenants, and conditions under the lease, the tenant will peacefully, quietly occupy, and enjoy the full possession of the premises without molestation or hindrance by the landlord or any other party claiming by, through, or under the landlord [or alternatively, "the tenant's possession of the premises will not be disturbed by the landlord or any party claiming by, through, or under the landlord"].

The tenant must be wary of additional language specifying that the quiet enjoyment clause is effective only as long as the tenant is not in default under the lease. This provides a broad "out" for the landlord and virtually no protection for the tenant.

The basic clause is often adjusted to satisfy particular tenant or landlord concerns, each usually in conflict with what would benefit the other party. A landlord might want to begin with a watered-down ending that limits the landlord's liability for disturbing the tenant's possession or puts in an exception. An example of this would be limiting the disturbing of a tenant's possession to the landlord, his or her successors, and assigns. Even more weakening is to add limiting language such as "except as subject to mortgages and deed-of-trust (and ground leases)," or even worse, "except as subject to the terms of this lease and any interests of record to which this lease may be, or become, subject and subordinate."

The additional language weakens the quiet enjoyment rights of the tenant. However, the landlord cannot (or would be foolish to) accept an all-encompassing and simplifying provision stating that the landlord promises the tenant's possession will not be bothered during the lease term. From a landlord's perspective, this would provide too broad a right to a tenant. (Theoretically, the landlord could not do anything, even if the tenant stopped paying rent.)

Nondisturbance

The landlord's quiet enjoyment lease clause only gives assurances regarding the nondisturbance of the tenant's possession of the premises. There is nothing in this clause, especially when coupled with other lease clauses, to keep the institution holding the building's mortgage, for example, from foreclosing on the property in the event of the landlord's default. And because of the subordination lease clause, the tenant could well find his or her possession severely disturbed—the lease might be terminated.

For total protection the tenant needs to have additional "quiet enjoyment" clauses from any third parties—not otherwise working with or in an ownership relationship with the landlord—who have the potential to affect a tenant's possession at some future time. Specifically, this should be a mortgage lender or a future building purchaser.

To create a total package that would protect the tenant's right to continued possession of the premises throughout the lease term, the tenant needs to have a nondisturbance certificate (or lease addendum). The nondisturbance certificate or agreement will have an associated lease clause, which is usually incorporated into the subordination and attornment clause. The actual nondisturbance certificate or agreement will be separate from the lease and will come directly from the mortgage lender to the tenant. In effect, the lender enters into an agreement with the tenant whereby, as long as the tenant is not in default under the terms, conditions, and covenants of the landlord's lease (this can often be modified to state merely that the tenant is up-to-date and continues to pay rent and any other money due under the lease), the lender agrees not to disturb the tenant's possession of the premises. This agreement provides the tenant full security in the event of foreclosure.

Many tenants and far too many PREBs push the landlord into putting a nondisturbance clause into the lease. For those who succeed, the value of the clause is questionable. The landlord, by him- or herself, cannot create a liability for or ensure actions on behalf of another party, in this case the mortgage lender, unless the landlord happens to hold an appropriate power of attorney (a remote possibility at best). Therefore, such a clause may carry no weight.

What many landlords wisely do is put in a modified nondisturbance provision that enables the landlord to "use his or her best efforts" to secure from the holder of the building's mortgage and deliver to the tenant an agreement stating that as long as the tenant is not in default of the lease, the tenancy and possession of the tenant under the lease will not be disturbed by an action or proceeding to foreclose on the mortgage or by a sale or foreclosure. With this toothless provision, the tenant should require that if the landlord is unable to obtain such an agreement, the reason for failure should be furnished to the tenant in writing.

This modified provision offers little solace to a tenant who is concerned about the most important issue, the possibility of having business operations interrupted or the business environment disturbed. Depending on how strongly the tenant feels about the need for a nondisturbance agreement and on the tenant's market power, the tenant's options are limited.

Obviously, a tenant should not enter into a lease unless a non-disturbance provision has been included. However, in many cases, depending on the size of the space being leased, this will not even be a tenant's option—many landlords do not want to be bothered with getting a nondisturbance agreement.

A second option is not to have a subordination and attornment clause in the lease. Instead, an addendum combining subordination, attornment, and nondisturbance can be created and signed by the landlord, the tenant, and the mortgage lender. This is the same as a separate nondisturbance agreement, but for some reason it goes over better with landlords.

A third option is for the tenant to insist on an addition to the landlord's "will try to get a nondisturbance" provision stating that the tenant has the option to terminate the lease in the event the landlord is unable to obtain a nondisturbance agreement from the mortgage lender.

Still another option is to adjust the attornment clause to state that the tenant is not required to attorn to a mortgage lender, unless the lender agrees that it will take no action to interfere with the rights of the tenant in, or to, the premises as long as the tenant is not in default of the lease.

A PREB who is unable to secure a nondisturbance agreement for a tenant will quickly explain, "The clause is not really needed anyway. Even in the event of a foreclosure, you, the tenant, will be perfectly safe and undisturbed in the space. After all, the lender will not want an empty building any more than the landlord. The lender will want cash flow as much as, perhaps even more than, the landlord. So, don't worry."

Worry just a little. A lot depends on economic conditions and real estate markets, as well as on any ulterior motives the lender might have. In a good market there probably would not have been a foreclosure in the first place. But if there is, the lender will more likely want to scrutinize every lease carefully and keep only those of the greatest economic value. In other circumstances the lender may want to take over the building for his or her own use and terminate every tenant's lease in the building. Or the lender may have an important client who wants to occupy or purchase the building. In the world of commercial real estate there are no certainties and no assurances, especially from a virtually powerless PREB.

Tenant peace of mind regarding any potential building disruptions requires a package concept. The package consists of a lease that includes a subordination clause, an attornment clause, a well-worded quiet enjoyment clause, and a supplemental nondisturbance clause as a lease addendum. Without a complete package, the tenant remains at risk.

36

Lien on Tenant's Property

This lease clause is one of the landlord's remedies for a tenant's default under the terms of the lease. Various applicable state laws will determine whether it needs to be included in a lease document. If it is included and agreed to by the tenant, it provides quick remedies in the event of certain tenant defaults and helps the landlord avoid the vagaries of the courtroom.

The PREB who fails to explain this lease clause is doing the tenant a disservice. The PREB should be aware of the legal default remedies that are available to a landlord and need not be included in a lease document and should advise a tenant accordingly.

Even more important, it is the PREB's responsibility to the tenant to reduce or eliminate, at least to the extent possible, the specific areas in a lease document that can create a default situation for the tenant. The clause pertaining to a lien on the tenant's property (also referred to as the "landlord's lien" in a lease document) can create an onerous burden for the tenant. Therefore, a tenant should under no circumstances sign a lease with this clause in it, unless it has been adjusted to meet the tenant's needs. Both the PREB and the landlord will attempt to overcome the tenant's objections to it. They will cite the "reasonableness" of this clause, explain that it is a "standard" landlord's clause and much needed for the landlord's protection, and absolutely swear

411

that there is only the most remote chance that it will ever need to be used. In the end, most resolve is worn down and tenants allow the clause to stay.

Everything Belongs to the Landlord

The lease clause specifies that the landlord will have a lien (or that the tenant grants the landlord a lien) on all the personal property of the tenant, including, but not limited to, all of the goods, wares, chattels, fixtures, furniture, equipment, and machinery of the tenant placed in or upon the premises. (There may be an additional provision stating that the tenant specifically waives any and all exceptions that may be allowed by law.) All the tenant's property will be subject to the lien of the landlord for the payment of rent, "additional rent," or any other monetary sums owed and unpaid to the landlord for services or costs related to the premises or for the tenant's default of any other lease obligations. Furthermore, the property may not be removed from the premises without the prior written consent of the landlord excepting as it may be exchanged, replaced, or sold from time to time in the ordinary course of doing business.

Under this lease provision the landlord is almost like a silent partner. However, just to be sure, an additional provision may state:

> The landlord may seize and take possession of the tenant's personal property found on the premises. The landlord, with 10 days' written notice to the tenant, may sell the seized property at public or private sale, subject to whatever terms and conditions the landlord shall solely deem to be in the landlord's best interests. The sale proceeds will be used, first, to pay off the tenant's monetary obligation to the landlord, with any remainder being paid over to the tenant.

Finally, just to be sure that nothing gets missed, a provision will state that the granted lien will be in addition to, and cumulative of, the landlord's lien right provided by law.

Effects on the Tenant

This clause may have no effect at all, unless the tenant does suffer some financial difficulty. The tenant should consider how this lease clause may affect what would otherwise be standard and normal business operations. Take, for example, the normal business practice of buying a new piece of office equipment through a lease, on time payments, or by borrowing the money. The business selling or leasing the equipment or lending the money will itself want to have a lien on the equipment and in some instances to record the existence of that lien (as, for example, when a loan is taken out for an automobile). The presence of this lease clause or knowledge of its existence will often create business conflicts. A leasing company may refuse to place equipment because of the conflict caused by an already existing, potentially all-encompassing, lien against the tenant's property. Equipment owners don't want to become embroiled in legal difficulties should the purchaser default on the payments. They want to be able to come and get their equipment. They don't want to argue with a landlord who has already seized the property, nor do they want legal entanglements regarding the party with a superior lien or priority ownership rights or the legal costs these difficulties entail.

The wrong time to find out what difficulties this lease clause can cause is when the tenant is trying, perhaps under the pressure of time, to make critical business decisions.

When It Can't Be Avoided

The ideal clause for the tenant would have the landlord waiving any rights for placing a lien on, or incurring a security interest in, any of the tenant's personal property. It would be better yet to have no clause at all.

When the tenant absolutely cannot avoid putting in this type of lease clause because the landlord insists on it and the tenant refuses to walk away from the transaction, it should be constructed in as limiting a way as possible. For example, limits can be placed on the type of monetary default that would put the lease clause into effect, for example, only for the nonpayment of rent.

The tenant must limit what personal property can be seized or attached. Any blanket statement including all of the tenant's personal property should be replaced with one limiting seizure to such things as fixtures, furnishings, and tenant improvements. In this way, the landlord would not be able to immediately attach (without court or legal actions) machines, office equipment, and any needed continuing business property, such as merchandise for sale or special products produced for clients (or constituents, such as the membership publications of an association).

There are two key points to remember regarding the landlord lien:

1. The tenant should absolutely never allow any lease language to be included that permits the landlord to seize anything other than tangible personal property that exists in or on the premises. If this is not done, it may be possible—at least made much easier by the tenant—for the landlord to seize tenant property that is not located on the premises, such as merchandise stored in a warehouse. Nontangible personal property may be interpreted to include financial assets and thus leave the tenant unable to conduct business. For example, the landlord might be able to seize accounts receivables or funded pension liabilities whose ownership remains with the tenant (e.g., deferred compensation accounts) or other special fund accounts maintained separately. The tenant should never enter into a lease that provides for this type of seizure and should be prepared to break off negotiations immediately and walk away from the transaction.

2. The tenant must be sure that the landlord's lien rights extend only to the personal property of the tenant. If the tenant has or maintains property on the premises other than the tenant's, this must be clearly specified in the lease clause, and the landlord must agree that such property will be exempt from the lien.

37
Holding Over

A tenant who "holds over" remains in possession of the premises beyond the expiration date of the lease. The holdover tenant creates a significant impact on both him- or herself and the landlord.

The Tenant's View

The tenant may be in a holdover situation for various reasons:

- The tenant forgot or did not kept track of the expiration date of the lease. Thirty days before a lease is scheduled to expire, the landlord sends a notice informing the tenant that the space has been leased to another business and the landlord expects the tenant to vacate the premises in a timely manner. The tenant, in a panic, is unable to find new space in time. Result: The tenant finds him- or herself in a holdover situation.

- The tenant intends to relocate to another building. A new lease is signed, and the expected move date is well before the current lease is to expire. However, as is often the case, the new landlord is delayed in getting the new space ready. Perhaps the construction or delivery of materials was delayed, or another tenant is holding over and has not yet vacated the space. Whatever the reasons, the tenant is in a holdover situation.

- The tenant may be negotiating with the landlord for a renewal of the lease or for a new lease on the expectation of staying in the building. However, a new lease agreement takes longer than either the tenant or the landlord planned. Result: The tenant is in a holdover situation.

- The tenant's business has grown significantly and he or she has been searching for new premises. However, operating a business and also looking for new space is time-consuming. Before the tenant realizes it, the expiration date of the current lease has come and gone, leaving the tenant in a holdover situation.

It is not too difficult to get into a holdover situation, despite the tenant's best intentions. The tenant therefore needs a fallback position, in the form of a holdover clause in the lease document. Although the holdover situation will not be a pleasant one for the tenant, at least he or she will know exactly what to expect.

The Landlord's View

For the landlord, a holdover tenant can be a mixed blessing, depending on the situation. For example:

- The landlord may have already re-leased the premises. A holdover tenant forces the landlord to delay preparing the space for a new tenant. With a holdover, the landlord is unable to deliver the premises to a new tenant. If the possibility of a prior tenant's holdover has been accounted for in the new tenant's lease, the landlord will not be significantly hurt by the holdover. The new tenant will be forced to endure the delay and take possession at a later date. Depending on the holdover tenant's lease clause, the landlord will undoubtedly receive unanticipated additional income.

- The landlord may have attempted to time the expiration of a tenant's lease with the expansion option of another tenant; although the tenant with the expansion option may not yet need the space, the landlord is convinced that the tenant will shortly want it. In this situation the holdover of the tenant with the expired lease provides the landlord with continued leasing and rent payments for what would otherwise be vacant space.

- The landlord has known that the current tenant intended to vacate the premises; however, because of market conditions and despite the best efforts of the landlord, a new tenant is not found by the time the current lease expires. The holdover tenant continues to provide a steady income to the landlord, who is thus able to avoid the cash drain a vacant space would impose.

When it comes to negotiating a holdover clause, the landlord may have a variety of straightforward and ulterior motives whose purposes may be best served when the tenant is in a holdover situation. Even if a holdover is not a preferred alternative, the landlord has usually had more experience with leasing (or contract) law, not to mention experience with previous holdover tenants. This gives the landlord some insight regarding a holdover clause that will not initially be available to the tenant or that a tenant's normal business legal counsel may not be aware of without the advice of an expert. Knowledge of actual and common law in a region, as applied to previous tenant holdover cases, is vital in structuring a clause to the benefit of the tenant. Otherwise, a tenant could be forced into a new minimum lease period of one or more years, without any opportunity to negotiate any of the lease terms or the rent.

The Holdover Concept

The holdover lease clause may include some expensive traps for the unwary tenant (the landlord may have a significant monetary stake in the outcome as well).

The clause will start out by stating the obvious, that in the event the tenant does not immediately surrender the premises on the expiration date of the lease (or at the end of the lease term), the tenant will become a tenant "at will," or the tenant will become a tenant "by the month," or the tenant will be deemed to be occupying the premises as a tenant-at-sufferance (that is, the permission to remain in the space will be implied only because it is not specifically prohibited).

The tenant would normally be best served with a month-to-month holdover. Being a tenant-at-sufferance is the weakest possible tenant occupancy of a space. In fact, being at sufferance is interpreted to mean having no valid status regarding the possession of the premises. Without validity, the tenant not only has no rights, but would have no recourse (e.g., for collecting insurance) if the premises or contents were to suffer damage.

Lease Covenants Continue

The other provisions in this lease clause will normally benefit only the landlord. The tenant must determine what, if anything, will serve his or her needs and must also make sure that there is room for some negotiation in virtually every provision (that is, before the original lease is signed).

The landlord will insist that, in spite of the holdover, the tenant will still be bound by the covenants of the lease. One of the better clauses, from the tenant's viewpoint, will state that the tenant, as a monthly tenant, shall be subject to all of the conditions and covenants of the lease as though the lease had originally been a monthly tenancy. In addition, the tenant will be required to give the landlord at least 30 days' written notice of any intention to quit the premises. The tenant should be sure that he or she will also be entitled to 30 days' written notice by the landlord to quit the premises. Landlord exception to the 30 days' notice will include the tenant's nonpayment of rent and the breach of any other lease covenant.

Actually, this provision is not too bad for the tenant or for the landlord. It creates a month-to-month tenancy, with the same lease in effect. Up to this point, the landlord has not really exacted anything from the tenant who has held over.

Rent Adjustment

A landlord will clearly expect to receive a rent adjustment from a tenant who has held over. The simplest version of a new or adjusted rent provision would have the tenant agree to pay rent by the month at a rate "twice" that in effect during the last month of the tenant's lease. An alternative would be a new rent calculated at "twice" the highest monthly rent paid during the entire lease term.

The tenant would prefer to pay a holdover rent equal to the

amount paid in the last month under the unexpired lease; the landlord will want at least twice the last rent. Moreover, the landlord may also want to specify that the doubling multiplier will be against the greater of either (1) the base rent plus any "additional rent" and any other sums that would have been payable according to the terms of the lease if the lease term had continued or (2) the fair market rent for the premises. The greater amount will be computed at the landlord's discretion. The latter rent increase is the more onerous. A fairer version for the tenant would specify that the multiplier (which is negotiable) would apply only against the base rent. Then the new rent to be paid would be the greater of either that amount or the increased fair market value.

Whatever rent increase provision prevails, it will be a significant cost to the tenant. This is why tenants are hurt by holding over and why landlords benefit.

How does a landlord justify doubling, or even more than doubling, the rent? A modified sentence taken from a lease clause helps explain:

> The tenant acknowledges that if he or she fails to surrender the premises at the expiration (or termination) of the lease term, it will be conclusively presumed that the value to the tenant of remaining in possession and the loss that will be suffered by the landlord as a result far exceed the amount of annual rent and additional rent that would have been payable had the lease term continued.

Extra Landlord Protection

Additional provisions that may be required to enable the landlord to retain legal rights to the premises will be detrimental to the tenant. The following is one of two usual additions:

> At the end of the lease term, at any time prior to the landlord's acceptance of the rent from the tenant as a monthly tenant, the landlord, at his or her option, may reenter and take possession of the premises without process, or by any legal process available under governmental laws and regulations.

An alternative to this provision states:

Acceptance by the landlord of the rent after lease termination does not constitute a lease renewal and shall not limit the landlord's right to sue for, and obtain possession of, the premises or any other landlord's rights as provided by law.

A second provision, one that no tenant should ever agree to, authorizes the landlord to dispose of any property remaining within the premises at the expiration of the lease as the landlord may desire, without any landlord liability for compensation or damages to the tenant, regardless of whether the property belongs to the tenant or to his or her employees, guests, or clients or customers:

If the tenant fails to surrender the premises upon the expiration of the lease, despite demand to do so by the landlord, the tenant shall indemnify and hold the landlord harmless from all loss or liability, including, without limitation, any claim made by a succeeding tenant.

Alternatively this provision may state:

The tenant shall be liable for any and all damages and expenses that the landlord may sustain by virtue of the tenant's not vacating the premises as required at the end of the lease term, including, but not limited to, any amount for which the landlord may be liable as a result of any other lease the landlord entered into for a term beginning at the expiration of the tenant's lease.

And to be certain that the landlord has not contemplated any unilateral extension or renewal of the lease, this lease clause will typically state that nothing contained in the lease will be construed as a consent by the landlord to the occupancy or possession of the premises by the tenant beyond the expiration date of the lease.

Can a PREB Help?

The holdover clause can create difficulty for a PREB, in that any broker's commission or fee may be contingent on when a new tenant actually moves into a space. If an older tenant is able to hold over, that will delay payment. Therefore, tenant holdover rights may not be in a PREB's future best interests.

For simplicity, the PREB will see the holdover provision as a landlord's business right to maintain control over a building and its tenants. However, many PREBs do not really understand the fine points and implications of the clause for both the tenant and the landlord. They too often and too quickly brush off the importance of the clause or incorrectly assume that a tenant's legal counsel will catch and fix the clause if there is a significant implication for the tenant (this will not be the case unless the tenant's legal counsel is experienced in commercial real estate).

The Day-to-Day Benefit

Tenants should add the day-to-day provision to all new lease documents. It can also be appended to current lease documents, especially if circumstances warrant it. The provision permits a day-to-day delay in the actual expiration date of the lease. In other words, it delays the landlord's right to invoke any provisions of the holdover lease clause, especially any increase in the tenant's rent. The day-to-day delay provision would only be valid at the end of a lease term and would be considered to be in force only during any period in which the tenant and landlord were negotiating in good faith the extension of the lease term or a renewal for the same premises. Or they may even be talking over the leasing of other premises in the same building or in another building owned by the landlord.

The main difficulty with this provision is defining what constitutes good faith intentions and negotiations on behalf of both parties. The day-to-day delay would show the good faith intentions of the landlord. Without the delay, a tenant would, because of a doubling or more of the rent expense, be put under intense pressure to concede to a landlord's demands, even if they were not in the tenant's best interests.

38
Surrender of Premises

Because a lease is written for a fixed term, it theoretically and automatically ends at the lease expiration date or the date determined by the lease commencement date and the lease term. A lease expiration is designed to take place without any special notices or other required action by either the tenant or the landlord. Why, then, bother to include a lease clause about the surrender of the premises? This is an example of a "keeping it neat and clean" type of clause that specifies what is, or should be, otherwise understood.

From a tenant's point of view this clause can be quite important because it specifies the disposition of fixtures, furnishings, and leasehold improvements in the premises. A general surrender of premises lease clause is a simple concept. It states:

> The tenant, upon the expiration of the lease term (or for whatever reasons the lease may be terminated), shall quit and surrender possession of the premises to the landlord and deliver all keys to the premises and any locks within the premises to the landlord (and make known to the landlord any access codes to combination type locks or security devices in the premises). The tenant will return the premises and all equipment and fixtures of the landlord within the premises in good repair and order and in broom-clean condition, with ordinary and reasonable wear and tear, use, damage by fire or other ca-

sualty (insurable or not) not caused by the tenant's actions or neglect, or acts of God excepted. Otherwise, the landlord may restore the premises, appropriate equipment, and fixtures to a reasonably acceptable condition, and the tenant shall be liable for and pay such costs and related expenses, on demand, to the landlord.

Tenant Furnishings and Improvements

The basic surrender clause is straightforward and merely puts in writing what is supposedly understood to occur at lease expiration. The landlord may add an additional provision regarding a tenant's furnishings and improvements that, without careful analysis, may be detrimental to the tenant. However, this is also the place where the tenant should insist on appropriate language regarding certain furniture, fixtures, or improvements important to the tenant.

An additional landlord provision may target the removal of tenant fixtures, furnishings, and improvements in one of three ways:

1. All such items may not be removed. That is, all fixtures, furnishings, and improvements are to become the property of the landlord.

2. The items must be removed. The tenant must remove all fixtures, furnishings, and improvements and restore the premises to their original condition (excepting normal wear and tear). If the tenant does not remove the improvements, the landlord may do so, and the tenant will be liable for all costs and related expenses, payable on demand to the landlord.

3. The items may be removed. The tenant has the option to remove the fixtures, furnishings, and improvements, but if he or she does not, they become the property of the landlord, who may or may not then remove them. If the landlord does remove these items, the costs and related expenses of doing so will be borne by the tenant.

Typical Language

The actual language of this provision varies but will state:

> All removable trade fixtures, furniture, furnishings, and other removable personal property owned by the tenant and located on, or used in connection with, the premises may be removed at the tenant's expense at the expiration of the lease. However, the tenant shall repair all damage to the premises caused by such removal. All installations, additions, partitions, hardware, light fixtures, floor coverings, nontrade fixtures, and improvements, temporary or permanent, in or upon the premises, whether placed there by the tenant or the landlord, will become the landlord's property and will remain within the premises. The landlord will provide no compensation, monetary allowance, or credit to the tenant for these items. The landlord may, however, in his or her sole discretion and prior to the lease expiration date or within 30 days thereafter, require the tenant, at his or her sole expense, to remove any and all such fixtures, equipment, improvements, and any other items of work installed within the premises by the tenant or his or her agents, and to repair all damage caused by the removal. In the event that the tenant does not promptly comply with the landlord's written request or notice, the landlord may remove any and all items so specified and cause appropriate and necessary repairs to be made to the premises, with the costs and related expense becoming the responsibility of the tenant, who shall pay such costs on demand, to the landlord.

An Itty-Bitty Problem

Depending upon the extent of the fixtures, furnishings, and improvements made by the tenant, the landlord's version of the improvements provision of this lease clause may be perfectly acceptable. However, in the majority of instances the landlord's plain vanilla version is not acceptable. Many business or trade fixtures are quite expensive and must be installed or otherwise attached to the premises during the term of the lease. Such attachment can change the status of the fixtures to "improvements" that the landlord is entitled to own upon the expiration of the lease.

The tenant will be particularly concerned about the legal confusion that can arise over the ownership of the fixtures, furnishings, and improvements when a lease term is extended, as opposed to when a new lease is drawn up between the tenant and landlord, as in a lease renewal, even though the same premises are involved. Depending on how the original lease clause is worded and because a lease renewal is (in the strictest interpretation) a new lease drawn up after the original lease expired, everything in the premises that the tenant thought he or she owned really belongs to the landlord. Why? Because, as specified, it was not properly removed by the tenant prior to the expiration of the lease.

Is this one of those itty-bitty points that do not really matter? Maybe—maybe not. It depends on the personality and trustworthiness of the landlord.

Continuing Tenant Ownership

The savvy tenant will have the appropriate lease provisions adjusted to reflect the tenant's continued ownership of all removable fixtures, trade fixtures, furnishings, equipment, machinery, and so on, during tenant-landlord negotiations for new space or for continued possession of the current premises.

For example, a tenant version of the appropriate provision will state:

> All articles of personal property and all business and trade fixtures, machinery and equipment, furniture, and movable partitions (and other appropriate items, such as supplemental air-conditioning units) owned by the tenant or installed by the tenant or his or her agents at his or her expense (or by the landlord on the tenant's behalf) will be considered and accepted by the tenant and the landlord to be the tenant's property and may be removed by the tenant at any time during the lease term, or with written notice to the landlord within 30 days of the expiration of the lease term, or with written notice to landlord within 30 days after any negotiations between the landlord and the tenant have concluded, successfully or not, regarding any extension or renewal of the lease term, and shall upon any lease extension or renewal remain the property of the tenant. The tenant shall be entitled to remove his or

her property at any time during the lease term or extended
time periods, provided the tenant is not in default of the lease
[the default provision will be a requirement of a landlord]
and provided that tenant will repair any damage to the premises caused by such removal.

Tenant Specificity

The details the tenant may wish to add to the improvements provision will depend on his or her needs and requirements. The following are some items a tenant may want to specify. When the following items are to be removed, the tenant should include a
statement indicating that the premises will be repaired and any
and all holes in floors, ceilings (including floor and ceiling slabs),
the roof, and walls will be properly patched.

1. *Security system.* Especially related computer controls, transformers, special wiring and security hardware (e.g., electric
   door locks)

2. *Computer room equipment.* Typically, supplemental HVAC packages, fire suppression systems and related equipment, power
   generators and related equipment, monitoring systems, and any
   special removable room improvements, such as raised floors

3. *Improvements to the base building.* Especially supplemental
   HVAC systems (e.g., in conference rooms); supplemental
   power and electrical equipment, such as transformers, telephone equipment, and wiring; computer and related system
   wiring; and audiovisual equipment and systems (e.g., projec-
   tors, monitors)

4. *Telecommunication equipment.* Roof towers, antennas, power
   transformers, special wiring, and transmission equipment and
   systems

5. *Food service.* Sinks, freezers, refrigerators, ovens, grills, dishwashers, storage and serving equipment, and other related
   kitchen or cafeteria equipment

This tenant-preferred addition provides the tenant with specific rights of ownership of furnishings and improvements. Any

required landlord boilerplate will be appended to the tenant's
provision addition (the tenant should be sure the boilerplate also
reflects his or her concerns). The landlord boilerplate will specify
what the tenant is required to do in the way of repairing damages
to the premises caused by the removal of the various items.

However, the tenant must be wary of an addition in the
landlord's provision stating that if the items are not removed, the
landlord, at his or her option, may remove and store the items
without any liability to the tenant for any losses, and that the tenant will be responsible for, and pay for, related removal, repair,
attorney, and storage costs, on demand. As an even more onerous
addition, the landlord would be permitted not only to remove the
items but to sell them, without any additional legal process (depending on appropriate governmental laws and regulations), and
apply the proceeds to any amounts due under the lease or for the
expenses related to the removal, repair of the premises, and sale.

39
Estoppel
Certificate

Not many tenants fully understand the estoppel certificate clause. The usual clause is fairly straightforward, so the tenant's legal counsel should have no problem with it. The tenant, thinking it is standard legal jargon necessary in a lease document, generally ignores this clause (especially if the legal counsel says nothing about it). Some PREBs may not understand the full import of the certificate themselves and may simply accept it. Other brokers may not want to rock the boat by giving a tenant any information that could be used against a landlord.

The concept behind the estoppel certificate is relatively simple. Depending on the region of the country, the clause may appear in every one of a landlord's leases or only in those for newly constructed buildings that have yet to receive permanent financing. The certificate is designed to meet the needs of a mortgage lender or a building purchaser. It provides the tenant's verification of a landlord's statements to a purchaser or a lender. The lender must have such a certificate from the landlord to verify that the leases presented by a landlord show the actual or potential cash flow commitment of a building. Depending on the lender, continuing certificates requests can, over time, act as a check on a landlord's overall performance and thereby safeguard the lender's investment.

The typical estoppel certificate lease clause will include a number of points:

1. The required time in which the tenant must respond to the landlord's request for the certificate. This time period can range from 5 to 30 days or more, depending on the landlord's needs.

2. A requirement that the tenant respond not just once, but from time to time, as requested in writing by the landlord.

3. An agreement by the tenant that he or she will acknowledge, execute, and deliver to the landlord a completed and signed certificate to a lender, purchaser, or other person so designated by the landlord. This provision may also include the general intent of what the tenant is certifying, for example:

   - That the lease is in full force and the tenant has possession
   - The amount of space being leased
   - That the lease is unmodified, or if modified, that the tenant agrees to the modifications
   - Whether there are any setoffs or unfulfilled obligations by the tenant or the landlord
   - Whether the tenant has any knowledge of any defaults either by the landlord or the tenant and whether any notices of default have been issued either to the landlord or to the tenant
   - The dates up to which rent has been paid or for which it has been paid in advance
   - The existence of any tenant security deposit or other advanced payments and whether such amounts are to be returned to the tenant, and if so, when
   - Whether the tenant has any knowledge of a past or imminent event that will permit him or her to terminate the lease
   - That the address for the tenant's receipt of any notices issued under the lease is correct
   - That an actual up-to-date lease document and any written modification will be attached to, and made part of, the estoppel certificate
   - That any other matters that may be reasonably requested will be attended to

4. A sample certificate as an addendum to the lease document. This provision may further specify that the sample certificate is agreed to and approved by both the landlord and the tenant. However, there will also be supplemental language stating that, notwithstanding the attached certificate, the tenant will execute any other landlord-submitted estoppel certificate that substantially and reasonably sets forth the statements asked for within this clause.

5. A requirement that the landlord will create and fill out the certificate for the tenant's execution.

6. A statement indicating that if the tenant does not return the executed landlord-supplied certificates within the stated time period, either

   ▪ The tenant is in full agreement with all of the statements made in the proffered estoppel certificate, or
   ▪ The tenant acknowledges that the lease is in full force and effect, that it is unmodified, that rent is fully paid, and so on (see the items in item 3).

7. An optional provision that in effect appoints, after a stated period of time, the landlord as the tenant's attorney-in-fact. This provision authorizes the landlord to execute and deliver the estoppel certificate on the tenant's behalf. This statement does not always appear or will be taken out when a tenant's lawyer strenuously objects.

After reading all the statements included in the estoppel certificate, the tenant should have a sense of its importance to the landlord. The legalese and the attorney-in-fact provision are the result of too many tenants ignoring landlords' requests that the certificate be executed and returned. For the landlord, the matter is too important to let slip.

In fact, most landlords will insist on preparing the certificate. However, they may also want to add language stating that the tenant will make no alterations, modifications, or additions to the estoppel certificate. The landlord will want this statement to be an absolute prohibition and require the tenant to notify the landlord of any disagreement.

The landlord-prepared certificate, while relatively simple, will be set up in such a way that every inch is accounted for in writing, with barely enough room for the tenant's signature.

Important Tenant Rights

Given the contents of this lease clause and the importance placed on it by the landlord, the tenant should stop to consider his or her own rights in the matter. If everything between the tenant and landlord is agreeable and for all intents and purposes the tenant is quite satisfied with the space, and if the estoppel certificate is as specified, there is no reason for the tenant not to execute and return the certificate without delay.

But what if everything is not so perfect? What if the tenant and landlord disagree on significant points? For example, what if the premises have not been maintained as promised, regardless of countless tenant calls to the landlord. Or what if the landlord has refused to comply or has delayed in complying with a final square-foot measurement requirement? Without a final determination of the actual amount of square feet contained in the premises, the tenant may be overpaying rent and his or her percentage share of the building's operating and other expenses.

Whatever the reasons, tenants should be aware and well advised that they have the *absolute right* to make any modifications and to add any statements to the estoppel certificate. Nothing should prohibit or be permitted to limit the tenant's right to indicate or specify disagreement with the landlord-provided information.

The estoppel certificate is a certification by the tenant. While the landlord may disapprove of and feel annoyed with the tenant-prepared alternative certificates or with the changes or additions made by the tenant, the tenant is the one who is signing the document. The tenant has the right to recopy, retype, or—if there is room—write his or her changes directly on the certificate. If the tenant is going to make changes, it is important that they be made quickly and that the tenant send the certificate directly to the lender or return it to the landlord (using certified mail). The tenant does not want to miss a deadline that creates, through lack of timely action, implicit tenant approval of a certificate.

Getting the Landlord's Attention

Depending on the disagreements and problems the tenant specifies on an estoppel certificate, the landlord may have difficulty getting a lender to issue permanent financing or may be unable to sell a property. Lenders want to protect their investments. Purchasers often will not accept buildings with tenant problems or bad tenant-landlord relations.

A tenant-altered or -supplied estoppel certificate may be exactly what is needed to get the landlord to respond to the tenant's previously ignored complaint or concerns.

40
Waiver of Trial by Jury

It is hard to imagine anyone giving up the basic right to a trial by a jury of his or her peers. But time and again tenants have signed leases with just such a clause.

Why? In many instances a PREB has, intentionally or unintentionally, misrepresented the value of this clause and has sold the tenant on one of two views; either that not having a jury trial can be an advantage, because the tenant will have a professional, a judge, interpreting the law and business terms without emotion, or that the clause does not really matter, because the tenant cannot give up his or her constitutional right to a jury trial.

The latter is by no means certain. In fact, by signing the lease, the tenant has said, without being coerced, that he or she is willing to give up this right by agreeing to include the lease clause. However, courts have some, if not a great deal, of sympathy for the tenant. Often a judge will permit a jury trial after all. It depends on what is being decided, whether third parties are involved, and whether the claims involve more than business interpretations. The wise tenant, however, will not rely on being able to find a sympathetic judge. In more instances than not, the waiver to a jury trial that has been agreed to in advance will be upheld.

The Waiver

This lease clause will state: "The landlord and the tenant agree to and do waive trial by jury in any action, proceeding, or counter-claim [and sometimes also cross claims and third-party claims] brought by either the landlord or the tenant against the other." An additional restrictive provision may state: "Included is any matter whatsoever arising out of, or in any way connected with, the lease, the relationship between the landlord and tenant, the tenant's use or occupancy of the premises, and any claim of injury or damage occurring on the premises."

What's In; What's Out

If the tenant is unable to have this lease clause eliminated altogether, there are a number of tenant-preferred adjustments. The waiver of trial should apply only to matters related to the lease document. The tenant should not accept a waiver of a jury trial for matters such as tenant-landlord relations, injury, or damage. These areas should either be excluded from the clause or, better yet, be included in a lease provision as specific exceptions to the waiver.

Sometimes a Landlord Is Right

Depending on the restrictiveness of the basic lease clause (and past experiences), the landlord may want an additional provision stating: "In the event that the landlord commences any proceedings for nonpayment of rent, minimum rent, or additional rent, the tenant will not interpose any counterclaim of whatever nature or description in any such proceedings." Because this provision has to do with the tenant's payment (or nonpayment) of rent, it is hard to argue against the landlord's position in attempting to collect what is properly owed by, and previously agreed to be paid by, the tenant, notwithstanding any other tenant-landlord disagreements.

But the tenant has certain rights, too. To the landlord's provision the tenant should add a statement indicating that the tenant's agreement not to interpose any counterclaim in the proceedings will not constitute, nor be construed to be, a waiver of the tenant's rights to assert his or her claim in any separate action or actions brought by him or her.

The tenant's adjustment should be perfectly acceptable to the landlord, since the tenant's action would not occur until after the landlord's action has been settled.

In Whose Best Interest?

The landlord's interests may best be served if there is no jury trial. The reason is also the reason that a jury trial may be better for the tenant. Landlords believe that most juries will be biased against them. They feel that most people are highly suspicious of landlords, seeing them as ogres (undoubtedly because of the negative publicity surrounding tenant-landlord relations in residential properties). Landlords believe that juries view them as malevolent beings who are already too rich. Any actions against the "poor" tenant is only a ruse to gain further riches.

Landlords truly believe that because disputes with tenants revolve around fine points of law and the interpretation of business transactions, the cumulative effects of these relations are beyond the comprehension of the typical jury. A knowledgeable judge is needed for a proper ruling on the merits of the landlord's arguments.

It is true that the tenant is often viewed as the underdog in a tenant-landlord encounter. Because the issues are so complex, the jury tends to side with the tenant emotionally, even when the tenant is at fault. The jury tends to relate better to the tenant; the tenant is one of them.

Right or wrong, the tenant is the person in the white hat. Therefore, the tenant's interests are best served by not having a lease clause waiving trial by jury.

41
Brokerage Commissions

The clause pertaining to brokerage or leasing commissions provides protection for both the landlord and the tenant. It sets forth the names of the PREBs, if any, engaged by each party to negotiate or help with the lease transaction. It can have any one of four basic versions.

No PREBs

The first version specifies that no brokers were used by either party for the transaction. This provision will state:

> The landlord and tenant represent and warrant to each other that neither of them has employed any broker in carrying out the negotiation relating to this lease. The landlord shall indemnify and hold the tenant harmless, and the tenant shall indemnify and hold the landlord harmless, from and against any claim for brokerage or other commission arising from or out of any breach of the specified representation and warrant.

Only a Landlord's PREB

A second version of this lease clause specifies that there is only a landlord's broker, that the tenant has not used a broker. This provision will state:

The tenant represents and warrants that he or she has not employed any broker in carrying out the negotiations relating to this lease. The tenant shall indemnify and hold the landlord harmless from and against any claim from brokerage or other commissions arising from or out of any breach of the foregoing representation and warranty. The landlord acknowledges that he or she has engaged "XYZ Company" as leasing agent in connection with this lease, and the landlord agrees to be responsible for the payment of all leasing commissions owed to the said agent.

An alternative version states:

The landlord recognizes "XYZ Company" as the sole broker procuring this lease and shall pay this broker a commission in accordance with a separate agreement between the broker and the landlord. The landlord and the tenant represent and warrant to each other that, except as stated above, neither of them has employed any broker, agent, or finder in carrying on the negotiations relating to the lease.

In addition, the mutual no-liability and hold-harmless provisions will be included.

When a landlord's broker is involved in a transaction, the landlord will insist on a provision stating that any representation or statement by a broker (or leasing company) or other third party (or employee) engaged by the landlord that is made with regard to the premises or the building will not be binding on the landlord or serve as a modification of the lease. The landlord will have no liability for representation or statements of any broker except for those contained in the lease or otherwise approved in writing by the landlord.

Both the Tenant and the Landlord Have PREBs; Each Pays

A third version of this clause will be needed if both the tenant and the landlord have their own brokers. The wording of this lease clause is important to the landlord, since it specifies who will pay for the brokers' services. This clause will state:

The landlord and the tenant represent and warrant to each other that if either has employed any broker or agent acting in any capacity for this transaction, each agrees to be responsible for any brokerage commission or fee payable to his or her own agent or broker.

The lease clause will then contain the usual mutual waiver of liability and hold-harmless provisions, as well as the landlord's statement of no liability for any statement or representation, except if in writing by the landlord.

Tenant's PREB:
The Landlord Pays

The fourth version of this lease clause specifies that the brokerage commission or other fees of the tenant's broker will be paid by the landlord. This clause may be worded in various ways, but it will generally state:

The tenant represents and warrants to the landlord that only the "PREB Company" has worked on behalf of the tenant for the leasing transaction and that the tenant has not engaged any other broker, agent, or other third party that would require a broker's commission or fee or any finder's or other fee that the landlord would be required to pay with respect to the transaction. The tenant agrees to indemnify and hold the landlord harmless from claims of any other party for brokerage commission or other fees, except that landlord shall be responsible for and agrees to pay "PREB Company" the required brokerage commission or other fees.

Also often included is the percentage fee being paid, the actual dollar amount, or some formula for calculating the amount of fee to be paid. The other standard provision regarding landlord statements and mutual waivers of liability and hold-harmless statements will also be included.

From a landlord's perspective, this clause clearly sets forth any additional monetary amounts he or she may be responsible for regarding the particular leasing transaction. Given the brokerage business and the possible cutthroat competition between PREBs (and the past experiences of the landlord), he or she does not want to have different brokers claiming a piece of a brokerage commission or fee because they talked with the tenant or perhaps even showed the tenant the space.

It's Not Really "Free"

In the commercial real estate brokerage business any required leasing commission or fee is usually paid directly to the PREB by the landlord, not by the tenant. The tenant pays, indirectly, through the rental rate or reduced value of the landlord concession package. The point is not that the tenant does not get full value and more from a PREB, only that the tenant must be aware that nothing is really free. (Many PREBs, especially the newer, less experienced agents, incorrectly state that their services are free to the tenant because their fee is paid by the landlord.)

The tenant's benefit from this clause is that the lease document clearly states that the landlord will pay the appropriate brokerage commission or other fees for the transaction. For simplicity, it is in the tenant's best interests to have a written agreement with only one PREB. Tenants should, in addition, maintain any correspondence declining the services of any other PREBs they may have talked to regarding the transaction. It is not unusual for a PREB to feel "unjustly" cut out of a share of a leasing commission or fee just because of a conversation with the tenant. An angry broker has been known to threaten, and actually follow through with, legal action against a tenant. Documentation is vital where the tenant is concerned.

42
Notices

The notices clause is the one that both tenants and PREBs ignore most. This is probably because the clause is short and simple. It may consist of only two or three lines stating:

> All notices required to be given by the lease, by either party to the other, will be given by certified or registered mail, first-class postage prepaid, return receipt requested. Notice to the respective parties shall be addressed as follows: [tenant and landlord addresses].

This clause specifies where notices are to be sent and to whom. An important additional provision would define what constitutes delivery and what constitutes the effective date of delivery of any notices.

The clause is particularly important when the notices pertain to sending or receiving the rent; the landlord's notice of a tenant's default; the tenant's notice of his or her intention to renew the lease, sublet the premises, or pick up an expansion option; and any other notices legally required under the terms of the lease.

It is in both the tenant's and landlord's best interest to include more than just the minimum amount of detail. For example, a more detailed clause would state:

> All notices, requests, consents, approvals, waivers, legal documents, or other communications that are required or permitted to be given by either the landlord or the tenant under the lease shall be given only in writing and shall be delivered ei-

ther in person or sent by registered or certified mail, return receipt requested, first-class postage prepaid. For the landlord all notices shall be delivered to: [address]. For the tenant, notice shall be delivered to: [leased premises or other tenant-provided headquarter or legal address]. Delivery shall also occur at any other address that may be given by the landlord or tenant to the other by notice, as specified.

The clause should also indicate an effective date for the delivery of all notices, including rent and other monetary payments.

All tenant payments of rent or any other monetary payments required under the lease and due to the landlord, and any tenant statements required to be submitted to the landlord, shall be made or delivered to the landlord at the stated address or any other address the landlord may specify or designate by written notice to the tenant. If sent by registered or certified mail, all payments will be considered made on the date mailed to the landlord; if delivered by other means, they will be considered made on the date received by the landlord.

How modern technology will affect the notices lease clause remains to be seen. It may eventually provide for the acceptable delivery of certain notices via a transmission device capable of faithfully and exactly duplicating the contents and required authorizations, signatures, and seals of the designated notices.

43
Parking

The subject of parking has been singled out on purpose to show the reader that virtually anything related to space occupancy can create problems if not properly accounted for, in writing, in the lease document. There is no reason why any important consideration of the tenant's cannot be covered in a separate clause in the lease document.

Parking is a necessity for most businesses. It helps attract and maintain employees and customers. All too often the tenant ignores the subject of parking (or the lack of it) until he or she has moved in; then it may be too late to correct the problem. It is not that tenants do not understand the importance of parking; rather, they tend to assume (wrongly) that what they see during a visit to the premises or building is what they will get.

For example, the tenant may have seen a large covered parking area adjacent to the building, with vacant spaces, unimpeded access from the building to the parking structure, and a weather-protected·entrance to the building. It is not until the tenant moves in (after the building has been fully leased) that he or she discovers there are not enough parking spaces for the firm's employees, much less its customers. Moreover, the landlord rented out the parking structure to an independent parking lot operator, who has installed entry and exit gates and an attendant for collecting hourly parking fees. This situation occurs all too often, either because the tenant did not have enough experience to know what could happen and relied on and accepted visual cues or because the tenant's broker did not fully or properly explain all the possibilities to the tenant.

Many times the subject of parking is buried in another lease clause, such as the premises clause; is briefly mentioned as a related common area; or is listed under the building's rules and regulations.

Parking provisions come in a wide variety of alternatives. The more typical ones are open-space parking (also known as surface parking), rooftop parking, underground parking (usually in the lower portion of the building), parking in a nearby or attached structure (a multistoried building devoted exclusively to parking), or some combination of these. Because of the many possibilities, no one lease clause will work equally well in every situation. The tenant must tailor the lease clause to his or her particular needs.

Generally, the landlord-required parts of this lease clause will state:

> The parking area will be under the exclusive control of the landlord and shall be available for general use, in common, by all tenants, their employees, guests, invitees, and customers subject to reasonable rules and regulations for its use as may from time to time be determined by the landlord.

The landlord will also retain the right to designate certain parking areas for particular uses (e.g., employee parking), to control ingress and egress, to locate and arrange spaces, and to establish rates for parking (if any) and any other matters necessary for maintaining the parking area(s) that, in the sole discretion of the landlord, are in the best interests of the tenants. Finally, the landlord will want to reserve the right to maintain and operate the parking areas him- or herself, to use an independent parking lot operator, or to lease the parking area to an independent parking lot operator.

Exactly What Does a Tenant Get?

Although none of these landlord requirements is particularly onerous, the tenant must make sure that current or future landlord determination will not conflict with the tenant's needs. Depending on the particular parking area situation, the tenant may have a number of concerns.

1. *Will the existing surface parking areas always remain parking areas?*
   Tenants must be assured that the wide-open and extensive parking areas that currently exist will remain parking areas. Often a landlord will create a parking area for convenience only until he or she can afford to build another building or have land use and zoning regulations changed.

2. *Will there be designated parking areas for tenants, guests, and customers? Will all or only certain tenants be permitted to reserve parking areas for their employees, guests, and customers?*
   Since the landlord retains control over the parking areas, nothing can be taken for granted concerning where special parking areas are to be established or how long any arrangement will last. A tenant can, however, have specific parking areas designated for the term of the lease.

3. *Is parking to be free? If it is to be at a cost, will there be any cost controls?*
   Parking that starts out free does not always remain that way unless the tenant has been able to have this specified in the lease. As a general rule, if parking is provided at no cost initially, the tenant should be able to have no-cost parking throughout the term of the lease.
   A bigger problem exists when the tenant starts out with paid parking. The tenant can expect at least three problems: how to control parking costs for the employees, how to control parking costs for the customers, and how to control increases in parking costs in general.
   To avoid the problems associated with the maintenance and control of parking areas, and especially to avoid having to negotiate the parking situation with tenants, the landlord may turn paid parking over to a professional garage or parking lot operator. In this way, the landlord can distance him- or herself from any increases in parking rates.
   In fact, as many large space users with market power have discovered, the landlord, despite protestations to the con-

trary, still exercises considerable control over the parking area. This is especially true for newly constructed buildings and the initial building tenants. It remains true throughout the life of the building.

So what can a tenant do? The range of options varies, depending on the amount of parking space available and the absolute needs of the tenant. For example, in major urban downtown areas, where much of the parking is either underground (below the building) or in a parking structure located elsewhere, the amount of parking space may be so restricted to begin with that landlords have only limited options. In suburban locations, where surface parking and attached parking structures are more prevalent and parking areas are usually (but not always) more abundant, landlords have a greater number of options.

Before negotiating parking, the tenant should examine his or her motives for choosing the premises in a particular building. The tenant will often find that a principal reason is the convenience of the location for conducting business. That is, it is easy for employees to go to and from work and both for customers to visit and for salespeople to reach customers. Once the tenant clearly understands this point, negotiations become easier. The parking situation is critical to the convenience and efficiency of the tenant's business operations. When a building's looks and "prestige" are put aside and the tenant can rationally assess the building or premises strictly for business value, the parking area becomes part of the total premises lease package.

To keep a sense of perspective, the tenant should ask whether the building was built because of the parking areas or whether the parking areas were built because of the building. If it is the latter, the parking is obviously an amenity and an inducement for getting the space in the building leased. The landlord or broker will want to work out the premises lease first so that it is "out of the way." They know that if the parking issue can be separated from other lease issues, more often than not the tenant will give in more easily to paid parking or less-than-best reserved parking areas.

Tenants should press for the following items:

- No-cost parking for a specific number of parking spaces for employees
- Reduced-cost parking for all employees
- No-cost parking for a specific number of parking spaces for customers
- Reduced-cost parking for all customers
- Limits to the increase that can occur for parking spaces for both hourly rates and monthly or annual parking contracts

4. *How many parking spaces will tenants get when the total parking area is limited (e.g., in an urban underground parking area)? And which tenants will get these spaces?*
   One method for allocating a limited number of parking spaces is to use a ratio based on the number of parking spaces available to the total amount of rentable square feet in the building. There are numerous ways to express the ratio, but the easiest is to say how many spaces are available per 1000 sq ft of space of leased premises. For example, a ratio of 1 per 1000 sq ft would allot at least 10 spaces to a 10,000-sq-ft user.
   Tenant needs vary. Some will want all of their allotted parking space, some will not, and some will need more than their allotment. Therefore, the long-term rights to parking spaces needs to be specified in the lease clause.
   If space is limited, the landlord may want each tenant, within some limited period of time (e.g., 90 days), to provide written notice of the number of spaces required, up to the maximum allotted by the parking ratio. This "right" may only permit the tenant to rent the spaces on a monthly or annual basis from the garage operator, at a rate to be determined. An additional "reasonableness" provision may specify that the rate will not be in excess of that charged in similar buildings or nearby parking garages.
   From the viewpoint of a growth-oriented tenant, not having access to additional parking spaces for new employees may be unacceptable. The tenant should be sure the lease clearly states that he or she will retain the right to rent all of his or her allowable parking spaces at any time throughout the term of the lease.
   Another possibility for the landlord is to specify the overall

ratio of compact to noncompact cars to determine the total
number of spaces available and then to allocate a specific ratio
to each tenant. Similarly, the landlord may permit the parking
area to be stacked or piggybacked so that cars are packed in,
one in front of the other, in order to maximize limited space.
Car stacking makes it awkward to enter and exit from the
parking area. This in turn restricts the at-will usefulness of the
parking area.

Restricted parking would be unacceptable for service-ori-
ented tenants, such as those with salespeople who need con-
tinual in-and-out access to parking areas. The tenant must be
sure to include a provision stipulating that a certain number
of parking spaces will be available for at-will access.

The tenant will also want to have a number of spaces in reserved areas for certain employees or customers and an option to obtain additional parking spaces from other tenants
not using their full allotment.

5. *Will the landlord establish a separate set of rules and regulations
   for the parking areas? Will they be included in the lease
   document?*
   The tenant should be sure that, just as there are rules and regulations and a char and janitorial cleaning schedule for the
   premises and the building, there are either similar documents
   for the parking area or the parking area is added to the general building documents. At a minimum, the tenant needs to
   be concerned with the following issues:

   ▪ *Control of specially marked parking areas.* Whether reserved
     for the tenant's employees or customers or available as gen-
     eral building visitor parking spaces, how will these areas be
     policed? How will parking restrictions be enforced? Will the
     landlord provide towing service for improperly parked cars?
     If so, how does the tenant request this service? Will a list of
     tenant employee cars and license plate numbers be re-
     tained so that the tenant can be notified of improperly
     parked employee cars before towing occurs?

   ▪ *Cleaning and maintenance of the parking area.* What cleaning
     and maintenance services will be performed for the parking
     areas, and how often? Will trash containers be strategically
     located throughout the area, and will they be emptied

nightly? Will the parking surface be brush cleaned or washed? How often (nightly, weekly, etc.)? How often will parking surfaces be repaired? How often will they be resurfaced? What will be the schedule for repainting the lines delineating the parking spaces? What spacing standard will be used to determine the distance between lines and between cars?

- *Parking area safety.* What standards, if any, will be established for removing snow and ice from the parking area? What standard will be used for the treatment of ice?
- *Parking area security.* What security will be provided for the parking areas? Will there be a roving guard to check parking areas at night? During the day? What type of lighting will be provided? Who is responsible for maintaining the lights? Will public parking access be restricted in all or only certain parking areas?
- *Parking area accessibility.* Will the parking area be accessible at all times to the general public? What will be the hours of operation or availability? If parking areas are leased to an independent operator, will building tenants still have egress and ingress rights beyond the lot operator's hours? Will building tenants have access 24 hours, seven days a week? When the parking area is an integral part of the building, will the area security be comparable to building security? Will there be direct access from the parking areas into the building?
- *Concierge or special services in the parking areas.* The tenant needs to specify that any initial services will remain during the tenant's lease term. These services might include automotive washing and waxing or attendants to take vehicles to repair shops on site or at a visiting garage (for oil changes while you work).

What You See Is Not Necessarily What You Get

The tenant must constantly remind him- or herself that what he or she sees is not always what he or she gets. Just because a service or other amenity existed during an initial visit to a building or premises, it will not necessarily be there when the tenant moves in—unless the tenant got the assurance in writing.

All too often many of the extraneous, but still important, factors that led the tenant to choose a particular building are left out of lease documents or are handled in a cavalier manner by brokers and landlords. The landlord wants to retain as much control as possible over the level of services and the mix of amenities offered in the building, as well as where and when they will be available. That leaves many things, including important items like parking, to the whims of the landlord and the vagaries of the market.

The tenant will want to include specific provisions for maintaining or including the services, amenities, and other items that attracted him or her to the building in the first place. The tenant cannot afford to trust in a vague statement, such as "as may be determined from time to time by the landlord" (under the rules and regulations lease clause) or "in accordance with other first-class buildings" (in a general building services lease clause).

44
No Representations of Landlord

The no representations lease clause is known by a variety of names and is often part of another clause. The intent of the clause is to specify that any and all agreements between the tenant and the landlord are limited to, and solely contained in, the lease document. That is, the lease document represents the "entire agreement" between the tenant and the landlord.

The basic lease clause will state:

> The tenant acknowledges that neither the landlord nor any broker, agent, or employee of the landlord has made any representation or promises with respect to the premises or the building except as expressly included in the lease document. The lease document represents the entire agreement between the tenant and the landlord, and no rights, easements, privileges, or licenses are acquired by the tenant except as expressly stated in the lease document.

An additional provision often found in this lease clause will specify that the tenant, by taking (or accepting) possession of the premises, accepts the premises in "as is" condition. The tenant's taking (or accepting) possession is considered conclusive evidence that the premises and the building are in good and satisfactory condition at the time of the possession, minor punch-list items being excepted.

From the tenant's perspective, there is nothing wrong with this clause. It is a perfectly appropriate ending to a legal document.

If It's Not in Writing, It Doesn't Exist

What is important to the tenant is the age-old business advice the clause conveys: If any agreement between two parties is not in writing, it does not exist. This lease clause clearly states that the tenant agrees that all tenant-landlord representations and agreements are included in the lease document. Regardless of what a tenant signs, however, if material misrepresentation was made, for example, by the landlord's broker, and it enticed the tenant to sign the lease, the tenant may have some legal recourse in a court of law.

Save the Evidence

The tenant, or the tenant's broker, should be sure to save (and to file permanently with the final lease document) every scrap of paper ever sent by (or to) the landlord or the landlord's representatives, including any promotional, public relations, or advertising material regarding the building or premises. In addition, there should be a written record of every conversation, whether in person or by telephone. This is especially important when it comes to any verbal agreements or representations made by the landlord or his or her representatives.

The collecting, collating, and recording of all the information pertaining to a leasing transaction is an important aspect of the work the PREB is expected to handle. In effect, the PREB should be the official recording secretary of the transaction; this role is a primary reason for the broker's existence.

Although it is a responsibility of the PREB, the tenant should also review every scrap of paper even remotely connected with the transaction. It is the tenant's ultimate responsibility to be sure that everything ever agreed to, especially any verbal representation, has properly been interpreted and included, in writing, in the lease document.

An essential part of both the landlord's and the broker's jobs is selling. They are there to sell the tenant on the building, the premises, and the neighborhood. When selling, they are likely to "stretch" the truth or even to make a promise they know the tenant wants to hear, in order to lease the space. Some favorite lines of the broker are "Don't worry," "I've got it covered," "Of course, that will be included," "Almost every building in the area has that," "It's guaranteed to be there by the time you move in," and "The landlord will usually give that to the tenants in the building."

Statements abound about supposed health clubs for a building, great retail shops, food shops, gourmet restaurants, excellent parking facilities, no-cost parking, special building finishes, special tenant finishes, upgraded premises, proposed building improvements, nearby building construction ("It will be built," "It won't be built"), nearby shopping, employee convenience areas, planned nearby public transportation, and major road construction or reconstruction ("It's just a rumor; it'll never happen," or "It'll be the best road system to reach a building—when it's built").

The tenant must never assume that amenities or certain building facilities will be permanent. Examples of building amenities that quickly disappear are a health club, a sauna room, and an on-site restaurant.

Get It in Writing

For the tenant, verbal assurances mean nothing. Even if something is in writing, that does not necessarily make it valid. The tenant must be sure everything is in writing *and* is included within the lease document or as an addendum to the lease. If the landlord or his or her representative hesitates or refuses to put something in writing in the lease document (saying, for example, "Oh, don't worry; no need to clutter up the document with that; the landlord always gives that to the tenants"), whatever that something is, it does not exist. It will more often than not prove to be a figment of the tenant's imagination.

45
Guarantee of Lease

The guarantee of lease is actually an addendum to or a certificate included with the lease document and is not a lease clause as such. The lease document is an agreement between the landlord and the individual(s) leasing space (be it a corporation, a sole proprietor, a partnership, a joint venture, or another kind of business organization). The guarantee, however, will be between the landlord and a third party, who may or may not own or work for the business organization. This third party personally guarantees (depending on the type of guarantee) either or both the rent payments and the business organization's performance of all obligations and other requirements under the lease, for the full term of the lease.

The Landlord Wants Tenant Stability

To the extent reasonably possible, the landlord wants to protect his or her business investment. Every time a tenant moves in or out of the premises, the landlord incurs a cost. This cost is related to having vacant (and thus non-income-producing) space in a building, having to repair and otherwise prepare the premises for reoccupancy, and having to attract another tenant (which may entail advertising fees and broker commissions).

For these reasons, as well as the need for a continuous cash flow, a landlord wants to find stable tenants. These are tenants who are able to pay the rent, who will be in business a long time, whose products or services are sold by the business, and who have a large and stable customer base. Even when a tenant appears to meet these criteria, the landlord, in order to allay any fears about renting the premises to the tenant, may still require a third party to guarantee the tenant's lease. A guarantor (someone providing guarantees) is usually sought for a new business venture or a company just starting up.

When the new business has no previous track record, the landlord will want the financial investors to provide the guarantees. When it is a new subsidy of a well-established corporation, the landlord will expect the parent corporation to provide the lease guarantee. When the business is relatively new, whether a corporation or not, the landlord will expect the owners (or principal stockholders) to individually and personally guarantee, by signing, the lease obligations (especially the rent). Guarantees will usually be required for:

- *A small business.* Because small businesses are often family-type ventures or are highly dependent on one or a few special individuals, these individuals may be asked to personally guarantee the lease. The landlord knows that if just one key individual or family member leaves the business, there may no longer be a business.

- *An established business undergoing or anticipating growth.* Even though the business may be well established, have strong financial reports, and seem to be able to afford the rent, the landlord may require a parent corporation or individual owner to provide a personal guarantee of the lease. All too often a business will expand, hiring new staff and leasing more space, on the expectation of winning a new government contract or on the basis of high public acceptance of a new product or service. And all too often the expansion proves to be too much, too soon. The contract does not come through, or the new product or service is not accepted by enough people to make it a success.

Although he or she may be sympathetic to the plights of a business, the landlord is renting space, not helping a business grow or sell products or services. The guarantee of the lease provides at least some protection for the landlord.

Potential Embarrassment to a Tenant

From the tenant's perspective, the guarantee of a lease is at best a slight annoyance. It means involving a third party, often with some embarrassment, depending on who guarantees the payment of rent and performance of lease obligations.

However, a lease guarantee does not come into play unless the tenant is unable to continue with the lease obligations. If that occurs, the tenant, as a business, may no longer be in a position to care, and the lease will become the problem of the guarantor. The extent to which this may be an embarrassment or a problem for the tenant depends on the identity of the guarantor(s).

Possibly even more embarrassing, because of potential loss, a guarantee may be difficult even to obtain. No third party (acceptable to the landlord) may be willing to intercede and guarantee the lease liability. Or worse, the third party may be the owner (or major stockholder) of the business, and his or her personal financial guarantees and credit may not satisfy the landlord's requirements.

Further embarrassment can occur when the third party has no personal or direct interest in the business but is the guarantor of both rent payments and the performance of lease obligations. Suppose that the tenant and landlord have a disagreement and that the tenant rightly or wrongly, legally or illegally, for whatever reason, holds back on a monetary payment due to the landlord or otherwise does not honor some covenant of the lease. The landlord can then approach and demand the tenant's payment or performance of the lease obligations from the guarantor.

Protecting the Guarantor's Best Interests

Before signing, a guarantor should be sure to have his or her own independent legal counsel review and evaluate a certificate of guarantee to a lease. At the same time, in accordance with good and ethical business practices, the tenant should negotiate a guarantee agreement that offers the most protection possible for the guarantor.

How restrictive the landlord will want the guarantee to be will depend on market conditions and how badly the landlord needs to rent the premises. Some guarantees will include the following provisions:

1. *An initial agreement that sets out the overall obligation(s) of the guarantor.* This is where the guarantor's responsibility is spelled out—for the rent payments alone or for the performance of all obligations under the lease. Obviously, the guarantor would be best off if obligated only for the rent payments.

The provision will state: "The guarantor unconditionally and without reservation guarantees that the tenant will faithfully and punctually perform and fulfill all its obligations, covenants, and agreements of the lease. In the event the tenant defaults, then the guarantor guarantees to pay rent and all other monetary sums due to the landlord."

2. *A provision stating that the guarantor will pay not only any monetary sums due under the lease but also all damages, claims, demands, costs, and expenses that the landlord may sustain as a consequence of a breach, nonperformance, or other default by the tenant.* This provision works much like a blank check from the guarantor, paying for virtually anything the landlord deems to be a cost or related expense of the tenant default.

The tenant should have this clause tempered so that it specifically lists anything a guarantor will be responsible for above and beyond what is specified in the lease document. For example, it should include a statement regarding reasonable legal costs and other related expenses incurred by the landlord for the tenant's default or a statement enforcing the guarantee.

3. *A provision specifying that the guarantee will remain in effect for any modifications or amendments that are made to the lease by the landlord and the tenant.* In addition, this provision may state that the guarantor waives both the right to receive notice of any change and the need for the guarantor's consent.

From a guarantor's point of view, not knowing about changes to the lease or not being able to influence them can be detrimental to his or her future financial and economic health. The guarantor should insist that his or her written consent or agreement be required for any changes or modifications to the lease.

This provision may also cover lease renewals and extensions. Since a renewal is actually a new lease, it would not seem that the guarantor could be held responsible for something not yet in existence. Nonetheless, the guarantor should insist these items be deleted from the provision or require guarantor approval in writing and a new guarantee of the lease among the tenant, the landlord, and the guarantor.

4. *A provision requiring that the guarantor's obligations under the guarantee of lease agreement remain binding, even though the landlord may have, for example, waived a tenant default, extended the time requirement for the tenant to meet a lease obligation, or released the tenant from being required to perform a particular lease obligation.* This provision offers broad general coverage to the landlord but little protection to the guarantor.

The most troubling aspect of this clause is that there is no counterrelease for the guarantor. The guarantor should have equal treatment to that of the tenant and be released from the same obligations as the tenant.

5. *A provision ensuring that the landlord will not lose anything in the event a tenant closes his or her doors, goes bankrupt, or otherwise ceases to do business and voluntarily or involuntarily leaves the premises.* This provision ties the guarantor to continued lease liability. Specifically, the provision will state: "The guarantee remains in full force and effect whether or not the tenant is forced or voluntarily enters bankruptcy, reorganization, receivership, or insolvency and whether or not such proceedings void the lease document." In effect, the guarantor remains on the hook for the premises, no matter what, supposedly even if a court invalidates the lease document. Whether this provision will hold up in a particular state's court of law remains to be seen. However, like any other agreement between individuals, it is better not to have to go into court because of disagreement. There is no way to predetermine what the legal outcome will be, and legal costs can be prohibitively expensive.

It is better for the guarantor to eliminate, or at least modify, this statement. At a minimum, a court's actions invalidating the lease document should automatically carry over to the guarantee of lease certificate.

The provision should not be open-ended; it should list the specific types of major tenant defaults the guarantor would be responsible for. The guarantor would also like the provision to stipulate a time limit. If the lease document has been in force at least up to some specified time period, then after that specified time, any major tenant default would not require continued guarantor liability and responsibility.

This clause may contain some other landlord-inspired provisions; for the most part, they should be general housekeeping statements. Even so, each additional provision should be carefully read and adapted to meet the guarantor's needs. As with every other clause in a lease document, there is no such thing as a "standard," nor should the guarantor accept the verbal assurance "It's the same clause everyone uses."

Index

About the Author

Stanley M. Wolfson is a founding partner and former COO of Barrueta & Associates, a full service commercial real estate brokerage firm in Washington, D.C. He is currently a consultant, lecturer, and writer on real estate topics.

Mr. Wolfson, author of several previous business books, has written numerous articles on aspects of the corporate real estate field, and is the creator of innovative commercial real estate broker programs for both junior- and senior-level personnel. His unique and extensive background—featuring experience preparing and negotiating leases as a tenant, first-hand involvement with developers and building owners, and intimate knowledge of the commercial real estate brokerage business—forms the basis upon which this pioneering work is built.